Just the
Arguments

Edited by
Michael Bruce and Steven Barbone

JUST THE ARGUMENTS

100

of the Most
Important
Arguments
in Western
Philosophy

WILEY-BLACKWELL

A John Wiley & Sons, Ltd., Publication

Blackwell Publishing was acquired by John Wiley & Sons in February 2007. Blackwell's publishing program has been merged with Wiley's global Scientific, Technical, and Medical business to form Wiley-Blackwell.

Registered Office
John Wiley & Sons Ltd, The Atrium, Southern Gate, Chichester, West Sussex, PO19 8SQ, United Kingdom

Editorial Offices
350 Main Street, Malden, MA 02148-5020, USA
9600 Garsington Road, Oxford, OX4 2DQ, UK
The Atrium, Southern Gate, Chichester, West Sussex, PO19 8SQ, UK

For details of our global editorial offices, for customer services, and for information about how to apply for permission to reuse the copyright material in this book please see our website at www.wiley.com/wiley-blackwell.

Library of Congress Cataloging-in-Publication Data

Just the arguments : 100 of the most important arguments in Western philosophy / edited by Michael Bruce and Steven Barbone.
     p. cm.
  Includes bibliographical references and index.
  ISBN 978-1-4443-3637-5 (hardcover : alk. paper) – ISBN 978-1-4443-3638-2 (pbk. : alk. paper)
  1. Philosophy–Introductions. I. Bruce, Michael. II. Barbone, Steven.
  BD21.J87 2011
  190–dc22
                                    2011012212

A catalogue record for this book is available from the British Library.

This book is published in the following electronic formats: ePDFs 9781444344400; Wiley Online Library 9781444344431; ePub 9781444344417; mobi: 9781444344424

Set in 10/12pt Sabon by Toppan Best-set Premedia Limited
Printed and bound in Singapore by C.O.S. Printers Pte Ltd

7 2015

In Memory of Mark Bruce (1961–2001). Never Forget.

Contents

Acknowledgments

First, we would like to thank the contributors. This was a massive project, and the authors have been patient and enthusiastic. We are impressed with quality of their entries and their ability to work within the format of the book. We appreciate that the authors worked during the precious summer time and met short deadlines.

Second, we would like to thank our publisher, Wiley-Blackwell. We especially are grateful to Jeff Dean, who believed in the concept and helped develop the project over the last year. This is the first book of its kind, and we are grateful to Jeff for his confidence in us to bring it to fruition.

Third, Michael would like to thank Steven for his continued optimism and support. Steven was Michael's graduate advisor at San Diego State, and when Michael talked to him about his little idea for this book in 2007, Steven not only encouraged him but offered to help in any way he could. Without Steven's positive outlook, the project would have never made it off the ground. At the same time, as Steven is quick to point out, the true genius and engine of this very original project is Michael.

We also wish to acknowledge our respective partners, Karen Hull and Stephen Russell, for their somehow managing to endure us while we absented ourselves to prepare this manuscript.

Introduction: Show Me the Arguments

Michael Bruce and Steven Barbone

"We are going to ruin undergraduate philosophy." That was what we told our friends and teachers when we pitched the idea of this book to them. It was our experience that for almost any given philosophy class that we took as undergraduates, there were only a handful of arguments, totaling no more than a few pages of carefully crafted notes, that we needed to know. We imagined a rolodex of arguments in front of us, which we could spin through with ease to find the argument and move on. Midterm or final examinations in one of these classes would be reduced to presenting a philosopher's argument, followed by a critique – usually another philosopher's argument. The ability to state an argument clearly and concisely, in a term paper, for example, demonstrates that one succinctly understands the material. The following arguments can be viewed as answers to such test questions and also to some of life's questions as well.

"Show me the argument" is the battle cry for philosophers. Everyone has subjective personal experiences, sentiments, and opinions, so philosophy appeals to the common ground of reason to evaluate claims objectively. Logical reasoning is independent of political and religious commitments. Put simply, an argument is valid or it is not. (Whether or not it is convincing is another issue.) When one analyzes a position in terms of its argument, one responds with a certain level of rigor and attention. Uncompelling arguments can be dismissed out of hand as absurd and forgotten; however, arguments that evoke strong reactions, often due to the potential consequences of the argument, are countered by a restatement of the initial argument, explicitly displaying the inferences, assumptions, and justifications and why the conclusions do not follow. When things become serious, one wants *just the arguments*.

Just the Arguments: 100 of the Most Important Arguments in Western Philosophy,
First Edition. Edited by Michael Bruce and Steven Barbone.
© 2011 Blackwell Publishing Ltd. Published 2011 by Blackwell Publishing Ltd.

The time has long passed when it was possible for one to read the entire Western philosophical canon. Philosophy needs new didactic tools to address the fact that the quantity of influential arguments will increase while the number of hours that a student at any level has will remain relatively the same. Philosophy as a formal discipline will increasingly need to "get smart" about how it selects which arguments deserve more attention than others in the classroom and then how to teach them. Outside of the classroom, there are little-to-no resources that function as study guides. Detailed study guides are made for everything – the Bible, calculus, grammar, biology – except for philosophy. There are laminated sheets in bookstores that list all the standard mathematical equations, sheets that have common Spanish verbs, and even one on "Golf for Women," but not one has arguments on the existence of God, free will, or moral responsibility. Many books present important philosophical arguments, but it is often the case that these books outline only a single argument or a string of related arguments. Encyclopedias of philosophy are great for limited descriptions of philosophers and concepts, but there is a need for reference tools that offer specific arguments. In the end, these secondary sources often bury the argument in commentary and analysis and do not lend themselves to concise and efficient referencing. It can take just as long to find an argument in the analysis as it would to go to the original text. This volume acts as a compact and accessible companion to both sources.

It deserves to be underscored that this volume showcases 100 of the most important arguments and that this list is not exhaustive or uncontroversial. This is the first project of its kind. There are not standardized accounts of arguments that are univocally accepted in the field. Experts in every field disagree – perhaps even more so in philosophy. Arguments that are valued now may not be considered to be as equally important in the future. Even when there is an agreement that an argument is important, it can be far from clear how the argument goes or what the correct conclusion is. Authors in this volume have selected representative quotations in support of their versions of the arguments. The following arguments are not ranked against each other as more or less important. Aquinas' Five Ways should not be considered more important than other arguments based on the fact that it comes first. There are many more, important arguments that are not included here, and we hope to provide these in forthcoming installments.

We have selected arguments that an undergraduate philosophy major would be likely to encounter, though many of the issues arise in general education classes outside of philosophy. A majority of the arguments employ intuitive logical inferences, allowing readers without formal training in logic to follow the argument. The inference rule used to draw each conclusion is named to enable the reader to see explicitly the argument's valid structure. We provide an overview of the inferences in the appendices. There are a few arguments that require a more advanced understanding of logic, and readers will benefit from the introduction and commentary that provide the general strategy.

This volume is divided into six parts: philosophy of religion, metaphysics, epistemology, ethics, philosophy of mind, and philosophies of science and language. There are more branches of philosophy than there are sections in the volume, and there are other important arguments within the given domains than those presented here. It is common that arguments in one area are also important and influence arguments in another. Many arguments could have been included in multiple sections. These divisions are provisional, and arguments will reference related arguments in the book, signaled by "#" and then the number of the argument. The bibliographic information in each article will also be instructive for further reading. The following are introductions to the arguments in the form of the questions that they address. In other words, we provide the questions that would naturally lead one to the argument. For example, "Is change real (#14)?" directs readers to the article "Parmenides' Refutation of Change," argument #14.

Philosophy of Religion

What were Aquinas' "Five Ways" to prove the existence of God (#1)? Must there be at least one self-existent being that explains why there is something rather than nothing (#2)? If something begins to exist, then does it have a cause (#3)? If God is something than which nothing greater can be thought, does that mean that God must exist in reality (#4)? What was Pascal's Wager (#5)? Is it rational to have religious belief without sufficient evidence (#6)? Does the existence of evil in the world disprove the existence of God (#7)? What if God permits evil so that humans have the greater good of free will (#8)? Does free will entail the power to sin (#9)? Is it justifiable to believe in a miracle on the basis of empirical evidence (#10)? Is what is holy holy because the gods approve it, or do they approve it because it is holy (#11)? What did Nietzsche mean when he said "God is dead" and where does this leave truth (#12)? What is Ockham's Razor (#13)?

Metaphysics

Is change real (#14)? If change is not real, then is time real (#15)? Are only things that are perceived real (#16)? How did Kant argue against this kind of idealism and skepticism (#17)? What is the relationship between necessity and possibility in terms of the past, present, and future (#18)? If things could have been different in the past, does that mean that there are different possible worlds (#19)? What are "persons" and what makes a person maintain her numerical identity over time (#20)? Is there a decisive factor – for example, body mass, brain mass, or memories – for personal identity (#21)? In what way do things both persist over time and change (#22, 23)? Do humans have nonbodily immaterial parts called souls (#24)? Is it irrational to fear death (#25)? How do we know things if they are in constant flux (#26)? How did Aristotle argue against Plato's Forms (#27)? Is the same logical theory to be applied in all domains, or do different domains require different logics (#28)? Can there be a totality of true propositions without running into paradoxes (#29)? What is the connection between free will and moral responsibility (#30)? Do I have free will only if I had the option to do otherwise (#31)? Are free will and determinism compatible (#32)? If everything is either going to happen or not, isn't fatalism tenable (#33)? How does Sartre's existentialism – "Man is condemned to be free" – enter into the conversation (#34)?

Epistemology

How do I know that I exist (#35)? Am I certain that I am not dreaming (#36)? Am I directly conscious of features of sensations or experiences (#37)? Does every belief need to be justified by other beliefs and will that lead to an infinite regress (#38)? Isn't there a commonsense response to skepticism (#39)? If there can be no justified procedure for normatively distinguishing among competing epistemic views, then are all accounts are epistemically equal (#40)? How does the traditional account of knowledge being a true justified belief fail (#41)? Is something true solely because people agree that it is true (#42)? Is it possible to differentiate knowledge or experience between a conceptual component and an empirical component (#43)? Is there a sharp division between analytic truths and synthetic truths (#44)? Is there a rational justification for inductive inferences and the foundation of modern science (#45)? If things are similar in certain observable or identified cases, are they are also similar in some other unobservable or unidentified cases (#46)? Should philosophy look to science to explain and justify our knowledge of the world (#47)? Are some cognitive states in direct contact with reality and form a firm foundation that supports the rest of our knowledge (#48, #49)? Are there limitations to what reasoning can accomplish (#50)?

Ethics

Does the just life bring happiness (#51)? Is the happy life one in accord with reason (#52)? Is the Good one thing or many (#53)? What is the best possible life that a person can lead (#54)? Did Kant have an argument for the categorical imperative (#55)? And why did he think that autonomy deserves respect (#56)? Should the Good be conceived of in terms of utility (#57)? Are humans just hedonists, who champion pleasure over everything else (#58)? Is all morality relative or are there objective principles across cultures (#59)? Can the good be defined (#60)? Should we accept the authority of the state (#61)? Is taxation forced labor (#62)? Do we have a moral duty to give to charity (#63)? Would it be better if, in the future, a greater rather than lesser number of people lived (#64)? Is a great loss to one person justified by smaller benefits to a great many others (#65)? Is it better to bring everyone down to the same level than to accept an inequality (#66)? Does justice demand preserving a patterned distribution of property (#67)?

What are the central arguments of liberal feminism (#68)? What is the moral status of marginal cases; that is, when is there not a clearly drawn line between human and nonhuman animals (#69)? What is the most robust argument in favor of vegetarianism (#70)? What does a famous violin player have to do with the most discussed argument in the abortion debate (#71)? Is abortion immoral due to the loss of future experiences, activities, projects, and enjoyments (#72)? Does something need to be able to desire or conceive of something in order to have the right to something; for example, life (#73)? Is there an ethical difference between active and passive euthanasia (#74)?

Philosophy of Mind

Is the mind a blank slate or are there innate ideas (#75)? What is Cartesian dualism and is the mind distinct from the body (#76)? What is the mind–body problem (#77)? What is property dualism and how is it different than substance dualism (#78)? Are mental events identical with physical events (#79, #80)? Is every mental property realized in exactly one physical way (#81)? How does the nonphysical mind move the physical body (#82)? Do I have privileged access to my mental states and can I know the mental states of others (#83)? Does physicalism capture all the essential facts of experience (#84, #85)? If a zombie world is metaphysically possible, how would that critique physicalism (#86)? Does the sensation of color reveal intrinsic features about color (#87)? If a computer had the right programs, would it have a mind; in other words, is true artificial intelligence possible (#88)?

Science and Language

How do we discern science from pseudo-science (#89)? Do scientific paradigms build from previous ones; that is, are they commensurable (#90)? Is the shift from one paradigm to another a rational process (#90)? Is scientific realism the only way that makes progress in science and technology not miraculous (#91)? How did Galileo know that all objects fall at the same rate of speed regardless of their respective weights without experimenting (#92)? If a theory is fallible, should it be eliminated (#93)?

Is there such a thing as a completely private language (#94)? Does learning a language require learning a rule (#95)? Does learning a rule require learning a language (#96)? When there is translation, is there also interpretation (#97, #98)? If there are true statements that contain abstract objects, does that mean those abstract objects exist (#99)? Is mathematical Platonism the best way to explain mathematical knowledge (#100)?

How to Use This Book

> In the boxed area that precedes the arguments, you will find a reference list of original and secondary sources.

Block quotations are provided to show how the argument is presented in the text.

P1. Premises are marked "P."
P2. A premise is a statement that is either true or false and is given as evidence or a reason for accepting the conclusion; a conclusion is the statement that is argued for and supported by the premises.
  C1. Conclusions, of which there may be many, are marked with "C" and are indented. Conclusion indicators – for example, "therefore" and "hence" – have been omitted. The rule of inference or replacement is listed after deductive conclusions.

Part I
Philosophy of Religion

1

Aquinas' Five Ways

Timothy J. Pawl

All quotations from Aquinas are taken from Alfred Freddoso's translation of the *Summa theologiae*, available online at www.nd.edu/~afreddos/summa-translation/TOC-part1.htm

Baisnee, Jules. "St. Thomas Aquinas's Proofs of the Existence of God Presented in Their Chronological Order," in *Philosophical Studies in Honor of the Very Reverend Ignatius Smith, O.P.,* edited by John K. Ryan, 29–64. Westminster: The Newman Press, 1952.
Bochenski, Joseph M. "The Five Ways," in *The Rationality of Theism,* edited by Adolfo García de la Sierra, 61–92. Atlanta, GA: Rodopi, 2000.
Kenny, Anthony. *The Five Ways: Saint Thomas Aquinas' Proofs of God's Existence.* Oxford: Oxford University Press, 1969.
Pawl, Timothy. "The Five Ways," in *The Oxford Handbook of Thomas Aquinas,* edited by Brian Davies and Eleonore Stump. Oxford: Oxford University Press, 2011.

St. Thomas Aquinas (1224/5–74) offered his Five Ways, or five proofs for the existence of God, near the beginning of his *magnum opus*, the *Summa theologiae* (Part 1, Question 2, Article 3, the response). The *Summa* (ST), as it is often called, was written as a textbook for men in their priestly formation. It is well over 2,500 pages in a standard English translation from the Latin, but the Five Ways take up only slightly more than one page.

Just the Arguments: 100 of the Most Important Arguments in Western Philosophy,
First Edition. Edited by Michael Bruce and Steven Barbone.
© 2011 Blackwell Publishing Ltd. Published 2011 by Blackwell Publishing Ltd.

Nevertheless, they are almost assuredly the most commented on section of the *Summa* and some of the most well-known arguments for the existence of God.

One should note that while each Way concludes with some variation of "and this we call God," Aquinas did not intend the Five Ways to be demonstrations of a uniquely Christian God. In fact, he warns against attempts to prove, for instance, that God is triune (three persons but one being, as Christians affirm), since such arguments, he explains, will fall short and lead unbelievers to scoff (see his *Summa contra gentiles*, Book 1, Chapter 9, paragraph 2). Furthermore, Aquinas did not take the Five Ways to show that this thing we call "God" is perfect, good, immutable, eternal, powerful, knowledgeable, or even that there is just one such thing. As a consequence, some common criticisms of the Ways – for instance, that they do not demonstrate an omnipotent being – clearly miss the mark. Aquinas goes on later to devote many pages to whether the thing we call "God" in the Five Ways is omnipotent. And the same is true for the other abovementioned attributes. Rather, Aquinas' intent in the Five Ways is to show that there is something-or-other that, for instance, causes things but is itself uncaused, or something that is necessary and does not have that necessary existence from another. In fact, he does not argue that the Five Ways conclude to the same thing – rather than five different things – until later in the *Summa* (Part 1, Question 11, Article 3, the response).

Finally, it is important to note that while the Five Ways are Aquinas' most often cited arguments for the existence of God, they are not his most detailed or nuanced. The *Summa*, as said above, is a textbook of sorts, and written for an audience of common men in formation for the priesthood – not academics, scholars, atheists, or agnostics. To judge Aquinas' best and most powerful arguments for the existence of God, one would do better to look at the parallel passages from his other works rather than at his *Summa* (see Baisnee for a helpful list of these passages). That said, it is the arguments in the *Summa* that have received the most attention and have become, by any reasonable standard, some of the most important arguments in the Western intellectual tradition.

The First Way – The Argument from Motion

The First Way focuses on motion. By "motion," Aquinas means the three sorts of accidental change that Aristotle differentiates: change of location (e.g., moving across the room), change in quality (e.g., heating up), and change in quantity (e.g., getting fatter). The general thrust of the argument is that anything changed in one of these ways is changed by something else. That something else, in changing the first thing, either is itself changed or remains changeless. A series of changing changers cannot proceed infinitely. So there must be some first, unchanging being. That being we call "God."

The argument below uses 'F' as a variable governing end states of being correlated with the three sorts of motion mentioned above. For instance, one could substitute "across the room," "hot," or "fat" for F. Aquinas provides three detailed defenses of C3 in the *Summa contra gentiles*, Part 1, Chapter 13. He considers the common objection that a thing can move itself (e.g., the runner moves himself when sprinting from the starting line) by saying that such cases are instances of a part moving a whole and not a thing moving itself. In P3, Aquinas says that the mover must be in a state of actuality relevant to F in order to make something F. The argument would be more forceful if Aquinas could say that the mover must be actually F, but he cannot say that, at least not with perfect generality. For Aquinas thinks that God can move things in many ways that God is not actually: God can fatten a man without himself being fat. In that case, God is said to be virtually F, where something is "virtually F" if it is not itself F but it has the power to make others F. One may say, then, that something is in a state of actuality relevant to F when it is either actually F or virtually F.

> It is certain, and obvious to the senses, that in this world some things are moved. But everything that is moved is moved by another. For nothing is moved except insofar as it is in potentiality with respect to that actuality toward which it is moved, whereas something effects motion insofar as it is in actuality in a relevant respect. After all, to effect motion is just to lead something from potentiality into actuality. But a thing cannot be led from potentiality into actuality except through some being that is in actuality in a relevant respect; for example, something that is hot in actuality – say, a fire – makes a piece of wood, which is hot in potentiality, to be hot in actuality, and it thereby moves and alters the piece of wood. But it is impossible for something to be simultaneously in potentiality and in actuality with respect to same thing; rather, it can be in potentiality and in actuality only with respect to different things. For what is hot in actuality cannot simultaneously be hot in potentiality; rather, it is cold in potentiality. Therefore, it is impossible that something should be both mover and moved in the same way and with respect to the same thing, or, in other words, that something should move itself. Therefore, everything that is moved must be moved by another.
>
> If, then, that by which something is moved is itself moved, then it, too, must be moved by another, and that other by still another. But this does not go on to infinity. For if it did, then there would not be any first mover and, as a result, none of the others would effect motion, either. For secondary movers effect motion only because they are being moved by a first mover, just as a stick does not effect motion except because it is being moved by a hand. Therefore, one has to arrive at some first mover that is not being moved by anything. And this is what everyone takes to be God. (ST I, q2, a3, response)

P1. Some things are moved.

P2. If something is moved to being F, then it is potentially but not actually F.

P3. If something moves a thing to be F, then it (the mover) is in a state of actuality relevant to F.

    C1. If something were to move itself to be F (e.g., be both moved and its own mover), then it would be both potentially but not actually F and also in a state of actuality relevant to F (conjunction, and *modus ponens*, P1, P2, P3).

P4. But it is not possible for something to be both potentially but not actually F and also in a state of actuality relevant to F.

    C2. It is not possible for something to move itself to be F (*modus tollens*, C1, P4).

P5. If it is not possible for something to move itself to be F, then if something is moved, it is moved by something else.

    C3. If something is moved, it is moved by something else (*modus ponens*, C2, P5).

P5. If B moves A and B is moved, then B must be moved by some other thing, C. And if C is moved, then C must be moved by still some other thing, D. And so on.

P6. If the series of movers were to go on to infinity, then there would be no first mover.

P7. If there were no first mover, then there would be no motion.

    C4. There is a first mover (*modus tollens*, P1, P7).

    C5. That first mover is the thing that everyone takes to be God (definition).

The Second Way – The Argument from Causation

Whereas the First Way focused on accidental changes, the Second Way focuses on ordered series of efficient causation. An efficient cause is that which produces something or an alteration in something. The composer is the efficient cause of the sonata; the fire is the efficient cause of the heating of the kettle. An ordered series is a series in which the causal work of later members in the series depends on the simultaneous causal work of earlier members in the series. If the fire heats the kettle and the kettle heats the water, it is an ordered series, since the kettle's heating the water depends upon the causal activity of the earlier cause, the fire. Likewise, a system of gears is an ordered causal series, since the causal action of one intermediate gear spinning another, later gear depends upon the causal activity of previous gears in the system. Aquinas argues in the Second Way, to continue with the gear image, that the system cannot be gears all the way back. An infinite series of gears, without a first cause of their spinning, would not be in motion.

> We find that among sensible things there is an ordering of efficient causes, and yet we do not find – nor is it possible to find – anything that is an efficient cause of its own self. For if something were an efficient cause of itself, then it would be prior to itself – which is impossible.
>
> But it is impossible to go on to infinity among efficient causes. For in every case of ordered efficient causes, the first is a cause of the intermediate and the intermediate is a cause of the last – and this regardless of whether the intermediate is constituted by many causes or by just one. But when a cause is removed, its effect is removed. Therefore, if there were no first among the efficient causes, then neither would there be a last or an intermediate. But if the efficient causes went on to infinity, there would not be a first efficient cause, and so there would not be a last effect or any intermediate efficient causes, either – which is obviously false. Therefore, one must posit some first efficient cause – which everyone calls God. (ST I, q2, a3, response)

P1. There is an ordered series of efficient causes.
P2. Necessarily, if X is an efficient cause of Y, then X is prior to Y.
   C1. Necessarily, if X is an efficient cause of X, then X is prior to X (instantiation, P2).
P3. It is not possible for X to be prior to X.
   C2. It is not possible for X to be an efficient cause of itself (*modus tollens*, C1, P3).
P4. If something is an ordered series of efficient causes, then the first cause causes the intermediate cause(s), and the intermediate cause(s) cause(s) the last effect.
P5. If a cause is removed from an ordered series of efficient causes, then the effects after that cause are removed as well.
   C3. If there were no first cause, then there would be no subsequent effects (instantiation, P4, P5).
P6. If an ordered series of efficient causes could precede infinitely, then there would be no first cause.
   C4. If an ordered series of efficient causes could precede infinitely, then there would be no subsequent effects (hypothetical syllogism, C3, P6).
P7. But there are subsequent effects.
   C5. An ordered series of efficient causes cannot precede infinitely (*modus tollens*, C4, P7).
P8. An ordered series of efficient causes either precedes infinitely, terminates in a cause that causes itself, or terminates in an uncaused cause.
   C6. An ordered series of efficient causation terminates in an uncaused cause (disjunctive syllogism, C2, C5, P8).
   C7. We call that uncaused cause "God" (definition).

The Third Way – The Argument from Possibility and Necessity

Aquinas has a specific understanding of possibility and necessity in mind in the Third Way, and it is not the common understanding in today's philosophical discussions. When Aquinas calls something "necessary," in this argument, he means that it is not subject to generation or corruption. A necessary being exists, but it does not come into existence by composition, and it cannot cease existing by way of decomposition. Similarly, a possible being, in this context, exists, but it does or could have come into existence by way of composition, and it can cease to exist by way of decomposition. The most debated inference in this argument is the inference from P3 to C2. Most commentators who attempt to justify it do so by arguing that Aquinas had in mind an implicit premise which, together with P3, entails C2. As it stands, without the help of an implicit premise, the inference is invalid and commits the fallacy of composition.

> Certain of the things we find in the world are able to exist and able not to exist; for some things are found to be generated and corrupted and, as a result, they are able to exist and able not to exist.
> But it is impossible that everything should be like this; for that which is able not to exist is such that at some time it does not exist. Therefore, if everything is such that it is able not to exist, then at some time nothing existed in the world. But if this were true, then nothing would exist even now. For what does not exist begins to exist only through something that does exist; therefore, if there were no beings, then it was impossible that anything should have begun to exist, and so nothing would exist now – which is obviously false. Therefore, not all beings are able to exist [and able not to exist]; rather, it must be that there is something necessary in the world.
> Now every necessary being either has a cause of its necessity from outside itself or it does not. But it is impossible to go on to infinity among necessary beings that have a cause of their necessity – in the same way, as was proved above, that it is impossible to go on to infinity among efficient causes. Therefore, one must posit something that is necessary *per se*, which does not have a cause of its necessity from outside itself but is instead a cause of necessity for the other [necessary] things. But this everyone calls God. (ST I, q2, a3, response)

P1. Some things are able to be generated or corrupted.
P2. If some things are able to be generated or corrupted, then it is possible for those things either to exist or not to exist.
  C1. It is possible for some things to exist or not to exist (*modus ponens*, P1, P2).

P3. If, for each thing, it is possible that it not exist, then at some time it does not exist.

C2. If, for each thing, at some time it does not exist, then at some time nothing exists (universal generalization, P3).

P4. If at some time nothing exists, then there would have been nothing to cause another thing to exist.

P5. If there had been nothing to cause another being to exist, then nothing could have come into existence.

P6. If nothing could have come into existence, then nothing would exist even now.

P7. But something does exist now.

C3. Something could have come into existence (*modus tollens*, P6, P7).

C4. There had to have been something to cause another thing to exist (*modus tollens*, P5, C3).

C5. At no time did nothing exist (*modus tollens*, P4, C4).

C6. It is not true that, for each thing, at some time it does not exist (*modus tollens*, C2, C5).

C7. There must be something that is not possible not to exist – that is, there must be a necessary being (*modus tollens*, P3, C6).

P8. A necessary being has a cause for its necessity from something else or it does not.

P9. It is not possible for there to be an infinite series of beings with their necessity from something else.

C8. There must be some necessary being with its necessity not from something else (disjunctive syllogism, P8, P9).

C9. We call that necessary being whose necessity comes from nothing else "God" (definition).

The Fourth Way – The Argument from Gradation

In the Fourth Way, Aquinas relies on two arguments from Aristotle, which he does not provide in the text, to justify two of his premises (P3 and P4). P1 is observably true. P2 requires a scope restriction. Aquinas seems to be saying that any comparative predications of a property entail that there exists something that is maximally that property. If this were true, then if Bob is fatter than Tom, then there must be something that is maximally fat. Worse still, from P4, it would follow that this fattest thing would be the cause of all other fat things. It seems better to restrict P2 to perfections and then take heat (his example) to be a form of perfection (note that this is just an example; one can grant his point while denying that heat is a perfection). C4 seems to commit the fallacy of composition. Even if it were proven that there is a thing that is most good, and a thing that is most noble, and a thing that is most true, it has yet to be shown why this must be the same thing. Aquinas perhaps had in mind a principle requiring the cause of a thing's being also to be the cause of its other positive attributes or the cause of its perfections. If so, such a premise would need to be inserted into the argument before C4.

> In the world some things are found to be more and less good, more and less true, more and less noble, etc. But *more* and *less* are predicated of diverse things insofar as they approach in diverse ways that which is maximal in a given respect. For instance, the hotter something is, the closer it approaches that which is maximally hot. Therefore, there is something that is maximally true, maximally good, and maximally noble, and, as a result, is a maximal being; for according to the Philosopher in *Metaphysics* 2, things that are maximally true are maximally beings.
>
> But, as is claimed in the same book, that which is maximal in a given genus is a cause of all the things that belong to that genus; for instance, fire, which is maximally hot, is a cause of all hot things. Therefore, there is something that is a cause for all beings of their *esse*, their goodness, and each of their perfections – and this we call God. (ST I, q2, a3, response)

P1. There are some things that are more or less good, more or less true, or more or less noble.
P2. If something is more or less F, then there is something maximally F.
   C1. There is something maximally good, something maximally true, and something maximally noble (substitution, and *modus ponens*, P1, P2).
   C2. There is something maximally true (simplification, C1).
P3. If something is maximally true, then it is maximally being.
   C3. Something is maximally being (*modus ponens*, C2, P3).
P4. If something is maximally F, then it is the cause of all things that are F.
   C4. There is something that is the cause for all beings, their goodness, and each of their perfections (*modus ponens*, C1, P4).
   C5. We call that thing which is the cause of the being, goodness, and perfection of all other things "God" (definition).

The Fifth Way – The Argument from the Governance

Aquinas argues in the Fifth Way that if things always or for the most part act for a particular end, that is evidence of their being directed at that end by an intelligent agent. In nature, most natural things act always or for the most part for a particular end, and so nature is directed by an intelligent agent. Note that, for Aquinas, to act for the sake of an end does not require intentionality. In Aquinas' way of speaking, fire acts for the sake of the end when it burns upwards and the stone acts for the sake of the end when falling down to the earth. One might think that evolutionary biology allows a way out of the design or chance dilemma, since, given evolutionary biology, something could always or for the most part act for the sake of an end but not due to either design or chance but rather natural selection. Aquinas' argument, however, is not aimed solely at biological entities. An electron, for instance, attracts positively charged particles always or for the most part, but it did not acquire this property via some evolutionary process. So even if natural selection narrows the scope of Aquinas' argument, it alone does not defeat the argument.

> We see that some things lacking cognition, viz., natural bodies, act for the sake of an end. This is apparent from the fact that they always or very frequently act in the same way in order to bring about that which is best, and from this it is clear that it is not by chance, but by design, that they attain the end.
>
> But things lacking cognition tend toward an end only if they are directed by something that has cognition and intelligence, in the way that an arrow is directed by an archer. Therefore, there is something intelligent by which all natural things are ordered to an end – and this we call God. (ST I, q2, a3, response)

P1. If something always or for the most part acts in the same way in order to bring about that which is best, then it acts for the sake of an end.

P2. Beings in nature always or for the most part act in the same way in order to bring about that which is best.

C1. Beings in nature act for the sake of an end (*modus ponens*, P1, P2).

P3. If beings in nature act for the sake of an end, then beings in nature are directed by something that has cognition and intelligence.

C2. Beings in nature are directed by something that has cognition and intelligence (*modus ponens*, C1, P3).

C3. We call that director of unthinking things "God" (definition).

2

The Contingency Cosmological Argument

Mark T. Nelson

Clarke, Samuel. *A Demonstration of the Being and Attributes of God and Other Writings*, edited by Enzio Vailati. Cambridge, UK: Cambridge University Press, 1998.

Rowe, William L. *The Cosmological Argument*. Princeton, NJ: Princeton University Press, 1975.

____. *Philosophy of Religion: An Introduction*. Belmont, CA: Wadsworth, 1978.

The Contingency Argument is a version of the cosmological argument for the existence of God, proposed by Samuel Clarke (1675–1729) and rescued from obscurity by William Rowe (b. 1931). The cosmological argument is not, in fact, a single argument but a family of arguments that attempt to prove, or at least render plausible, the existence of God based on the existence of the cosmos. Typically, these arguments have two stages: the first arguing from the existence of the cosmos to the existence of a necessary being or first cause of this cosmos; the second arguing that this necessary being or first cause is God. Regarding the first stage of the argument, scholars sometimes distinguish between two versions: those based on the idea that infinite causal regresses do not exist and those not based on this idea. The first three of Thomas Aquinas' (1224/5–74) "Five Ways" (#1) are examples of the former; Clarke's contingency argument is an example of the latter. Aquinas argues, for example, that an uncaused first cause of

Just the Arguments: 100 of the Most Important Arguments in Western Philosophy, First Edition. Edited by Michael Bruce and Steven Barbone.
© 2011 Blackwell Publishing Ltd. Published 2011 by Blackwell Publishing Ltd.

"sensible beings with efficient causes" must exist, because, if it did not, there would be an infinite regress of caused causes, but such infinite causal regresses do not in fact exist. Many critics find Aquinas' argument on this point unconvincing, so one advantage of Clarke's argument is that it simply sidesteps this issue. According to Clarke, the problem with the idea of everything's being just an infinite regress of dependent beings caused by other dependent beings (equivalent to Aquinas' "sensible beings with efficient causes") is not that such regresses are impossible but that this would violate the Principle of Sufficient Reason, an intuitive principle according to which (roughly) there is an explanation for every being and every fact. In such a case, there would be an explanation of the existence of every particular dependent being, and there would even be an explanation of the existence of that particular collection of dependent beings. There would not, however, be an explanation of the fact that there are any dependent beings at all, since no particular existing dependent being (or set of dependent beings) could explain this. That is, we would lack an explanation of the fact that there is something rather than nothing. Thus, there must be at least one self-existent being that explains why there is something rather than nothing. Elsewhere, Clarke undertakes to prove that this being has the other attributes that we normally associate with divinity.

> There has existed from eternity some one unchangeable and independent being. For since something must needs have been from eternity, as has been already proved and is granted on all hands, either there has always existed some one unchangeable and independent being from which all other beings that are or ever were in the universe have received their original, or else there has been an infinite succession of changeable and dependent beings produced one from another in an endless progression without any original cause at all. Now this latter supposition is so very absurd that, though all atheism must in its accounts of most things [. . .] terminate in it, yet I think very few atheists ever were so weak as openly and directly to defend it. For it is plainly impossible and contradictory to itself. I shall not argue against it from the supposed impossibility of infinite succession, barely and absolutely considered in itself, for a reason which shall be mentioned hereafter. But, if we consider such an infinite progression as one entire endless series of dependent beings, it is plain this whole series of beings can have no cause from without of its existence because in it are supposed to be included all things that are, or ever were, in the universe. And it is plain it can have no reason within itself for its existence because no one being in this infinite succession is supposed to be self-existent or necessary (which is the only ground or reason of existence of anything that can be imagined within the thing itself [. . .]), but every one dependent on the foregoing. And where no part is necessary, it is manifest the whole cannot be necessary – absolute necessity of existence not being an extrinsic, relative, and accidental denomination but an inward and essential property of the nature of the thing which so exists. (Clark, 10)

Rowe's terminology:

"*dependent being*" = "a being whose existence is explained by the causal activity of other things"
"*self-existent being*" = "a being whose existence is explained by itself, that is, by its own nature"
"*positive fact*" = "a fact whose obtaining entails the existence of at least one contingent being"
"*contingent being*" = "a being such that it is logically possible for that being to exist and it is logically possible for that being not to exist"

Principle of Sufficient Reason (PSR):

PSR1. For every being that exists or ever existed, there is an explanation of the existence of that being.
PSR2. For every positive fact, there is an explanation of that fact.

P1. Every being (that exists or ever existed) is either a dependent being or a self-existent being.
P2. Not every being is a dependent being.
　　C1. There exists a self-existent being (disjunctive syllogism, P1, P2).

The argument is valid if it is interpreted as follows:

P1*. Every being is a dependent being or some being is a self-existent being. [Or: If no being is a self-existent being, then every being is a dependent being.]
P2*. It is not the case that every being is a dependent being.
　　C1*. Some being is a self-existent being (disjunctive syllogism, P1*, P2*).

The case for P1*:

P1 may appear to be a tautology, but it is not, because it rules out one type of case, namely, things whose existence is explained by nothing at all. Thus, it is equivalent to PSR1.

The case for P2*:

P3. If every being is a dependent being, then if there is an explanation for the fact that any dependent beings exist (rather than nothing at all), this will be in terms of the existence of either the totality of dependent beings or some subset of that totality.
P4. That any dependent beings exist at all (rather than nothing) is a positive fact (definitions of "dependent being", "positive fact").

P5. There is an explanation of every positive fact (PSR2).

C2. There is an explanation for the fact that any dependent beings exist at all (instantiation, P4, P5).

C3. If every being is a dependent being, then there is an explanation for the fact that any dependent beings exist (rather than nothing at all), in terms of the existence of either the totality of dependent beings or some subset of that totality (instantiation, P3, C2).

P6. It is not possible to explain the fact that any dependent beings exist at all (rather than nothing) simply in terms of the existence of either the totality of dependent beings or of some subset of that totality.

C4. It is not the case that every being is a dependent being (*modus tollens*, C3, P6).

Thus, P1* depends on PSR1 and P2* depends on PSR2, so, according to Rowe, the success of Clarke's contingency argument turns on the truth or rational acceptability of the Principle of Sufficient Reason itself.

3

The Kalam Argument for the Existence of God

Harry Lesser

Craig, William L. *The Kalam Cosmological Argument*. London: Macmillan, 1979.

One of the most interesting arguments for the existence of God was developed by the philosopher–theologians of the Kalam, the tradition of mediaeval Muslim theology, and has recently been revived by William Craig, among others. It is a version of the cosmological argument, being an argument from the mere existence of the universe to the existence of God, as opposed to arguing from the concept of God, as the ontological argument does, or from particular features of the universe, such as evidence of design. William Craig's formulation of the argument is particularly concise, and runs as follows:

> Whatever begins to exist has a cause.
> The universe began to exist.
> Therefore, the universe has a cause. (63)

This argument is clearly a valid *modus ponens*; but how certain is the truth of the premises? The major premise seems unproven. It is not self-contradictory to assert that something could, or did, begin to exist without any cause. There is, of course, a powerful empirical inductive argument

Just the Arguments: 100 of the Most Important Arguments in Western Philosophy,
First Edition. Edited by Michael Bruce and Steven Barbone.
© 2011 Blackwell Publishing Ltd. Published 2011 by Blackwell Publishing Ltd.

from the fact that there are billions upon billions of examples of something beginning to exist and having a cause of its existence, and not a single observed or recorded example of something coming to exist without a cause. But this is insufficient for proof for two reasons. First, no inductive argument gives us more than very good evidence that something is always the case: however many confirming instances we find, an exception is always a possibility, even if an unlikely one. Second, even if every individual entity in the universe that began to exist has a cause of its existence, it does not follow that this is true of the universe as a whole, since what is true even of every part is not necessarily true of the totality and vice versa.

A third argument for the claim that whatever begins to exist has a cause would be that though it is not self-contradictory that something might come into existence without a cause, it is unimaginable. To this two replies might be made. One is that this might be a feature of our minds rather than a feature of how the world really is, that is, simply a limit on what we can conceive and not a limit on what can happen. Secondly, the universe as a whole is something totally beyond our experience: hence it might be said that we simply have no idea what might or might not be possible. Hence, the major premise of the argument cannot be proven by either logic or experience. Nevertheless, the notion that something could come into being from nothing, without a cause, seems close to incredible, so that the premise, though unproven, seems very plausible.

On the other hand, the minor premise, that the universe has a beginning, for a long time looked very vulnerable: there seemed to be no reason to assert that the universe came into being rather than having always existed, as most of the Greeks, including Aristotle, thought. The Kalam philosophers themselves, and those who followed them, tried to argue that the notion of an infinite series of events back in time, with no first event, is incoherent or in some way impossible, but no convincing argument on these lines has been produced. It is true that the idea that time has no beginning creates problems for the mind, but there are equal problems in supposing that it does have a beginning, since one can always ask, "What happened before that?" What has reestablished the argument in a contemporary version, by no means confined to Muslims, is the increasing scientific evidence that the universe did have a beginning. This does not yet amount to proof: indeed, it is not clear what astronomical or other observations could absolutely prove the "big bang" theory of the beginning of the universe. But it makes the proposition, that the universe had a beginning, plausible, something for which there is evidence and which is believed by many who have studied the evidence. So the Kalam argument for the existence of God is a valid argument from two premises of which neither is proven nor certain, but both are plausible. The jury is still out, and much depends on how science develops and whether the minor premise looks increasingly plausible.

We should note, though, that the argument is incomplete. Even if the universe has a cause outside itself, further argument is needed to establish that the cause is an eternal and good being; in other words, that it is God. Some who accept the argument think that one also has to show that the cause is a personal being and have offered arguments for this. Certainly it could be argued that only an eternal being could precede the universe and therefore only an eternal being could cause it. It can also be argued that the only kind of cause that could operate on the universe from outside, as opposed to being part of it, would be the act of a personal being and only a good personal being would wish to create a universe. But it is fair to say, I think, that we have not yet got a full and rigorous working-out of this part of the argument, though the above indicates the lines it might take. Once again, we might say that it is plausible, but not proven, that the cause of the universe is a good personal Creator, just as it is plausible, but not proved, that the universe has a cause.

P1. If something begins to exist, then it has a cause.
P2. The universe began to exist.
  C1. The universe has a cause (*modus ponens*, P1, P2).

4

The Ontological Argument

Sara L. Uckelman

Anselm of Canterbury. *Proslogion,* in *S. Anselmi Cantuariensis Archiepiscopi Opera Omnia,* vol. 1, edited by F. S. Schmitt, 93–104. Seccovii: Abbatia, 1938–61.

Anselm of Canterbury. *Proslogion,* in *Anselm of Canterbury: The Major Works,* edited by B. Davies and G. R. Evans, translated by M. J. Charlesworth, 82–104. Oxford: Oxford University Press, 1998.

Davies, Brian. "Anselm and the Ontological Argument," in *The Cambridge Companion to Anselm,* edited by B. Davies and B. Leftow, 57–178. Cambridge, UK: Cambridge University Press, 2004.

In philosophy of religion, arguments that attempt to prove the existence of God on the basis of God's essence are called ontological arguments because they appeal only to the nature or essence of God's being. The first such argument was given by Saint Anselm of Canterbury (1033–1109) in Chapter II of his *Proslogion* (written *c.*1077–8). Saint Anselm defines God as "that than which nothing greater can be thought" and seeks to derive from this definition a contradiction with the assumption that God does not exist. Some modern commentators have also found another similar argument in *Proslogion* III, which purportedly shows not only that God exists but that God's existence is necessary. However, it is the argument in *Proslogion* II that is usually referred to simply as "the ontological argument."

Just the Arguments: 100 of the Most Important Arguments in Western Philosophy, First Edition. Edited by Michael Bruce and Steven Barbone.
© 2011 Blackwell Publishing Ltd. Published 2011 by Blackwell Publishing Ltd.

Many authors since Anselm have objected to the argument on the strength of its conclusion and have attempted to show that it is either invalid or unsound. During Anselm's lifetime, Gaunilo, a monk from Marmoutier, criticized the argument by showing that an argument of the same structure could be used to demonstrate the existence of the best possible island, which conclusion is taken to be absurd. While this criticism does not point to a specific error in Anselm's argument, it casts some doubt on its structure, since the same structure can be used to derive absurd conclusions. One famous counterargument is given by Immanuel Kant (1724–1804), who argues that Anselm mistakenly uses "existence" as a predicate, which it is not. However, there is no agreement as to the status of the validity of the argument or the soundness of its premises; even among those who believe the argument is problematic do not agree on what is the problem.

> Well then, Lord, You who give understanding to faith, grant me that I may understand, as much as You see fit, that You exist as we believe You to exist, and that You are what we believe You to be. Now we believe that You are something than which nothing greater can be thought. Or can it be that a thing of such a nature does not exist, since 'the Fool has said in his heart, there is no God' [Ps. 13: 1; 52: 1]? But surely, when this same Fool hears what I am speaking about, namely 'something-than-which-nothing-greater-can-be-thought', he understands what he hears, and what he understands is in his mind, even if he does not understand that it actually exists. For it is one thing for an object to exist in the mind, and another thing to understand that an object actually exists. Thus, when a painter plans beforehand what he is going to execute, he has [the picture] in his mind, but he does not yet think that it actually exists because he has not yet executed it. However, when he has actually painted it, then he both has it in his mind and understands that it exists because he has now made it. Even the Fool, then, is forced to agree that 'something-than-which-nothing-greater-can-be-thought exists in the mind, since he understands this when he hears it, and whatever is understood is in the mind. And surely that-than-which-a-greater-cannot-be-thought cannot exist in the mind alone. For if it exists solely in the mind, it can be thought to exist in reality also, which is greater. If then that-than-which-a-greater-cannot-be-thought exists in the mind alone, this same that-than-which-a-greater-cannot-be-thought is that-that-which-a-greater-can-be-thought. But this is obviously impossible. Therefore there is absolutely no doubt that something-than-which-a-greater-cannot-be-thought exists both in the mind and in reality. (Anselm trans. Charlesworth, 87)

P1. God is something than which nothing greater can be thought (definition).

P2. Existence in the understanding and existence in reality are two separate things.

P3. Existence in reality is greater than existence in the understanding.

(P3a. Something existing in reality is greater than something that only exists in the understanding.)

P4. Even the fool understands the concept of "something than which none greater can be imagined."

P5. If something is understood, then it exists in the understanding (definition).

    C1. "Something than which none greater can be imagined" exists in the understanding (*modus ponens*, P4, P5).

P6. "Something than which none greater can be imagined" can exist only in the understanding (assumption for *reductio*).

P7. It is greater for "something than which none greater can be imagined" to exist in reality than for it to just exist in the understanding.

    C2. There is something greater than "something than which none greater can be imagined" (instantiation, P6).

    C3. "Something than which none greater can be imagined" cannot exist only in the understanding. It must also exist in reality (*reductio*, P6–C2).

    C4. God exists (substitution of *definiendum* for *definiens*, C3, P1).

5

Pascal's Wager

Leslie Burkholder

Pascal, Blaise. *Pensées*, translated by John Warrington. London: Dent, 1960.

Hacking, Ian. "The Logic of Pascal's Wager." *American Philosophical Quarterly* 9 (1972): 186–92.
McClennan, Edward F. "Pascal's Wager and Finite Decision Theory," in *Gambling on God*, edited by Jeff Jordan, 115–33. London: Rowman & Littlefield, 1994.
Whyte, Jamie. *Crimes against Logic*. New York: McGraw-Hill, 2004.

Unlike some other arguments about God's existence, Pascal's Wager doesn't try to prove that God exists. It is intended to show that you are better off believing that God exists and leading the life of a believer than not doing so. More particularly, it tries to show that it is worthwhile to believe in the existence of a Christian God and lead the life of a Christian believer.

The following is a modern presentation of Pascal's thinking. The Christian God either exists or does not. It is difficult to prove the existence of God by philosophical argument. Is it worthwhile for you to live a Christian life – acting as though you are a believer – in the hope of attaining eternal life and of becoming a believer in the process of living that life? If God exists and if you live the Christian life, you will be saved. This has nearly infinite value to you. If God exists and if you do not lead the Christian life, you will be damned, a result whose negative utility is also large. If God does not exist and if you live the Christian life, you lose at most a little worldly pleasure compared to what you would get if God did exist. Hence the expected gain from living the Christian life is higher than that of living otherwise, so long as the probability of God's existence is greater than 0. It is foolish not to lead the Christian life.

Parts of the wager argument – whether in Pascal's own version or this modern one – are best presented using a device called a "decision table" (below). The words at the top of each column describe a possible state of the world or universe. There are just two, and each one has some chance or probability of being the truth. We can't eliminate either, according to Pascal. Each box tells the result you get if the state named in the column is true and you make the choice in the row. So, for example, the result for you if the Christian God exists and you lead the Christian life and believe this God exists is a gain or benefit of all – in Pascal's words – or infinite positive value – in the words of the modern argument – and a loss of either nothing – which seems to be what Pascal thinks – or something very small, some worldly pleasure – as the modern argument has it. Pascal doesn't explicitly tell us what goes into some of the boxes. For example, he doesn't say what the results for you are if the Christian God exists but you don't believe this. The modern statement of the wager fills this in for us.

The third and fourth premises of the argument below are implicit or hidden. This argument is certainly deductively valid once these hidden premises are added. Each simple step in the reasoning in the argument is truth-functionally valid. So any criticism of the argument must tell us that one or more of the premises are false. Here are some examples of criticisms:

(a) The first premise says that anyone who leads the Christian life and believes, no matter why he does this, gets the benefit. That's what is in Table 1 and the first premise tells us that everything in the table is true. But it's false. The Christian God would not reward someone who believes or leads the life of a believer solely in order to gain the benefit of infinite happiness.

(b) According to the reasoning, the table completely describes the possible states of the world and says what will result in each of these states if you do believe and lead an appropriate life or you don't believe and do not lead the Christian life. But is that correct? Suppose, when the Christian God doesn't exist, it is also true that another type of god does. This god punishes severely those who believe in the Christian God or lead a Christian life. This is a possibility; it is not ruled out by logic any more than the existence of the Christian God is ruled in or out by logic. If that happens, then what is said in Table 1 down column 2 aren't certain results. They are merely one among many possible sets of results. These are the results that would happen when the Christian

Table 1

	Christian God exists (Prob > 0)	*Christian God doesn't exist (Prob > 0)*
Lead Christian life and believe Christian God exists	Gain = all, infinite good; loss = small or nothing	Gain = nothing; loss = small or nothing
Don't lead Christian life and believe Christian God exists	Gain = nothing; loss = all, infinite bad	Gain = nothing; loss = nothing

God doesn't exist and no other god does either. What is said about the state when the Christian God doesn't exist also holds for when that God does exist. Other kinds of gods could possibly exist as well, even when the Christian God exists. The results listed in column 1 of the table are only the ones that happen when the Christian God exists and no other kind of god does. So either premise 1 is false because what the table states is that the results are really only one of indefinitely many possible results, or premise 2 is false because the columns do not cover all the possibilities. They only really cover the case when the Christian God exists and no other does and the case when the Christian God does not exist and no other does either.

(c) Suppose that there is no problem with either premise 1 or premise 2. Then there is a problem with the implicit or hidden premise 3. According to the table, the benefit gained from believing in the case when the Christian God exists is infinitely positive and the loss from not believing in this case is infinitely negative. Using these facts and the rest in the table, we are supposed to be able to calculate that we are better off believing in the existence of the Christian God than not believing. But there is no way to make sound calculations involving infinite gains and losses. So premise 3 may be false – or at least it is very uncertain that it is true.

God is, or He is not. Reason can decide nothing here. [. . .] A game is being played at the extremity of this infinite distance where heads or tails will turn up. [. . .] Which will you choose then? [. . .] Let us weigh the gain and the loss in wagering that God is. [. . .] If you gain, you gain all; if you lose, you lose nothing. Wager, then, without hesitation that He is. (§233)

P1. The information in Table 1 is true.
P2. The information in Table 1 is complete.
  C1. The information in Table 1 is true and the information in Table 1 is complete (conjunction, P1, P2).

P3. If the information in Table 1 is true and the information in Table 1 is complete, then you are better off having the life of a believer and believing in the Christian God than not doing so.

C2. You are better off having the life of a believer and believing in the Christian God than not doing so (*modus ponens*, C1, P3).

P4. If you are better off having the life of a believer and believing in the Christian God than not doing so, then you logically should choose the Christian kind of life and believe in God.

C3. You logically should choose the Christian kind of life and believe in God (*modus ponens*, C2, P4).

6

James' Will to Believe Argument

A. T. Fyfe

James, William. *The Will to Believe and Other Essays in Popular Philosophy.* New York: Dover, 1956.

Welchman, Jennifer. "William James's 'The Will to Believe' and the Ethics of Self-Experimentation." *Transactions of the Charles S. Pierce Society* 42, 2 (Spring 2006): 229–41.
Wernham, James C. S. *James' Will-to-Believe Doctrine: A Heretical View.* Montreal: McGill-Queen's University Press, 1987.

William James (1842–1910), in his 1896 lecture, "The Will to Believe," gave an argument for holding onto religious belief even in the face of insufficient evidence that is second in prominence only to Pascal's Wager (#5). James' stated target in his lecture is W. K. Clifford (1845–79), a philosopher who had recently argued in his "The Ethics of Belief" that "It is wrong always, everywhere and for everyone to believe anything upon insufficient evidence." James' strategy in "The Will to Believe" is first to identify what he thought would be a point of agreement with Clifford; specifically, that our two fundamental duties as believers are to believe truth and avoid falsehood. James then goes on to agree partially with Clifford that at least ordinarily, when someone believes upon insufficient evidence, he is irrational. This is because while believing upon insufficient evidence does con-

Just the Arguments: 100 of the Most Important Arguments in Western Philosophy, First Edition. Edited by Michael Bruce and Steven Barbone.
© 2011 Blackwell Publishing Ltd. Published 2011 by Blackwell Publishing Ltd.

tribute to the pursuit of true belief (since the belief might be true), when someone believes upon insufficient evidence, he is usually violating his duty to avoid false belief (since he didn't wait for sufficient evidence before believing).

Where James disagrees with Clifford is on whether believing upon insufficient evidence always involves violating our duty to avoid false belief. Specifically, James argues that there exist beliefs for which the evidence of their truth (if they were true) would only become available after we believed them and, therefore, waiting to believe until we had sufficient evidence would be a self-defeating wait. To illustrate with an example, suppose that you have just finished medical school and that you are trying to decide whether to join a research team working to discover a cure for cancer. Now, to make such a substantial commitment to the search for a cure, James would argue that you must believe that a cure exists to be found. That is, you'd be fooling yourself if you thought you could make such a momentous career choice while continuing to suspend belief about the existence of the cure you're looking for. At the very least, most people would need such a belief to sustain them during the times in which their research was going poorly. That being said, sufficient evidence that such a cure exists won't be available until well into the search for one. Therefore, a belief in the existence of a cure for cancer is a belief for which the evidence of its truth (if it is true) only becomes available after we believe a cure exists.

Similar to a cancer researcher's belief in the existence of a cure, James holds that religious belief is required before evidence of its truth (if it is true) can become available. While this would seem to justify religious belief only for those who make a career of religious research, James argues that religious belief is justified even for ordinary believers in virtue of the peculiar way its evidence depends upon their belief. In the preface to the published version of his "The Will to Believe" lecture, James fills in this last step of his argument:

> If religious hypotheses about the universe be in order at all, then the active faiths of individuals in them, freely expressing themselves in life, are the experimental tests by which they are verified, and the only means by which their truth or falsehood can be wrought out. The truest scientific hypothesis is that which, as we say, 'works' best; and it can be no otherwise with religious hypotheses. Religious history proves that one hypothesis after another has worked ill, has crumbled at contact with a widening knowledge of the world, and has lapsed from the minds of men. Some articles of faith, however, have maintained themselves through every vicissitude, and possess even more vitality to-day than ever before [...]. [T]he freest competition of the various faiths with one another, and their openest application to life by their several champions, are the most favorable conditions under which the survival of the fittest can proceed. (XII)

P1. It is not rational to have religious belief without sufficient evidence if and only if having religious belief without sufficient evidence violates our duty to avoid false belief.

P2. Having religious belief without sufficient evidence violates our duty to avoid false belief if and only if I could withhold religious belief for the purpose of waiting until I had sufficient evidence.

C1. If it is not rational to have religious belief without sufficient evidence, then having religious belief without sufficient evidence violates our duty to avoid false belief (equivalence, simplification, P1).

C2. If having religious belief without sufficient evidence violates our duty to avoid false belief, then I could withhold religious belief for the purpose of waiting until I had sufficient evidence (equivalence, simplification, P2).

C3. If it is not rational to have religious belief without sufficient evidence, then I could withhold religious belief for the purpose of waiting until I had sufficient evidence (hypothetical syllogism, C1, C2).

P3. Access to the evidence for religious belief requires already having religious belief.

P4. If access to the evidence for religious belief requires already having religious belief, then I cannot withhold belief for the purpose of waiting until I had sufficient evidence.

C4. I cannot withhold religious belief for the purpose of waiting until I had sufficient evidence (*modus ponens*, P3, P4).

C5. It is rational to have religious belief without sufficient evidence (*modus tollens*, C3, C4).

7

The Problem of Evil

Michael Bruce and Steven Barbone

Inwood, Brad, and L. P. Gerson. *Hellenistic Philosophy*. Indianapolis: Hackett, 1988.

Hume, David. *Dialogues Concerning Natural Religion*. Indianapolis: Hackett, 1980.

Mackie, J. L. "Evil and Omnipotence." *Mind* 64 (1955): 200–12.

In the philosophy of religion, the "problem of evil" (sometimes referred to as "theodicy") is one of the oldest and most interesting areas of study. There have been numerous reformulations and solutions proposed, most of which try to reconcile the existence of evil in the world with the concept of God as omnipotent, omniscient, and omnibenevolent (all powerful, all knowing, and all loving). Epicurus (341–270 BCE) is usually cited as the first author to articulate this tension. Following Epicurus, we present a generic argument that more explicitly shows the inferences. Starting with the premise of an omnipotent, omniscient, and omnibenevolent God, the argument shows only that the definition is incoherent by conflict with the existence of evil and the relevant collective attributes of God. A common mistake in interpreting this argument is to suppose that it shows that "God" does not exist *tout court*; what this argument in fact shows is that "God" as defined in a certain way is contradictory and therefore cannot exist as such.

Just the Arguments: 100 of the Most Important Arguments in Western Philosophy,
First Edition. Edited by Michael Bruce and Steven Barbone.
© 2011 Blackwell Publishing Ltd. Published 2011 by Blackwell Publishing Ltd.

God either wants to eliminate bad things and cannot, or can but does not want to, or neither wishes to nor can, or both wants to and can. If he wants to and cannot, he is weak – and this does not apply to god. If he can, but does not want to, then he is spiteful – which is equally foreign to god's nature. If he neither wants to nor can, he is both weak and spiteful and so not a god. If he wants to and can, which is the only thing fitting for a god, where then do bad things come from? Or why does he not eliminate them? (Epicurus as recounted by Lactantius, qtd. in Inwood and Gerson, 94)

P1. God is omnipotent, omniscient, and morally perfect.

P2. If God is omnipotent, then God has the power to eliminate all evil.

C1. God has the power to eliminate all evil (*modus ponens*, P1, P2).

P3. If God is omniscient, then God knows evil exists.

C2. God knows evil exists (*modus ponens*, P1, P3).

P4. If God is morally perfect, then God has the desire to eliminate all evil.

C3. God has the desire to eliminate all evil (*modus ponens*, P1, P4).

P5. Evil exists.

P6. If evil exists, then either God doesn't have the power to eliminate all evil or doesn't know evil exists or doesn't have the desire to eliminate all evil.

C4. God doesn't have the power to eliminate all evil or doesn't know evil exists or doesn't have the desire to eliminate all evil (*modus ponens*, P5, P6).

P7. If God doesn't have the power to eliminate all evil or doesn't know evil exists or doesn't have the desire to eliminate all evil, then God does not exist.

C5. God does not exist (*modus ponens*, P7, C4).

8

The Free Will Defense to the Problem of Evil

Grant Sterling

van Inwagen, Peter. *The Problem of Evil*. Oxford: Clarendon Press, 2006.

The free will defense is a response to the problem of evil (#7). This defense is designed to show that there is no contradiction in supposing that God would allow evil to exist (even if God is omnipotent, omniscient, and perfectly good), because even a perfectly good being might have reason to permit an evil to exist if there is some greater good that cannot be achieved without allowing it. The proponent of the free will defense thinks that free will is such a good – it is logically impossible for even God to give a creature free will and at the same time guarantee that it will always choose rightly, and yet free will is a very great good (or is necessary for the existence of great goods).

Note that for many advocates of this argument, it is only necessary to show that such a story is coherent, not that it is true. That is, since the problem of evil claims that it is impossible for God and evil both to exist, to refute the argument, it is only necessary to show that the existence of both God and evil is a coherent possibility. On this understanding, a "defense" claims to lay out a coherent possibility, whereas a philosopher who undertakes a "theodicy" aims to show that this possibility is the actual reason God allows evil.

Just the Arguments: 100 of the Most Important Arguments in Western Philosophy,
First Edition. Edited by Michael Bruce and Steven Barbone.
© 2011 Blackwell Publishing Ltd. Published 2011 by Blackwell Publishing Ltd.

I grant that, in some sense of the word, the non-existence of evil must be what a perfectly good being wants. But we often don't bring about states of affairs we can bring about and want to bring about. Suppose, for example, that Alice's mother is dying in great pain and that Alice yearns desperately for her mother to die today and not next week or next month. And suppose it would be easy for Alice to arrange this – she is perhaps a doctor or a nurse and has easy access to pharmaceutical resources that would enable her to achieve this end. Does it follow that she will act on this ability that she has? It is obvious that it does not, for Alice might have reasons for not doing what she can do. Two obvious candidates for such reasons are: she thinks it would be morally wrong; she is afraid that her act would be discovered, and that she would be prosecuted for murder. And either of these reasons might be sufficient, in her mind, to outweigh her desire for an immediate end to her mother's sufferings. So it may be that someone has a very strong desire for something and is able to obtain this thing, but does not act on this desire – because he has reasons for not doing so that seem to him to outweigh the desirability of the thing. The conclusion that evil does not exist does not, therefore, follow logically from the premises that the non-existence of evil is what God wants and that he is able to bring about the object of his desire – since, for all logic can tell us, God might have reasons for allowing evil to exist that, in his mind, outweigh the desirability of the non-existence of evil. (van Inwagen, 64–5)

God made the world and it was very good. An indispensable part of the goodness he chose was the existence of rational beings: self-aware beings capable of abstract thought and love and having the power of free choice between contemplated alternative courses of action. This last feature of rational beings, free choice or free will, is a good. But even an omnipotent being is unable to control the exercise of the power of free choice, for a choice that was controlled would ipso facto not be free. In other words, if I have a free choice between x and y, even God cannot ensure that I choose x. To ask God to give me a free choice between x and y and to see to it that I choose x instead of y is to ask God to bring about the intrinsically impossible; it is like asking him to create a round square, a material body that has no shape, or an invisible object that casts a shadow. Having this power of free choice, some or all human beings misused it and produced a certain amount of evil. But free will is a sufficiently great good that its existence outweighs the evils that have resulted and will result from its abuse; and God foresaw this. (van Inwagen, 71–2)

Problem of Evil, Conclusion 3: *C3*. God has the desire to eliminate all evil.

P1. God is omnipotent, omniscient, and morally perfect.
P2. If God is morally perfect, then if it is impossible to secure a great good without permitting an evil, God will not desire to eliminate that evil.

P3. Free will in created beings is a great good (or is a necessary precondition for great goods).

P4. It is impossible to secure the existence of free will in created beings without permitting evil to exist.

    C1. If it is impossible to secure a great good without permitting an evil, God will not desire to eliminate that evil (*modus ponens,* P1, P2).

    C2. It is impossible to secure a great good (free will) without permitting an evil (semantic substitution, P3, P4).

    C3. God will not desire to eliminate all evil (*modus ponens,* C1, C2, with slight semantic variation).

    C4. *C3* (Conclusion 3 of the Problem of Evil) is false (double negation, C3).

    C5. The Problem of Evil is unsound. (All arguments with a false premise are unsound by definition.)

9

St. Anselm on Free Choice and the Power to Sin

Julia Hermann

S. Anselmi Cantuariensis Archiepiscopi Opera Omnia. Edited by Franciscus
Salesius Schmitt, 3 vols. Stuttgart – Bad Cannstatt: Friedrich Fromann
Verlag, 1968. (S)
Anselm. *Three Philosophical Dialogues*, translated by Thomas Williams.
Indianapolis: Hackett, 2002. (*Dialogues*)

Anselm's argument for the claim that freedom of choice does not entail the power to sin is still of great philosophical interest regarding the problem of free will. Interested in how free will bears on the human responsibility for sin and the need for grace, Anselm's reasons for dealing with the issue differ from those of contemporary philosophers. Yet, we do not have to share his interests in order to see the force of his arguments.

The argument presented here can be found at the beginning of Anselm's dialogue "On Freedom of Choice," which is the second of three "treatises pertaining to the study of Holy Scripture" (S I: 173; *Dialogues*, 1), all of which deal with closely related subject matters: truth and justice (*De Veritate*), freedom of choice (*De Libertate Arbitrii*), and the fall of the devil (*De Casu Diaboli*). The speakers are the same in all three dialogues: a teacher asking questions and a student responding to them.

At the beginning of the second dialogue, the teacher rejects the view put forward by the student that "freedom of choice is 'the ability to sin and not to sin'" (S 208; *Dialogues*, 32). He starts with a *reductio ad absurdum*:

Just the Arguments: 100 of the Most Important Arguments in Western Philosophy,
First Edition. Edited by Michael Bruce and Steven Barbone.
© 2011 Blackwell Publishing Ltd. Published 2011 by Blackwell Publishing Ltd.

If freedom of choice was that ability, "neither God nor the angels, who cannot sin, would have free choice – which it is impious to say" (ibid.). He then provides a further argument for the claim that "the power to sin is neither freedom nor a part of freedom," which will be reconstructed below (ibid.).

Initially, the student believes that a will capable of both sinning and not sinning is freer than a will which lacks the former capacity. This reveals the assumption, prominent in recent debates about the compatibility of free will and determinism, that the capacity to do otherwise is a necessary condition for freedom of will ("Principle of Alternative Possibilities," #31). Anselm rejects this assumption, holding that freedom does not depend on the possibility to will both what is just and what is unjust but on the ability to initiate one's own actions. It is a necessary condition for a person's will to be free that his actions have their origin in him and not in any external power (S I: 209f; *Dialogues*, 33f.). Freedom of will (or choice) is only impeded by external compulsion, not by the lack of alternative possibilities. Today, we find elaborated versions of this idea in accounts of "agent-causality."

Starting from the premise that "if someone has what is fitting and expedient in such a way that he cannot lose it, he is freer than someone who has it in such a way that he can lose it and be seduced into what is unfitting and harmful," Anselm argues that a will that lacks the ability to sin is freer than a will that has it. He then continues arguing that since something that diminishes the will's freedom when added to the will cannot be freedom or a part of it, and since the power to sin diminishes freedom when added to the will, that power is neither freedom nor a part of freedom.

Initially, the first premise of the argument seems controversial. It must be seen in the light of Anselm's teleological conception of freedom. Later in the dialogue, freedom of choice is defined as "the power to preserve rectitude of will for the sake of rectitude itself" (S I: 212; *Dialogues*, 36). This definition, in turn, cannot be understood independently of Anselm's discussion of truth in the first dialogue. There he argues that truth consists in rectitude, or correctness (*rectitudo*, S I: 177; *Dialogues*, 5). He speaks of truth not only in statements and opinions but also in actions, the will, the senses, and the essences of things. According to his teleological understanding of rectitude, a will has rectitude if it wills what it ought to will, that is, what God wants it to will (S I: 181f; *Dialogues*, 8f).

Anselm then defines justice as "rectitude of will preserved for its own sake" (S I: 194; *Dialogues*, 24). Given that in the second dialogue freedom of choice is defined as "the power to preserve rectitude of will for the sake of rectitude itself," freedom of choice turns out to be identical with a capacity for justice. This illuminates why the ability to sin, when added to the will, diminishes its freedom. Also, we can now see clearly that, like his understanding of truth, Anselm's understanding of freedom is teleological. This distinguishes him from most contemporary philosophers.

In the way in which Anselm presents his argument, it is incomplete. To be formally and semantically valid, it has to be supplemented by a number of premises that are merely implicit in the text. The original argument is contained in the following passage from "On Free Will":

> T: Which will do you think is freer: one whose willing and whose ability not to sin are such that it cannot be turned away from the rectitude of not sinning, or one that in some way can be turned to sin?
> S: I don't see why a will isn't freer when it is capable of both.
> T: Do you not see that someone who has what is fitting and expedient in such a way that he cannot lose it is freer than someone who has it in such a way that he can lose it and be seduced into what is unfitting and inexpedient?
> S: I don't think anyone would doubt that.
> T: And you will say that it is no less indubitable that sinning is always unfitting and harmful.
> S: No one in his right mind thinks otherwise.
> T: Then a will that cannot fall away from the rectitude of not sinning is freer than a will that can abandon that rectitude.
> S: I don't think anything could be more reasonably asserted.
> T: Now if something diminishes freedom if it is added and increases freedom if taken away, do you think that it is either freedom or a part of freedom?
> S: I cannot think so.
> T: Then the power to sin, which if added to the will diminishes its freedom and if taken away increases it, is neither freedom nor a part of freedom.
> S: Nothing could be more logical. (S I: 208f; *Dialogues*, 32f)

P1. If someone has what is fitting and expedient in such a way that he cannot lose it, he is freer than someone who has it in such a way that he can lose it and be seduced into what is unfitting and harmful.

P2. Rectitude is fitting and expedient.

   C1. If someone has rectitude in such a way that he cannot lose it, then he is freer than someone who has it in such a way that he can lose it and be seduced into what is unfitting and harmful (substitution, P1, P2).

P3. Sinning is always unfitting and harmful.

   C2. If someone has rectitude in such a way that he cannot lose it, then he is freer than someone who has it in such a way that he can lose it and be seduced into sinning (substitution, C1, P3).

P4. Someone who has rectitude in such a way that he cannot lose it is someone who has a will that cannot fall away from the rectitude of not sinning.

P5. If someone has a will that cannot fall away from the rectitude of not sinning, then he is freer than someone who has it in such a way that he can lose it and be seduced into sinning (substitution, C2, P4).

   C3. Someone who has a will that cannot fall away from the rectitude of not sinning is freer than a will that has rectitude in such a way that he can lose it and be seduced into sinning (*modus ponens*, P5, P4).

P6. A will that can abandon rectitude is a will that has rectitude in such a way that it can lose it and be seduced into sinning.

   C4. A will that cannot fall away from the rectitude of not sinning is freer than a will that can abandon rectitude (substitution, C3, P6).

P7. The power to sin diminishes freedom if it is added to the will and increases freedom if it is taken away from it (implied by C2).

P8. If something diminishes freedom if it is added and increases freedom if taken away, then it is neither freedom nor a part of freedom.

   C5. The power to sin is neither freedom nor a part of freedom (*modus ponens*, P7, P8).

10

Hume's Argument against Miracles

Tommaso Piazza

Hume, David. *An Inquiry concerning Human Understanding*. Indianapolis: Hackett, 1997.

Buckle, Stephen. *Hume's Enlightenment Tract: The Unity and Purpose of An Inquiry Concerning Human Understanding*. Oxford: Oxford University Press, 2001.
Fogelin, Robert J. *A Defense of Hume on Miracles*. Princeton, NJ: Princeton University Press, 2003.
Levine, Michael P. *Hume and the Problem of Miracles: A Solution*. Dordrecht: Kluwer, 1989.
____. "Miracles." *The Stanford Encyclopedia of Philosophy* (Winter 2005 edn.), edited by Edward N. Zalta, available at http://plato.stanford.edu/entries/miracles/#Hum
Swinburne, Richard. *The Existence of God*. Oxford: Oxford University Press, 2004.

Originally planned to appear in the earlier *Treatise of Human Nature* (1739–40), Hume's argument against miracles first went to press as Chapter X of *An Inquiry concerning Human Understanding* in 1748. Since then, mainly as a separate text, it has been granted continued attention. The argument is part of Hume's philosophy of religion. In particular, it is inserted within a discussion about whether some religious belief could be

Just the Arguments: 100 of the Most Important Arguments in Western Philosophy, First Edition. Edited by Michael Bruce and Steven Barbone.
© 2011 Blackwell Publishing Ltd. Published 2011 by Blackwell Publishing Ltd.

established by revelation; the argument purports to vindicate a negative answer to this question, by showing that miracles – the very foundation of revealed religion – are not (could not be) credible. Importantly, it is independent of any metaphysical claim about whether a miracle is or is not possible, and it is just premised on Hume's empiricist views in epistemology. Here is how Hume summarizes the argument:

> A miracle is a violation of the laws of nature [DEF-m]; and as a firm and unalterable experience has established these laws [DEF-l], the proof against a miracle, from the very nature of the fact, is as entire as any argument from experience can possibly be imagined. (Hume, 76)

It is scarcely controversial, although it has not remained unchallenged (see Swinburne), that Hume's argument is to be read as addressing the question about whether we could be justified in believing in a miracle on the basis of empirical evidence; in fact, he leaves to a different part of the *Inquiry* a discussion of whether we could have knowledge of God (and so, on its basis, indirectly of miracles) other than by revelation. It is a bit more controversial, though, whether Hume is trying to establish the conclusion that we could be justified in believing in a miracle on the basis of no empirical evidence whatsoever – and so, in particular, not even if we had an experience of a miracle – or the considerably weaker conclusion that we could not be justified in believing in a miracle on the basis of the testimony of others. In what follows, the argument will be presented as it is more customarily discussed, that is, as aimed to establish the weaker conclusion. It is also unclear whether Hume's argument is meant to be *a priori* or *a posteriori*. This difference is worth taking into consideration for the following reason: while many philosophers think that *a priori* justification is indefeasible by experience, it is quite uncontroversial that *a posteriori* justification can be so defeated; since the conclusion of an argument cannot be justified more firmly than its premises, this implies that Hume's argument, depending on whether we read it as *a priori* or *a posteriori*, is aimed to establish a conclusion that cannot – respectively can – be overturned by further experiences. A possible irenic solution that will be adopted here is to divide Hume's argument in two parts (corresponding to the parts into which Chapter X is divided),[1] and to read the first of them as aimed to assess the question whether testimony (possibly) justifies belief in a miracle (at least in part) in light of *a priori* considerations, and to read the second

---

[1] Buckle explains that both parts reflect to some degree a division of probability arguments which was common in Hume's time: that among "internal" and "external" evidences. The internal part of any such argument examines the internal credibility of a claim, the external part examines this claim in light of the evidence available.

as aimed to assess the very same question in light of additional considerations of a clearly *a posteriori* nature. As we will see, the (sub)conclusion of the first part is logically weaker than the conclusion of the second. By the same token, the conclusion of the first argument has appeared more resistible than the conclusion of the second. (For this reason, Fogelin contends that Hume just wanted to offer the second argument and not the first.) The first argument purports to show that no testimony could ever provide evidence that is strong enough to undermine our expectation that events that have always been experienced in conjunction with one another will not (and did not) appear in conjunction with one another; the second argument aims just to show that no testimony has provided such evidence. Finally, it is worth mentioning that some controversy surrounds the scope of the conclusion that (the first part of) Hume's argument, if successful, would actually establish. In particular, it has been suggested that the argument quickly (and undesirably) generalizes to the conclusion that it is always irrational to accept testimony of something which is very unlikely in light of past experience (such as water's becoming ice, if you live in a very warm region). Hume's insistence on the distinction among extraordinary (yet natural) events and miracles is often invoked to resist this objection (Levine): given its supernatural origin, a miracle cannot be judged to be analogous to any other event in experience; on the contrary, an extraordinary event can bear the relevant similarity to past experience and then become acceptable by analogy. Yet, it is controversial whether this strategy – since it implies that Hume's argument should feature as a premise the claim that we could not have had an experience of a miraculous event – creates more problems for Hume's argument than it helps to solve.

P1. That A is the case provides evidence E for B's being the case if and only if the number of times in which we have observed A, and then have observed B, is greater than the number of times in which we have observed that A was not followed by B.

P2. The strength of E is proportional to the ratio among the number of times in which we have observed A, and then have observed B, and the number of times in which we have observed that A was not followed by B.

P3. The existence of testimony of type K (henceforth K-testimony) to the effect that B was not the case provides evidence ET for the proposition that B was not the case only if the number of times in which we have received K-testimony for a proposition, and then have observed that the proposition was true, is greater than the number of times in which we have received K-testimony for a proposition and then have observed that the proposition was not true (instantiation, P1).

P4. The strength of ET is proportional to the ratio among the number of times in which we have received K-testimony for a proposition and then have observed that the proposition was true and the number of times in which we have received K-testimony for a proposition and then have observed that the proposition was not true (instantiation, P2).

P5. Whenever one's global evidence is constituted by E1 and E2, and E1 is evidence in favor of a given p, and E2 is evidence for non-p, it is rational to believe that p only if E1 is stronger than E2, it is rational to disbelieve that p only if E2 is stronger than E1, and it is rational to withhold belief as to whether p only if the strength of E1 is the same as the strength of E2.

P6. There is K-testimony to the occurrence of a miracle M.

P7. There is a law of nature L – say that every A is followed by B – and the K-testimony is to the effect that A was not followed by B (DEF–m).

P8. It is rational to accept that M occurred (assumption for *reductio*).

P9. That A was the case provides evidence E* for the proposition that B was the case, which is weaker than the evidence ET, provided by the K-testimony, for the proposition that B was not the case.

P10. If it is rational to accept that M occurred, then that A was the case provides evidence E* for the proposition that B was the case, which is weaker than the evidence ET, provided by the K-testimony, for the proposition that B was not the case (instantiation, P8, P9).

P11. L has been established by a "firm and unalterable experience" of many instances of A's that were followed by many instances of B's without exception (DEF-1).

P12. That A was the case provides the strongest possible evidence E* for the proposition that B was the case (instantiation, P2, P11).

P13. ET is stronger than the strongest possible evidence E* (conjunction P9, P12).

C1. It is not the case that ET is stronger than E*.

C2. It is not rational to accept that M occurred (*modus tollens*, P10, C1).

The (sub)conclusion above is derived without further specifying the nature of the K-testimony in favor of a miracle (namely, independently of the number, reliability, opportunity, etc. of the witnesses reporting M that identify the relevant K). So, at least to this extent, the argument is *a priori*. Importantly, the conclusion is still compatible with its being rational, on the basis of testimony, to withhold belief as to whether a miracle occurred. As already anticipated, however, in the second part of Chapter X of the *Inquiry*, Hume presents empirical considerations about the K-testimony which is actually available that allow one to derive a logically stronger conclusion.

> There is not to be found, in all history, any miracle attested by a sufficient number of men, of such unquestioned good-sense, education and learning as to secure us against all delusion. [...] The passion of surprise and wonder, arising from miracles, being an agreeable emotion, gives a sensible tendency towards the belief of these events. (Hume, 78)

Empirical observation of the nature of the witnesses who have testified to a miracle and the general psychological remark that men are far too prone to believe in the marvelous suggest that the testimony for a miracle that is actually available is of a kind K that is unable to deliver evidence ET that is strong enough to equal to (not to say to outweigh) the evidence we have to expect nature to proceed along the course we have always experienced. So, it arguably enforces:

C1. Evidence ET is weaker than E^*.
C2. It is (more) rational to believe that M did not occur (*modus ponens*, P5, C1).

11

The Euthyphro Dilemma

David Baggett

Plato. *The Collected Dialogues of Plato*, edited by Edith Hamilton and Huntington Cairns. Princeton, NJ: Princeton University Press, 1961.

Adams, Robert. *Finite and Infinite Goods: A Framework for Ethics*. Oxford: Oxford University Press, 2000.
Baggett, David, and Jerry L. Walls. *Good God: The Theistic Foundations of Morality*. New York: Oxford University Press, 2011.

Antony Flew once said that the test of one's aptitude in philosophy is one's ability to grasp the force and point of the "Euthyphro Dilemma," a traditional objection to theistic ethics traceable to an early Socratic dialogue. The dilemma has long been thought to be an effective refutation of the effort to locate the authority of morality in the will or commands of God (or the gods). In the original context, the dilemma referred to the Greek pantheon of gods and what they loved and hated, whereas in more recent times the formulation is typically in terms of God and God's commands. The point of the dilemma is that God, even if God exists, does not function as the foundation of ethics. At most, God satisfies a prudential or epistemic function when it comes to morality, but not an ontological one, if the argument goes through.

About halfway into Plato's *Euthyphro*, Socrates asks the young Euthyphro a question that has come to be known as the "Euthyphro Dilemma." Expressed in contemporary and monotheistic terms, it can be put like this:

Just the Arguments: 100 of the Most Important Arguments in Western Philosophy,
First Edition. Edited by Michael Bruce and Steven Barbone.
© 2011 Blackwell Publishing Ltd. Published 2011 by Blackwell Publishing Ltd.

Does God command something because it is moral, or is something moral because God commands it? In the original context, Euthyphro, a firm believer in the Greek pantheon of gods, argues that the essence of holiness is what the gods love. After Socrates elicits from Euthyphro the admission that the gods, according to legend, could disagree, Euthyphro's view became that the holy is what all the gods loved and the unholy what all the gods hated. At this point, Socrates shifts gears and introduces the Dilemma, both horns of which are problematic for the theistic ethicist: for either God is merely reporting what's moral apart from God or God can render as moral whatever God's whim happens to choose.

Many classical theists find both horns of the dilemma unacceptable, because as moral realists they are unwilling to think of morality as infinitely malleable, and as robust supernaturalists they resist the notion that God is essentially irrelevant to a matter so important as moral truth. One common effort at the solution is to disambiguate "morality" between its deontic and axiological dimensions, distinguishing between obligation and value, and rooting God's commands only in the former. God's commands thus provide a way to delimit among what's good what's also obligatory, since some such mechanism is necessary because not everything that's morally good is also morally obligatory (otherwise there would no room for the category of supererogation, moral actions that go above and beyond the call of duty, a category that act utilitarians have a notoriously hard time accommodating).

A principled affirmation of divine impeccability (sinlessness) helps resolve arbitrariness and vacuity concerns, because if God is essentially good and loving, then God would never issue commands in irremediable tension with nonnegotiable moral intuitions.

A series of six additional distinctions can also be useful in diffusing the Euthyphro Dilemma. A scope distinction between definition and analysis, a semantic distinction between univocation and equivocation, a modal distinction between conceivability and possibility, an epistemic distinction between difficulty and impossibility, a metaethical distinction between knowing and being, and an ontological distinction between dependence and control collectively can enable the theistic ethicist to defend her view against the Euthyphro Dilemma. Therefore, God's commands can provide the right analysis of moral obligations even if not a definition of "moral obligation," which allows atheists to use deontic language meaningfully without believing in God. God would, moreover, retain moral prerogatives that human beings wouldn't, so God's behavior, though ultimately recognizable as moral, need not be exactly like human morality (contrary to John Stuart Mill's claim to the contrary). Although God's issuing irremediably evil commands is vaguely conceivable, it wouldn't be genuinely possible; reconciling God's commands with ineliminable moral intuitions may be difficult but can't be impossible if it's rational to believe in God's moral perfection; and our grasp of necessary moral facts is an epistemic issue that would under-determine the metaphysical foundations of morality. And finally, the dependence of morality on God does not entail God's volitional control over the contents of morality to make it just anything at all; divine impeccability would rule some things out. Armed with such distinctions, the theistic ethicist and divine command theorist has not been shown to be irrational in light of the Euthyphro Dilemma.

> Is what is holy holy because the gods approve it, or do they approve it because it is holy? (Plato, 10a)

P1. What is moral is either moral because God commands it or it is not.
P2. If what is moral is moral because God commands it, then morality is arbitrary and vacuous.
P3. If what is moral is moral for reasons other than that God commands it, then God is superfluous from the standpoint of morality.
   C1. Either morality is arbitrary and vacuous or God is superfluous to morality (constructive dilemma, P1, P2, P3).

12

Nietzsche's Death of God

Tom Grimwood

Nietzsche, Friedrich. *The Gay Science*, translated by Josefine Nauckhoff. Cambridge, UK: Cambridge University Press, 2001.

While Nietzsche resists easy logical formulation, the significance of his critique of the ideas of truth and morality in Western philosophy makes him one of the most important thinkers in modern times. Perhaps no other philosopher has been defined through his legacy as has been Nietzsche: the assault on the metaphysical nature of truth in this argument not only lays foundations for existentialism, poststructuralism, and postmodernism, but it also provides moral philosophy with an emblematic figure of moral skepticism (in the work of MacIntyre or Williams, for example).

For Nietzsche, the contemporary age (Northern Europe at the end of the nineteenth century) was witnessing a radical undermining of its philosophical foundations. On the one hand, the traditional beliefs in God were rendered unbelievable by developments in science. But on the other hand, the gap this left in existence had merely being filled by a substitute, science itself, which for Nietzsche maintained the same illusory suppositions over the sacred nature of "truth." On the one hand, the rise of the middle classes in the industrial age was undermining traditional structures of society, revealing the importance and malleability of power to the development of humanity. On the other hand, Nietzsche saw that this great shift had produced not radical change but only apathy. The real problem, Nietzsche argued, was not that God had ceased to be believable, but – given the way

Just the Arguments: 100 of the Most Important Arguments in Western Philosophy, First Edition. Edited by Michael Bruce and Steven Barbone.
© 2011 Blackwell Publishing Ltd. Published 2011 by Blackwell Publishing Ltd.

in which science seamlessly slotted into the same foundational space – nobody had really noticed the significance of the event. Nietzsche is not a nihilist: for him, the death of God is the greatest event of recent times, enabling "Free Spirits" to throw off their metaphysical shackles and embrace a genuinely open future (although Nietzsche's – necessary – ambiguity over the precise nature of this future has undeniably led to such diverse readings of his work).

Hence, despite its subject matter, Nietzsche does not argue for the Death of God itself in his work in a way that would engage traditionally with the philosophy of religion – it is, rather, a proclamation of an event which is witnessed or reported (for example, in *The Gay Science*, §125, §343, and in the prologue to *Thus Spoke Zarathustra*). He is more interested in how we, as humans, react to the event: whether we embrace its full significance or continue to place a similar "faith" in concepts that remain dependent upon the same metaphysical assumptions, such as science and/or morality. Central to these assumptions is the affirmation of "another world," that of "truth," which lies behind our immediate world of experience (for Christianity, this is "heaven"; for morality, the abstract "good"; for science, atomic structures; and so on). This "beyond" removes us from our own sensibilities and retains us in a quasi-religious state in reverence to the scientific and/or the moral. Given that such an ordering of the world infects both our language and practice, Nietzsche consequently views the importance of truth as metaphorical rather than rational: the sense we make of the world is always limited by our perspective (indeed, in his early work he argues that truth is itself a mixed metaphorical construction, a point much elaborated on by later poststructuralists), and as such images, figures, and motifs authorize this sense long before we construct a justificatory logic for it. Nietzsche's style of arguing is at once rigorously philological, tracing the historical development of concepts with intense academic skill, and at the same time almost hopelessly generalizing, aiming broad shots across the bows of our expectations of what a philosophical argument should be. This style must be borne in mind when approaching the logic of Nietzsche's argument: his argument over the Death of God is far more a polemic than it is an exercise in close reasoning, and at least one of its aims is to open our eyes to a world without fixed parameters of meaning and truth, and in its place, a raw flux of energy and power.

The greatest recent event – that "God is dead"; that the belief in the Christian God has become unbelievable – is already starting to cast its first shadow over Europe. [...] But in the main one might say: for many people's power of comprehension, the event is itself far too great, distant, and out of the way even for its tidings to be thought of as having arrived yet. Even less may one suppose many to know at all what this even really means – and, now that this faith has been undermined, how much must collapse because it was built on this faith, leaned on it, had grown on it – for example, our entire European morality. (§343)

Wouldn't the cultivation of the scientific spirit begin when one permitted oneself no more convictions? That is probably the case; only we need still ask: *in order that this cultivation begin,* must there not be some prior conviction – and indeed one so authoritative and unconditional that it sacrifices all other convictions to itself? We see that science, too, rests on a faith; there is simply no "presuppositionless" science. The question whether *truth* is necessary must get an answer in advance, the answer "yes", and moreover this answer must be so firm that it takes the form of the statement, the belief, the conviction: "*Nothing* is *more* necessary than truth; and in relation to it, everything else has only secondary value." [...] But why not deceive? But why not allow oneself to be deceived? Note that the reasons for the former lie in a completely different area from those for the latter: one does not want to let oneself be deceived because one assumes it is harmful, dangerous, disastrous to be deceived; in this sense science would be a long-range prudence, caution, utility, and to this one could justifiably object: How so? Is it really less harmful, dangerous, disastrous not to want to let oneself be deceived? [...] Precisely this conviction could never have originated if truth *and* untruth had constantly made it clear that they were both useful, as they are. So, the faith in science, which after all undeniably exists, cannot owe its origin to such a calculus of utility; rather it must have originated *in spite of* the fact that the disutility and dangerousness of the "will to truth" or "truth at any price" is proved to it constantly. [...] Consequently, "will to truth" does not mean "I do not want to let myself be deceived" but – there is no alternative – "I will not deceive, not even myself"; *and with that we stand on moral ground.* (§344)

Thus the question "Why science?" leads back to the moral problem: *Why morality at all,* if life, nature, and history are "immoral"? No doubt, those who are truthful in that audacious and ultimate sense which faith in science presupposes *thereby affirm another world* than that of life, nature, and history; [...] it is still a *metaphysical faith* upon which our faith in science rests – that even we knowers of today, we godless anti-metaphysicians, still take *our* fire, too, from the flame lit by the thousand-year old faith, the Christian faith which was also Plato's faith, that God is truth; that truth is divine [...] But what if this were to become more and more difficult to believe, if nothing more were to turn out to be divine except error, blindness, the lie – if God himself were to turn out to be our longest lie? (§344)

The opening part of this reconstructed argument is not Nietzsche's but rather a standard motif of modernity, which Nietzsche takes to task:

P1. If we accept or commit to something as an organizing principle of our lives, then it should be rational, true, or believable.

P2. God's existence is not rational, true, or believable ("The belief in the Christian God has become unbelievable," §343).

    C1. We should not accept and commit to God as an organizing principle of our lives (*modus tollens*, P1, P2).

The majority of people are happy with this, Nietzsche thinks, because they substitute other, more believable principles – science, morality, and so on – in the place of 'God's existence'. P2 then becomes an affirmation rather than a negation – 'science is rational', for example – albeit creating a fallacy of affirming the consequent. It is these substitutions that Nietzsche sees as remnants of belief that are really challenged by the idea of the Death of God. Thus, Nietzsche is not interested in discussing the existence or nature of God (P2 or C1). His issue is rather with the claim made in P1: our desire to seek a "truth" in the world beyond our immediate sensations, or, as Nietzsche terms it, the Will to Truth, and why this conditions our lives in the way it does.

P3. If science, morality, or religion contains assumptions, then these will affect the outcome of its inquiry.

Again, here Nietzsche is using the principles of the Enlightenment (the "scientific spirit") that knowledge should be objective and without assumptions (or, in Nietzsche's words, "convictions"). "Wouldn't the cultivation of the scientific spirit begin when one permitted oneself no more convictions?" But Nietzsche probes this premise, "we need still ask: *in order that this cultivation begin*, must there not be some prior conviction – and indeed one so authoritative and unconditional that it sacrifices all other convictions to itself?" (§344).

P4. Science, morality, and religion contain the same assumption: the Will to Truth (the unspoken assumption of science, for example, is that truth is worth discovering: the "yes" in advance); "There is simply no 'presuppositionless' science."

    C2. The Will to Truth affects the outcome of (moral, scientific, religious) inquiry (*modus ponens*, P3, P4).

Nietzsche is noting here that our understanding is conditioned by the need to discover a "truth" beyond our immediate perception, which he considers most moral, scientific, and religious understanding to do (he writes more on this in the section of *Beyond Good and Evil* entitled "On the prejudices of philosophers").

P5. If the Will to Truth is essential to our understanding (i.e., we can have no knowledge without it), then we will have a reason for following it.

P6. But we do not have a moral or utilitarian reason for following it.

When Nietzsche asks whether it is "really less harmful, dangerous, disastrous not to want to let oneself be deceived?" we can see that lying and deception can, in fact, be very useful (e.g., when raising children, absolute truth is unnecessary and sometimes unhelpful).

C3. The Will to Truth is not essential to our understanding (*modus tollens*, P5, P6).

As Nietzsche reflects, "you only have to ask yourself carefully, 'Why do you not want to deceive?' especially if it should seem – and it does seem! – as if [...] life on the largest scale has actually always shown itself to be on the side of the most unscrupulous *polytropoi*." (201) "*Polytropoi*" means devious, cunning, deceptive. It comes from *The Odyssey*, where it is used to describe the hero who uses these traits to survive the wrath of the gods. In other words, Nietzsche is suggesting that "life" in general does not favor truth in the way that scientific or moral knowledge seems to.

The argument then makes two interrelated points surrounding the status of "truth" itself:

P7. If we do not have moral or utilitarian reasons for following the Will to Truth, our reasons must be other than these.

"Should both be necessary – a lot of trust as well as a lot of mistrust – then where might science get the unconditional belief or conviction one which it rests?" (200–1).

C4. Our reasons for following the Will to Truth are other than moral or utilitarian (*modus ponens*, P7, P6).
P8. If we do not have moral or utilitarian reasons for following the Will to Truth, then it cannot be rational, true, or believable
C5. The Will to Truth cannot be rational, true, or believable (*modus ponens*, P8, P6).

In the place of "rational" justification, which is but an aspect of the Will to Truth, Nietzsche suggests that "truth" is merely a guise for the expression of our power. It rests on a metaphysical faith which is no different, at heart, to the Christian belief in God. The Will to Truth is, thus, a means for limiting our expression of such power: this is symptomatic in the "slave morality" of Christianity. With this connection established between science, morality, and faith, Nietzsche returns to the first part of the argument. If God has become unbelievable, then our faith in the divinity of "truth" is also placed in question. The question that Nietzsche leaves us with suggests that this is what the death of God "really means."

13

Ockham's Razor

Grant Sterling

William of Ockham. *Theory of Terms: Part I of the Summa Logicae*, translated by Michael J. Loux. Notre Dame, IN: University of Notre Dame Press, 1974.
____. *Scriptum in librum primum Sententiarum (Ordinatio)*, Distinctiones XIX–XLVIII, in *Opera Theologica*, vol. IV, edited by Girard Etzkorn and Francis Kelly. St. Bonaventure, NY: St. Bonaventure University, 1979.

"Ockham's Razor" is frequently cited as an argument and attributed to William of Ockham. It is typically rendered as "Entities are not to be multiplied without necessity." It is sometimes understood to mean that when given a choice between two theories, one should choose the one that employs fewer entities (or, sometimes, fewer different types of entities). At other times, it is understood to state that if a given entity is not necessary to explain anything, then we should deny its existence. This common conception, however, is a misunderstanding in several ways.

First, Ockham never said those words – the name "Ockham's Razor" was invented in 1852, and the words attributed to Ockham do not appear in any of his known works. (The two statements above represent Ockham's actual position.) Second, the idea that we shouldn't believe in things without a good reason is by no means original to Ockham or distinctive of him. Third, the Razor is not really an argument but rather a premise or principle used to create arguments of a certain form. Finally, Ockham himself did not actually use the argument to deny the existence of any possible entities, only to doubt them. Ockham allowed for three sources of knowledge

Just the Arguments: 100 of the Most Important Arguments in Western Philosophy, First Edition. Edited by Michael Bruce and Steven Barbone.
© 2011 Blackwell Publishing Ltd. Published 2011 by Blackwell Publishing Ltd.

(self-evidence, empirical evidence, and biblical revelation), and held that if we cannot know that something exists through one of these three sources, we should not believe that the thing exists (which does not necessarily mean that we believe that it doesn't exist – without positive evidence that the thing is not there, we should simply remain neutral).

> Plurality should not be postulated without necessity. (*Commentary on the Sentences of Peter Lombard*, Part I, dist. 1, q. 1 and 2)

> For nothing ought to be posited without a reason given, unless it is known through itself or known by experience or proven by the authority of Sacred Scripture. (*Commentary on the Sentences of Peter Lombard*, Part I, dist. 30, q. 1)

"Ockham's Razor" as it is commonly employed:

P1. Two theories, T1 and T2, explain the observed facts equally well (and better than all rival theories), and T1 requires us to postulate the existence of more entities (or more types of entities) than T2.

P2. "Ockham's Razor": If two theories explain the observed facts equally well (and better than all rival theories), believe the theory that postulates fewer entities than a rival theory with no loss in explanatory force.

C1. We ought to believe T2 and disbelieve T1 (*modus ponens*, P1, P2).

Or

P1. We do not need to postulate the existence of object X in order to explain any of the phenomena we are attempting to explain.

P2. "Ockham's Razor": If we do not need to postulate the existence of any particular object in order to explain any of the phenomena we are attempting to explain, we should disbelieve the existence of any putative object not needed to explain phenomena.

C1. Disbelieve the existence of X (*modus ponens*, P1, P2).

Ockham's Razor as Ockham himself would employ it:

P1. The existence of object X is not self-evident, nor do we have empirical evidence for its existence, nor is it required by the Bible.

P2. Ockham's Razor: If the existence of object X is not self-evident, nor do we have empirical evidence for its existence, nor is it required by the Bible, then we should not believe in the existence of object X.

C1. Do not believe in the existence of object X (though it is still possible that X does exist) (*modus ponens*, P1, P2).

Part II
Metaphysics

14

Parmenides' Refutation of Change

Adrian Bardon

Palmer, John. *Parmenides and Presocratic Philosophy*. Oxford: Oxford University Press, 2009.

Hoy, Ronald. "Parmenides' Complete Rejection of Time." *Journal of Philosophy* 91 (1994): 573–98.

Parmenides was a Greek scholar living in the Italian colony of Elea in the fifth century BCE. The Eleatic school that he championed was known for its claim that reality is a timeless unity. Change, along with the passage of time, is just an illusion or projection of the mind. Only fragments of Parmenides' work survive; they include his refutation of change, which may constitute the earliest surviving example of extended philosophical argumentation.

The main fragment contains a series of connected points intended to show the impossibility of change. According to Parmenides, any change involves destruction or creation, in that it either involves an item going from being to not being (or vice versa) or a property going from being (instantiated) to not being (uninstantiated) (or vice versa). So any change involves something that both is and is not, which is an apparent contradiction. He anticipates the obvious proposed resolution to this claim: there is no contradiction in an item or property both being and not being, since it can, say, "be" in the present while "not be" in the future or past. He replies that this just relocates the contradiction inherent in change to the level of change

Just the Arguments: 100 of the Most Important Arguments in Western Philosophy, First Edition. Edited by Michael Bruce and Steven Barbone.
© 2011 Blackwell Publishing Ltd. Published 2011 by Blackwell Publishing Ltd.

over time. Taking change seriously requires us to think in terms of past and future times as real; but the past and future are distinguished from the present in that the present "is" while the past and future "are not." The only way to think of the past and future as real (Parmenides would claim) is to think of them as real now, which would make them present. So thinking about change requires us to think about the past and future as both present and not present, real and not real.

Parmenides' resolution of the contradiction is to deny the reality both of change and of the passage of time. (Note this line of reasoning is a very close precursor to J. M. E. McTaggart's (#15) early-twentieth-century argument to the same conclusion. Sense-perception is characterized by change, so sensation is fundamentally deceptive. The only way to know the truth about the world is by disregarding sensation and using reason and logic alone.

Note that Parmenides does not consider rejecting P2 or P4 instead of P1; he does not, in other words, consider any definition of change that would be consistent with a static theory of time. The static theory denies dynamic nonrelational temporal properties (such as past/present/future) but allows static relational temporal properties (such as earlier/simultaneous/later). This is the same omission later made by McTaggart. This omission does not affect the validity of this argument when considered as an attack specifically on the dynamic theory of time.

> As yet a single tale of a way
> remains, that it is; and along this path markers are there
> very many, that *What Is* is ungenerated and deathless,
> whole and uniform, and still and perfect;
> but not ever was it, nor yet will it be, since it is now together entire,
> single, continuous; for what birth will you seek of it?
> How, whence increased? From not being I shall not allow
> you to say or to think: for not to be said and not to be thought
> is it that it is not. And indeed what need could have aroused it
> later rather than before, beginning from nothing, to grow?
> Thus it must either be altogether or not at all.
> Nor ever from not being will the force of conviction allow
> something to come to be beyond it: on account of this neither to be born
> nor to die has Justice allowed it, having loosed its bonds,
> but she holds it fast. And the decision about these matters lies in this:
> it is or it is not; but it has in fact been decided, just as is necessary,
> to leave the one unthought and nameless (for no true
> way is it), and [it has been decided] that the one that it is indeed is genuine.
> And how could *What Is* be hereafter? And how might it have been?
> For if it was, it is not, nor if ever it is going to be:
> thus generation is extinguished and destruction unheard of.
>
> (Parmenides, qtd. in Palmer, 143)

P1. Change is real (assumption for *reductio*).

P2. If change is real, then it involves either (a) an object's coming into exist-
    ence or beginning to have some property or (b) an object's becoming
    nonexistent or ceasing to have some property.

P3. If (P2), then there are different times, that is, past/present/future.

    C1. There are different times, that is, past/present/future (hypothetical
    syllogism, P1,P2, P3).

P4. There are not different times – only the present exists.

    C2. There are different times and there are not different times (conjunc-
    tion C1, P4).

    C3. Change is not real (*reductio*, P1–C2).

15

McTaggart's Argument against the Reality of Time

M. Joshua Mozersky

McTaggart, J. M. E. *The Nature of Existence*, vol. II. Cambridge, UK: Cambridge University Press, 1927.

Broad, C. D. *An Examination of McTaggart's Philosophy*, vol. II. Cambridge, UK: Cambridge University Press, 1938.
Le Poidevin, Robin, and Murray MacBeath (eds.). *The Philosophy of Time*. Oxford: Oxford University Press, 1993.

McTaggart's argument begins with the rather simple observation that there are two ways in which moments and events in time may be characterized. First, they may be past, present, or future, in which case they form what McTaggart calls the "A-series" (this is a series because these properties order events with respect to each other). Second, times or events may be earlier than, simultaneous with, or later than other times/events; McTaggart calls this ordering the "B-series." These two series differ. A-series properties are transitory; an event might be future, but soon it will be present, then past. B-series relations are permanent. If, for example, it is true that X follows Y, then it is always true that X follows Y; there is never a time at which X precedes Y or at which X and Y are simultaneous. On the B-series, McTaggart concludes, there is no genuine change – no temporal variation in facts – since whatever is true is always true. McTaggart also claims, however, that time can only exist if change exists; hence, if time is real, then

Just the Arguments: 100 of the Most Important Arguments in Western Philosophy, First Edition. Edited by Michael Bruce and Steven Barbone.
© 2011 Blackwell Publishing Ltd. Published 2011 by Blackwell Publishing Ltd.

moments and events in time must be characterized by A-series properties. In short, any series that is ordered solely by B-series relations could not be temporal in nature.

The problem, according to McTaggart, is that the assumption that anything exhibits A-series properties leads to a contradiction. On the one hand, these properties are mutually incompatible: if something is present, for example, it is neither past nor future. On the other hand, each event in time must possess all three A-series properties: anything present, for instance, was future and will be past. McTaggart notes that one may object that there is no difficulty here, for surely it is not really a contradiction to suppose that an event is present, was future, and will be past. He responds as follows. Suppose that an event, M, is present, was future, and will be past. To say that M will be past is to say that at some future time, T, M is past. Nonetheless, since M is present, there is no moment of past time at which M is past. However, T itself will eventually be past, and when it is, M will then be past at a moment of past time. So it turns out that M is not past at a moment of past time but is past at a moment of past time, namely T, and this is a contradiction. Now, of course, one will want to reply that when T is finally past, then it is possible for M to be past at a moment of past time, so there is no contradiction even if now M cannot be past at any moment of past time. This move, replies McTaggart, simply reintroduces the contradiction, because if T itself will be past, then T must be past, present, and future, and to make that coherent we must suppose that it is past, present, and future at different times. But each of those times will be past, present, and future, which is a contradiction unless we suppose that they are past, present, and future at different times; and so on. Every attempt to eliminate the contradiction leads back to it.

Accordingly, the A-series does not escape contradiction and, therefore, cannot characterize anything. But time is real only if moments and events are characterized by A-series properties. Hence, concludes McTaggart, time itself is unreal.

McTaggart's argument is valid, but there are three main sources of concern over its soundness. First, McTaggart presents the first premise without substantial support. In fact, his defense is simply the following: "It would, I suppose, be universally admitted that time involves change [...] there could be no time if nothing changed" (11). But even if this were universally admitted, perhaps universal opinion is wrong. It is, moreover, not universally admitted. Some philosophers have argued that it is possible for time to exist without change (see Le Poidevin and MacBeath 63–79).

Additionally, the second premise has been questioned. McTaggart argues that if it is always true that, say, a fireplace poker is hot on Monday and cold on Tuesday, then nothing has changed because the sum total of truths remains unchanged. But it is beliefs, sentences, or propositions that are true;

in other words, truth, whatever it is, is a property of entities that represent something else. But couldn't something have a property that our representation of it lacks? After all, we can represent a red flower with black and white words, so perhaps we can represent a changing world with a set of nonchanging, eternal truths. In other words, it seems that McTaggart is wrong to assume that the B-series is incompatible with real change, and as a result many philosophers have rejected the A-series without rejecting the existence of time. Such philosophers are typically called "B-theorists."

Finally, premise six is controversial. Many philosophers have wondered why we should follow McTaggart and analyze "M will be past" as "M is past at a moment of future time, T" (see Broad). Perhaps tense modifiers such as 'was' and 'will be' have no need of further analysis and are easily understood as they are. In other words, if we allow for tensed descriptions of time such as 'M is present', 'M was future', and 'M will be past' to stand as basic and fundamental, then no contradiction arises that needs to be eliminated by McTaggart's suggested analysis, because all such descriptions are mutually compatible. "A-theorists" agree with McTaggart that the B-series is inadequate as a description of time but reject his claim that there is a contradiction in the A-series.

To this day, most philosophers who think about time are either A-theorists or B-theorists. Though few agree with the whole of McTaggart's reasoning, almost every subsequent philosopher of time has been influenced by it. It truly stands as one of the most important arguments in Western philosophy.

> Past, present and future are incompatible determinations. Every event must be one or the other, but no event can be more than one. If I say that any event is past, that implies that it is neither present nor future, and so with the others. And this exclusiveness is essential to change, and therefore to time. For the only change we can get is from future to present, and from present to past. The characteristics are, therefore, incompatible. But every event has them all. If M is past, it has been present and future. If it is future, it will be present and past. If it is present, it has been future and will be past. Thus all the three characteristics belong to each event [...]. The attribution of the characteristics past, present and future to the terms of any series leads to a contradiction, unless it is specified that they have them successively. This means, as we have seen, that they have them in relation to terms specified as past, present and future. These again, to avoid a like contradiction, must in turn be specified as past, present and future. And, since this continues infinitely, the first set of terms never escapes from contradiction at all [...]. The reality of the A series, then, leads to a contradiction, and must be rejected. And, since we have seen that change and time require the A series, the reality of change and time must be rejected. And so must the reality of the B series, since that requires time. (McTaggart, 20–2)

P1. If time is real, then change is real.

P2. If change is real, then what is true at one time differs from what is true at other times.

    C1. If time is real, then what is true at one time differs from what is true at other times (hypothetical syllogism, P1, P2).

P3. If moments and events are characterized only by B-series relations, then it is not the case that what is true at one time differs from what is true at other times.

    C2. If it is not the case that what is true at one time differs from what is true at other times, then it is not the case that time is real (transposition, C1).

    C3. If moments and events are characterized only by B-series relations, then it is not the case that time is real (hypothetical syllogism, P3, C2).

    C4. If time is real, then it is not the case that moments and events are characterized only by B-series relations (transposition, C3).

P4. If it is not the case that moments and events are characterized only by B-series relations, then moments and events have A-series properties.

    C5. If time is real, then moments and events have A-series properties (hypothetical syllogism, C4, P4).

P5. A-series properties are mutually incompatible.

P6. If A-series properties are mutually incompatible, then the attribution of A-series properties to moments and events entails a contradiction.

    C6. The attribution of A-series properties to moments and events entails a contradiction (*modus ponens*, P5, P6).

P7. If the attribution of A-series properties to moments and events entails a contradiction, then it is not the case that moments and events have A-series properties.

    C7. It is not the case that moments and events have A-series properties (*modus ponens*, C6, P7).

    C8. It is not the case that time is real (*modus tollens*, C5, C7).

16

Berkeley's Master Argument for Idealism

John M. DePoe

Berkeley, George. *Principles of Human Knowledge and Three Dialogues*, edited by R. S. Woolhouse. London: Penguin, 1988.

Much of the philosophical writings of George Berkeley (1685–1753) is dedicated to arguing for metaphysical idealism, the position that everything that exists is composed of thought, mind, or God. As Berkeley understood it, being composed of thought is contrary to being composed of matter, and therefore he aimed to show that believing in the existence of matter is unreasonable, if not unintelligible. Matter, according to Berkeley, exists independently of thought. He described matter as inert, senseless, and having what the British empiricists called "primary qualities," roughly defined as properties that exist independently of a mind's perception of them (e.g., mass, extension, motion, etc.).

One of Berkeley's most famous arguments against the existence of matter is commonly called "the master argument" because if it is successful, it refutes the existence of matter with a single masterstroke. The argument can be summed up with a challenge: can you imagine or conceive of a tree's (or any material object's) existing without its being perceived (or thought about)? While you might think you have succeeded in conceiving of a tree that is not being perceived, a little reflection will reveal that you haven't done so, because in the process of conceiving of the tree, you are perceiving

Just the Arguments: 100 of the Most Important Arguments in Western Philosophy, First Edition. Edited by Michael Bruce and Steven Barbone.
© 2011 Blackwell Publishing Ltd. Published 2011 by Blackwell Publishing Ltd.

it. So, it seems that it is impossible to conceive of something's existing truly unperceived. But if it isn't even possible to conceive of something existing unperceived, why should we think that matter can and does exist this way? Since it is impossible to conceive of matter's unperceived existence, Berkeley concluded that the existence of matter is unreasonable.

> But say you, surely there is nothing easier than to imagine trees, for instance, in a park, or books existing in a closet, and no body by to perceive them. I answer, you may so, there is no difficulty in it: but what is all this, I beseech you, more than framing in your mind certain ideas which you call books and trees, and at the same time omitting to frame the idea of any one that may perceive them? But do not you your self perceive or think of them all the while? This therefore is nothing to the purpose: it only shows you have the power of imagining or forming ideas in your mind; but it doth not shew that you can conceive it possible, the objects of your thought may exist without the mind: to make out this, it is necessary that you conceive them existing unconceived or unthought of, which is a manifest repugnancy. When we do our utmost to conceive the existence of external bodies, we are all the while only contemplating our own ideas. But the mind taking no notice of itself, is deluded to think it can and doth conceive bodies existing unthought of or without the mind; though at the same time they are apprehended by or exist in it self. (Berkeley, 60)

P1. If material objects exist, then material objects exist independently of any mind's thinking of them.

P2. If material objects exist independently of any mind's thinking of them, then it is conceivable for material objects to exist without any mind thinking of them.

P3. It is not the case that it is conceivable for material objects to exist without any mind thinking of them.

    C1. It is not the case that material objects exist independently of any mind's thinking of them (*modus tollens*, P2, P3).

    C2. It is not the case that material objects exist (*modus tollens*, P1, C1).

17

Kant's Refutation of Idealism

Adrian Bardon

Kant, Immanuel. *Critique of Pure Reason*, translated by Paul Guyer and Allen Wood. Cambridge, UK: Cambridge University Press, 1998.

Dicker, Georges. "Kant's Refutation of Idealism," *Noûs* 42, 1 (2008): 80–108.

Guyer, Paul. *Kant*. New York: Routledge, 2006.

In the second edition of his *Critique of Pure Reason*, Kant offers a refutation of Cartesian epistemological skepticism that draws (albeit somewhat cryptically) on his insights regarding the necessary conditions of time-consciousness. While the details remain under dispute, the key claim seems to be that we would be unable to order all or some of our subjective experiences in time unless we were relating their sequence in some way to changes in objects external to the mind. The contents of our perceptual states do not come marked with the time of their occurrence; further, all experience is successive in form regardless of whether it represents sequences of events or static states of affairs. Thus we need some guide to reconstructing past events beyond the mere subjective contents of perception and memory. Only objective states of affairs and events – conceived of as part of a law-governed system – could function as a guide to this reconstruction by dictating one interpretation over another. Consequently, the fact that we are

Just the Arguments: 100 of the Most Important Arguments in Western Philosophy, First Edition. Edited by Michael Bruce and Steven Barbone.

able to assign a determinate order to our experiences shows that they are the result of contact with states of affairs and events independent of the mind.

Kant's refutation of idealism is a classic example of an argument form known as a "transcendental argument." Transcendental arguments are usually aimed at some form of epistemological skepticism. They begin with some uncontroversial fact about our mental life – such as our having some knowledge, belief, or cognitive capacity – and add the claim that some fact about the extra-mental world questioned by the skeptic is a necessary condition of that indisputable fact about our subjective mental life.

Many contemporary commentators think that transcendental arguments are not likely to be successful as proofs of any extra-mental fact since they characteristically involve an implausible leap from knowing how we must represent the world to knowing how the world must really be. However, some also think that more modest versions of similar arguments may hold promise. A "modest" transcendental argument attempts to show only that some conceptual framework is indispensable to experience as we know it, not that the world must actually conform to that framework. The most common contemporary objection to Kant's reasoning in the refutation of idealism is that it establishes, at best, that we must conceive of our experiences as being related to external objects and events, not that those experiences are actually caused by external objects and events. Kant's apparent lack of concern over the difference between these conclusions may be due to his "transcendental idealism," according to which the distinction between how things are and how we must, constitutionally, represent them to be is intelligible on a certain level but inoperative from any experiential or practical standpoint.

> I am conscious of my own existence as determined in time. All determination of time presupposes something *persistent* in perception. This persistent thing, however, cannot be an intuition in me. For all grounds of determination of my existence that can be encountered in me are representations, and as such require something persistent that is distinct even from them, in relation to which their change, thus my existence in the time in which they change, can be determined. Thus the perception of this persistent thing is possible only through a thing outside me and not through the mere *representation* of a thing outside me. Consequently, the determination of my existence in time is possible only by means of the existence of actual things that I perceive outside myself. Now consciousness in time is necessarily combined with the consciousness of the possibility of this time-determination. Therefore it is also necessarily combined with the existence of the things outside me, as the condition of time-determination; i.e., the consciousness of my own existence is at the same time an immediate consciousness of the existence of other things outside me. (Kant, B276)

P1. I am aware of myself as a subject of experiences with a determinate temporal order that represent a world of objects and events distinct from my mental states; that is, I have self-consciousness.

P2. If (P1), then I make judgments about the temporal order of my own mental states.

C1. I make judgments about the temporal order of my own mental states (*modus ponens*, P1, P2).

P3. There are no grounds for ordering my own mental states to be found either in the form or content of those states.

P4. If (P3), then if I have self-consciousness, then there is something distinct from my mental states to which their changes can be referred and their order thereby determined.

C2. If I have self-consciousness, then there is something distinct from my mental states to which their changes can be referred and their order thereby determined (*modus ponens*, P3, P4).

C3. There is something distinct from my mental states to which their changes can be referred and their order thereby determined (*modus ponens*, C2, P1).

P5. If (C3), then objects of experience exist outside me.

C4. Objects of experience exist outside me (*modus ponens*, C3, P5).

P6. If objects of experience exist outside me, they must exist in space.

C5. Objects of experience exist in space (*modus ponens*, P6, C4).

18

The Master Argument of Diodorus Cronus

Ludger Jansen

Aristotle. *The Complete Works of Aristotle: The Revised Oxford Translation*, edited by Jonathan Barnes, 2 vols. Princeton, NJ: Princeton University Press, 1984.

Boethius. *Commentarii in librum Aristotelis Perihermeneias*, vols. I–II, edited by C. Meiser. Leipzig: Teubner, 1877–80.

Cicero. *De Fato*, translated by H. Rackham. Cambridge, MA: Harvard University Press, 1982.

Epictetus. Discourses, in *The Hellenistic Philosophers*, edited and translated by A. Long and D. Sedley, vol. 1. Cambridge, UK: Cambridge University Press, 1987.

Gaskin, Richard. *The Sea Battle and the Master Argument: Aristotle and Diodorus Cronus on the Metaphysics of the Future*. Berlin: de Gruyter, 1995.

Psellos, Michael. *Theologica*, Vol. I., edited by P. Gautier. Leipzig: Teubner, 1989.

Sedley, David. "Diodorus Cronus and Hellenistic Philosophy." *Proceedings of the Cambridge Philological Society* 203 (1977) 74–120.

Vuillemin, Jules. *Necessity or Contingency: The Master Argument*. Stanford, CA: CSLI, 1996.

Weidemann, Hermann. "Aristotle, the Megarics, and Diodorus Cronus on the Notion of Possibility." *American Philosophical Quarterly* 45 (2008) 131–48.

Just the Arguments: 100 of the Most Important Arguments in Western Philosophy, First Edition. Edited by Michael Bruce and Steven Barbone.
© 2011 Blackwell Publishing Ltd. Published 2011 by Blackwell Publishing Ltd.

The "Master argument" (*ho kurieuôn logos*) is usually credited to Diodorus Cronus, a philosopher of the Dialectical school in the fourth century BCE. Its name is probably derived from the stock example used but connotes also its sophistication: It was a masterly argument about a master (see Michael Psellus, *Theologica*, 3.129–35). Together with Aristotle's sea-battle argument (*De Interpretatione* 9), it belongs to a series of arguments pertaining to the discussion of possibility and necessity and their bearing on the determination of the future. The master argument hinges on the alleged logical incompatibility of three intuitively valid conceptions:

(1)   The necessity of the past: What is past cannot be changed; thus truths about the past seem to be necessary.
(2)   The closure of the possible over entailment: A possible proposition does not entail any impossible propositions but only possible ones; this can be used as a test for checking whether something is indeed possible (cf., Aristotle, *Metaphysics* IX 3–4).
(3)   The existence of unrealized possibilities: There seem to be plenty of unrealized possibilities. For example, it seems both to be possible that I sit at noon and that I stand at noon, but at most one of these possibilities will be realized.

Diodorus' aim is to disprove (3), that is, to show that it is inconsistent to assume that a statement such as "You are a master" may be possible, although it neither is nor will be true. On this basis, Diodorus was able to argue for his characterization of the possible in temporal terms as that which either is or will be (Cicero, *On Fate* 13; Boethius, *On De Interpretatione* 234.22). But it leads also to a form of "logical determinism," because if there are no unrealized possibilities, everything is necessary. His fellow Dialectician Panthoides and others, however, used (2) and (3) to reject (1), and the Stoic Chrysippus used (1) and (3) to reject (2). Anterior to this debate, Aristotle was able to hold all three ideas by distinguishing absolute necessity (of, e.g., logical truth) from time-relative necessity. For it is only now that singular past facts are unchangeable; when they were still in the future, they were contingent and thus nonnecessary, because they could have been changed. As we have no ancient sources about the structure of Diodorus' argument, its reconstruction is somewhat speculative, and several competing reconstructions have been suggested, using different modern logical systems such as tense logic or quantified temporal logic with or without indexicals.

These seem to be the sort of starting-points from which the Master Argument is posed. The following three propositions mutually conflict: 'Every past truth is necessary'; 'Something impossible does not follow from something possible'; and 'There is something possible which neither is nor will be true.' Diodorus saw this conflict and exploited the convincingness of the first two to establish the conclusion that 'Nothing which neither is nor will be true is possible.' (Epictetus, 38A)

P1. If α is or has been the case, then it is necessary that α is or has been the case.

    C1. If α is or has at least once *not* been the case, then it is not possible that α is and has always been the case (contraposition, P12).

P2. If α necessarily implies β, and α is possible, then β is possible.

    C2. If α necessarily implies β, and β is not possible, then α is not possible (contraposition, P2).

P4. There is a proposition, *p*, that is possible but neither is nor will be the case (assumption for *reductio*).

    C3. *p* is possible (simplification, P4).

    C4. *p* neither is nor will be the case (simplification, P4).

P5. If *p* neither is nor will be the case, then it is or has at least once not been the case that *p* will be true (tense logic).

    C5. It is or has at least once not been the case that *p* will be true (*modus ponens*, C4, P5).

    C6. It is not possible that it is and has always been the case that *p* will be true (*modus ponens*, C1, C5).

P6. *p* necessarily implies that it is now and has always been the case that *p* will be true (tense logic).

    C7. *p* is not possible (*modus ponens*, conjunction, C2, P6, C6).

    C8. There is no proposition that is possible but neither is nor will be true (*reductio*, P4–C7).

19

Lewis' Argument for Possible Worlds

David Vander Laan

Lewis, David. *Counterfactuals*. Cambridge, MA: Harvard University Press, 1973.
____. *On the Plurality of Worlds*. Malden, MA: Blackwell, 1986.

van Inwagen, Peter. "Two Concepts of Possible Worlds," in *Ontology, Identity and Modality: Essays in Metaphysics*. Cambridge, UK: Cambridge University Press, 2001.
Lycan, William. "The Trouble with Possible Worlds," in *The Possible and the Actual: Readings in the Metaphysics of Modality*, edited by Michael J. Loux, 274–316. Ithaca, NY: Cornell University Press, 1979.

In the middle of the twentieth century, the notion of possible worlds demonstrated its power by providing a semantics for modal logic, and the idea has since become standard equipment in the analytic philosopher's toolbox. Naturally, the notion of possible worlds raises ontological questions. Are there really such things? If so, what kinds of things are they? David Lewis was one of the first to take on these questions. In *Counterfactuals*, Lewis defended the ontological foundations of his possible worlds analysis of counterfactual conditionals. Later, in *On the Plurality of Worlds*, Lewis made a sustained case for possible worlds and more fully developed his "modal realist" account of what possible worlds are.

Just the Arguments: 100 of the Most Important Arguments in Western Philosophy, First Edition. Edited by Michael Bruce and Steven Barbone.
© 2011 Blackwell Publishing Ltd. Published 2011 by Blackwell Publishing Ltd.

Lewis' earlier argument for possible worlds is characteristically concise. Lewis notes that we already believe that there are many ways things could have been, takes this as an affirmation that certain entities exist, and calls these entities "possible worlds."

One reason the argument has been controversial is that Lewis took the actual world to be what we ordinarily call "the universe" and took other possible worlds to differ from the universe "not in kind but only in what goes on in them" (Lewis *Counterfactuals*, 85). Worlds are thus concrete objects, and anything that could possibly happen really does happen in some world or another. The thought that Lewis' argument establishes such a view has seemed incredible to some philosophers. Peter van Inwagen, for one, writes, "[T]o suppose that the existence of a plurality of universes or cosmoi could be established by so casual an application of Quine's criterion of ontological commitment has been regarded by most of Lewis's readers as very exceptionable indeed" (87).

Others have suggested that Lewis' argument is not even an argument, properly speaking, at all. For example, William Lycan calls it a "brief paean to the hominess and familiarity of nonactual worlds" and goes on to say that Lewis' "'natural as breathing' talk, like Meinong's, thinly masks a formidable theoretical apparatus which must be evaluated on theoretical grounds" (277 n.7).

The argument Lewis later offered in *On the Plurality of Worlds* was an argument from utility: the notion of possible worlds is useful, and this is a reason to think that there are possible worlds. The earlier argument, as construed below, anticipates the later one in at least two ways. First, the earlier argument concludes not that there are possible worlds but rather that there is a presumption in favor of accepting the existence of possible worlds. Similarly, Lewis' argument from utility was not intended as a conclusive case for the existence of possible worlds (Lewis *On the Plurality*, viii). Second, premise four of the below argument stands in clear need of further support. Much of *On the Plurality of Worlds* consists of a defense of modal realism and a critique of the alternatives and thus attempts to provide the support that premise four needs. Lewis' later argument might thus been seen as a development of his earlier one.

> I believe that there are possible worlds other than the one we happen to inhabit. If an argument is wanted, it is this. It is uncontroversially true that things might have been otherwise than they are. I believe, and so do you, that things could have been different in countless ways. But what does this mean? Ordinary language permits the paraphrase: there are many ways things could have been besides the way they actually are. On the face of it, this sentence is an existential quantification. It says that there exist many entities of a certain description, to wit 'ways things could have been'. I believe that things could have been different in countless ways; I believe permissible paraphrases

of what I believe; taking the paraphrase at its face value, I therefore believe in the existence of certain entities that might be called 'ways things could have been'. I prefer to call them 'possible worlds'. (Lewis *Counterfactuals*, 84)

P1. Things could have been different in many ways.

P2. If things could have been different in many ways, then there are many ways things could have been besides the way they actually are.

C1. There are many ways things could have been besides the way they actually are (*modus ponens*, P1, P2).

P3. If (C1), then if it is not the case that both (i) taking (C1) at face value is known to lead to trouble, and (ii) taking (C1) in some other way is known not to lead to trouble, then there is a presumption in favor of accepting (C1) at face value.

C2. If it is not the case that both (i) taking (C1) at face value is known to lead to trouble, and (ii) taking (C1) in some other way is known not to lead to trouble, then there is a presumption in favor of accepting (C1) at face value (*modus ponens*, C1, P3).

P4. It is not the case that both (i) taking (C1) at face value is known to lead to trouble, and (ii) taking (C1) in some other way is known not to lead to trouble.

C3. There is a presumption in favor of accepting (C1) at face value (*modus ponens*, C2, P4).

P5. "There exist many possible worlds" expresses (C1) taken at face value.

C4. There is a presumption in favor of accepting that there exist many possible worlds (substitution, C3, P5).

20

A Reductionist Account of Personal Identity[1]

Fauve Lybaert

Descartes, René. *Meditations on First Philosophy*. New York: Classic Books America, 2009.

Locke, John. *An Essay concerning Human Understanding*. Indianapolis: Hackett, 1996.

Nagel, Thomas. *The View from Nowhere*. Oxford: Oxford University Press, 1986.

Parfit, Derek. "Experiences, Subjects and Conceptual Schemes," *Philosophical Topics* 26, 1/2 (1999): 217–70.

____. "Is Personal Identity What Matters?" The Ammonius Foundation. http://www.ammonius.org/assets/pdfs/ammoniusfinal.pdf (accessed December 31, 2007).

____. *Reasons and Persons*. Oxford: Oxford University Press, 1984.

____. "The Unimportance of Identity," in *Identity*, edited by H. Harris, 13–46. Oxford: Oxford University Press, 1995.

Quine, W. V. "Identity and Individuation." *The Journal of Philosophy* 69 (1972): 488–97.

Shoemaker, Sydney. "Persons and Their Pasts." *American Philosophical Quarterly* 7 (1970): 269–85.

Williams, Bernard. *Problems of the Self*. Cambridge, UK: Cambridge University Press, 1973.

Wittgenstein, Ludwig. *Zettel*. Oxford: Blackwell, 1967.

[1] The exposition of this account draws heavily on the work of Derek Parfit. The exposition of the different kinds of reductionism is in large part inspired by Parfit's "Experiences, Subjects and Conceptual Schemes" as well as his "Is Personal Identity What Matters?" in which he slightly revises the argument which he makes about personal identity in *Reasons and Persons*. The formalized argument at the end of this chapter is an abbreviated version of the argument which Parfit develops in his *Reasons and Persons*. Both the commentary and the formalized argument have benefited from the comments of Derek Parfit, Cheryl Chen, Filip Buekens, Lorenz Demey, and Roger Vergauwen.

For ages, philosophers have argued over the nature of persons and what is involved in the numerical identity of persons over time. To understand the concept of numerical identity, consider this. The two chairs at my kitchen table, which look exactly alike and are made of the same material, may be qualitatively identical, but they are not numerically identical. Contrast this with the one chair in my room. If someone paints that chair while my eyes are closed, then the chair I see when I open my eyes will be qualitatively different from but numerically the same as the chair I saw before.

Apply this to persons. When a relative tells you that you have changed over the years, he recognizes that you are still numerically the same person. He does not think that you have passed away. But he sees that you are qualitatively a bit different now.

There is more debate over whether someone is still numerically the same person when complete loss of memory and radical change of character occur. Philosophers disagree over whether the resulting person is only qualitatively different or also numerically different than the person before having a brain hemorrhage. Philosophers, such as Derek Parfit, who hold that we are only the same as long as there is psychological continuity, say that we would in such a case be confronted with a numerically different entity. Philosophers, such as Bernard Williams, who state that someone stays the same as long as there is bodily continuity, claim the opposite.

How do we decide what determines the numerical identity of someone? We will first have to agree on how the concept "person" gets its meaning. John Locke (*An Essay*, 148 II.xxvii.26) stated that the concept 'person' is a forensic concept. "Forensic" is often equivocated with "legal", but its meaning stretches further than this. The term is derived from the Latin term '*forum*' and means "public". Locke refers to "person" as a public concept because he takes its meaning to be determined by how we use it – or, to be more precise, by how we ought to use it if we want our speaking to be in accordance with our common beliefs, attitudes, and practices. The meaning of the word 'person' in a legal context is one instance of this. It has, for example, been held that, in this context, someone cannot be found guilty of committing a crime unless he remembers committing it. One idea behind this is that it only makes sense to penalize someone for doing something if he can take responsibility for doing this. Remembering what you did is supposed to be a precondition for the latter.

However, not all philosophers agree on whether the meaning of the concept "person" is determined by our common use of it. Derek Parfit, for instance, contests this assumption. He warns that our use of this term may be wrongheaded and holds that philosophers are in a position to assess this. They can unveil inconsistencies in our use of this concept, examine whether there is a real entity in the world to which it refers, as well as determine whether this concept names what matters when we are concerned about our survival – as we usually think it does.[2]

This being said, philosophers will mostly start their examination of what the concept "person" refers to with an assessment of how we commonly use this concept. They will either describe our use of this concept as precisely as possible and let this description function as a determination of the meaning of this term, or they will explain why our application of this concept is not entirely accurate.

This has led to two main philosophical approaches to the questions of what persons are and what makes a person maintain her numerical identity over time: the reductionist and the nonreductionist approach.

There are different versions of reductionism. Constitutive reductionism[3] is likely to be the most defensible version of reductionism with regard to persons. Constitutive reductionists admit that persons exist but argue that they are fully constituted by their physical and/or psychological continuity, and nothing over and above these continuities.

To say that persons are fully constituted by their physical and/or psychological continuity is not to say that persons are nothing but this continuity. According to Sydney Shoemaker, the case is analogous to the relationship between a statue and the lump of clay of which it is made. The statue is constituted by the clay and has no separate existence apart from the clay. Yet it is not the same as the lump of clay. For, if this lump loses its shape, it will still be there, but the statue will not be.[4]

Constitutive reductionists are metaphysical reductionists, not conceptual reductionists.[5] They claim that persons are not separately existing entities over and above their physical and/or psychological continuity, even though we may not be able to get rid of the term "person" when we want to give a complete description of the world. It is possible that we ascribe experiences to subjects and that we should call these subjects "persons" not "physical" and/or "psychological continuities."

Another way to state what constitutive reductionists hold is this. They claim that what makes different experiences belong to one person is not the fact that they belong to a single separately existing entity. Rather, what makes experiences intrapersonal should be explained in terms of other facts, such as the fact that they are psychologically continuous with one another or the fact that they are associated with a single body.

---

[2] This is why Parfit calls for a revisionary metaphysics, rather than a descriptive metaphysics: he claims that we have to revise the use of certain of our concepts (see, e.g., Parfit *Reasons*, ix).

[3] For the term 'constitutive reductionism,' see Parfit "Experiences" and Parfit "Is Personal".

[4] For this reference to Shoemaker, see Parfit "Experiences" (268 n.9).

[5] For a distinction between these two kinds of reductionism, see Parfit "Experiences" (223).

A metaphysical nonreductionist, on the other hand, claims that persons are separately existing entities over and above their physical and psychological continuity. An example of a metaphysical nonreductionist would be someone who identifies persons in accordance with their soul and does not take this soul to be fully constituted by any combination of further entities. This metaphysical nonreductionist could believe in the transmigration of the soul: perhaps she believes that she is identical to some past person from whom her soul has migrated, even though that person's body is not continuous with her current body, that person's character is radically different, and she has no memory of that person's experiences.

Let's return to reductionism. Within constitutive reductionism, there is still one big division to be made. Some reductionists, such as Bernard Williams and Thomas Nagel, argue that a person stays the same person as long as there is a certain degree of physical continuity. Other reductionists, such as Sydney Shoemaker and Parfit, hold that a person stays the same as long as there is a certain degree of nonbranched psychological continuity.

Below, we will look at Parfit's argument for his position. Parfit argues for his view by stating that we should be either nonreductionists or reductionists, by advancing that there is no evidence for the nonreductionist view, and by demonstrating how we can describe psychological continuity in a way that does not presuppose personal identity.

Even when Parfit's argument is considered formally valid, discussion about the truth of his premises and his method is possible.

Two of the premises that could be questioned are premise 6 and premise 7. Can quasi-memories really be called 'memories', or are they only bits of information? If the latter is the case, could quasi-memory then still be said to be an instance of psychological continuity?

As far as Parfit's method is concerned, one could question his appeal to a thought experiment. Parfit imagines a world in which we could have memories of experiencing an event at which we were in fact not present. Philosophers develop thought experiments like these to become clear on our intuitions about a certain concept. They ask something like "If x were the case, what would we then think about A?" There is controversy over whether it is legitimate to appeal to thought experiments in philosophical arguments. Some philosophers, such as Quine ("Identity," 490) and Wittgenstein (*Zettel*, proposition 350), claim that doing so would mean that we attribute a power to words which they in fact do not have. They argue that, being in this world, we cannot really predict what our attitudes in another world would be. They also question what our attitudes in a world unlike ours could possibly say about our attitudes in the world in which we actually live.

We are not separately existing entities, apart from our brains and bodies, and various interrelated physical and mental events. Our existence just involves the existence of our brains and bodies, and the doing of our deeds, and the thinking of our thoughts, and the occurrence of certain other physical and mental events. Our identity over time just involves (a) Relation R – psychological connectedness and/or psychological continuity – with the right kind of cause, provided (b) that this relation does not take a 'branching' form, holding between one person and two different future people. (Parfit *Reasons*, 216)

Defining Premises

P1. When we ask what persons are, and how they continue to exist, the fundamental choice is between two views: the nonreductionist view and the reductionist view (Parfit *Reasons*, 273).

P2. "On the non-reductionist view, persons are separately existing entities, distinct from their brain and bodies and their experiences" (ibid., 275). On this view, persons are entities whose existence must be all-or-nothing (cf., ibid., 273).

P3. On the reductionist view, "persons exist. And a person is distinct from his brain and body, and his experiences. But persons are not separately existing entities. The existence of a person, during any period, just consists in the existence of his brain and body, the thinking of his thoughts, the doing of his deeds, and the occurrence of many other physical and mental events" (cf., ibid.).

Arguments in Defense of the Reductionist View

P4. The reductionist view is true (A) if the occurrence of psychological continuity does not presuppose that a person holds these psychological events together and (B) if we should reject the belief that persons are separately existing entities.

A. The occurrence of psychological continuity does not presuppose that a person holds these psychological events together.

P5. We could think of memories as instantiations of quasi-memories.

P6. I would have an "accurate quasi-memory of past experience if I seem to remember having an experience; someone did have this experience; and my apparent memory is causally dependent on that past experience" (ibid., 220). An example of my quasi-memory of another person's past experience could be this: this person experiences something; a memory of this experience is formed; this memory gets stored on some device and is then downloaded to my brain.

P7. The continuity of quasi-memory is an instantiation of psychological continuity. Or, in other words: if there is continuity of quasi-memory $(P(x))$, then there is an instantiation of psychological continuity $(Q(x))$. Formalized, this gives: $(\forall x(P(x) \to Q(x)))$.

P8. If we were aware that our quasi-memories may be of other people's past experiences, as well as of ours, these quasi-memories would and should not be automatically combined with the belief that these memories are about our own experiences. In logical language, this means that the continuity of quasi-memory (P) is consistent with the idea that this continuity can be shared by different persons (R). This relationship of consistency can be formalized as: $\exists x(P(x) \ \& \ R(x))$.

    C1. A certain continuity of quasi-memory can be shared by different persons. Or: $P(a) \ \& \ R(a)$ (elimination of the existential quantifier, P8).

    C2. There is continuity of quasi-memory $(P(a))$ (simplification, C1).

    C3. The occurrence of a certain continuity of quasi-memory implies the occurrence of a certain psychological continuity: $P(a) \to Q(a)$ (elimination of the universal quantifier, P7).

    C4. There is an instantiation of psychological continuity $(Q(a))$ (*modus ponens*, C2, C3).

    C5. Something has the property of being shared by different persons $(R(a))$ (simplification, C1).

    C6. The property of being psychologically continuous is consistent with the property of being shared: $Q(a) \ \& \ R(a)$ (conjunction, C4, C5).

    C7. Psychological continuity is consistent with this continuity not being shared by different persons: $\exists x(Q(x) \ \& \ R(x))$. Or, in other words: the occurrence of psychological continuity does not presuppose that one person holds these psychological events together) (introduction of the existential quantifier, C6).

B. We should reject the belief that persons are separately existing entities.

P9. If we do not have evidence for the claim that persons exist as separately existing entities, then we should reject this belief (ibid., 224).

P10. We do not have any awareness of the continued existence of a separately existing subject.

P11. We do not have "evidence for the fact that psychological continuity depends chiefly, not on the continuity of the brain, but on the continuity of some other entity" (ibid., 228).

P12. We do not have good evidence for the belief in reincarnation (ibid.). Neither do we have evidence for the existence of Cartesian egos (i.e., thinking nonmaterial substances); it seems like they are neither "publicly observable" nor "privately introspectible facts" (ibid.).

P13. There are no other reasons than the ones in P10, P11, and P12 to believe in the existence of a separately existing subject of experiences.

 C5. We have no evidence for the claim that we are separately existing entities (P10, P11, P12, P13).

 C6. We should reject the belief that persons exist as separately existing entities (*modus ponens*, P9, C5).

 C7. The reductionist view is true (*modus ponens*, P4, C1, C6).

21

Split-Case Arguments about Personal Identity

Ludger Jansen

Parfit, Derek. *Reasons and Persons*. Oxford: Oxford University Press, 1984.
Shoemaker, Sydney, and Richard Swinburne. *Personal Identity (Great Debates in Philosophy)*. Oxford: Blackwell 1984.

In the empiricist tradition, it is a common move to account for the diachronic identity of a person in terms of shared mental properties or continuity of memories (e.g., Locke) or in terms of shared matter, especially of the brain. But all these criteria allow for "split cases," that is, for two or more candidates fulfilling the requirements, which cause trouble with the formal properties of the identity relation (i.e., reflexivity, symmetry, and transitivity). For example, a brain can be divided and both halves implanted in different bodies: which of these, if any, is the same person as the original one? Two individuals could even share most of their memories – but this does not make them the same person. Thus, none of these criteria can be the decisive factor for personal identity. Some philosophers, such as Richard Swinburne (#24), argue for dualism and conclude that there must be some immaterial factor, the soul, that accounts for personal identity. Others, such as Derek Parfit, conclude that we should discard the concept of personal identity altogether and rather replace it with a nonsymmetric successor relation that allows for such split cases.

Just the Arguments: 100 of the Most Important Arguments in Western Philosophy,
First Edition. Edited by Michael Bruce and Steven Barbone.
© 2011 Blackwell Publishing Ltd. Published 2011 by Blackwell Publishing Ltd.

There are no logical difficulties in supposing that we could transplant one of [a person] P_1's [brain] hemispheres into the skull from which a brain had been removed, and the other hemisphere into another such skull, and that both transplants should take, and it may well be practically possible to do so. [...] If these transplants took, clearly each of the resulting persons would behave to some extent like P_1, and indeed both would probably have some of the apparent memories of P_1. Each of the resulting persons would then be good candidates for being P_1. After all, if one of P_1's hemispheres had been destroyed and the other remained intact and untransplanted, and the resulting person continued to behave and make memory claims somewhat like those of P_1, we would have had little hesitation in declaring that person to be P_1. The same applies, whichever hemisphere was preserved [...]. But if it is, that other person will be just as good a candidate for being P_1. [...] But [...] that cannot be – since the two persons are not identical with each other. (Shoemaker and Swinburne, 15)

P1. A_1 and A_2 are two distinct persons.

P2. At $t_2 > t_1$, A_1 and A_2 are such that each of A_1 and A_2 share exactly the same amount of the X that A had at t_1.

P3. X is the decisive factor for personal identity (e.g., body mass, brain mass, memories, character traces), that is, for any persons A_1 and A_2 and any times t_1 and t_2, if A_2 has at t_2 most of the X that A_1 had at t_1, then A_1 and A_2 are the same person (assumption for *reductio*).

C1. A_1 is the same person as A (*modus ponens*, P3, P2).

C2. A_2 is the same person as A (*modus ponens*, P3, P2).

P4. If X is the same person as Y, then Y is the same person as X (symmetry of identity).

C3. A is the same person as A_2 (*modus ponens*, P4, C2).

P5. If A_1 is the same person as A and A is the same person as A_2, then A is the same person as A_2 (transitivity, C1, C3).

C4. A_1 is the same person as A_2 (*modus ponens*, conjunction, P5, C1, C3).

C5. No such X can be the decisive factor for personal identity (*reductio*, P1–C4).

22

The Ship of Theseus

Ludger Jansen

Hobbes, Thomas. "*De corpore,*" in *The English Works of Thomas Hobbes*, Vol. 1, edited by Sir William Molesworth. London: John Bohn, 1839.

Plato. *Phaedo*, in *Five Dialogues*, 2nd edn., translated by G. M. A. Grube, revised by J. M. Cooper, 93–154. Indianapolis: Hackett, 2002.

Plutarch. "Life of Theseus," in *Lives*, translated by Bernadotte Perrin, vol. I, 1–87. Cambridge, MA: Harvard University Press, 1967.

The "Ship of Theseus" is an intriguing puzzle about identity through time. It is based on the custom of the Athenians to send Theseus' ship each year on a sacred voyage to Delos, because it was believed that Apollo once saved the lives of Theseus and his fourteen fellow-travellers. The ritual was annually repeated for a long time, and hence the ship needed continual repair, new planks being substituted for the old ones. Plutarch relates to us that already the Athenian philosophers had discussed whether the ship is still the same ship although it consists, after a while, entirely of new planks (Plutarch, "Life of Theseus" §22–3; cf., Plato, *Phaedo* 58a–c). Hobbes put a sophisticated twist to the story: Suppose, he said, that someone collected the old planks and put them together again in the end, thus restoring the old ship. The same ship, then, seems to exist twice, which is absurd. Hobbes used this argument to support his version of relative identity: the original ship T1 and the restored ship T2 share the same matter, whereas the original ship and the repaired ship T3 share the same form.

Just the Arguments: 100 of the Most Important Arguments in Western Philosophy,
First Edition. Edited by Michael Bruce and Steven Barbone.
© 2011 Blackwell Publishing Ltd. Published 2011 by Blackwell Publishing Ltd.

[I]f, for example, that ship of Theseus, concerning the difference whereof made by continual reparation in taking out the old planks and putting in new, the sophisters of Athens were wont to dispute, were, after all the planks were changed, the same numerical ship it was at the beginning; and if some man had kept the old planks as they were taken out, and by putting them afterwards together in the same order, had again made a ship of them, this, without doubt, had also been the same numerical ship with that which was at the beginning; and so there would have been two ships numerically the same, which is absurd. (Hobbes Chapter 11, 136)

P1. T1 is identical with T2.
P2. It is not the case that T2 is identical with T3.
P3. T3 is identical with T1 (assumption for *reductio*).
   C1. T3 is identical with T2 (transitivity of identity, P1, P3).
   C2. T2 is identical with T3 (symmetry of identity, C1).
   C3. It is not the case that T2 is identical with T3 and T2 is identical with T3 (conjunction, P2, C2).
   C4. It is not the case that T3 is identical with T1 (*reductio*, P3–C3).

23

The Problem of Temporary Intrinsics

Montserrat Bordes

Lewis, David. *On the Plurality of Worlds*. Oxford: Blackwell, 1986.

Lowe, E. J. "The Problems of Intrinsic Change: Rejoinder to Lewis." *Analysis* 48 (1988): 72–7.

Moore, G. E. *Philosophical Studies*. London: Oxford University Press, 1922.

Our pre-theoretic beliefs tell us that ordinary things such as trees, people, or chairs change their properties during their existence. We can say that ordinary things persist – they exist at different times – and change; that is, they persist and have complementary properties (P, not-P) at distinct times. What remains controversial, however, is the way in which ordinary things persist. We commonly distinguish between ordinary things and events. Some think that unlike football games, weddings, and smiles, ordinary things persist by having only spatial, not temporal parts; they appear to endure rather than perdure. Something endures if and only if it persists by being wholly present at different times; something perdures if and only if it persists by having distinct temporal parts at different times (Lewis). Opponents of endurantism think that ordinary things endure, whereas their histories, which are types of events, perdure (Lowe). Perdurantists hold that both events and ordinary things have not only three spatial dimensions but also a temporal one: they have (the worm view) or are (the stage view) temporal parts.

Just the Arguments: 100 of the Most Important Arguments in Western Philosophy, First Edition. Edited by Michael Bruce and Steven Barbone.
© 2011 Blackwell Publishing Ltd. Published 2011 by Blackwell Publishing Ltd.

Is there a rationale for preferring one theory of persistence to another? Lewis thought that the argument from temporary intrinsics (ATI) shows compellingly that endurantism is untenable. His reasoning can be presented as follows. Ordinary things undergo change of their temporary intrinsic properties; that is, they gain or lose (monadic) properties, that they have in virtue of the way they themselves are, not in virtue of their relations to other things. Put differently, A's intrinsic properties are properties shared by every duplicate of A (Moore and Lewis).

Endurantist and perdurantist explanations of change are incompatible. To illustrate this, let us suppose that A is P at time *t* and that A also existed at a past time *t'* when A was not-P. For a perdurantist, this amounts to A's having a temporal part that is P at *t* and A's having another part that is not-P at *t'*. For an endurantist, A itself (not a proper part of it) is P at *t* and not-P at *t'*. Supporters of endurantism, then, face a contradiction, that A itself is both P and not-P, that is also at odds with Leibniz' Law of the Indiscernibility of Identicals: given that A endures from *t'* to *t*, A must therefore be the same from *t'* to *t* (A at *t'* is diachronically identical to A at *t*), and A should have the same properties at both times (A at *t'* should be indiscernible from A at *t*). Lewis states that endurantism cannot account for the existence of temporary intrinsic properties demanded by ATI, since the efforts to solve the contradiction deny either the nonrelational nature of properties, their instrinsicality, or their temporality.

P1. Ordinary things change their intrinsic properties (properties that ordinary things have in virtue of the way they themselves are, not in virtue of their relations to other things).

P2. Properties can be either of two mutually exclusive types: extrinsic or intrinsic.

P3. If ordinary things change their intrinsic properties, then ordinary things persist; that is, they exist at different times.

C1. Ordinary things persist (*modus ponens*, P1, P3).

P4. If ordinary things persist, then they either endure (persist by being wholly present and numerically identical at more than one time) or perdure (persist by having temporal parts or being partially present at more than one time).

C2. Ordinary things either endure or perdure (*modus ponens*, P4, C1).

P5. Indiscernibility (having the same intrinsic properties) is a necessary condition of numerical identity (the Law of Indiscernibility of Identicals implied by Leibniz' Law).

P6. If ordinary things endure, then ordinary things cannot remain numerically identical if they have incompatible (like P and not-P) intrinsic properties (general instantiation, P5).

P7. If ordinary things cannot remain numerically identical if they have incompatible properties, then either intrinsic properties are either disguised relations to times or the only intrinsic properties of ordinary things are those they have in the present.

    C3. If ordinary things endure, then either intrinsic properties are either disguised relations to times or the only intrinsic properties of ordinary things are those they have in the present (hypothetical syllogism, P6, P7).

P8. If ordinary things perdure, then their incompatible properties belong to different things (i.e., their different temporal parts).

P9. If intrinsic properties are disguised relations to times, then all properties are extrinsic.

    C4. Intrinsic properties are not disguised relations to times (*modus tollens*, P9, P2).

P10. If intrinsic properties are those properties which ordinary things have in the present, then there is no other time than the present; that is, presentism is true.

P11. If presentism is true, then ordinary things do not persist.

    C5. Presentism is false (*modus tollens*, P11, C1).

    C6. Ordinary things do not endure (*modus tollens*, P9, C4, C5).

    C7. Ordinary things perdure (disjunctive syllogism, C2, C6).

    C8. The incompatible properties of ordinary things belong to their different temporal parts (*modus ponens*, P8, C8).

24

A Modern Modal Argument for the Soul

Rafal Urbaniak and Agnieszka Rostalska

Alston, W. P., and T. W. Smythe. "Swinburne's Argument for Dualism." *Faith and Philosophy* 11 (1994): 127–33.

Hasker, W. "Swinburne's Modal Argument for Dualism: Epistemically Circular." *Faith and Philosophy* 15 (1998): 366–70.

Nagasawa, Y. 2005. "Critical Notice of Richard Swinburne's 'The Evolution of the Soul (Revised Version)'." Available at www.infidels.org/library/modern/yujin_nagasawa/soul.html (accessed 27 July, 2010).

Reames, K. "A Response to Swinburne's Latest Defense of the Argument for Dualism." *Faith and Philosophy* 16 (1999): 90–7.

Stump, E., and N. Kretzmann. "An Objection to Swinburne's Argument for Dualism." *Faith and Philosophy* 13 (1996): 405–12.

Swinburne, Richard. *The Evolution of the Soul*. Oxford: Clarendon Press, 1986.

____. "Dualism Intact." *Faith and Philosophy* 13 (1996): 968–77.

Swinburne, Richard, and Sydney Shoemaker. *Personal Identity*. Oxford: Blackwell, 1984.

Urbaniak, R., and A. Rostalska. "Swinburne's Modal Argument for the Existence of a Soul: Formalization and Criticism." *Philo* 12 (2009): 73–87.

Zimmerman, D. W. "Two Cartesian Arguments for the Simplicity of the Soul." *American Philosophical Quarterly* 3 (1991): 217–26.

Just the Arguments: 100 of the Most Important Arguments in Western Philosophy, First Edition. Edited by Michael Bruce and Steven Barbone.
© 2011 Blackwell Publishing Ltd. Published 2011 by Blackwell Publishing Ltd.

Richard Swinburne, one of the most prominent representatives of dualism in the twentieth century, formulated his modal argument for the existence of the soul as an improvement of Descartes' (#76) analogous argument. Roughly speaking, Swinburne argues that human beings currently alive have nonbodily immaterial parts called souls, using the assumption that it is logically possible that a human being survives the destruction of the body (and a few additional supposedly quite innocent premises). The modern twist to the argument that makes it technically interesting is that it employs a quantified propositional modal logic. The argument raises also a general philosophical interest, like all seemingly simple and correct philosophical arguments for strong conclusions.

The argument employs quantified propositional modal logic T, a rather straightforward extension of classical propositional logic. We extend the language with two modal operators: '◊' read as "it is possible that," and '□' read as "it is necessary that" and quantifiers binding propositional variables. On top of the classical rules of inference, one needs to add two axiom schemata (called traditionally K and T):

(K)	$\Box(A{\rightarrow}B){\rightarrow}(\Box A{\rightarrow}\Box B)$
(T)	$\Box A{\rightarrow}A$

We also add two rules of inference: necessitation, which tells us that if something is a thesis of the system, it is necessary, and propositional universal quantifier elimination, which works like universal quantifier elimination in classical predicate logic, except that it applies to propositional variables and formulae. We'll start with a brief presentation of the argument in its original formulation. Then, we'll reconstruct the argument in more detail. Next, we'll describe main known objections to the argument, describe how one of the objections (usually considered to be lethal) can be avoided, and finally, provide our own brief assessment of what we think the main weakness of the argument is.

The argument was originally designed to prove that I [Swinburne] have a soul in 1984, and I leave it in that form. Updating is always possible for any year in which Premiss one is manifestly true. Likewise any name or other referring expression can be substituted for 'I', so long as Premiss 1 remains manifestly true. [...] I define:

p = 'I am a conscious person and I exist in 1984'
q = 'my body is destroyed in the last instant of 1984'
r = 'I have a soul in 1984'
s = 'I exist in 1985'
x ranges over all consistent propositions compatible with $(p\&q)$ and describing 1984 states of affairs.

'(x)' is to be read in the normal way as 'for all x'.

The argument is then as follows:

p (Premiss 1)

$(x)\Diamond(p\&q\&x\&s)$ (Premiss 2)

$\sim\Diamond(p\&q\&\sim r\&s)$ (Premiss 3)

Premiss 2 says that it is possible that I survive into 1985, given that I am conscious in 1984, even if my body is totally destroyed and whatever else might be the case in 1984, compatible with these last two suppositions. Premiss 3 says that it is not possible that I who am conscious in 1984 survive into 1985 if my body is totally destroyed, unless there is a non-bodily part of me in 1984, namely, a soul. It follows from Premiss 2 and Premiss 3 that $\sim r$ is not within the range of x. But since $\sim r$ describes a 1984 state of affairs it follows that it is not compatible with $(p\&q)$. Hence $(p\&q)$ entails r. But the addition to p of q, which describes what happens to my body at the end of 1984 can hardly affect whether or not p entails r. So I conclude that p by itself entails r. Hence, from Premiss 1, r. (Swinburne *Evolution*, 322–3)

Once we point out tacit assumptions, the argument comes out valid in a rather modest modal logic T with universal propositional quantifier elimination. First, a few abbreviations:

$C \Leftrightarrow$ Swinburne is a Conscious person and exists in 1984.

$D \Leftrightarrow$ Swinburne's body is (completely) Destroyed in the last instant of 1984.

$S \Leftrightarrow$ Swinburne has a Soul in 1984.

$E \Leftrightarrow$ Swinburne Exists in 1985.

$84(p) \Leftrightarrow$ Sentence p is about 1984.

Now, the premises are as follows:

P1. C.

P2. $\forall p[84(p)\&\Diamond(p\&C\&D)\rightarrow\Diamond(C\&D\&p\&E)]$.

P3. $\sim\Diamond(C\&D\&\sim S\&E)$.

P4. $84(\sim S)$.

P5. $\Box((C\&D)\rightarrow S)\rightarrow\Box(C\rightarrow S)$.

The first premise is straightforward. The second one now incorporates the restrictions that Swinburne put on quantification in metalanguage (now we are able to substitute any proposition whatsoever for p). (2) says that any proposition about 1984 compatible with the claim that Swinburne is conscious and his body is (afterwards) destroyed is compatible with his being conscious, his body being (afterwards) destroyed, and his having a soul in 1984. P3 says that it's impossible for Swinburne to survive the complete destruction of his body if he doesn't have a soul. P4 says that the claim that he doesn't have a soul in 1984 is a claim about year 1984. P5 says that if his being conscious and his body's being destroyed entail that he has a soul, his being conscious itself entails the same claim (thus capturing the intuition that whether his body is destroyed has no impact on whether he has a soul).

P6. $84(\sim S)\&\Diamond(\sim S\&C\&D)\rightarrow\Diamond(C\&D\&\sim S\&E)$ (universal quantifier, P2).
P7. $\sim(84(\sim S)\&\Diamond(\sim S\&C\&D))$ (*modus tollens*, P3, P6).
P8. $\sim84(\sim S)\vee \sim\Diamond(\sim S\&C\&D)$ (De Morgan' s Law, P7).
P9. $\sim\Diamond(\sim S\&C\&D)$ (disjunctive syllogism, P8, P4).
P10. $\Box\sim(\sim S\&C\&D)$ (definition of $\Box$, P9).
P11. $\Box((C\&D)\rightarrow S)$ (substitution of provable equivalents, P10).
P12. $\Box(C\rightarrow S)$ (*modus ponens*, P5, P11).
    C1. S (schema T; i.e., $\Box A\rightarrow A$; *modus ponens*, P1, P12).

The argument has been attacked from various angles. Swinburne and Shoemaker (*Personal Identity*) point out that P2 involves a *de re* possibility claim that cannot be justified by bare thought experiments. They complain that no conclusion about the actual world can follow from mere possibility claims. Swinburne (1996) insists that not all premises are merely modal (P1 isn't). Swinburne also argues that the story in which he himself survives is consistent and that this is enough to support the *de re* claim.

Hasker argues that Swinburne's argument is epistemically circular. Swinburne (1996) attempted to defend against this sort of insinuation that someone may accept premise 2 without even understanding the conclusion or without accepting premise 3. The strength of this criticism is rather unclear because the notion of epistemic circularity is rather vague.

Reames gives a parallel argument for the opposite conclusion, switching ~S with S and E with ~E. Some space is still left for Swinburne, for he can argue that one of the premises is false on this reading.

Nagasawa disagrees with the so-called "quasi-Aristotelian premise," which says that there is no identity through time between two objects if they have no part in common (Swinburne used it to defend P3).

Probably the best known objection, which is most often considered to be lethal, is the substitution objection formulated against the truth of P2 (Zimmerman, Alston, Smythe, Stump, and Kretzmann). These authors point out that if we substitute for *p* a sentence that states 'Swinburne is purely material in 1984' (let's abbreviate it by M) or 'Swinburne is identical with his body or some part of it', premise 2 comes out false, for (arguably) it is not possible that Swinburne is purely material and yet he survives the destruction of his body, even though it is possible that he is purely material and yet conscious.

Dealing with the substitution objection proceeds as follows. First of all, one cannot try to save P2 by insisting that the consequent of the problematic substitution instance is true, for on the assumption that being material entails not having a soul, this move would falsify P3.

Swinburne himself tried a slightly different strategy. He insisted that no such p is compatible with C&D, for any such p amounts to the denial of his conclusion. This defense doesn't seem too convincing. To say that it is possible that Swinburne is conscious and material (and his body is later destroyed) is not to state a philosophical thesis about the very issue in dispute. One can admit such a possibility without asserting that conscious beings actually are (purely) material. Another worry is that if you reject the compossibility of being material and conscious, you no longer even need Swinburne's argument: from the mere claim that Swinburne is conscious, you'll be able to conclude that he is not purely material.

As it turns out, a slight modification to one of the premises yields a valid argument that doesn't fall prey to the substitution objection. Instead of 'being about 1984', let's use 'being true about 1984' in P2 and let's leave other premises intact. If we use 84(p) &p instead of 84(p) we get: P2*. ∀ p[84(p)&p&◊(p&C&D)→◊(C&D&p&E)], which says that no true sentence about 1984 compatible with C&D excludes C&D&E. The first thing to observe is that we still can derive S (see Urbaniak and Rostalska for more details).

The second thing to note is that P2*, as a case of strengthening the antecedent, is properly weaker than P2. Last but not least, P2* is not susceptible to the substitution objection. For to believe that substituting M for p will falsify P2*, one has to believe that the antecedent of such an instance will be true:

84(M) &M&◊ (M&C&D).

Does this move completely immunize the argument to criticism? Alas, it only shows that the main fault doesn't lie where the substitution objection claimed it did. Clearly, the key premises here are P2* and P3. The former says that no true sentence about 1984 excludes Swinburne's survival in 1985, and the latter says that such a survival is impossible if one doesn't have a soul. If presented with those sentences separately, we might feel compelled to say, Sure, there is no (logical) reason why sentences purely about 1984 should exclude sentences about 1985! Sure, there is no way one could survive the complete and instantaneous destruction of one's body if one didn't have a soul! The key question here is whether the modalities underlying those intuitions are the same. It seems that the modality that motivates us to accept P3 is a rather strong metaphysical modality with quite a few metaphysical assumptions built in, whereas the one that compels us to buy into P2* looks definitely weaker (would a modality that makes it impossible to survive into 1985 if you didn't have a soul in 1984 make you think that no true sentence about 1984 excludes your survival into 1985?)

Swinburne (*Evolution*, 314) himself admits only one type of possibility and explicitly identifies the metaphysical and the logical. The mere fact, however, that Swinburne didn't want to accept such a distinction doesn't mean that we ourselves should make no distinction between the kinds of modalities involved in the intuitive assessment of P2* and P3. And in fact, if this distinction is made, we not only have an explanation of why the argument initially might seem compelling (we don't notice that our intuitions employ two different modalities), but also the argument itself cannot be interpreted as a sound argument.

25

Two Arguments for the Harmlessness of Death

Epicurus' Death is Nothing to Us Argument

Steven Luper

> Epicurus. "Letter to Menoeceus," in *Greek and Roman Philosophy after Aristotle*, edited by Jason Saunders, 49–52. New York: The Free Press, 1966.

Epicurus (341–270 BCE) is most famous for arguing that death is nothing to us. His position is still discussed today, partly because it is not immediately clear where his argument fails and partly because the implications of his conclusion would be important. For example, it seems to follow that we have no reason to avoid death and also that if we save people from death, we are not doing them any good. If death is not bad for us, it seems, living is not good for us.

Epicurus makes his argument in the course of defending a more substantial thesis, namely that anyone can achieve, and then maintain, *ataraxia*, or perfect equanimity. The achievement of complete equanimity requires so situating ourselves that nothing will harm us, so that we have nothing to dread. Since death appears to be harmful indeed, and hence something that a reasonable person will dread, Epicurus needed to explain why it is not.

His argument can be found in the following passage, taken from his "Letter to Menoeceus":

> Death [...], the most awful of evils, is nothing to us, seeing that, when we are, death is not come, and, when death is come, we are not. (50)

Unfortunately, it is not clear that this argument accomplishes what Epicurus wanted it to do. The problem is that the term 'death' might mean

Just the Arguments: 100 of the Most Important Arguments in Western Philosophy, First Edition. Edited by Michael Bruce and Steven Barbone.
© 2011 Blackwell Publishing Ltd. Published 2011 by Blackwell Publishing Ltd.

at least two different things. First, it might signify an event: our ceasing to live. Call this "dying." Second, it might signify a state of affairs: the state of affairs we are in as a result of our ceasing to live. Call this "death." Both dying and death appear to harm us, and hence both threaten our equanimity. But Epicurus' argument shows, at best, that death is nothing to us.

This argument is directed at death rather than dying, but it is possible to substitute 'dying' for 'death'.

P1. We are not affected by an event or state of affairs before it happens.
P2. Death is an event or state of affairs.
  C1. Death does not affect us before it happens (instantiation, P1, P2).
P3. If death affects us while we are alive, it affects us before it happens.
  C2. Death does not affect us while we are alive (*modus tollens*, P3, C1).
P4. If death affects us while we are dead, it affects us when we do not exist.
P5. We are not affected by anything when we do not exist.
  C3. We are not affected by death when we do not exist (instantiation, P5).
  C4. Death does not affect us while we are dead (*modus tollens*, P4, C3).
  C5. It is not the case that death affects us while we are alive or while we are dead (conjunction, C2, C4).
P6. If death affects us, it affects us while we are alive or while we are dead.
  C6. Death does not affect us (*modus tollens*, P6, C5).
P7. What does not affect us is nothing to us.
  C7. Death is nothing to us (*modus ponens*, P7, C6).

It is possible to substitute 'dying' for 'death' in this argument, but the resulting argument will clearly be unsound. The problem, of course, is P6, which can easily be challenged on the grounds that dying can affect us while we are dying.

Lucretius' Symmetry Argument

Nicolas Bommarito

Luctretius. *On the Nature of Things*, translated by Martin Ferguson Smith. Indianapolis: Hackett, 2001.

Kaufman, Frederick. "Death and Deprivation; or, Why Lucretius' Symmetry Argument Fails." *Australasian Journal of Philosophy* 74, 2 (1996): 305–12.

Nagel, Thomas. "Death" in *Mortal Questions*. Cambridge: Cambridge University Press, 1997.

Warren, James. *Facing Death*. Oxford: Oxford University Press, 2004.

Symmetry arguments attempt to show the fear of death to be irrational by appeal to similarities between time before our birth and the time after our death. This type of argument has its origin in the philosophy of Epicurus (341–270 BCE), but its most famous statement is in Lucretius' (*c*.99 BCE–*c*.55 BCE) philosophical epic *De Rerum Natura* (*On the Nature of Things*). The scope of the poem is wide, dealing with physics, metaphysics, psychology, and other fields. The clearest statement of the symmetry argument comes near the end of book III:

> Look back now and consider how the bygone ages of eternity that elapsed before our birth were nothing to us. Here, then, is a mirror in which nature shows us the time to come after our death. Do you see anything fearful in it? Do you perceive anything grim? Does it not appear more peaceful than the deepest sleep? (Lucretius III, 972–75)

The argument draws a similarity between pre-natal nonexistence and post-mortem nonexistence; they both are simply states in which we fail to exist. It then notes that we do not fear the time before our birth in which we did not exist, so the time after our death warrants a similar attitude. It is important to remember that the argument is about the fear of death (the state of nonexistence), not the fear of dying (the process of going out of existence).

There are several criticisms of this kind of argument. Thomas Nagel suggests that post-mortem nonexistence is a deprivation in a way that pre-natal nonexistence is not; one who dies is robbed of life in a way that those yet to be conceived are not. Someone whose watch has just been stolen is not in the same state as someone who never owned a watch; they are both watch-less, but one of them has lost something. One might also think that fear itself has a temporal aspect and is essentially future-directed in the way it is natural to fear being fired next week but not to fear having been fired last week.

Another response to the argument is to grant the symmetry, but use our fear of death as a premise rather than our lack of fear of the time before we existed. Another way to have similar attitudes toward both states is to fear both the time before we existed and the time after our death.

P1. The pre-natal state is a kind of nonexistence.
P2. The post-mortem state is a kind of nonexistence.
    C1. Pre-natal and post-mortem states are relevantly similar; both are states of nonexistence (conjunction, P1, P2).
P3. If states are relevantly similar, then they warrant similar attitudes.
    C2. The pre-natal and post-mortem states warrant similar attitudes (*modus ponens*, C1, P3).
P4. The pre-natal state does not warrant fear.
    C3. Post-mortem nonexistence does not warrant fear (instantiation, C2, P4).

26

The Existence of Forms: Plato's Argument from the Possibility of Knowledge

Jurgis (George) Brakas

Plato. *The Collected Dialogues of Plato*, edited by Edith Hamilton and Huntington Cairns. New York: Bollington Foundation, 1963.

Cornford, F. M. *The Republic of Plato*. Oxford: Oxford University Press, 1941.
Ross, William David. *Plato's Theory of Ideas*. Oxford: Clarendon Press, 1951.

The existence of Forms is at the heart of Plato's philosophy. Take them away, and no philosophy that could reasonably be called Plato's would remain. To the layman (not to mention many philosophers), they are strange creatures indeed. This demands that any discussion of them attempt not only to make clear what these Forms are supposed to be like but also why we should believe they exist at all. Plato gives us several arguments for their existence, but the most important one is arguably what may be called his "argument from the possibility of knowledge." Its premises can be found in several of his dialogues. The argument, naturally enough, is the product of his own passionate convictions and the influence of his predecessors upon his thinking.

Deeply influenced by Socrates, he took from him the love of wisdom, the love of genuine knowledge, with its corresponding withering contempt

---

Just the Arguments: 100 of the Most Important Arguments in Western Philosophy, First Edition. Edited by Michael Bruce and Steven Barbone.
© 2011 Blackwell Publishing Ltd. Published 2011 by Blackwell Publishing Ltd.

for pretensions to it – including the relativism and subjectivism of many of his contemporary thinkers, the Sophists. He also realized that he had to come to grips with the views of two other major thinkers, Heraclitus and Parmenides – Heraclitus claiming that nothing is, only becoming, Parmenides (#14) claiming that change does not exist, only what does not change (a certain One). If – as Plato believed with Heraclitus – everything in this world is constantly changing in every way, constantly "morphing," never, ever remaining what it is, how could it ever be possible for us to "grasp" anything, to know what any thing is? By the time you think you have grasped it, it has already slipped out of your hands.

To know something must therefore be to know something that does not change, something that always remains what it is (something Parmenidean). Only such a thing can be known, and only such a thing – Plato agrees with Parmenides – is really real. Since such things do not exist in this world, they must exist in, and constitute, a nonspatial, nontemporal dimension. These are what Plato calls "Forms." (Note that the structure of Plato's argument is not that Forms exist because knowledge exists; it is, rather, that knowledge exists because Forms exist. Knowledge is not the source of the existence of Forms; the reverse is true: the existence of Forms makes the existence of knowledge possible. Plato's argument, therefore, is not epistemic; it is ontological.) They are also perfect, eternal, the source of the existence of this world, and many other things as well, but Plato gives other reasons for their possession of these attributes.

> [Socrates asks Cratylus] Tell me whether there is or is not any absolute beauty or good, or any other absolute existence? Certainly, Socrates, I think there is. Then let us seek the true beauty, not asking whether a face is fair, or anything of that sort, for all such things appear to be in flux, but let us ask whether the true beauty is not always beautiful. Certainly [. . .]. Then how can that be a real thing which is never in the same state? [. . .]. They cannot. Nor yet, can they be known by anyone; for at the moment that the observer approaches, then they become other and of another nature, so that you can no longer know their nature or state. [. . .]. Nor can we reasonably say [. . .] that there is knowledge at all, if everything is in a state of transition and there is nothing abiding. For knowledge too cannot continue to be knowledge unless continuing always to abide and to exist. But if the very nature of knowledge changes, at the time when the change occurs there will be no knowledge, and if the transition is always going on, there will always be no knowledge. (*Cratylus*, qtd. in Ross, 439C–440C; Ross's trans., slightly modified using Jowett's in *The Collected Dialogues*)

In the *Republic*, Plato gives us the same argument in more explicit form – or, if you like, a different version of the same argument in more explicit form.

> [Addressing Glaucon, Socrates asks] [If] a man believes in the existence of beautiful things, but not of Beauty itself [. . .], is he not living in a dream? [. . .]. Contrast him with the man who holds that there is such a thing a Beauty itself and can discern that essence as well as the things that partake of its character, without ever confusing the one with the other – is he a dreamer or living in a waking state? He is very much awake. So we may say that he knows, while the other has only a belief in appearances; and might we call their states of mind knowledge and belief? Certainly. [. . .] When a man knows, must there not be something that he knows? [. . .] [T]here must. Something real or unreal? Something real. How could a thing that is unreal ever be known? [. . .]. So if the real is the object of knowledge, the object of belief must be something other than the real. Yes. Can it be the unreal? Or is that an impossible object even for belief? Consider: if a man has a belief, there must be something before his mind; he cannot be believing nothing, can he? No. [. . .]. So what he is believing cannot be real nor yet unreal. True. [. . .]. It seems, then, that what remains to be discovered is that object which can be said both to be and not to be and cannot properly be called either real or purely unreal. If that can be found, we may justly call it the object of belief [. . .]. (Plato *Republic*, 476C–479A; Cornford's trans.)

Socrates then goes on to identify that object as the world in which we live, a world which he earlier implicitly referred to as a world of appearances. Although one of the basic operating premises here is not that all things in this world are in constant flux, but rather that they are neither fully real nor fully unreal, it is not a far stretch to argue that they are neither fully real nor fully unreal because they are in constant flux. If so, then the argument is fundamentally the same as the one given in the *Cratylus*; if not, then it is another version of it. In the latter case, premise 4 would have to be modified accordingly as well as the wording in all the lines relying on it.

P1. Knowledge is possible.

P2. Knowledge is knowledge of some object. That is, if a (putative) piece of knowledge does not have an object, then that (putative) piece of knowledge does not exist.

P3. All knowledge (unlike opinion) is stable. That is, all pieces of knowledge are stable: they do not change, being one thing at one time, another at another.

P4. If the object of knowledge could change (for example, if beauty, the object I know, could become something other than beauty), then the knowledge of that object would not be stable (my knowledge of beauty would not be stable).

P5. All things in this world, as Heraclitus says, are in constant flux. That is, all things in this world are things that are always changing in every way, or, all things in this world are not things that are stable.

P6. Some objects of knowledge exist among things in this world (assumption for *reductio*).

C1. Some objects of knowledge change; they are not stable (syllogism, P5, P6).

C2. Some pieces of knowledge are not stable (*modus ponens*, P4, C1).

C3. All knowledge (unlike opinion) is stable and some pieces of knowledge are not stable (conjunction, P3, C2).

C4. No objects of knowledge exist among things in this world (*reductio*, P6–C3).

P7. If objects of knowledge do not exist in this world and do not exist in another, then objects of knowledge do not exist.

P8. Objects of knowledge do not exist in another world (assumption for indirect proof).

C5. Objects of knowledge do not exist in this world, and objects of knowledge do not exist in another (conjunction, C4, P8).

C6. Objects of knowledge do not exist (*modus ponens*, P7, C5).

C7. Knowledge is not possible (*modus ponens*, P2, C6).

C8. Knowledge is possible, and knowledge is not possible (conjunction, P1, C7).

C9. Objects of knowledge – called "Forms" – do exist in another world (*reductio*, P6–C8).

27

Plato, Aristotle, and the Third Man Argument

Jurgis (George) Brakas

Aristotle. *Peri Ideon* (*On Ideas*), in *Aristotle Fragmenta Selecta*, edited by William D. Ross. Oxford, 1963: 84.21–85.6.

Fine, Gail. "Owen, Aristotle and the Third Man." *Phronesis* 27 (1982): 13–33.

Lewis, Frank A. "On Plato's Third Man Argument and the 'Platonism' of Aristotle," in *How Things Are*, edited by J. Bogen and J. McQuire, 133–74. Dordrecht: Reidel, 1985.

Plato. *Plato: Parmenides*, translated by R. E. Allen. New Haven, CT: Yale University Press, 1998.

Strang, Colin. "Plato and the Third Man." *Proceedings of the Aristotelian Society*, vol. 1 (1963): 147–64.

Many scholars believe that the Third Man Argument (the TMA) is one of the most powerful arguments against the existence of Plato's Forms, many going so far as to maintain that it is successful. It exists in two versions. One, preserved to us only in a commentary on Aristotle's *Metaphysics* by Alexander of Aphrodisias, uses the Form Man as an example; the other – offered first, to his great credit, by Plato himself – uses the Form Large. The difference between the versions is significant, because the first uses Forms of entities or substances as examples whereas the second uses attributes or properties.

Just the Arguments: 100 of the Most Important Arguments in Western Philosophy, First Edition. Edited by Michael Bruce and Steven Barbone.
© 2011 Blackwell Publishing Ltd. Published 2011 by Blackwell Publishing Ltd.

Both versions use just three major premises (in addition to five that most people would find uncontroversial) to generate a regress that is vicious. For any group of things to which the same "name" (word) may be truly applied, there exists a Form having the same "name" in virtue of which that "name" may be truly applied to them. (This may be called the "Existence Assumption" or "One-over-many Assumption.") This Form is not a member of the group of things of which it is the Form. (This is usually called the "Non-identity Assumption.") Finally, this Form may be predicated of itself. (This is usually called the "Self-predication Assumption." It should be pointed out that both the formulation of this premise and its name are misleading. It is not the very same Form that is predicated of itself but rather another Form having the same name as the first, with the same point applying as the regress proceeds.) Since an infinite regress is impossible (at least, so both Plato and Aristotle agree), one or more of the three major premises must be false, if we take the additional five to be uncontroversial. The problem is that it is extremely difficult, if not impossible, to see how Plato could give up any of those premises and be left with anything that resembles his philosophy.

Controversy does surround both versions. Scholars interpret them differently, and, while some find one or both to be successful, others do not (see Strang, Fine, and Lewis).

> The third man is proven also in the following way. If the thing predicated of some group of things also is another thing in addition to the things of which it is predicated, having been separated from them (for this [is what] those who posit the Forms think they prove; this is why, according to them, a certain man-itself exists – because the man being truly predicated of the many individual men also is other than the individual men) – if this is so, there will be a third man. For if the thing predicated is other than the things of which it is predicated, and exists on its own, and man is predicated both of the individual men and of the Form, there will be a third man in addition to both the individuals and the Form. In the same way, [there will be] also a fourth man, predicated of both this [man] – that is, the Form – and the individual [men], and in the same way also a fifth, and so on to infinity. (Aristotle, 84.21–85.6; author's translation)

P1. If a group of things exists (individual men,[1] for example) to each member of which the same name ("man") may be truly applied, then a Form (Man or man-himself) exists in virtue of which that name may be truly applied to them (existence or one-over-many assumption).

---

[1] "Men" and "man" are used in a gender-neutral sense.

P2. If a Form (Man) exists in virtue of which the same name may be truly applied to a group of things (individual men), then the Form in virtue of which the same name may be truly applied to that group is not included in it (nonidentity assumption).

P3. If the same name ("man") may be truly applied to each member of a group of things (individual men), then the name that may be truly applied to each member of that group may also be truly applied to the Form in virtue of which that name may be applied to each member of that group (self-predication assumption).

P4. A group of things (e.g., men) exists to each member of which the name "man" may be truly applied.

   C1. A Form, Man, exists (in virtue of which "man" may be truly applied to each member of the group of individual men) (*modus ponens*, P1, P4).

   C2. The Form Man is not included in the group of individual men (*modus ponens*, P2, C1).

   C3. The name "man" may be truly applied to the Form Man. That is, the Form Man is [a][2] man (*modus ponens*, P3, P4).

P5. The Form (Man) in virtue of which the same name ("man") may be applied to a group of things (individual men) is added to that group.

P6. If the Form (Man) in virtue of which the same name ("man") may be applied to a group of things (individual men) is added to that group, then the Form and that group constitute a new, different group.

   C4. Man and the group of individual men constitute a new, different group (*modus ponens*, P6, P5).

   C5. The name "man" may be truly applied to Man and each of the individual men. In other words, a group of things exist (Man and the individual men) to each member of which the same name ("man") may be truly applied (conjunction, C3, P4).

   C6. Another Man (The Third Man[3]) exists (in virtue of which "man" may be truly applied to each member of this new group) (*modus ponens*, P1, C5).

P7. If a third Man exists, then also a fourth Man exists (by the same reasoning that the third Man exists: P1–C6).

   C7. A fourth Man exists (*modus ponens*, P7, C6).

P8. If a fourth Man exists, then an infinite number of such Forms exist.

   C8. An infinite number of such Forms exist (*modus ponens*, P8, C7).

---

[2]   Brackets are placed around "a" because the indefinite article does not exist in ancient Greek. Depending on the context, the Greek would therefore allow the same set of words to be translated as "Man is a man" or "Man is man." Clearly, the argument will not go through if "self-predication" is understood along the lines of "Man is man."

[3]   Although this Form is not the third Form Man to appear, it is the third man to appear if we take any one of the individual men to be the first man – as Aristotle does.

P9. If an infinite number of Forms exist, then an infinite regress is possible.

C9. An infinite regress is possible (*modus ponens*, P9, C8).

P10. An infinite regress is not possible.

   C10. An infinite regress is possible and an infinite regress is not possible (conjunction, C9, P10).

   C11. One or more of P1, P2, P3, P4, P5, P6, P7, P8, P9, or P10 are false (*reductio*, P1–C10).

Plato presents what may be called the "self-characterization" version of the TMA in the *Parmenides*. Parmenides is questioning Socrates:

> "[W]hen some plurality of things seem to you to be large, there perhaps seems to be some one characteristic that is the same when you look over them all, whence you believe that the large is one."
>
> "True," he said.
>
> "What about the large itself and the other larges? If with your mind you should look over them all in like manner, will not some large one again appear, by which they all appear to be large?"
>
> "It seems so."
>
> "Therefore, another character of largeness will have made its appearance alongside largeness itself and the things that have a share of it; and over and above all those, again, a different one, by which they will all be large. And each of the characters will no longer be one for you, but unlimited in multitude." (Plato, 132a–b; Allen's translation)

In reconstructing this argument, I have used beautiful things and their corresponding Forms instead of the "larges" and their Forms. This should make Plato's argument more "down to earth," without distorting it in any way.

P1. If a group of things exists (individual beautiful things, for example) to each member of which the same name ("beautiful") may be truly applied, then a Form (the beautiful itself or Beauty) exists in virtue of which that name may be truly applied to them (existence or one-over-many assumption).

P2. If a Form (Beauty) exists in virtue of which the same name may be truly applied to a group of things (individual beautiful things), then the Form in virtue of which the same name may be truly applied to that group is not included in it (non-identity assumption).

P3. If the same name ("beautiful") may be truly applied to each member of a group of things (individual beautiful things), then the name that may be truly applied to each member of that group may also be truly applied to the Form in virtue of which that name may be applied to each member of that group ("self-predication" assumption).

P4. A group of things (individual beautiful things, for example) exists to each member of which the name ("beautiful") may be truly applied.

   C1. A Form, Beauty, exists (in virtue of which "beautiful" may be truly applied to each member of the group of individual beautiful things) (*modus ponens*, 1, 4).

   C2. The Form Beauty is not included in the group of individual beautiful things (*modus ponens*, P2, C1).

   C3. The name "beautiful" may be truly applied to the Form Beauty. That is, the Form Beauty is beautiful (*modus ponens*, P3, P4).

P5. The Form (Beauty) in virtue of which the same name ("beautiful") may be applied to a group of things (individual beautiful things) is added to that group.

P6. If the Form (Beauty) in virtue of which the same name ("beautiful") may be applied to a group of things (individual beautiful things) is added to that group, then the Form and that group constitute a new, different group.

   C4. Beauty and the group of individual beautiful things constitute a new, different group (*modus ponens*, P6, P5).

   C5. The name "beautiful" may be truly applied to Beauty and each of the individual beautiful things. In other words, a group of things exist (Beauty and the individual beautiful things) to each member of which the same name ("beautiful") may be truly applied (conjunction, C3, P4).

   C6. Another Beauty (The Third Beauty) exists (in virtue of which "beautiful" may be truly applied to each member of this new group) (*modus ponens*, P1, C5).

P7. If a third Beauty exists, then also a fourth Beauty exists (by the same reasoning that the third Beauty exists: P1–C6).

   C7. A fourth Beauty exists (*modus ponens*, P7, C6).

P8. If a fourth Beauty exists, then an infinite number of such Forms exist.

   C8. An infinite number of such Forms exist (*modus ponens*, P8, C7).

P9. If an infinite number of Forms exist, then an infinite regress is possible.

   C9. An infinite regress is possible (*modus ponens*, C8, P7).

P10. An infinite regress is not possible.

   C10. An infinite regress is possible and an infinite regress is not possible (conjunction, C9, P10).

   C11. One or more of P1, P2, P3, P4, P5, P6, P7, P8, P9, or P10 are false (*reductio*, P1–C10).

28

Logical Monism

Luis Estrada-González[1]

Beall, J. C., and Greg Restall. *Logical Pluralism*. Oxford: Oxford University Press, 2006.
Haack, Susan. *Philosophy of Logics*. Cambridge, UK: Cambridge University Press, 1978.
Priest, Graham. *Doubt Truth to Be a Liar*. Oxford: Oxford University Press, 2006.
Read, Stephen. "Monism: The One True Logic," in *A Logical Approach to Philosophy*, edited by David DeVidi and Tim Kenyon, 193–209. Dordrecht: Springer, 2006.

Logical monism is the view that there is only one correct logic or, alternatively, the view that there is only one genuine consequence relation, only one right answer to the question on whether and why a given argument is valid, only one collection of valid inferences (or of logical truths), or only one right way of reasoning. Logic is at the center of philosophy and many theoretical and practical pursuits, for they proceed by the way of argument, inference, and their evaluation. Thus, the problem of knowing whether there is only one correct logic is central in philosophy and of crucial importance to philosophy and other activities.

There is a simple argument for logical monism, put forward, among others, by Graham Priest and purported to follow from the pre-theoretical notion of validity – an inference is valid if and only if whenever its premises

[1] Thanks to Axel Barceló, John Corcoran, Claudia Olmedo-García, Agustín Rayo, and Stephen Read for valuable comments on earlier versions of this text. Needless to say, those mistakes that remain are mine alone.

are true, so is the conclusion. He works with a broad notion of logic in the sense that he is ready to accept that inferential tools for certain particular cases or domains augmented with principles specific to those domains count as logics, but he says that there is nonetheless one true logic, a logic whose inferences are valid in all domains and that lacks principles depending on specific domains.

Some logical pluralists try to wriggle out of this monist argument by claiming that the quantification "all cases (domains)" is not absolute but should be read "all cases (domains) of a kind." For example, classical predicate logic would stem from taking cases to be the consistent and complete worlds, whereas constructive logic would be given when cases are taken to be possibly incomplete bodies of information or warrants or constructions, and relevance logic would be given when cases are taken to be possibly incomplete or inconsistent (or both) ways the world might or might not be. Thus, there could be different collections of inferences valid in all cases, for they could be valid in all cases but of different kinds.

This pluralist reply seems not to be a good one, for then 'all the cases' does not mean "all the cases" and makes logic dependent on the content or particularities of the case under consideration, which goes against the generality and topic-neutrality expected from logic. Moreover, the inferences valid in all the (different kinds of) cases would be regarded as the real valid inferences, for they are indeed valid in all cases, do not vary from case to case, and hence hold independently of the particularities of each case.

Another pluralist option, not very well developed yet, is to bite the bullet, to take the pre-theoretical notion of validity at face value and then try to show that it might be inapplicable. The logical monist assumes that the collection of valid inferences, defined as inferences holding in all cases, is not empty. We have seen in the preceding paragraph that a logical monist might insist on the existence of one true logic, claiming that the inferences valid across all the cases of every kind are the real valid inferences. This move rests on the third premise below. But what if it were false; that is, what if there were no inferences valid in all cases (of all kinds)? Would there be no logic at all? Some arguments by trivialists and possibilists seem to imply that there are no inferences holding in all cases. However, this hardly entails the inexistence of any logic at all. Even though there were no inferences valid in all of them, cases might need special inferences as inferential patterns ruling right reasoning in them. To complicate things, premise 3 requires further an "enough" number of valid inferences, for even though if the collection of valid inferences were not empty – if it consisted of, say, only one or just few inferences – it would be vacuous in practice to call "logic" to such a small number of valid inferences. However, the greater the collection of inferences, the more likely that they could not hold together in all cases.

It seems, then, that logic should be better characterized as an inferential device and the universal quantifier on the notion of validity should be explicitly restricted:

An inference X⊢Y is *k*-valid if and only if it holds in all *k*-cases. As it is, this notion of validity is compatible with both the existence of one true logic (since it does not prevent the nonemptiness of the case of all cases) and the idea that logics may be inferential devices for specific domains.

Priest rejects the idea that, in practice, every principle of inference – or at least a large amount of them so as to make speaking of a logic vacuous – fails in some situation. His argument for this, premise 3, is that to the extent that the meanings of connectives are fixed, there are some principles that cannot fail. The discussion of this reply would lead us quite far from our present concern, though, for it introduces the problem of the meaning of logical connectives.

The pluralist replies considered hitherto tried to provide a special account of the phrase 'all cases (or domains)' or attempted to give reasons to reject premise 3. There is an additional way of challenging logical monism, not necessarily incompatible with the former and just recently being taken into account in the specialized literature. It consists of challenging premises 1 and 2, that is, challenging at least the uniqueness of the pre-theoretical notions of holding in a case and validity. For example, the following characterizations of validity turn out to be equivalent in classical logic, which has just two, sharply separable truth values (true and false), but in general they are not:

V1. An inference X⊢Y is valid if and only if in all cases in which X is true then Y is true too.
V2. An inference X⊢Y is valid if and only if in all cases in which X is not false then Y is true.
V3. An inference X⊢Y is valid if and only if in all cases in which X is true then Y is not false.

These different notions of validity may give rise to different collections of valid inferences and hence to a plurality of logics with very different properties. This last pluralist strategy surely has its shortcomings, but in order to discuss it in detail, it is necessary to introduce further and more technical remarks on truth values and the ways the collections of truth values can be partitioned. However, I hope this brief note is helpful for anyone looking to enter the fascinating problem of whether there is only one correct logic.

Priest expresses his logical monism in the following terms:

> Is the same logical theory to be applied in all domains, or do different
> domains require different logics? [...] Even if modes of legitimate inference do
> vary from domain to domain, there must be a common core determined by the
> syntactic intersection of all these. In virtue of the tradition of logic as being
> domain-neutral, this has good reason to be called *the* correct logic. But if this
> claim is rejected, even the localist must recognise the significance of this core.
> Despite the fact that there are relatively independent domains about which we
> reason, given any two domains, it is always possible that we may be required
> to reason *across* domains. (Priest, 174f; emphasis in the original)

I hereby present a version of the argument using valid inferences, but it
can be easily turned into an argument about logical truths. 'X⊢Y' is read
"Y is inferred from X." I use also the word 'case', but you can read 'domain'
if you prefer.

P1. An inference X⊢Y holds in a case if and only if, in that case if X is true,
then Y is true (the pre-theoretical notion of holding in a case).

P2. An inference X⊢Y is valid if and only if it holds in all cases (the pre-
theoretical notion of validity.)

P2′. X⊢Y is not valid if and only if it does not hold in all cases (contraposi-
tion, P2).

P3. There is at least one collection of (enough) inferences holding in all
cases (existence of a logic).

P4. If two collections of all inferences holding in all cases are different, then
there is at least one inference X⊢Y such that it belongs to a collection
but not to the other (extensionality of collections).

P5. There are at least two different collections of all inferences holding in
all cases (logical pluralism, hypothesis to be reduced).

C1. Since they are different collections of valid inferences, there is an
inference X⊢Y belonging to one of the collections but not to the other
(*modus ponens*, P4, P5).

C2. If X⊢Y is a valid inference, then it holds in all cases (equivalence,
simplification, P2).

C3. If X⊢Y is not a valid inference, then it does not hold in all cases
(equivalence, simplification, P2′).

C4. X⊢Y holds in all cases (*modus ponens*, C1, C2).

C5. X⊢Y does not hold in all cases (*modus ponens*, C1, C3).

C6. X⊢Y holds in all cases and X⊢Y does not hold in all cases (conjunction, C4, C5).

C7. There are not even two collections of inferences that are different
and hold in all cases (*reductio*, P5–C6).

C8. There is exactly one collection of inferences holding in all cases
(disjunctive syllogism, P3, C7).

29

The Maximality Paradox

Nicola Ciprotti

Adams, Robert. "Theories of Actuality," *Noûs* 8 (1974): 211–31. Reprinted in *The Possible and the Actual. Readings in the Metaphysics of Modality*, edited by Michael Loux, 190–209. Ithaca, NY: Cornell University Press, 1979. (All subsequent references are to this edition.)

Chihara, Charles. *The Worlds of Possibility: Modal Realism and the Semantics of Modal Logic*. Oxford: Clarendon Press, 1998.
Davies, Martin. *Meaning, Quantification, Necessity: Themes in Philosophical Logic*. London: Routledge & Kegan Paul, 1981.
Divers, John. *Possible Worlds*. London: Routledge, 2002.
Grim, Patrick. *The Incomplete Universe. Totality, Knowledge, and Truth*. Cambridge, MA: The MIT Press, 1991.

The suggested label for the argument to follow, the "maximality paradox," is tentative. As a matter of fact, there currently is no consensus as to what the most appropriate label might be; what's more, there is not even consensus as to who first formulated it. Robert Adams is credited with having been the first to touch on it in print, while the first detailed formulation is due to Martin Davies.

Such uncertainties about name and origin have possibly to do with the fact that the maximality paradox is actually a family of closely related, yet distinct, arguments. For, while each argument relies on a common body of tenets, namely, well-established facts of standard set theory, it nevertheless is the case that the salient targets of maximality paradox can, and do, differ. What is common to each argument, and so what the maximality paradox essentially consists in, is that a *reductio* of the hypothesis that a set A exists of a given sort, namely a totality-set, is arrived at. Different maximality

Just the Arguments: 100 of the Most Important Arguments in Western Philosophy, First Edition. Edited by Michael Bruce and Steven Barbone.
© 2011 Blackwell Publishing Ltd. Published 2011 by Blackwell Publishing Ltd.

paradox-style arguments can be wielded, however, against the existence of distinct set-theoretic (or set-like) totalities, such as, for example, the set of all possible worlds, the set of all truths, or the set of all states of affairs (whether or not the maximality paradox also threatens the existence of the members of such sets, not only the sets themselves, is an issue we shall briefly address in closing).

In what follows, we shall focus on Adams' original outline of maximality paradox as subsequently given rigorous shape by John Divers. This version of the maximality paradox is specifically concerned with a particular conception of possible worlds as world-stories, namely, peculiar sets of propositions. After due modifications, however, the argument can be conferred wider in scope so as to apply to set-like totalities including elements that are different from possible worlds.

According to a good deal of philosophers (#99), abstract entities of various sorts exist. Among them are sets, numbers, states of affairs, propositions, and properties, to name the ones referred to most often. The majority of philosophers who believe in abstract objects also include possible worlds among them. In particular, the suggestion is that possible worlds can be analyzed as world-stories, that is, sets of propositions that are both (i) consistent and (ii) maximal collections thereof.

Generally speaking, a set A is consistent if and only if it is possible for its members to be jointly true (or jointly obtain); a set A is maximal if and only if, for every proposition p, either A includes p or A includes the contradiction of p. Such two conditions seem constitutive of the notion of a possible world: a possible world ought to be possible, that is, a contradiction-free entity; a possible world ought to be maximal, that is, a complete alternative way things might be, or have been – one filled in up to the minutest detail.

According to this conception, then, the explicit definition of "possible world" is as follows:

(DF) w is a possible world $=_{df}$ w is a set A of propositions such that: (i) for every proposition p, either p is an element A or p is not an element A (maximality condition); (ii) the conjunction of the members of A is consistent (consistency condition).

The main asset of (DF) is that, through it, the existence of possible worlds is made compatible with an ontology that eschews quantification over nonactual objects, generally regarded as *entia non grata*. *Qua* sets of propositions, in fact, it is alleged that no more than actually existing abstract objects – indeed, sets and propositions – is needed for accommodating possible worlds within a respectable actualist ontology; that is, one free of mere *possibilia*. (DF), though, gives rise to the maximality paradox.

Notoriously, the development of a satisfactory logic theory of propositions [. . .] is also beset by formal problems and threats of paradox. One such threat particularly concerns the [. . .] theory [of possible worlds as maximal sets of propositions]. The theory seems to imply that there are consistent sets composed of one member of every pair of mutually contradictory propositions. Furthermore, it follows from the theory, with the assumption that every possible world is actual in itself, that every world-story, *s*, has among its members the proposition that all the members of *s* are true. Here we are teetering on the brink of paradox [. . .]. This may give rise to a suspicion that the [. . .] theory could not be precisely formulated without engendering some analogue of the semantical paradoxes. (Adams, 207–8)

Adams' point is as follows. If w is a possible world, namely, a maximal consistent set of propositions (call it 'S'), then *qua* set S must have a size – in set-theoretic jargon, a cardinality. What is the cardinality of S? We know from standard set theory that the power set of S – that is, the set whose members are all of the subsets of S – has a cardinality that is greater than S's. It follows that for each member B of the power set, there is the proposition that B is a set (in fact, it is true that B is a set). Accordingly, there is a consistent set of propositions that has a cardinality greater than S, which was supposed to be a maximal consistent set – *reductio*. Thus, we have started from the supposition that w was a maximally comprehensive object, one "than which nothing greater can be conceived," and we have ended up with an object greater than w. (Taking the union of S and B as the real maximal consistent set won't do, of course, since by standard set theory again, there is a set whose cardinality is greater than the union of S and B.) This is the maximality paradox.

As already hinted at, the maximality paradox has possibly more bite; while the case below is only concerned with possible worlds as maximal consistent sets of propositions, structurally identical arguments can be constructed to question the existence of other set-like totalities. As soon as some given totality is construed set-theoretically, in fact, there follows by Cantor's Theorem that such a totality cannot exist. Thus, parallel arguments have been mounted for proving, for example, that: (i) there is no set of all truths (Grim); and (ii) there is no set of all possible states of affairs (Chihara).

Notice that, strictly speaking, maximality paradox-style arguments do not rule out the (possibility of the) existence of the members involved. As regards, for example, possible worlds as maximal consistent sets of propositions, their nonexistence actually follows from the maximality paradox only if the further premise is taken aboard that, for every possible world, there necessarily is a corresponding maximal consistent set of propositions. In other words, the stronger conclusion – that is, the nonexistence of the worlds themselves – would follow only if the further principle is assumed that, for every domain of discourse, the objects in that domain necessarily make up a set or some set-like object. Unless this is assumed, a possible way out of the maximality paradox is to treat possible worlds not as sets but proper classes, that is, such that they cannot in turn be members of a more inclusive collection. Maximality paradox-style arguments cannot exclude by themselves the (possibility of the) existence of all-inclusive domains of discourse of a given sort (e.g., the domain of all possible worlds, the domain of all existent objects, the domain of all truths, etc.), provided that such domains be (treated as) nonsets. What maximality paradox-style arguments do rule out is the existence of a set (or set-like entity) of which all objects of the domain of discourse at stake are members. Notice finally though that regarding possible worlds, the suggested way out is not trouble free because it seems to undermine a basic tenet of possible-worlds semantics, that is, that a set W of possible worlds is both mathematically well defined and manageable. This strategy would then require us to revise robustly our views on what constitutes an acceptable applied semantical system, like possible-worlds semantics.

The power set of A, symbolized as $\wp(A)$, is the set of all subsets of a set A. Thus, $\wp(A)$ is short for $\{B \mid B \subseteq A\}$. $\wp(A)$ has 2^n members if A has n members.

(Example: suppose that A = $\{1, 2, 3\}$. Hence, $\wp(A)$ = $\{A, \{1, 2\}, \{1, 3\}, \{2, 3\}, \{1\}, \{2\}, \{3\}, \emptyset\}$.)

Theorem (so-called "Cantor's Theorem," CT): For any set A, every subset of A is smaller than $\wp(A)$. (Emphasis on "every" because every set A is a subset of itself.)

The Proposition Assumption, PA: For each set A_i that is a member of $\wp(A)$, a proposition p exists that is about that set, namely, the proposition that A_i is a set; if $A_i \neq A_j$, then the proposition that A_i is a set and the proposition that A_j is a set are different propositions.

P1. There is a maximal consistent set S of propositions (assumption for *reductio*).

P2. For each set S_i that is a member of $\wp(S)$, there is the proposition p that S_i is a set (Proposition Assumption).

P3. For each such p, either p is an element of S or p is not an element of S (definition of maximality condition).

P4. S includes at least as many propositions as there are elements in $\wp(S)$ (P2, P3).

P5. S is a subset of S (standard set theory).

P6. S has a subset that is at least as large as $\wp(S)$ (P4, P5).

P7. S has no subset as large as $\wp(S)$ [CT].

C1. There is no maximal consistent set S of propositions (*reductio*, P1–P7).

30

An Argument for Free Will

Gerald Harrison

Clarke, Randolph. "Toward a Credible Agent-Causal Account of Free Will." *Noûs* 27 (1993): 191–203.

van Inwagen, Peter. *An Essay on Free Will.* Oxford: Oxford University Press, 1983.

____. "How to Think about the Problem of Free Will." *Journal of Ethics* 12 (2008): 327–41.

Reid, Thomas. *Essays on the Active Powers of the Human Mind.* Cambridge, MA: The MIT Press, 1969.

Strawson, Peter F. "Freedom and Resentment." *Proceedings of the British Academy* 48 (1962): 1–25.

Some philosophers think that our decisions are free only if uncaused, others that causation is needed to prevent our decisions being uncontrolled; some think that the causation needs to be indeterministic, others that it needs to be deterministic, and others that it does not matter either way.

Nevertheless, there is near unanimous agreement that free will is needed to ground moral responsibility. That is to say, free will is required if we are to deserve praise, blame, reward, or punishment for our deeds, and if a host of so-called "reactive attitudes" such as resentment, guilt, and forgiveness are appropriate.

This common ground among disputants provides the basis for a positive argument for free will. Versions of this argument (which has no specific

Just the Arguments: 100 of the Most Important Arguments in Western Philosophy,
First Edition. Edited by Michael Bruce and Steven Barbone.
© 2011 Blackwell Publishing Ltd. Published 2011 by Blackwell Publishing Ltd.

name) have been presented by Thomas Reid, Randolph Clarke, Peter van Inwagen (*Essay*), and Peter Strawson, among others.

Just as it is widely agreed that moral responsibility requires free will, it is also widely agreed that we are morally responsible for at least some of what we do some of the time. For Reid, it was a first principle "that some aspects of human conduct deserve praise, others blame" (361). According to Peter Strawson, our commitment to moral responsibility is so deeply rooted that it is simply inconceivable that we could give it up, and thus the reality of moral responsibility sets a boundary condition for where rational argument can lead.

If our moral responsibility is beyond reasonable doubt, then it must be beyond reasonable doubt that we possess free will, as the former presupposes the latter. Thus, we get our positive argument for free will.

Not everyone accepts this argument. A significant minority of philosophers deny that we are morally responsible. There are, after all, powerful arguments both for thinking that free will is incompatible with determinism and for thinking that it is incompatible with indeterminism. Such arguments can be used to raise doubts about whether we have free will, and so to raise doubts about moral responsibility.

For most, however, the belief that we are morally responsible has greater initial plausibility than any of the premises of an argument leading to the denial of free will. Moral responsibility therefore provides the best positive argument for thinking that we do have free will.

> There are, moreover, seemingly unanswerable arguments that, if they are correct, demonstrate that the existence of moral responsibility entails the existence of free will, and, therefore, if free will does not exist, moral responsibility does not exist either. It is, however, evident that moral responsibility does exist: if there were no such thing as moral responsibility nothing would be anyone's fault, and it is evident that there are states of affairs to which one can point and say, correctly, to certain people: That's *your* fault. (van Inwagen "How to Think")

P1. If we are morally responsible then we have free will.
P2. We are morally responsible.
   C1. We have free will (*modus ponens*, P1, P2).

31

Frankfurt's Refutation of the Principle of Alternative Possibilities

Gerald Harrison

Frankfurt, Harry. "Alternate Possibilities and Moral Responsibility." *Journal of Philosophy* 45 (1969): 829–39.

Fischer, John M. "Frankfurt-Style Compatibilism," in *Free Will*, edited by Gary Watson, 190–211. Oxford: Oxford University Press, 2003.
Widerker, David, and Michael McKenna, (eds.). *Moral Responsibility and Alternative Possibilities*. Farnham, UK: Ashgate, 2006.

Endorsed by Aristotle, Hume, Kant, and many others the "Principle of Alternative Possibilities" (PAP for short) states:

PAP: A person is morally responsible for what she has done only if she could have done otherwise.

Historically, PAP has been one of the most popular routes to "incompatibilism" about moral responsibility (incompatibilism is the view that moral responsibility and causal determinism – the thesis that there is only one future compatible with the past and the laws of nature – are incompatible). After all, if determinism is true, there's a sense in which no one could ever have acted differently. "Compatibilists" (those who believe determinism and moral responsibility to be compatible) resisted this argument by arguing that PAP should be given a controversial "conditional" interpretation according to which an agent could have done otherwise if he would have done so had he desired.

Just the Arguments: 100 of the Most Important Arguments in Western Philosophy,
First Edition. Edited by Michael Bruce and Steven Barbone.
© 2011 Blackwell Publishing Ltd. Published 2011 by Blackwell Publishing Ltd.

But in 1969, the philosopher Harry Frankfurt devised an argument to refute PAP. Frankfurt argued that it is possible for circumstances to arise in which it is clear that a person could not have done otherwise yet also clear that he is morally responsible for his deed. The defining feature of what has now become known as a "Frankfurt-style case" is that an intervention device does not intervene in a process leading to an action but would have intervened if the agent had been about to decide differently. The presence of the intervention mechanism rules out the possibility of the agent's deciding differently, yet because the intervention mechanism plays no role in the agent's deliberations and subsequent action, it seems clear that the agent is fully morally responsible for his action; hence PAP is refuted.

By refuting PAP, Frankfurt's argument closes off one of the major routes to incompatibilism and allows compatibilists to bypass the debate over the correct interpretation of PAP.

Frankfurt's argument remains the focus of considerable debate, with detractors arguing that it is impossible to construct a Frankfurt-style case in which all relevant alternative possibilities have been expunged.

> Suppose someone, Black, let us say wants Jones to perform a certain action. Black is prepared to go to considerable lengths to get his way, but he prefers to avoid showing his hand unnecessarily. So he waits until Jones is about to make up his mind what to do, and he does nothing unless it is clear to him (Black is an excellent judge of such things) that Jones is going to decide to do something other than what he wants him to do. If it does become clear that Jones is going to decide to do something else, Black takes effective steps to ensure that Jones decides to do, and that he does do, what he wants him to do. Whatever Jones's initial preferences and inclinations, then, Black will have his way [...].
>
> Now suppose that Black never has to show his hand because Jones, for reasons of his own, decides to perform and does perform the very action Black wants him to perform. In that case, it seems clear, Jones will bear precisely the same moral responsibility for what he does as he would have borne if Black had not been ready to take steps to ensure that he do it. (Frankfurt, 835–6)

P1. An agent is morally responsible for what he has done only if he could have done otherwise (PAP).

P2. If PAP is true, then a Frankfurt-style case will absolve its subject from moral responsibility.

P3. Frankfurt-style cases do not absolve their subjects from moral responsibility.

C1. PAP is false (*modus tollens*, P2, P3).

32

Van Inwagen's Consequence Argument against Compatibilism

Grant Sterling

van Inwagen, Peter. *An Essay on Free Will*. Oxford: Clarendon Press, 1983.

One of the most famous recent arguments in the free will and determinism debate is Peter van Inwagen's consequence argument, which aims to show that compatibilism is false. Compatibilism is the view that all our actions could be fully determined by the laws of physics and yet at the same time we could have free will in the sense necessary for moral responsibility. Van Inwagen introduces the essence of this argument near the beginning of his book on free will and then goes on to gives three detailed technical versions of the argument. Included here is the simple version and the first technical formalization (which aims to show that under determinism we could never act in any way other than the way in which we do act).

> If determinism is true, then our acts are consequences of the laws of nature and events in the remote past. But it is not up to us what went on before we were born, and neither is it up to us what the laws of nature are. Therefore, the consequences of these things (including our present acts) are not up to us. (16)

> Consider any act that (logically) someone might have performed. If it should turn out that this act was incompatible with the state of the world before that person's birth taken together with the laws of nature, then it follows that that person could not have performed that act. Moreover, if determinism is true, then just any deviation from the actual course of events would be incompatible with any past state of the world taken together with the laws of nature. Therefore, if determinism is true, it never has been within

---

Just the Arguments: 100 of the Most Important Arguments in Western Philosophy,
First Edition. Edited by Michael Bruce and Steven Barbone.
© 2011 Blackwell Publishing Ltd. Published 2011 by Blackwell Publishing Ltd.

my power to deviate from the actual course of events that has constituted my history. (75)

P1. If determinism is true, then our acts are consequences of the laws of nature and events in the remote past.

P2. The laws of nature and events in the remote past are not up to us.

P3. If something is not up to us, then its consequences are not up to us.

    C1. If the laws of nature and events in the remote past are not up to us, then their consequences are not up to us (substitution, P2, P3).

    C2. Consequences of the laws of nature and events in the remote past are not up to us (*modus ponens*, P2, C1).

    C3. If determinism is true, then our acts are not up to us (in our control, within our ability) (substitution, C2, P1).

P4. If our acts are not up to us, then we're not responsible for them.

    C4. If determinism is true, we're not responsible for any of our acts (hypothetical syllogism, C3, P4).

Van Inwagen's First Formalization

Definitions:

Let 'U' be a complete description of the state of the universe right now.
Let 'U – 1' be a complete description of the state of the universe the day before some person 'X' was born.
Let 'A' be some action that X did *not* perform.
Let 'L' be the laws of nature.

P1. X cannot change U – 1 (no one can change the past state of the universe at a time before she was even born).

P2. X cannot change L (no one can change the laws of nature).

P3. If determinism is true, then {(U – 1 plus L), entails U} (follows from the concept of determinism).

P4. If X had done A, then not-U (A is an action that didn't occur, so if it had occurred the universe wouldn't be exactly the same as it is now).

    C1. If X could have done A, X could have made U false (follows semantically from P4).

    C2. If X could have made U false, then X could have made (U – 1 plus L) false (transposition, P3).

    C3. If X could have made (U – 1 plus L) false, then X could have made L false (De Morgan's, C2, P1, and disjunctive syllogism).

    C4. X could not have made L false (P2).

    C5. X could not do A (*modus tollens*, C3, C4, and a series of implicit hypothetical syllogisms).

33

Fatalism

Fernando Migura and Agustin Arrieta

Aquinas, Thomas. *Summa Theologiae*, translated by Fathers of the English Dominican Province, *The Summa Theologiae*, 2nd rev. edn., 22 vols. London: Burns, Oates & Washbourne, 1912–36. Reprinted in 5 vols., Westminster: Christian Classics, 1981. E-text in HTML available at www.newadvent.org/summa

Aristotle. *Aristotle Categories and De Interpretatione*, translated with notes and glossary by J. L. Ackrill. Oxford: Clarendon Press, 1961.

Augustine, Saint. *On Free Choice of the Will*, translated, with introduction by Thomas Williams. Indianapolis: Hackett, 1993.

Rice, Hugh. "Fatalism." *The Stanford Encyclopedia of Philosophy* (Fall 2009 edn.), edited by Edward N. Zalta, available at http://plato.stanford.edu/archives/fall2009/entries/fatalism

According to the philosophical doctrine called "fatalism," everything that happens does so inevitably. Suppose that something is going to happen tomorrow; let's say that it is going to rain. If it is true now that tomorrow it is going to rain, then it can't be true that it won't rain tomorrow, so it is necessary to rain tomorrow. On the other hand, if it is false now that tomorrow it is going to rain, then it can't be true that it will rain tomorrow, so it is impossible to rain tomorrow; that is, it is necessary that it won't rain tomorrow. Since the same reasoning can be applied to every event, everything that happens does so necessarily and inevitably.

Just the Arguments: 100 of the Most Important Arguments in Western Philosophy, First Edition. Edited by Michael Bruce and Steven Barbone.
© 2011 Blackwell Publishing Ltd. Published 2011 by Blackwell Publishing Ltd.

Let us see the structure of the argument from which fatalism is concluded. Let *p* be: "It is going to rain tomorrow" (or whatever declarative sentence that describes an event that you think that can happen tomorrow). Then the argument has the following structure:

P1. If it is true now that *p*, then necessarily *p*.
P2. If it is true now that not *p*, then necessarily not *p*.
P3. It is true now that *p* or it is true now that not *p*.
   C1. Necessarily *p* or necessarily not *p* (constructive dilemma, P1, P2, P3).

This argument is unsound because it is clear that the conclusion is false, but it is not so clear where it goes wrong. The classical solution has to do with a known ambiguity (amphiboly) associated with conditional sentences of the form: "If X, then, necessarily Y." This can be interpreted as (a) "It is a necessary truth that if X, then Y" or as (b) "If X, then it is a necessary truth that Y." On the one hand, if premises 1 and 2 are read as (a), they are clearly true but, then, the conclusion doesn't follow from premises. On the other hand, if premises 1 and 2 are interpreted as (b), the conclusion does follow from them, but they presuppose fatalism. So, either the argument is not logically valid or it begs the question.

The first and best known argumentative version of fatalism can be found in the sea-battle argument formulated by Aristotle in Chapter IX of *On Interpretation* (*Peri Hermeneias*, also *De Interpretatione*):

> For if every affirmation or negation is true or false it is necessary for everything either to be the case or not to be the case. For if one person says that something will be and another denies this same thing, it is clearly necessary for one of them to be saying what is true – if every affirmation is true or false; for both will not be the case together under such circumstances. [...] It follows that nothing either is or is not happening, or will be or will not be, by chance or as chance has it, but everything of necessity and not as chance has it (since either he who says or he who denies is saying what it is true).
>
> I mean, for example: it is necessary for there to be or not to be a sea-battle tomorrow, but it is not necessary for a sea-battle to take place tomorrow, not for one not to take place – though it is necessary for one to take place or not to take place. (Aristotle *On Interpretation*, IX 18a34, 19a23)

But there are also other known formulations due to St. Augustine and Thomas Aquinas relating to the associated problem of free will. St. Augustine in *On Free Choice of the Will* (Book Three), considers an argument that could be paraphrased as follows:

> If God foreknows that Pope Benedict XVI will sin tomorrow, then necessarily Pope Benedict XVI will sin tomorrow. God foreknows that Pope

Benedict XVI will sin tomorrow. So necessarily Pope Benedict XVI will sin tomorrow.

Another example of this is Thomas Aquinas' discussion of the argument that God's Providence (*Summa Theologiae*, First Part, Question 22) implies fatalism. The argument is built from a supposition like this: During the Creation, God foresaw everything, including, for example, Pope Benedict XVI sinning tomorrow. So, necessarily Pope Benedict XVI will sin tomorrow.

Assuming that what God foreknows or sees is always true, these versions of fatalist arguments are essentially analyzed in the same way. Both arguments count as *modus ponens*: "If X, then, necessarily Y, and X, so, necessarily Y." In both cases, the key issue has to do with the correct interpretation of conditional sentence properly understood as "It is necessarily true that X, then Y."

Let us consider a more familiar example:

(e) "If I know George Clooney is a bachelor, then necessarily George Clooney is unmarried."

Given that I know George Clooney remains Hollywood's most famous bachelor today (September 1, 2010), if I don't interpret correctly the conditional, I can conclude by *modus ponens*, "Necessarily, George Clooney is unmarried." But this conclusion would be equivalent to saying, "There are no possible circumstances in which George Clooney is married," and so a strong conclusion is not justified by the premises. Obviously the correct interpretation of (e) is, "Necessarily, if I know George Clooney is a bachelor, then George Clooney is unmarried."

One of the most known practical consequences of fatalism has to do with the uselessness of decision-making. If someone assumes fatalism, why should she bother making decisions if the outcome is already fixed? This direct consequence of fatalism is clearly illustrated in the famous "lazy argument." For instance, if you feel sick now, it is true now that you will either recover or it is now true that you will die. In any case, by direct application of the fatalist argument, necessarily you recover from your illness or necessarily you die because of it. So, why should you call the doctor or do anything at all? (As is easy to see, this argument has the form of a dilemma too.)

Aristotle was entirely aware of this consequence of fatalism when he said that if everything is and happens of necessity, there would be no need to deliberate or to take trouble thinking that if we do this, this will happen, but if we do not, it will not (see *On Interpretation*, IX 18b26).

34

Sartre's Argument for Freedom

Jeffrey Gordon

Sartre, Jean-Paul. *Being and Nothingness*, translated by Hazel Barnes. New York: Philosophical Library, 1956.

Sartre's argument for freedom is unique in the history of philosophy because it treats freedom as the essential characteristic of human consciousness as opposed to a property or capacity of consciousness or mind. In one of Sartre's famous formulations, "Man is freedom," the idea is that consciousness has no properties at all, that it is nothing more than a relation to real existent things, and it relates to those things by defining their significance. The conscious person must interpret the significance of the existent thing; he must construct a coherent world from what is given. The given has no meaning in itself; whatever meaning it will have derives from the agent's interpretation. For a given state of affairs to function as a cause of my conduct, I must first confer upon that state of affairs a certain meaning, which in turn informs that situation with its power to cause. I, then, am the source of its causal efficacy. But determinism requires that the nature and compelling power of the cause exist in themselves, quite independently of any characteristic of the entity undergoing the cause–effect process. Since this necessary condition of determinism is never met by consciousness, determinism is inapplicable to human experience. Experience cannot be caused. To experience is to appropriate, to interiorize the given, to make it

Just the Arguments: 100 of the Most Important Arguments in Western Philosophy, First Edition. Edited by Michael Bruce and Steven Barbone.
© 2011 Blackwell Publishing Ltd. Published 2011 by Blackwell Publishing Ltd.

one's own. In virtue of the relationship between consciousness and the given, my freedom to choose is inescapable. Sartre therefore concludes, "Man is condemned to be free" (439).

Suppose that a boy is born into poverty; that is, the socioeconomic condition of his family is much lower than the average. (The idea of poverty, fraught with connotations of disvalue, already presupposes an interpretation.) Trying to explain his later extraordinary drive, we might well cite this early circumstance as formative – indeed, as determinative. But Sartre would insist that such an explanation is quite misleading. The poverty could not have had this effect had the young boy not understood the condition as shameful. Had he thought of it instead as the source of the strong mutual dependency in his family and their consequent bonds of solidarity, the drive for wealth might very well have seemed to him an empty pursuit. Sartre's point would be that a given socioeconomic circumstance must await the interpretation of consciousness before it could function as a cause. Life circumstances cannot impel an effect without the assent of consciousness. Always to have to interpret the given, to have to forge of the given a motive and cause, is the inescapable condition of consciousness. The uncaused source of its own actions, the human being is irremediably free.

> No factual state whatever it may be (the political and economic structure of society, the psychological "state," etc.) is capable by itself of motivating any act whatsoever. For an act is the projection of [consciousness] toward what it is not, and what is can in no way determine by itself what is not. [. . .] This implies for consciousness the permanent possibility of effecting a rupture with its own past, of wrenching itself away from its past so as to be able to consider it in the light of a non-being and so as to be able to confer on it the meaning which it has in terms of the project of a meaning it *does not have*. Under no circumstances can the past in any way by itself produce an act [. . .]. In fact as soon as one attributes to consciousness this negative power with respect to the world and itself [. . .] we must recognize that the indispensable and fundamental condition of all action is the freedom of the acting being. (436)

P1. In order for a given state of affairs deterministically to cause a human action, the causal efficacy of that state of affairs would have to derive exclusively from characteristics of that state of affairs.
P2. A given state of affairs has no meaning in itself.
P3. If a given state of affairs has no meaning in itself, then its meaning must be conferred upon it by the person experiencing it.
    C1. The meaning of a given state of affairs must be conferred upon it by the person experiencing it (*modus ponens*, P2, P3).
P4. The meaning of the state of affairs is the source of its power to motivate (or cause) the action.

P5. If the meaning of the state of affairs is the source of its power to motivate (or cause) the action, then in the case of human action, the causal efficacy of the state of affairs does not derive exclusively from characteristics of that state of affairs.

C2. In the case of human action, the causal efficacy of the state of affairs does not derive exclusively from characteristics of that state of affairs (*modus ponens*, P4, P5).

C3. No given state of affairs can deterministically cause a human action (*modus tollens*, P1, C3).

P6. If no given state of affairs can deterministically cause a human action, then one's actions are free.

C4. Human beings are inescapably free (*modus ponens*, C3, P6).

Part III
Epistemology

35

The Cogito Arguments of Descartes and Augustine

Descartes' Cogito

Joyce Lazier

Descartes, René. *Meditations*, edited by David B. Manley and Charles S. Taylor, translated by John Veitch, available at www.wright.edu/cola/descartes/index.html (accessed June 2010).

Since Descartes' argument, "I think therefore I am," presented in Meditation II, is often taken as the foundation of idealism and also the source of the mind–body problem, it is a core philosophical argument. The *Meditations* are presented as a stream-of-consciousness style of writing, and the arguments are difficult to follow when just reading it straight through. When put in premise and conclusion form, it is easier to see both the argument as well as some of its flaws. After Descartes discards God as the cause of his thoughts in the first argument, the assumption of the "evil deceiver" in the fifth argument is the most obvious flaw, since it contradicts the logic given in the first argument. If we believe the first argument, that Descartes is capable of producing thoughts himself so he needn't presume a God, then we could also think Descartes is capable of producing his own deceit so he needn't presume a deceiver. So, either the evil demon could be discarded as the cause of Descartes' deceit along with God as the cause of his thoughts, or God could be presumed to exist along with the deceiver. Furthermore,

Just the Arguments: 100 of the Most Important Arguments in Western Philosophy, First Edition. Edited by Michael Bruce and Steven Barbone.
© 2011 Blackwell Publishing Ltd. Published 2011 by Blackwell Publishing Ltd.

besides deceit, which we could cause ourselves, we have no evidence for the evil deceiver and therefore good reason to doubt (by Descartes' own standard of knowledge) and throw out such an assumption. Another flaw that stands out after the reconstruction is an equivocation with "exist" as well as with "I." Most interestingly, this formulation shows that the typical "I think therefore I am" interpretation of Descartes' argument is too broad in two senses. First, as the argument shows, he claims to know he exists when he is thinking, which allows for the possibility of his not knowing he exists when he is not thinking. Second, the "I am" in "I think, therefore, I am" suggests existence of the "I" independent of thought. But Descartes' argument does not prove this "I"; it just proves thought. At most, his argument proves "thought exists."

> But how do I know that there is not something different altogether from the objects I have now enumerated, of which it is impossible to entertain the slightest doubt? Is there not a God, or some being, by whatever name I may designate him, who causes these thoughts to arise in my mind? But why suppose such a being, for it may be I myself am capable of producing them? Am I, then, at least not something? But I before denied that I possessed senses or a body; I hesitate, however, for what follows from that? Am I so dependent on the body and the senses that without these I cannot exist? But I had the persuasion that there was absolutely nothing in the world, that there was no sky and no earth, neither minds nor bodies; was I not, therefore, at the same time, persuaded that I did not exist? Far from it; I assuredly existed, since I was persuaded. But there is I know not what being, who is possessed at once of the highest power and the deepest cunning, who is constantly employing all his ingenuity in deceiving me. Doubtless, then, I exist, since I am deceived; and, let him deceive me as he may, he can never bring it about that I am nothing, so long as I shall be conscious that I am something. So that it must, in fine, be maintained, all things being maturely and carefully considered, that this proposition [*pronunciatum*] I am, I exist, is necessarily true each time it is expressed by me, or conceived in my mind.

P1. Either God or I cause thoughts to arise in my mind.
P2. If I can produce the thoughts myself, I needn't suppose such a God.
P3. I can produce the thoughts myself.
   C1. I needn't suppose God (*modus ponens*, P2, P3).
P4. If I can produce thoughts myself, then I am something.
P5. I can produce thoughts myself.
   C2. I am something (*modus ponens*, P4, P5).
P6. I was persuaded that there was nothing in the world.
P7. If I am persuaded, then I existed.
P8. I was persuaded.
   C3. I existed (*modus ponens*, P7, P8).

P9. There is an evil demon who is constantly deceiving me that I'm something.

P10. If I am deceived, then I am conscious that I am something.

P11. I am deceived.

C4. I am conscious that I am something (*modus ponens*, P10, P11).

P12. If I am conscious that I'm something, then I cannot be nothing.

P13. I am conscious that I'm something.

C5. I am not nothing (*modus ponens*, P12, P13).

P14. If I am not nothing, then I exist.

P15. I am not nothing.

C6. I exist (*modus ponens*, P14, P15).

Augustine's *"Si fallor, sum"* Argument (If I Am Mistaken, I Exist)

Brett Gaul

Augustine. *The City of God against the Pagans*, edited and translated by R. W. Dyson. Cambridge, UK: Cambridge University Press, 1998.

Descartes, René. *The Philosophical Writings of Descartes*, translated by John Cottingham, Robert Stoothoff, and Dugald Murdoch. Cambridge, UK: Cambridge University Press, 1999.

Menn, Stephen. *Descartes and Augustine*. Cambridge, UK: Cambridge University Press, 1998.

Saint Augustine of Hippo (354–430) occupies an interesting place in the history of philosophy. A bishop in the Roman Catholic Church, Augustine is one of the main figures responsible for incorporating elements of Greek and Roman philosophy into Christianity, and his ideas still exert a powerful influence in Christian philosophy even today. In *The City of God*, his longest and arguably his most important and influential work, Augustine defends Christianity against the criticisms of unbelievers and displays his considerable knowledge of classical thought. One of the many classical views Augustine addresses is skepticism – the belief that no genuine knowledge is possible. Augustine defends the possibility of genuine knowledge by arguing that he cannot be mistaken about his own existence (*"Si fallor, sum"*). The argument is significant because it predates by about 1,200 years Descartes' more famous French *"Je pense, donc je suis"* and Latin *"Cogito, ergo sum"* ("I think, therefore I am") arguments from the *Discourse on Method* and *Principles of Philosophy*, respectively. Although it is unclear whether Descartes bases his versions of the argument on Augustine's, we know from Descartes' own correspondence that he did read Augustine.

> It is, however, without any delusive representation of images or phantasms that I am wholly certain that I exist, and that I know this fact and love it. So far as these truths are concerned, I do not at all fear the arguments of the Academics when they say, What if you are mistaken? For if I am mistaken, I exist. He who does not exist clearly cannot be mistaken; and so, if I am mistaken, then, by the same token, I exist. And since, if I am mistaken, it is certain that I exist, how can I be mistaken in supposing that I exist? Since, therefore, I would have to exist even if I were mistaken, it is beyond doubt that I am not mistaken in knowing that I exist. (Augustine, 484)

P1. If I can consider whether I might be mistaken about my own existence, then I know that I exist because the ability to consider something is a sufficient condition for existence.
P2. I can consider whether I might be mistaken about my own existence.
C1. I know that I exist (*modus ponens*, P1, P2).

Alternatively:

P1. If I do not exist, then I cannot consider whether I might be mistaken about my own existence because existence is a necessary condition for the ability to consider anything.
P2. I can consider whether I might be mistaken about my own existence.
C1. I exist (*modus tollens*, P1, P2).

36

The Cartesian Dreaming Argument for External-World Skepticism

Stephen Hetherington

Descartes, René. "Meditation I," in *Meditations on First Philosophy*, in *The Philosophical Works of Descartes*, vol. I, edited and translated by E. S. Haldane and G. R. T. Ross. Cambridge, UK: Cambridge University Press, 1911.

____. *Discourse on the Method*, in *The Philosophical Works of Descartes*, vol. I, edited and translated by E. S. Haldane and G. R. T. Ross. Cambridge, UK: Cambridge University Press, 1911.

Sosa, Ernst. *A Virtue Epistemology*. Oxford: Clarendon Press, 2009.

Stroud, Barry. *The Significance of Philosophical Scepticism*. Oxford: Clarendon Press, 1984.

Wilson, M. D. *Descartes*. London: Routledge & Kegan Paul, 1978.

Descartes' was not the first worried philosophical reference to dreaming as an epistemological issue. But he made the worry especially famous. It has since developed into an argument – usually deemed Cartesian, at least in spirit – which many epistemologists regard as needing to be defeated if external-world knowledge is to be possible. (Descartes' use of the worry helped even to define the category of external-world knowledge in the first place. Such knowledge amounts, in his treatment of it, to knowledge of the physical world.) Even if not always in the suggestive but elliptical way used by Descartes, the skeptical argument is routinely taught in introductory

Just the Arguments: 100 of the Most Important Arguments in Western Philosophy, First Edition. Edited by Michael Bruce and Steven Barbone.
© 2011 Blackwell Publishing Ltd. Published 2011 by Blackwell Publishing Ltd.

philosophy courses – general ones, as well as metaphysics and epistemology ones.

This argument is epistemological, skeptically so. It challenges the thesis – one which, for most of us, is an unquestioned presumption – that people are able to have even some knowledge of a physical world, including of their own physical aspects. The argument is generally called "Cartesian" in honor of René Descartes (1596–1650), even though a much earlier version of the argument was advanced by Socrates in Plato's dialogue *Theaetetus* (at 158a–e). Descartes' version has been the historically influential one. Most famously presented in his 1641 *Meditations on First Philosophy* ("Meditation I"), it was a dramatic moment within philosophy's most celebrated expression and exploration of sustained doubt. These skeptical thoughts by Descartes – followed immediately within the *Meditations* by his attempts to resolve them – were pivotal in the formation of modern philosophy, let alone modern epistemology.

The argument has since been formulated more fully within contemporary epistemology, along the way acquiring the status of a paradigm form of skeptical challenge. Whenever contemporary epistemologists seek to defuse skeptical reasoning, this particular piece of skeptical reasoning – the Cartesian dreaming argument for external-world skepticism – often serves as their representative target. This is partly because knowledge of the physical world is something that people seem so manifestly and so often to have and to use.

The importance of the Cartesian argument is also due partly to its apparent metaphysical ramifications. It has either reflected or suggested the possibility of people living only as thinking things – within their "inner" worlds of thoughts and apparent sensations, not knowing if there is any "outer" world beyond these.

Descartes' argument reaches that stage by seizing upon the possibility of something – dreaming – that can strike us as being a vivid yet deceitful sort of experience. We believe we can be deceived, when dreaming, into thinking that we are really experiencing the physical world as it is. The skeptical argument challenges us to know that this is not happening whenever we think we are really experiencing the physical world. If we do not know that this is not happening, do we know that the world is at all as it seems to us to be? The skeptical conclusion is that we do not, even when everything seems normal to us.

That argument has inspired many attempted refutations because most epistemologists are not skeptics. Many, even so, treat it as an important way of challenging us, not to prove that we have knowledge of the physical world, but to explain how we have such knowledge. We seem to rely just on our sensory experiences. How could these be adequate, though, if they can be mimicked in dreaming?

At the same time I must remember that I am a man, and that consequently I am in the habit of sleeping, and in my dreams representing to myself the same things or sometimes even less probable things, than do those who are insane in their waking moments. How often has it happened to me that in the night I dreamt that I found myself in this particular place, that I was dressed and seated near the fire, whilst in reality I was lying undressed in bed! At this moment it does indeed seem to me that it is with eyes awake that I am looking at this paper; that this head which I move is not asleep, that it is deliberately and of set purpose that I extend my hand and perceive it; what happens in sleep does not appear so clear and distinct as does all this. But in thinking over this I remind myself that on many occasions I have in sleep been deceived by similar illusions, and in dwelling carefully on this reflection I see so manifestly that there are no certain indications by which we may clearly distinguish wakefulness from sleep that I am lost in astonishment. And my astonishment is such that it is almost capable of persuading me that I now dream. (Descartes Meditation I, 145–6)

Technical terms used in the ensuing argument:

Experience: an occurrence within someone's awareness or consciousness.
Sensory experience: an experience resulting from the use of one or more of the person's senses (sight, hearing, etc.)
Content (of an experience): the details of what (according to the experience) reality is like in some respect; how, in some respect, the experience portrays the world as being.
Conclusive: rationally conclusive: ruling out all possible rational doubts about the accuracy of the content at hand.
Certainty: rational certainty: having ruled out all possible rational doubts about the accuracy of the content at hand.

P1. Consider at random any actual or possible experience (call it E) that does or would feel like a sensory experience of the physical world.
P2. Any actual or possible experience that does or would feel like a sensory experience of the physical world has a content to the effect that the physical world is thus-and-so in some more or less specific respect.
  C1. E has a content to the effect that the physical world is thus-and-so in some more or less specific respect (instantiation, P2).
P3. For any actual or possible experience that does or would feel like a sensory experience of the physical world, if it has a content to the effect that the physical world is thus-and-so in some more or less specific respect, then it includes no further content.
  C2. If E has a content to the effect that the physical world is thus-and-so in some more or less specific respect, then E includes no further content (instantiation, P3).

C3. E includes no further content (*modus ponens*, C1, C2).

P4. For any actual or possible experience that does or would feel like a sensory experience of the physical world, if it includes no further content, then in particular it includes no further and conclusive mark or indication of not being an instance of dreaming.

    C4. If E includes no further content, then in particular E includes no further and conclusive mark or indication of not being an instance of dreaming (instantiation, P4).

    C5. In particular, E includes no further and conclusive mark or indication of not being an instance of dreaming (*modus ponens*, C3, C4).

P5. For any actual or possible experience that does or would feel like a sensory experience of the physical world, if in particular it includes no further and conclusive mark or indication of not being an instance of dreaming, then it is not providing conclusive evidence of not being an instance of dreaming.

    C6. If, in particular, E includes no further and conclusive mark or indication of not being an instance of dreaming, then E is not providing conclusive evidence of not being an instance of dreaming (instantiation, P5).

    C7. E is not providing conclusive evidence of not being an instance of dreaming (*modus ponens*, C5, C6).

P6. For any actual or possible experience that does or would feel like a sensory experience of the physical world, if it is not providing conclusive evidence of not being an instance of dreaming, then the person who is or would be having the experience does not know with certainty that it is not an instance of dreaming.

    C8. If E is not providing conclusive evidence of not being an instance of dreaming, then the person who is or would be having E does not know with certainty that it is not an instance of dreaming (instantiation, P6).

    C8. The person who is or would be having E does not know with certainty that it is not an instance of dreaming (*modus ponens*, C7, C8).

P7. For any actual or possible experience that does or would feel like a sensory experience of the physical world, if the person who is or would be having it does not know with certainty that it is not an instance of dreaming, then she does not know at all that it is not an instance of dreaming.

    C9. If the person who is or would be having E does not know with certainty that it is not an instance of dreaming, then she does not know at all that E is not an instance of dreaming (instantiation, P7).

    C10. The person who is or would be having E does not know at all that it is not an instance of dreaming (*modus ponens*, C8, C9).

P8. For any actual or possible experience that does or would feel like a sensory experience of the physical world, if the person who is or would be having it does not know at all that it is not an instance of dreaming, then he does not know at all that it is a sensory experience of the physical world.

    C11. If the person who is or would be having E does not know at all that it is not an instance of dreaming, then he does not know at all that E is a sensory experience of the physical world (instantiation, P8).

    C12. The person who is or would be having E does not know at all that it is a sensory experience of the physical world (*modus ponens*, C10. C11).

P9. For any actual or possible experience that does or would feel like a sensory experience of the physical world, if the person who is or would be having the experience does not know at all that it is a sensory experience of the physical world, then it is not providing her with any knowledge of the physical world.

    C13. If the person who is or would be having experience E does not know at all that it is a sensory experience of the physical world, then E is not providing her with any knowledge of the physical world (instantiation, P9).

    C14. E is not providing any knowledge of the physical world to the person who is or would be having experience E (*modus ponens*, C12, C13).

    C15. Any actual or possible experience that does or would feel like a sensory experience of the physical world is not providing any knowledge of the physical world to the person who is or would be having the experience (universal generalization, P1, C14).

    C16. No actual or possible experience that does or would feel like a sensory experience of the physical world is providing knowledge of the physical world to the person who is or would be having the experience (quantifier-negation, C15).

P10. If no actual or possible experience that does or would feel like a sensory experience of the physical world is providing knowledge of the physical world to the person who is or would be having the experience, then knowledge of the physical world is impossible.

    C17. Knowledge of the physical world is impossible (*modus ponens*, C16, P10).

37

The Transparency of Experience Argument

Carlos M. Muñoz-Suárez

Block, Ned. "Mental Paint and Mental Latex," in *Philosophical Issues 7, Perception*, edited by E. Villanueva, 19–49. Atascadero, CA: Ridgeview, 1996.

Dretske, Fred. *Naturalizing the Mind*. Cambridge, MA: The MIT Press, 1995.

Harman, Gilbert. "The Intrinsic Quality of Experience," in *Philosophical Perspectives* 4, Action Theory and Philosophy of Mind, edited by J. Tomberlin, 53–79. Atascadero, CA: Ridgeview, 1990.

____. "Explaining Objective Color in Terms of Subjective Reactions," in *Philosophical Issues 7*, Perception, edited by E. Villanueva, 1–17. Atascadero, CA: Ridgeview, 1996.

Kind, Amy. "What's so Transparent about Transparency?" *Philosophical Studies* no. 115 (2003): 225–44.

Moore, G. E. "The Refutation of Idealism." *Mind*, New Series 12, 48 (1903): 433–53.

Robinson, Howard. *Perception*. London: Routledge, 1994.

Russell, Bertrand. *The Problems of Philosophy*. Oxford: Oxford University Press, 1980.

Shoemaker, Sydney. "Color, Subjective Relations and Qualia," in *Philosophical Issues 7*, Perception, edited by E. Villanueva, 55–66. Atascadero, CA: Ridgeview, 1996.

Tye, Michael. *Ten Problems of Consciousness*. Cambridge, MA: The MIT Press, 1995.

____. *Consciousness, Color and Content*. Cambridge, MA: The MIT Press, 2000.

Just the Arguments: 100 of the Most Important Arguments in Western Philosophy, First Edition. Edited by Michael Bruce and Steven Barbone.
© 2011 Blackwell Publishing Ltd. Published 2011 by Blackwell Publishing Ltd.

This is one of the main arguments in the philosophy of perception and epistemology. It was canonically presented by G. E. Moore. This argument challenges the thesis that by having sensations we are directly conscious of features of sensations or experiences. It makes explicit a commonsense intuition on what appears to be diaphanous by having sensations, that is, sensory awareness relations – in the words of Moore: "in respect of which all sensations are alike" (444). In general, the argument is about what it is epistemically available by having sensations.

In principle, this is an epistemic argument, but it has metaphysical conclusions depending on the theoretical framework. In general, the transparency of experience argument (henceforth, TEA) is often understood as going against the reduction of the contents of sensations (say, colors) to a kind of "veil of perception" or "mental paint" (Harman, "Intrinsic Quality" and "Explaining") – in other words, in Berkeley's empiricism, something constituting the external world itself. Other philosophers have criticized such a conclusion (see Block).

The intuition framing the TEA was sketched by Moore as follows: when "we try to fix our attention upon consciousness and to see what, distinctly, it is, it seems to vanish: it seems as if we had before us a mere emptiness. When we try to introspect the sensation of blue, all we can see is the blue: the other element is as if it were diaphanous" (Moore 450). This quote is often used to uphold the following: (a) An epistemological inference: by merely having sensations, we are never able to introspect sensory awareness relations; therefore, we are directly aware of what our sensations are about, for example, the color green (Tye *Ten Problems*, 30). (b) A metaphysical inference: by merely having sensations, we are *never* able to introspect sensory awareness relations or features of sensations themselves; therefore, there are no perceptual intermediaries. The consequent of (a) is not necessarily the consequent of (b), despite the antecedent being the same. To clarify the relations between such antecedent and such consequents is the core issue in the debate (see Dretske, Harman "Explaining," Block, and Shoemaker). The antecedent was not defended by Moore. I shall return to this issue below.

The abstract structure of the reasoning behind the TEA is as follows:

P1. [Content Premise:] If a subject, S, has a sensation, v, v is a sensation of x.
P2. [Transparency Premise:] By having v, S only has direct knowledge of y.
    C1. [Epistemological conclusion] S is directly aware of y.
    C2. [Metaphysical conclusion]

(If $v = y$ or ($y = P$ and Pv)) There are y-like entities between S and x.
(If $v \neq y$ or ($y = P$ and $\neg Pv$)) There are no y-like entities between S and x.

The TEA is not an argument concluding that transparency is true but takes it as a premise. The argument has *ab initio* two plausible interpretations depending on the metaphysical character and role ascribed to that what sensation are about: (i) The strong content version: what figures as the content of a sensation is a subject-independent particular and its properties. (ii) The weak content version: what figures as the content of a sensation is a subject-dependent entity (e.g., sensory properties, *qualia*, and so on). Philosophers endorsing (i) appeal to TEA to justify objective (physical) relations between sensations and external mind-independent physical entities (Harman "Intrinsic," Dretske, and Tye *Consciousness*]. Accordingly, philosophers endorsing (ii) appeal to TEA to justify (mental) relations between sensations and mind-dependent entities (Robinson IX §3). Further on, "transparency" has *ab initio* two plausible interpretations depending on the epistemic role ascribed to sensations (see Kind): (i*) Strong transparency: by having a sensation, V, one cannot introspect features of v, but just what v is about. (ii*) Weak transparency: by having a sensation, V, one could introspect some feature of V. The latter was the version endorsed by Moore and the former is the antecedent of the epistemological inference and the metaphysical inference.

(i) and (i*) can be coupled, and we obtain a version of TEA motivating direct realism. Call this version strong TEA: by having a sensation, V, one cannot introspect features of V but just the subject-independent entity that v is about (Tye *Consciousness* and Harman "Intrinsic," 39). It might be synthesized as follows:

P1. If a subject, S, has the sensation, V, then, V is a sensation of a subject-independent entity, X (strong content version).
P2. By having V, S cannot introspect features of V but just what V is about (strong transparency).
  C1. There are no perceptual intermediaries between S and X (metaphysical inference*).

Accordingly, (ii) and (ii*) can be coupled, and we obtain a version of TEA motivating idealism. Weak TEA holds that by having a sensation, V, one is sensory aware of a mind-dependent entity and one could introspect features of V. The argument would be as follows:

P1. If a subject, S, has the sensation, V, then V is a sensation of a subject-dependent entity, Z (weak content version).
P2. By having V, S cannot introspect features of V, but just what V is about, that is, Z (strong transparency).
  C1. There are no perceptual intermediaries between S and Z (metaphysical inference**).

There is another version about content; this is a version of the weak content version. Call this the "property-content" version (iii): what figures as the content of a sensation are subject-dependent properties (say, colors) which look like being instantiated in subject-independent particulars (say, tables). This version can be coupled with weak transparency. We obtain a third version of TEA: call this "sense-data" TEA.

P1. If a subject, S, has the sensation, V, then V is a sensation of a subject-dependent property, Q, looking like instantiated on a mind-independent particular X (property-content version).
P2. By having a sensation, V, S could introspect Q (Weak Transparency).
   C1. There are perceptual intermediaries between S and X.

Sense-data TEA differs from weak TEA since the former specifies that perceptual intermediaries can only be sensory properties, say *qualia*, and cannot be concrete physical particulars (see Russell). The debate about transparency and the right comprehension of the content of sensations is far from being solved; however, there are many detailed theories trying to do it.

38

The Regress Argument for Skepticism

Scott Aikin

Sextus Empiricus. *Outlines of Scepticism*. Translated by Julia Annas and Jonathan Barnes. Cambridge, UK: Cambridge University Press, 2000.

Oakley, I. T. "An Argument for Scepticism Concerning Justified Beliefs." *American Philosophical Quarterly*, 13, 3 (1976): 221–8.
Cling, Andrew. "Reasons, Regresses and Tragedy." *American Philosophical Quarterly*, 46, 2 (2009): 333–46.

The basic thought behind the regress argument is familiar to anyone who has spoken with an inquisitive child, "Why?" is always a good question. Since the question can be asked of any answer, a recursive pattern very quickly emerges. For example, "Eat your vegetables." "Why?" "Because they are good for you." "Why?" "Because you want to he healthy." "Why?" And then we are off to the races. Translated to an epistemological context, the regress problem arises because of the simple requirement that if you are to hold reasonably a belief, you must be able to answer satisfactorily a "why" question with another reasonably held belief or group of beliefs. This, of course, invites another "why" question, which requires another satisfactory and justifiably held answer. And then the regress ensues (#49). It seems that the demand that we go on to infinity is excessive, that answers that go in a circle are vicious, and that anytime someone says she does not need to give further answers, she is acting unreasonably. Skepticism seems to follow – if we cannot give the adequate backing for our claims, we do not know those claims to be true.

Sextus Empiricus classically framed the regress problem in his *Outlines of Pyrrhonism* as the coordination of five "modes," or strategies, of skeptical argument. Two of these modes, sometimes called the "material modes," are those to challenge someone who believes something to defend it. These are the modes of relativity and dispute. Once a believer starts to defend the belief, there are only three options for the argument to proceed: either in (i) a vicious regress, which Sextus calls "*ad infinitum*," (ii) a question-begging circle, which Sextus calls "reciprocality," or (iii) unsupported dogmatic assertion, which Sextus calls "hypothesis." These three final modes for argument are called the "formal modes" or "the trilemma."

> According to the mode deriving from dispute, we find that undecidable dissension about the matter proposed has come about both in ordinary life and among philosophers. Because of this we are not able either to choose or to rule out anything, and we end up with suspension of judgment. In the mode of deriving from infinite regress, we say that what is brought forward as a source of conviction for the matter proposed itself needs another source, which itself needs another, and so ad infinitum, so that we have no point from which to begin to establish anything, and suspension of judgment follows. In the mode deriving from relativity, [...] the existing object appears to be such-and-such relative to the subject judging and to the things observed together with it, but we suspend judgment on what it is like in its nature. We have the mode from hypothesis from the Dogmatists, being thrown back ad infinitum, begin from something which they do not establish but claim to assume simply and without proof in virtue of a concession. The reciprocal mode occurs when what ought to be confirmatory of the object under investigation needs to be made convincing by the object under investigation; then, being unable to take either in order to establish the other, we suspend judgment about both. (Empiricus PH I.165–9)

Given the structural problems that come with knowing, we are forced to suspend judgment about our beliefs generally because they are not justified. Justification is structurally vexed, and as a consequence, something we cannot possess. General skepticism about knowledge, then, follows. The argument's premises are all inherently plausible. The principle of inferential justification is something that comes with being a responsible believer – if you believe something, then you should be able to explain why you do so; that is, you should be able to give a reason that counts in favor of the truth of your belief. This is simply what it is to be accountable for and in charge of your beliefs. The responsibility iterates, because the reasons we give must, themselves, pass this test. And so these chains of reasons are just part of what it is to be a rational being – we give justifying stories for what we do, what we say, and what we believe. Without those stories, it is hard to see ourselves as responsible, reasonable, or rational.

The principle of noncircular justification comes from the informal argumentative thought that arguments that have their conclusions function in their premises fail because they beg the question. Reasoning should be a kind of progress, where we get somewhere, increase our knowledge, resolve disagreements, and answer questions. If we assume our conclusions at the beginning and tell our justifying stories for them in light of them, we have at most been consistent, but that is about as much as we can say in favor of the reasoning.

The principle of finite justification is simply that infinite series of reasons are not completable by finite creatures such as us. We do not have infinite time, nor do we have infinite reasons for our beliefs – our minds are limited only to the things we've experienced, thought about, and learned. The requirement that knowledge be more than that is absurd. Further, it seems, as Sextus notes above, even were there an infinite chain of reasons, we are unsure how reasoning on such a chain of reasons could either ever get started or ever finish.

The corollaries of no unjustified justifiers and no unjustified chain-enders are contrapositives of the principle of inferential justification and the corollary of recursive justification. The requirement of inferential justification is that (in epistemology lingo) if S has a justified belief that p, S has a justified belief that q that justifies p. The corollary is that without a justified belief that q that justifies p, S does not have a justified belief that p. There are no unjustified justifiers.

The trilemma is that once chains of reasons begin to be extended, there are only three options: they either (a) stop with some belief or other, without further support, (b) circle back on themselves, or (c) go on to infinity. So long as we think that reasons must come in recursive chains, these are the only three options.

Despite the fact that all the premises of the argument are each individually appealing, they together entail an unappealing conclusion, namely, that we have no justification for any of our beliefs. This unacceptable conclusion has forced many to return to the premises of the argument with a more critical eye. One of the premises, if we do in fact know things, must be false. The project of anti-skepticism, in light of the regress problem, is that of making the case for the falsity of at least one of these premises.

The oldest and most widely favored anti-skeptical strategy is called "foundationalism." The foundationalist holds that premise 1 is false, or at least, that there are notable exceptions. There are some beliefs that stand on their own, and they can then serve as a foundation for further beliefs. Call these beliefs with autonomous justification "basic beliefs." The foundationalist accepts that reasons come in chains, but if the reasons are justifying, those chains of reasons all end with beliefs that are justified independently of other reasons. Take three examples, your beliefs: (i) that you exist, (ii) that you have a book in front of you, and (iii) that 2 + 2 = 4. Each of these beliefs is justified because you just see that they it is true. You, in believing (i), furnish the reason for its truth (it can't be false if you believe it). Your visual experiences of this book in front of you give you a reason to believe (ii), and you don't need more reasons for that. Your concepts of addition, equality, two, and four give you the understanding to make it so that you don't need any more reason to believe (iii) than just that you understand it. Beliefs such as these are regress-enders.

The "coherentist" accepts the principle of inferential justification and holds that only justified beliefs can justify beliefs. However, the coherentist denies the principle of the noncircularity of justification. Justifying stories come as packages, in that we reasonably believe things when they fit well enough with other things that we believe. And once these systems of belief are up and running, the beliefs in them are mutually supporting. For example, you believe that there are physical forces, such as gravity. You also believe that a bowling ball falling down on a fragile porcelain mouse will crush it. You also believe that the last time you dropped your keys, they fell on the ground. These beliefs all hang together, and they function, with many others, as a system for you to make sense of your past experiences and make predictions about future ones. Justification emerges from these interdependent and mutually supporting systems of beliefs.

The "contextualist," like the foundationalist, holds that there are exceptions to the principle of inferential justification. However, the beliefs that need no further reasons are dependent on what kinds of questions our justifications are out to answer. For example, if you're trying to decide whether to go to Las Vegas for your holiday, it may be reasonable to doubt that your year-old information about hotel prices is accurate. So you may go to a recent source. But you're not going to worry about whether they accept American dollars or whether you can expect that you can get service in English. But if you were thinking about going to Monte Carlo (in Monaco), instead, you'd not only want to get better information about hotel prices, but you'd also want to check into what kind of currency you'll need and whether you'll need to take a crash course in French. Depending on what's at issue, some questions aren't worth asking, because their answers are reasonably assumed in the context. But in others they are worth asking, because you cannot reasonably assume their answers.

"Infinitism" is a recent development in epistemology, as for the over 2,000 years folks have been thinking about the regress problem, it wasn't until the last 10 years that anyone's tried to work this view out in any detail. The infinitist denies the principle of finite justification. And so the infinitist holds that only an infinite series of reasons can yield justified belief. The basic thought is that the person who really knows something can answer "why" questions until there just aren't any more. And, in principle, there is no reason why such questions must end. This is certainly a heavy task, and it seems troublesome, because it is clear that we don't ever actually give those very long arguments. But the infinitist holds that one may not have to give those arguments but only be able to give them as far as they are needed by critical questioners. Persistent questioners are troublesome, but they are useful to us in that they allow us to plumb the depths of our reasons. They may break certain rules of context in questioning things we don't normally question, but that is how we really know – we can answer questions that otherwise we'd just say we'd assumed.

The success of the regress argument for skepticism hinges on whether these four anti-skeptical programs are correct in denying or modifying the argument's premises. If these anti-skeptical programs are right, they must be able to answer some simple questions. The question for the foundationalist is whether, in arguing that there are regress-ending basic beliefs, the foundationalist has actually continued the regress. This is sometimes called the "meta-regress problem" for foundationalism. The question for the contextualist is whether these systems of mutually supporting beliefs have anything to do with the truth, as it seems that systems of crazy beliefs (e.g., conspiracy theories) are coherent and function similarly but are terribly wrong. This is called the "alternate systems problem" for coherentism. The question for the contextualists is whether contextually appropriate assumption amounts to justification – surely some contexts are defined by the fact that people make assumptions in them, but that doesn't mean they have knowledge. This is called the "problem of credulity" for contextualists. The question for the infinitist is whether infinitism is simply another form of skepticism, as it seems that no one ever actually has an infinite series of justifying reasons and so no one actually knows anything. This is called the problem of "crypto-skepticism" for infinitists. The regress skeptic is, for lack of a better term, skeptical as to whether there are adequate answers to these challenges.

P1. If any believer is reasonably (or justifiably) to hold a belief, then that believer must do so on the justifying basis of another justified belief.

P2. If a believer reasonably holds a belief, then that believer must reasonably hold another belief to justify that first belief, and a third belief to hold that second one, and a further fourth belief to hold that third one, and so on. Call this a "chain of reasons."

   C1. If a believer reasonably holds a belief, that believer must have a justifying chain of reasons (hypothetical syllogism, P1, P2).

P3. If any believer is reasonably to hold a belief, it cannot be on the basis of a circular chain of reasons.

P4. If any believer is reasonably to hold a belief, it cannot be on the basis of an infinite chain of reasons.

P5. If any believer holds a belief on the basis of a belief without justification, that believer does not reasonably hold the first belief.

    C2. No believers with chains of reasons with unjustified beliefs at their ends are justified (universal generalization, P2, P5).

P6. Chains of reasons either (a) are circular, (b) end with unjustified beliefs, or (c) are infinite.

    C3. For any believer's chain of reasons, it either (a) goes in a circle, (b) ends with an unjustified commitment, or (c) goes on to infinity (instantiation, P6).

    C4. There are no beliefs for which believers are justified in holding them (destructive trilemma, P3, P4, P6).

39

Moore's Anti-Skeptical Arguments

Matthew Frise

Moore, G. E. "Four Forms of Scepticism," and "Proof of an External World," in *Epistemology: An Anthology*, edited by Ernest Sosa, Jaegwon Kim, and Matthew McGrath, 24–8. Malden, MA: Blackwell, 2000.

Reid, Thomas. *Philosophical Works*. Hildesheim: Olms, 1983.

External-world skepticism – the view that we do not know that anything outside our minds exists – has always been a central issue in epistemology. G. E. Moore, one of the most influential analytic philosophers of the twentieth century, popularized two types of arguments against skepticism that make reference to commonsense claims, claims such as "I know this is a pencil" and "Here is a hand." The strategy of the first type of argument is to point out that commonsense claims are more certain than the skeptic's assumptions (at least some of them). The conclusion is not that commonsense knowledge disproves skepticism, but that our commonsense knowledge is in no danger of being undermined by skepticism. The strategy of the second type of argument is to cite things in the external world that we clearly know to exist, thereby demonstrating knowledge that the external world itself exists. An argument of this type is formally valid, but many think it fails to disprove skepticism because it "begs the question"; knowledge of its premises allegedly presupposes knowledge of its conclusion.

Just the Arguments: 100 of the Most Important Arguments in Western Philosophy, First Edition. Edited by Michael Bruce and Steven Barbone.
© 2011 Blackwell Publishing Ltd. Published 2011 by Blackwell Publishing Ltd.

Below, we give the skeleton of both types of arguments, making the reasoning and conclusion of each explicit.

> What I want, however, finally to emphasize is this: Russell's view that I do not know for certain that this is a pencil or that you are conscious rests, if I am right, on no less than four distinct assumptions: (1) That I don't know these things immediately; (2) That they don't follow logically from any thing or things that I do know immediately; (3) That *if* (1) and (2) are true, my belief in or knowledge of them must be 'based on an analogical or inductive argument'; and (4) That what is so based cannot be *certain knowledge*. And what I can't help asking myself is this: Is it, in fact, as certain that all these four assumptions are true, as that I do know that this is a pencil and that you are conscious? I cannot help answering: It seems to me *more* certain that I do know that this is a pencil and that you are conscious, than that any single one of these four assumptions is true, let alone all four. That is to say, though, as I have said, I agree with Russell that (1), (2), and (3) *are* true; yet of no one even of these three do I feel as certain as that I do know for certain that this is a pencil. Nay more: I do not think it is rational to be as certain of any one of these four propositions as of the proposition that I do know that this is a pencil. (Moore, 28)

P1. The skeptic's assumptions imply that propositions such as "I know this is a pencil" are false.
P2. If proposition A is more certain than proposition B, B cannot falsify A.
P3. "I know this is a pencil" is more certain than any of the skeptic's assumptions.
   C1. The skeptic's assumptions cannot falsify that "I know this is a pencil" (*modus ponens*, P2, P3).

> I can prove now, for instance, that two human hands exist. How? By holding up my two hands, and saying, as I make a certain gesture with the right hand, 'Here is one hand', and adding, as I make a certain gesture with the left, 'and here is another'. (Moore, 24)

P1. Here is a hand, here is another.
P2. If hands exist, then external objects exist.
   C1. External objects exist (*modus ponens*, P1, P2).

40

The Bias Paradox

Deborah Heikes

Antony, Louise. "Quine as Feminist," in *A Mind of One's Own*, edited by
    Louise M. Antony and Charlotte Witt, 110–53. Boulder, CO: Westview,
    2002.
Heikes, Deborah. "The Bias Paradox: Why It's Not Just for Feminists
    Anymore." *Synthese* 138, 3 (2004): 315–35.

The bias paradox arises from arguments that reject or decisively revise standard Cartesian conceptions of pure objectivity and impartiality. Such conceptions require that we move beyond particularity and contingency in order to acquire knowledge that is free from bias. Feminist philosophers are generally concerned with rejecting notions of objectivity that require this complete elimination of subjectivity. As a rule, feminists believe that subjectivity can never be entirely eliminated. However, this rejection of a notion of pure (nonsubjective) neutrality has led the dilemma that Louise Antony calls the "bias paradox."

For feminists, two fundamental commitments give rise to a dilemma that seems to require a commitment either to objectivism or relativism. The first of these commitments is the explicit rejection of the concept of impartial objectivity, and the second one is the desire to assert the reality and injustice of women's oppression. The problem is that in the absence of impartiality (at least as an ideal), there appears to be a lack of principled, normative criteria for evaluating beliefs across differing epistemic perspectives. At the same time, feminist philosophers almost unanimously reject the possibility of impartiality. The dilemma, as Antony presents it, is this: either we endorse the ideal of objectivity so that we can provide a ground for evaluating bias or we cease criticizing bias (i.e., we cease distinguishing between "good" biases and "bad" biases), since there can be no standard for evaluating competing biases.

Just the Arguments: 100 of the Most Important Arguments in Western Philosophy,
First Edition. Edited by Michael Bruce and Steven Barbone.
© 2011 Blackwell Publishing Ltd. Published 2011 by Blackwell Publishing Ltd.

While this tension is dealt with most straightforwardly in discussions of naturalized feminist epistemology and feminist philosophy of science, the bias paradox is not merely a problem for feminists. Any view that rejects the Cartesian ideals of pure objectivity and value-neutrality will ultimately be forced to confront the dilemma that seemingly results from the paradox, namely, either to endorse pure impartiality or to accept an "anything goes" relativism. The problem, of course, is that most philosophical views deny that pure impartiality can be achieved, and many argue that it is not even useful as an ideal. However, the alternative view is that just about every claim to knowledge is as good as any other claim, and almost no one wishes to adopt this view. Hence, we encounter the bias paradox.

> According to many feminist philosophers, the flaw in the ideal of impartiality is supposed to be that the ideal itself is biased: Critics charge either that the concept of 'objectivity' serves to articulate a masculine or patriarchal viewpoint [...], or that it has the ideological function of protecting the rights of those in power, especially men. But how is it possible to criticize the partiality of the concept of objectivity without presupposing the very value under attack? Put baldly: If we don't think it's good to be impartial, then how can we object to men's being *partial*? (Antony, 114)

P1. Impartiality is untenable as an ideal of epistemic practice.
P2. If impartiality is untenable as an ideal of epistemic practice, then all epistemic practices are biased.
    C1. All epistemic practices are biased (*modus ponens*, P1, P2).
P3. If all epistemic practices are biased, there can be no impartial criteria for evaluating the epistemic worth of biases.
    C2. There can be no impartial criteria for evaluating the epistemic worth of biases (*modus ponens*, C1, P3).
P4. If there are no impartial criteria for evaluating the epistemic worth of biases, then all biases are equal.
    C3. All biases are equal (*modus ponens*, C2, P4).

Generic bias paradox:

P1. The ideal of impartiality should be rejected.
P2. If we reject the ideal of impartiality, there can be no justified procedure for normatively distinguishing among competing epistemic views.
    C1. There can be no justified procedure for normatively distinguishing among competing epistemic views (*modus ponens*, P1, P2).
P3. If there can be no justified procedure for normatively distinguishing among competing epistemic views, then all accounts are epistemically equal.
    C2. All accounts are epistemically equal (*modus ponens*, C1, P3).

41

Gettier's Argument against the Traditional Account of Knowledge

John M. DePoe[1]

Gettier, Edmund. "Is Justified True Belief Knowledge?" *Analysis* 23 (1963): 121–3.

The Gettier problem has drawn the attention of epistemologists since Edmund Gettier (1927–) published his three-page article in 1963. The point of Gettier's argument is to show that the concept of knowledge cannot be defined as justified true belief, and Gettier set out to disprove the traditional account of knowledge by showing that there are counterexamples to it. If the traditional account of knowledge is correct, then it is not possible for a person to have a justified true belief that isn't knowledge (P1). Since the account maintains that all instances of knowledge are justified true beliefs and vice versa, in order to refute the traditional account, Gettier needed to provide an example of a justified true belief that no one would think is an example of knowledge.

In order to understand Gettier's counterexample, it is first important to see how advocates of the traditional account understood justified belief. The correct analysis of justification is a matter of great controversy, but as a preliminary attempt it may be helpful to think of a person's having a justified belief as that person's having some evidence or good reasons to think that the belief is true or likely to be true. Importantly, to have a justi-

[1]   The author wishes to thank Michael O'Rouke (University of Idaho).

Just the Arguments: 100 of the Most Important Arguments in Western Philosophy, First Edition. Edited by Michael Bruce and Steven Barbone.
© 2011 Blackwell Publishing Ltd. Published 2011 by Blackwell Publishing Ltd.

fied belief, one's good reasons do not necessarily need to guarantee that the belief is true. For example, one may be justified in believing that one is seeing a zebra based on the evidence of a black-and-white-striped-equine sensory experience, and one would still be justified, in believing one is seeing a zebra, even if the animal were not a zebra but a cleverly painted mule instead. Consequently, for a belief to be justified, it is not necessary for the belief to be true. As (P2) states, it is possible for one to be justified in believing a false proposition.

The next part of Gettier's counterexample follows from the principle expressed by (P3): if one is justified in believing some proposition, then one is justified (at least to the same degree) in believing any proposition that one competently deduces from the original one. Since when deductive reasoning is performed competently it preserves truth infallibly, one's justification does not diminish across deductive inference. Perhaps this is best illustrated by a variation from one of Gettier's examples. Imagine a case where a trustworthy friend, Mr. Nogot, provides sufficiently strong evidence to his friend Jackson for being justified in believing that he (Nogot) owns a Ford. For example, imagine that in addition to his typically trustworthy testimony, Mr. Nogot shows Jackson his registration papers, he takes Jackson for a ride in the Ford, and Jackson has no reason to doubt his testimony or any of the additional evidence that he has to support the proposition that Mr. Nogot owns a Ford. Now, Mr. Nogot does not own a Ford (unbeknownst to Jackson), but this does not prevent Jackson from being justified in believing that Mr. Nogot owns a Ford, since according to (P2) it is possible for a person to be justified in believing a false proposition. And now to the part relevant to (P3) – suppose that as Jackson is pondering his justified belief (that Mr. Nogot owns a Ford) with Mr. Nogot in the room, he deductively reasons that if Mr. Nogot owns a Ford, then someone in the room owns a Ford; therefore, Jackson concludes, someone in the room owns a Ford. On the basis of (P3), Jackson is at least as justified in believing that someone in the room owns a Ford as he is for the proposition that Mr. Nogot owns a Ford since he deduced the former from the latter, which is stated in (C1).

The final claim needed to underwrite Gettier's counterexample is stated in (P4): If a person is justified in believing a proposition that is true by accident or luck, then her justified true belief is not knowledge. It has already been stipulated that Mr. Nogot does not own a Ford. Now let's suppose that at the time that Jackson deductively reasons from the proposition that Mr. Nogot owns a Ford to the proposition that someone in the room owns a Ford, Mr. Havit happens to be the room. Mr. Havit – a person Jackson has never met or has any justification for believing what kind of car he owns – is sitting quietly in the corner of the room, and he happens to own a Ford. So, it turns out that Jackson's belief that someone in the room owns a Ford is both justified and true. Recall that it is justified because he deduced it from a proposition that he is justified in believing. The belief is true since Mr. Havit owns a Ford and he is in the room. But since Jackson has no beliefs whatsoever about Mr. Havit, the truth of his justified belief appears to be accidental or lucky. After all, Jackson would have still believed that someone in the room owns a Ford even if Mr. Havit wasn't in the room. Thus, it seems that Jackson's justified belief is true by luck or accident. In other words, the belief's being true has nothing to do with the justification Jackson has for holding the belief. For this reason, it would be wrong to accept that Jackson's justified true belief (that someone in the room owns a Ford) counts as knowledge.

Since Jackson's belief that someone in the room owns a Ford is a justified true belief (C2), and it is plainly wrong to think that it counts as knowledge, Gettier's argument is widely accepted as demonstrating why knowledge cannot be defined as justified true belief (C3).

> These [. . .] examples show that definition (a) [knowledge is justified true belief] does not state a sufficient condition for someone's knowing a given proposition. (Gettier, 123)

P1. If knowledge is justified true belief, then it is not possible for a person to have a justified true belief that isn't knowledge.

P2. A person can be justified in believing a false proposition.

P3. If a person is justified in believing some proposition, then she is justified (at least to the same degree) in believing any proposition that she competently deduces from the original.

    C1. A person is justified (at least to the same degree) in believing any proposition that she competently deduces from the original (*modus ponens*, P2, P3).

P4. If a person is justified in believing a proposition that is true by accident or luck, then his justified true belief is not knowledge.

P5. Jackson is justified in believing that someone in the room owns a Ford, which is true by accident or luck.

    C2. It is possible for a person to have a justified true belief that isn't knowledge (*modus ponens*, P4, P5).

    C3. It is not the case that knowledge is justified true belief (*modus tollens*, P1, C2).

42

Putnam's Argument against Cultural Imperialism

Maria Caamaño

Putnam, Hilary. "Why Reason Can't Be Naturalized," in *Epistemology: An Anthology*, edited by Ernest Sosa, Jaegwon Kim, and Mathew McGrath, 314–24. Malden, MA: Blackwell, 1999.

Putnam introduces this argument in the context of criticizing the different attempts to naturalize reason by reducing it to those standards accepted by a culture. According to Putnam, reason always results from a balance between immanence to culture and traditions and transcendence to them. The first would be manifest in the inherited cultural background in which any reasoning always takes place; the second would become obvious in our ability to criticize such cultural background. Both cultural relativism and cultural imperialism would break the above balance as a result of their emphasis on immanence. However, facts related to the transcendent side of reason are precisely the ones that would show the self-refutability of both views. Cultural relativism would need to make, inconsistently, a transcendent assumption regarding the symmetry of the epistemic situation between different cultures. Cultural imperialism, on the other hand, would require us to assume an immanent agreement that is contradicted by experience. So while the argument for cultural relativism turns out to be analytically flawed, the one to support cultural imperialism proves empirically faulty. In this context, Putnam formulates his argument against cultural imperialism and continues by pointing out two of its important features: first, its contingent character, since the goodness of the argument depends on the

Just the Arguments: 100 of the Most Important Arguments in Western Philosophy, First Edition. Edited by Michael Bruce and Steven Barbone.
© 2011 Blackwell Publishing Ltd. Published 2011 by Blackwell Publishing Ltd.

contingent fact that people disagree about something – that is, about truth's dependency on cultural standards (P2 below); and second, its extensibility to all theories which equate truth or right assertability with what people (would) agree. The importance of the argument, therefore, does not only lie on its rebuttal of cultural imperialism but also on its more general refutation of any definition of truth in terms of (possible) agreement among people. The argument follows a *reductio ad absurdum* strategy, by reflexively applying the requirement established in the principle of cultural imperialisms to that very principle and thereby showing that the assumption violates the very requirement that it establishes. Finally, a more general aim of Putnam's argument consists in supporting the view that modern European and American culture does not have "norms" that decide philosophical questions, as would happen in totalitarian or theocratic cultures.

> A statement is true (rightly assertable) only if it is assertable according to the norms of modern European and American culture is itself neither assertable nor refutable in a way that requires assent by everyone who does not deviate from the norms of modern European and American culture. So, if this statement is true, it follows that it is not true QED. (Putnam, 319)

P1. A statement P is true (rightly assertable) only if it is assertable according to the norms of modern European and American culture (assumption for *reductio*).

    C1. If "A statement is true (rightly assertable) only if it is assertable according to the norms of modern European and American culture" is true (rightly assertable), then it is assertable according to the norms of modern European and American culture (substitution of 'P' with "A statement is true (rightly assertable) only if it is assertable according to the norms of modern European and American culture" in P1).

P2. "A statement is true (rightly assertable) only if it is assertable according to the norms of modern European and American culture" is not assertable according to the norms of modern European and American culture.

    C2. "A statement is true (rightly assertable) only if it is assertable according to the norms of modern European and American culture" is not true, that is, rightly assertable (*modus tollens*, C1, P2).

    C3. A statement is true (rightly assertable) only if it is assertable according to the norms of modern European and American culture and it is not the case that a statement is true (rightly assertable) only if it is assertable according to the norms of modern European and American culture (conjunction, P1, C2).

    C4. It is not the case that a statement is true (rightly assertable) only if it is assertable according to the norms of modern European and American culture (*reductio*, P1–C3).

Extension of Putnam's Argument

In order to bring Putnam's discussion of his own argument to completion, it may be interesting to show how it naturally extends to arguments equating truth with what people (would) agree. Let us see how the refutation would work in that case:

P1. A statement P is true (rightly assertable) only if everybody agrees with it (assumption for *reductio*).

   C1. If "A statement is true (rightly assertable) only if everybody agrees with it" is true (rightly assertable), then everybody agrees with it (Substitution of 'P' by "A statement is true (rightly assertable) only if everybody agrees with it" in P1).

P2. Not everybody agrees that "A statement is true (rightly assertable) only if everybody agrees with it."

   C2. "A statement is true (rightly assertable) only if everybody agrees with it" is not true, that is, rightly assertable (*modus tollens*, C1, P2).

   C3. A statement is true (rightly assertable) only if everybody agrees with it and it is not the case that a statement is true (rightly assertable) only if everybody agrees with it (conjunction, P1, C2).

   C4. It is not the case that a statement is true (rightly assertable) only if everybody agrees with it (*reductio*, P1–C3).

43

Davidson on the Very Idea of a Conceptual Scheme

George Wrisley

Davidson, Donald. "On the Very Idea of a Conceptual Scheme." *Proceedings and Addresses of the American Philosophical Association* 47 (1974): 5–20; reprinted in Davidson (2001).

Davidson, Donald. *Inquiries into Truth and Interpretation*, 2nd edn. Oxford: Clarendon Press, 2001.

Case, Jennifer. "On the Right Idea of a Conceptual Scheme." *Southern Journal of Philosophy* 35 (1997): 1–18.

Malpas, Jeff. "Donald Davidson." *The Stanford Encyclopedia of Philosophy* (Fall 2009 edn.), edited by Edward N. Zalta, available at http://plato.stanford.edu/archives/fall2009/entries/Davidson

One of Immanuel Kant's (1724–1804) central philosophical concerns was the relationship between mind and world. He famously inverted the idea that in knowing the world the mind attempts to mirror a "mind-independent" world, claiming instead that the world we experience necessarily conforms to certain categories of the mind. While such categories were essentially universal for Kant, later philosophers replaced the idea of the world's conforming to the categories of the mind with the idea of the world's conforming to linguistic or conceptual categories. This change allowed for the idea of a very strong conceptual/linguistic relativism whereby either the content of experience or the world itself is relativized to conceptual frameworks or

Just the Arguments: 100 of the Most Important Arguments in Western Philosophy, First Edition. Edited by Michael Bruce and Steven Barbone.
© 2011 Blackwell Publishing Ltd. Published 2011 by Blackwell Publishing Ltd.

schemes – the central idea of which is that different conceptual schemes result in different worlds.

Donald Davidson (1917–2003) argues that conceptual relativism is incoherent because the very idea of a conceptual scheme is incoherent. Davidson reaches these conclusions by arguing that the idea of a conceptual scheme depends on the notion of failure of translation between differing schemes. According to Davidson, sense cannot be made of either complete or partial failure of translation, and so it does not make sense to speak of different conceptual schemes. Since it does not make sense to speak of different conceptual schemes, he claims that it does not make sense to speak of there being only one conceptual scheme.

Davidson's argument against the intelligibility of the idea of a conceptual scheme, and thus the possibility of conceptual relativism, is important given its implications for the way that we know the world, the relationship between us and the world, and the relationship between language and world. For if he is right, then there is not a dualism of conceptual scheme and content (world/experience), and it becomes even more difficult to make sense of the idea that radically different accounts of what exists and how the world is could all be true, and those forms of skepticism that depend on a dualism of scheme and content are also called into question.

> We may accept the doctrine that associates having a language with having a conceptual scheme. The relation may be supposed to be this: where conceptual schemes differ, so do languages. But speakers of different languages may share a conceptual scheme provided there is a way of translating one language into the other. Studying the criteria of translation is therefore a way of focusing on criteria of identity for conceptual schemes. [. . .]
>
> I consider two kinds of cases that might be expected to arise: complete, and partial, failures of translatability. There would be complete failure if no significant range of sentences in one language could be translated into the other; there would be partial failure if some range could be translated and some range could not. [. . .] My strategy will be to argue that we cannot make sense of total failure, and then to examine more briefly cases of partial failure.[. . .]
>
> [Regarding partial failure], when others think differently from us, no general principle, or appeal to evidence, can force us to decide that the difference lies in our beliefs rather than our concepts.
>
> We must conclude, I think, that the attempt to give a solid meaning to the idea of conceptual relativism, and hence to the idea of a conceptual scheme, fares no better when based on partial failure of translation than when based on total failure. (Davidson *Inquiries*, 197)

Both the shorter version (Part I) and longer version (Part II) consist of three arguments: (1) an argument against the idea of complete failure of translation; (2) an argument against partial failure of translation; and

(3) a capstone argument drawing on (1) and (2) for the conclusion that the very idea of a conceptual scheme is unintelligible rather than its being false that there is only one conceptual scheme or that there could be different conceptual schemes.

Part I: Shorter Version (Leaves Key Premises Unsupported)

P1. If the idea of different conceptual schemes is intelligible, then we can make sense of a difference in conceptual schemes consisting in complete failure of translation between schemes, *or* If the idea of different conceptual schemes is intelligible, then we can make sense of a difference in conceptual schemes consisting in partial failure of translation between schemes.

P2. If the idea of complete failure of translation as a way to individuate conceptual schemes makes sense, then we can make sense of the idea of the scheme organizing the content, *or* If the idea of complete failure of translation as a way to individuate conceptual schemes makes sense, then we can make sense of the idea of the scheme fitting the content.

P3. We can neither make sense of the idea of the scheme organizing the content, nor the idea of the idea of the scheme fitting the content.

   C1. We cannot make sense of the idea of complete failure of translation as a way to individuate conceptual schemes (destructive dilemma, P2, P3).

P4. If the idea of partial failure of translation as a way to individuate conceptual schemes makes sense, then there is either a general principle or evidence that could determine whether our disagreement with those operating with a purportedly different scheme about the truth of sentences X, Y, Z is a difference in scheme or a difference in belief.

P5. There is neither a general principle nor evidence that could determine whether our disagreement with those operating with a purportedly different scheme about the truth of sentences X, Y, Z is a difference in scheme or a difference in belief.

   C2. We cannot make sense of the idea of partial failure of translation as a way to individuate conceptual schemes (*modus tollens*, P4, P5).

   C3. The idea of different conceptual schemes is not intelligible (destructive dilemma P1, C1, C2).

P6. If there is only one conceptual scheme, then it is false that there are different conceptual schemes.

P7. If the idea of different conceptual schemes is not intelligible, then it is not false that there are different conceptual schemes.

P8. It is not false that there are different conceptual schemes (*modus ponens*, C3, P7).

P9. There is not only one conceptual scheme (*modus ponens*, P6, P8).

P10. If the idea of different conceptual schemes is not intelligible and there is not only one conceptual scheme, then the very idea of a conceptual scheme is unintelligible.

    C4. Therefore, the very idea of a conceptual scheme is unintelligible (*modus ponens*, P10, C3, P9).

Part II: Detailed Version

P1. If the idea of different conceptual schemes is intelligible, then we can make sense of a difference in conceptual schemes consisting in complete failure of translation between schemes, *or* If the idea of different conceptual schemes is intelligible, then we can make sense of a difference in conceptual schemes consisting in partial failure of translation between schemes.

Complete Failure of Translation

P2. Let us consider the possibility of complete failure of translation between languages.

P3. A conceptual scheme implies a dualism of scheme and (uninterpreted) content. The scheme is the conceptual apparatus of a language, where a language consists of sentences held to be true. The content is either the world/reality or experience/evidence understood as uninterpreted, that is, a neutral something to which the scheme stands in a relation.

P4. If the idea of complete failure of translation as a way to individuate conceptual schemes makes sense, then we can make sense of the idea of the scheme's organizing the content, *or* If the idea of complete failure of translation as a way to individuate conceptual schemes makes sense, then we can make sense of the idea of the scheme's fitting the content.

P5. If sense can be made of the scheme's organizing the content, then the content is a nonindividuated object, or if the scheme organizes the content, then the content consists of parts.

P6. A nonindividuated object cannot be organized.

P7. The content cannot consist of parts prior to being organized by the scheme, since it is supposed to be the scheme that organizes the content into parts.

    C1. We cannot make sense of the idea that a scheme organizes the content (destructive dilemma, P5, P6, P7).

P8. Consider the possibility of the scheme's fitting the content. Saying that a scheme fits the content just means that it is borne out by the evidence, which simply means that the scheme is true (or largely true to allow for error).

P9. From P8, this means that a scheme X will be different from, for example, that of the English language if and only if X is (largely) true but untranslatable into English.

P10. However, we cannot separate the concepts of truth and translation in this way. Here is why, according to Davidson:

P11a. Following Alfred Tarski's work on the concept of truth (and Tarski's work gives us the best understanding of truth), the true sentences of a language must conform to Tarski's Convention T, which says that for every sentence s of (the language) L, a theorem can be given of the form 's is true if and only if p' where 's' is replaced by a description of s and 'p' by s itself if L is English, and by a translation of s into English if L is not English. An example using English and German: "'*Es schneit*' is true if and only if it is snowing." All true sentences of a language conforming to Convention T constitute a "theory of truth" for that language.

P11b. In the case we are considering, X is a conceptual scheme different from English, which means (a) X is true, but untranslatable. But (b) if X is true, then a theory of truth for X can be given. And (c) if a theory of truth for X can be given, then, by Convention T, translations of sentences of X into English can be given. However, by the supposition that X is a different conceptual scheme from English, its sentences are untranslatable into English.

P11c. We cannot make sense of the claim that X is true (two instances of *modus tollens* from 11b, beginning with (c) and (a), and then the negation of the antecedent of (c) together with (b)).

P12. We cannot make sense of the idea that a scheme fits the content, for if the scheme fits the content, then it is true and untranslatable into another language. But, by P11c, we cannot make sense of a true and untranslatable language.

C2. We cannot make sense of the idea of complete failure of translation as a way to individuate conceptual schemes (destructive dilemma P4, C1, P12).

Partial Failure of Translation

P13. Let us consider the possibility of partial failure of translation between languages. Two languages that have partial failure of translation will embody different schemes to the extent that they have parts that are not intertranslatable.

P14. The proper way to approach the translation of an unknown language into a known language is by interpreting the utterances of the speakers of the unknown language from the perspective of speakers of the known language. Such interpretation will consist in forming hypotheses as to what the speakers' utterances mean.

P15. The formation of such hypotheses requires attributions of both meaning and belief. As a matter of interpretation, we know what a person's utterances mean in relation to knowing what he believes in a given context. For example, if a speaker utters "Hartchep" right after a thunderclap, our hypothesizing that "Hartchep" means thunder consists in attributing the belief that the sound that occurred was thunder to the speaker. If we thought the speaker believed the sound to have been an explosion (even though we knew it had been thunder), we would likely not hypothesize that "Hartchep" means thunder.

P16. Assume that even when we cannot know what a speaker believes or means, we can know whether a speaker holds a particular utterance to be true.

P17. To facilitate the possibility of interpretation, we should employ the principle of charity and assume that the beliefs of the people we are interpreting are by and large true (by our lights).

P18. If it is a reasonable assumption that there will be sentences uttered by speakers of language X that those speakers reject as truths, and we are to interpret those rejected sentences, then depending on the evidence available, we will either translate them into sentences that we accept or sentences that we reject.

P19. If the evidence available for interpreting those rejected sentences of X leads us to translate them into sentences that we accept as true, then this can be taken to mean either that our schemes differ at this point or that our beliefs differ.

P20. If we are in a position in which we can either take our schemes to differ or our beliefs to differ at a particular point, then there is neither a general principle nor evidence that could possibly determine whether it is a difference in scheme or a difference in belief.

P21. If there is neither a general principle nor evidence that could possibly determine whether it is a difference in scheme or a difference in belief, then we could never be in a position to judge whether speakers of X have concepts or beliefs radically different from our own.

P22. If we could never be in a position to judge whether speakers of X have concepts or beliefs radically different from our own, then we cannot make sense of the idea of there being partial failure of translation.

P23. It is a reasonable assumption that there will be sentences uttered by speakers of language X that those speakers reject as truths, and we are to interpret those rejected sentences.

C3. We cannot make sense of the idea of partial failure of translation (hypothetical syllogism of P18–P22, and *modus ponens*, P22, P23).

The Unintelligibility of the Very Idea of a Conceptual Scheme

C4. The idea of different conceptual schemes is not intelligible (destructive dilemma, P1, C2, C4).

P24. If there is only one conceptual scheme, then it is false that there are different conceptual schemes.

P25. If the idea of different conceptual schemes is not intelligible, then it is not false that there are different conceptual schemes.

P26. It is not false that there are different conceptual schemes (*modus ponens*, C4, P25).

P27. There is not only one conceptual scheme (*modus tollens*, P24, P26).

P28. If the idea of different conceptual schemes is not intelligible and there is not only one conceptual scheme, then the very idea of a conceptual scheme is unintelligible.

P29. The idea of different conceptual schemes is not intelligible and there is not only one conceptual scheme (conjunction, P27, C4).

C4. The very idea of a conceptual scheme is unintelligible (*modus ponens*, P28, P29).

44

Quine's Two Dogmas of Empiricism

Robert Sinclair

Quine, W. V. "Two Dogmas of Empiricism," in *From a Logical Point of View*, 20–46. Cambridge, MA: Harvard University Press, 1981. Originally published in *Philosophical Review* 60 (1951): 20–43.

Hylton, Peter. *Quine*. New York: Routledge, 2007.
Kemp, Gary. *Quine: A Guide for the Perplexed*. New York: Continuum, 2006.
Russell, Gillian. "The Analytic/Synthetic Distinction." *Philosophy Compass* 2 (2007): 712–29.

There appears to be an intuitive difference between these two claims:

(1) All bachelors are unmarried.
(2) All bachelors are less than 15 feet tall.

While both of these statements are true, the way in which they are taken to be true highlights what many philosophers have seen as a significant difference. The first is an "analytic" truth, whose truth is determined solely through the meanings of the terms involved and independently of any empirical fact. The second "synthetic" truth is true because of empirical facts about the world. In his famous and widely read article, "Two Dogmas of Empiricism," W. V. Quine declared that the use of this distinction in modern empiricism was an unsupported dogma, and he further argued that

---

Just the Arguments: 100 of the Most Important Arguments in Western Philosophy, First Edition. Edited by Michael Bruce and Steven Barbone.
© 2011 Blackwell Publishing Ltd. Published 2011 by Blackwell Publishing Ltd.

what he calls "reductionism," roughly, the view that theoretical statements can be logically reduced to statements about experience, is a second dogma that should also be rejected. These criticisms target the views of Rudolf Carnap, C. I. Lewis, and others who used analyticity to make sense of the *a priori* elements of human knowledge and, more specifically, advocated its importance in clarifying and understanding the language of science.

In "Two Dogmas," Quine's main concern is with clearly explicating the distinction in question, and he argues that there is no such sharp division between analytic truths and synthetic truths. His argument has been usefully described as analogous to the kind one might find offered in the physical sciences (Kemp, 19–20). A scientist might reject a type of physical phenomena because it cannot be explained in ways that do not already assume its existence. It might be further argued that the evidence cited in support of such phenomena can be accounted for in other ways without them. In general, it is this type of attitude that informs the structure of Quine's overall argument, where he begins by surveying a number of attempts to explain the concept of analyticity and finds them all uninformative. Here, he appeals to what has been called the "circularity argument," where analyticity is defined in terms of sameness of meaning or synonymy (Russell, 718).

Two expressions are synonymous when sentences containing them remain true when one is substituted for the other, what is here described as interchangebility *salva veritate*. When applied to necessity statements in English, this view seems to work, since the sentence 'Necessarily, every unmarried man is unmarried' and 'Necessarily, every bachelor is unmarried' is a case where truth is preserved when we switch 'unmarried man' for 'bachelor,' and these terms are also synonyms. The problem is that such sentences are understood as true in virtue of being analytic. The attempt to explain analyticity by an appeal to synonymy is then circular.

Quine criticizes the second dogma of reductionism by claiming that theoretical sentences have connections to experience only as a collective body and not when isolated from each other. This then prevents the type of phenomenalist reduction of science to experience advocated by the logical empiricists and further prevents us from defining synthetic statements as true when confirmed by sets of experience and analytic truths as those confirmed by any experience whatsoever. With each of these attempts to clarify analytic truth found wanting, Quine claims that the reasonable thing to conclude is that the distinction itself is an unempirical dogma. In the last section of his paper, he outlines his alternative view of empiricism, often described as "epistemological holism," which is further developed in his later work. Here, he indicates how the alleged *a priori* necessity of mathematics and logic can be explained by its deep entrenchment within our overarching system of theoretical commitments rather than by an appeal to analyticity. This deep entrenchment is what further explains our reluctance to revise such truths. Quine would come to emphasize that the main issue surrounding the analytic–synthetic distinction turns less on the availability of its sharp delineation (he later suggests and endorses his own way of marking the difference), but rather with its general epistemological significance. Here he claims that no such distinction is of any real import in helping us to understand the structure of human knowledge (Hylton, 68–80).

Many philosophers influenced by logical empiricism and its specific conception of scientific philosophy viewed some form of the analytic–synthetic distinction as central for making sense of *a priori* truth. After Quine's famous criticisms, it became increasingly difficult simply to assume that some form of this distinction was viable. This also led to a fundamental change in conceptions of philosophy and philosophical practice. Carnap's use of the analytic–synthetic distinction supported his view of philosophy as concerned with the logical structure of scientific language and as distinct from empirical science. Quine's criticisms of analyticity further challenged this view of philosophy by rejecting any sharp difference between philosophy and empirical science. The result was Quine's influential naturalistic view of philosophy, which conceives of philosophical pursuits as continuous with those found in the empirical sciences.

There have been many critical responses to Quine's circularity argument against analyticity, and there are various ongoing attempts to resurrect alternative conceptions of analyticity. It has been recently suggested that new innovations in the theory of meaning offer support for an account of analytic truth in terms of meaning (Russell, 712–29).

> In formal and informal work alike, thus, we find that definition [. . .] hinges on prior relations of synonymy. Recognizing then that the notion of definition does not hold the key to synonymy and analyticity, let us look further into synonymy and say no more of definition [. . .] we must recognize that interchangeability *salva veritate*, if construed in relation to an extensional language, is not a sufficient condition of cognitive synonymy in the sense needed for deriving analyticity. [. . .] If a language contains an intensional adverb 'necessarily' [. . .] then interchangeability *salva veritate* in such a language does afford a sufficient condition of cognitive synonymy; but such a language is intelligible only in so far as the notion of analyticity is already understood in advance [. . .]. The dogma of reductionism, even in its attenuated form, is intimately connected with the other dogma – that there is a cleavage between the analytic and synthetic [. . .] the one dogma clearly supports the other in this way: as long as it is taken to be significant in general to speak of the confirmation and information of a statement, it seems significant to speak also of a limiting kind of statement which is vacuously confirmed, *ipso facto*, come what may; and such a statement is analytic [. . .].

My present suggestion is that it is nonsense, and the root of much nonsense, to speak of a linguistic component and a factual component in the truth of any individual statement. Taken collectively, science has its double dependence upon language and experience; but this duality is not significantly traceable into the statements of science taken one by one. (Quine 27, 31, 41–2)

P1. Analytic truths are defined as true in virtue of the meaning of their terms and independently of empirical fact.

P2. Meaning is not to be confused with reference (e.g., 'creature with a heart' and 'creature with kidneys' refers to the same class of objects, but the expressions differ in meaning).

P3. There is no need to appeal to a special set of things called "meanings" to explain this difference, since the concept of meaning can be shown to be theoretically adequate if we focus on cases of sameness of meaning or synonymy (where we say that x and y are alike in meaning). If we proceed to use the concept of "meaning" to define analyticity, we should then appeal to synonymy between terms.

    C1. We can now define analytic truths as logical truths achieved by substituting synonyms for synonyms ('No bachelor is married' becomes the logical truth 'No unmarried man is married' if we substitute 'unmarried man' for 'bachelor') (*modus ponens*, P1, P3).

P4. If truth-by-sameness of meaning (C1) relies on our understanding of truth-by-meaning, which in turn rests on a prior understanding of 'meaning', then this explanation of analyticity by use of synonymy is no clearer than our starting point.

    C2. This explanation of analyticity by use of synonymy is no clearer than our starting point (*modus ponens*, C1, P4).

P5. What if we understand synonymy as involving the definition of terms?

P6. If we understand synonymy as involving the definition of terms, then this only provides a report of which terms mean the same as others, but no further indication of what synonymy or sameness of meaning consists in.

    C3. Synonymy defined as definition is then no help in clarifying analyticity (*modus ponens*, P5, P6).

P7. What if we take two phrases or expressions as synonymous when sentences containing them remain true when one is substituted for the other?

P8. If we take two phrases or expressions as synonymous when sentences containing them remain true when one is substituted for the other, then in extensional languages, where substituting co-extensive expressions preserves truth-value, the interchangeability does not give us sameness of meaning (e.g., substituting 'creature with a heart' with 'creature with kidneys' preserves truth-value, but we would not claim that these expressions have the same meaning).

C4. In extensional languages, interchangeability does not give us sameness of meaning and is no help in understanding analyticity (*modus ponens*, P7, P8).

P9. However, English is not extensional and in such nonextensional languages, interchangeability *salva veritate* is the right criterion for synonymy; that is, it preserves sameness of meaning (e.g., 'Necessarily, every unmarried man is unmarried' and 'Necessarily, every bachelor is unmarried' is a case where truth value is preserved when we switch 'unmarried man' for 'bachelor', and they are also synonyms).

P10. But necessity statements of this kind are thought to be true precisely because the statement in question ('every unmarried man is unmarried') is already taken to be analytic. In this way, interchangeability *salva veritate* provides the right account of synonymy, but only by already relying on the intelligibility of analyticity. This is circular, and so analytic truth is still not clarified.

P11. If English is not extensional (P9), and necessity statements are taken to be analytic (P10), then this view of synonymy does not then explain analyticity.

C5. This view of synonymy does not then explain analyticity (*modus ponens*, P11, conjunction, P9, P10).

P11. Reductionism claims that any significant nonanalytic statement is equivalent to a statement about sensory experience. The meaning of a statement is then directly tied to a set of sensory experiences.

P12. Given this view, we can define analytic truths as those statements confirmed by every experience or, in other words, as statements that contain no empirical content or information.

P13. However, the reductionism project cannot be completed because of holistic considerations that prevent a simple reduction of theoretical sentences to specific sensory experiences.

P14. But if reductionism is untenable, then we cannot assign specific empirical content to individual sentences or then specify when a sentence is analytic in the sense of being confirmed by any experience whatsoever.

C6. There is then no way to use reductionism to clarify those statements which depend on sensory experience for their confirmation and those that do not, that is, analytic truths. Reductionism then fails to clarify the distinction between analytic and synthetic statements (*modus ponens*, P13, P14).

C7. A consideration of these various proposals for clarifying analytic truths has shown them all to be wanting. We have no reason to hold such a firm distinction or the form of reductionism often used to support it. Both are dogmas of modern empiricism that should be rejected (conjunction, C2, C3, C4, C5, C6).

45

Hume and the Problem of Induction

Editors' note: We have included two versions of Hume's argument concerning induction in order to highlight different approaches to the seminal issue.

Hume's Problem of Induction

James E. Taylor

Hume, David. *An Enquiry concerning Human Understanding*. Indianapolis: Hackett, 1993.

Hume's argument for skepticism about induction presupposes his distinction between "relations of ideas," which are intuitively or demonstratively certain because their denials are contradictory (e.g., "All bachelors are unmarried") and "matters of fact and existence," which are not certain because their denials are possibly true (e.g., "The sun will rise tomorrow"). Hume holds that all of our beliefs about matters of fact and existence are based on either the present testimony of our senses, our memories of what we have experienced on the basis of our senses, or reasoning about relations of cause and effect on the basis of our senses and memory beliefs. For instance, we infer that a friend of ours is in a distant place on the grounds that a letter we are currently looking at indicates that it was sent by our friend from that place; so we infer a currently unobserved cause from a currently observed effect of that cause. We also infer more generally from cause-and-effect relationships we have observed in the past that similar causes will have similar effects in the future. Thus, according to Hume, the foundation of all our reasoning about matters of fact and existence is experience. But Hume argues that these sorts of inferences from experience

Just the Arguments: 100 of the Most Important Arguments in Western Philosophy,
First Edition. Edited by Michael Bruce and Steven Barbone.
© 2011 Blackwell Publishing Ltd. Published 2011 by Blackwell Publishing Ltd.

are not based on any further reasoning. The way this claim is typically put today is that there is no rational justification for inductive inferences. If this claim is true, then no one can be rationally justified in believing anything that goes beyond what one is currently observing, and if that is the case, then there is no rational justification for any theory of empirical science. Since Hume was the first philosopher to make this claim and argue for it, the problem facing philosophers who deny it is called "Hume's Problem of Induction." Though many attempts have been made to solve this problem, none of these attempts is widely believed to be successful. Consequently, Hume's problem of induction continues to be a central topic of philosophical conversation.

> All reasonings may be divided into two kinds, namely, demonstrative reasoning, or that concerning relations of ideas, and moral reasoning, or that concerning matter of fact and existence. That there are no demonstrative arguments in the case seems evident; since it implies no contradiction that the course of nature may change, and that an object, seemingly like those which we have experienced, may be attended with different or contrary effects. May I not clearly and distinctly conceive that a body, falling from the clouds, and which, in all other respects, resembles snow, has yet the taste of salt or feeling of fire? Is there any more intelligible proposition than to affirm, that all the trees will flourish in December and January, and decay in May and June? Now whatever is intelligible, and can be distinctly conceived, implies no contradiction, and can never be proved false by any demonstrative argument or abstract reasoning *a priori*.
>
> If we be, therefore, engaged by arguments to put trust in past experience, and make it the standard of our future judgement, these arguments must be probable only, or such as regard matter of fact and real existence, according to the division above mentioned. But that there is no argument of this kind, must appear, if our explication of that species of reasoning be admitted as solid and satisfactory. We have said that all arguments concerning existence are founded on the relation of cause and effect; that our knowledge of that relation is derived entirely from experience; and that all our experimental conclusions proceed upon the supposition that the future will be conformable to the past. To endeavour, therefore, the proof of this last supposition by probable arguments, or arguments regarding existence, must be evidently going in a circle, and taking that for granted, which is the very point in question. (IV.ii)

An example of an inductive inference employed by Hume (which can represent all inductive inferences) is the inference from (a) "All the bread I have eaten has nourished me" to (b) "The bread I am about to eat will nourish me." I will refer to this example in my reconstruction of Hume's argument for his claim that no such inferences have a rational foundation.

P1. If the (inductive) inference from (a) to (b) has a rational foundation, then it must be based on intuition, reasoning that is based on intuition ("demonstrative" or deductive reasoning) or reasoning that is based on direct observation ("experimental" or inductive reasoning).

P2. The (inductive) inference from (a) to (b) is not based on intuition, reasoning that is based on intuition, or reasoning that is based on direct observation.

   C1. The (inductive) inference from (a) to (b) does not have a rational foundation (*modus tollens*, P1, P2).

Argument for P2:

P3. The connection between (a) and (b) of the example inference is not intuitive (i.e., it isn't self-evident that if (a) is true, then (b) is true).

P4. The inference from (a) to (b) is not based on demonstrative reasoning (since demonstrative reasoning can only establish claims that are not possibly false and the claim that if (a) is true, then (b) is true is possibly false).

P5. The inference from (a) to (b) is not based on experimental reasoning (because all experimental reasoning presupposes that similar causes have similar effects and the inference in question is an instance of this very presupposition, so an experimental (inductive) argument for that inference would be circular).

   C2. P2 is true: the (inductive) inference from (a) to (b) is not based on intuition, reasoning that is based on intuition, or reasoning that is based on direct observation (conjunction, P3, P4, P5; De Morgan's).

Hume's Negative Argument concerning Induction
Stefanie Rocknak

Hume, David. *A Treatise of Human Nature*, edited by D. F. and M. J. Norton. Oxford: Oxford University Press, 2002.

Arnold, N. Scott. "Hume's Skepticism about Inductive Inferences." *Journal of the History of Philosophy* 21, 1 (1983): 31–55.

Baier, Annette. *A Progress of Sentiments*. Cambridge, MA: Harvard University Press, 1991.

Beauchamp, Tom, and Alexander Rosenberg. *Hume and the Problem of Causation*. Oxford: Oxford University Press, 1981.

Broughton, J. "Hume's Skepticism about Causal Inferences." *Pacific Philosophical Quarterly* 64 (1983): 3–18.

Garrett, Don. *Cognition and Commitment in Hume's Philosophy*. Oxford: Oxford University Press, 1997.

Immerwahr, John. "The Failure of Hume's Treatise." *Hume Studies* 3, 2 (1977): 57–71.

Loeb, L. E. *Stability and Justification in Hume's Treatise*. Oxford: Oxford University Press, 2002.

Owen, David. *Hume's Reason*. Oxford: Oxford University Press, 1999.

Passmore, John. *Hume's Intentions*. Cambridge, UK: Cambridge University Press, 1952/1968.

Schmitt, F. E. *Knowledge and Belief*. London: Routledge, 1992.

Smith, Norman K. *The Philosophy of David Hume: A Critical Study of its Origins and Central Doctrines*. New York: Macmillan, 1941.

Stove, D. C. *Probability and Hume's Inductive Skepticism*. Oxford: Oxford University Press, 1973.

Strawson, P. F. *Introduction to Logical Theory*. London: Methuen, 1952.

Where does the necessity that seems to accompany causal inferences come from? "Why [do] we conclude that [...] particular causes must *necessarily* have such particular effects?" (Hume, 1.3.2.15) In 1.3.6 of the *Treatise*, Hume entertains the possibility that this necessity is a function of reason. However, he eventually dismisses this possibility, where this dismissal consists of Hume's "negative" argument concerning induction. This argument has received, and continues to receive, a tremendous amount of attention. How could causal inferences be justified if they are not justified by reason? If we believe that p causes q, isn't it reason that allows us to conclude with some assurance – that is, with some necessity – that q whenever we see p?

The responses to these questions are many, but they may be parsed into four groups. (1) Some argue that Hume's negative argument shows that he thought that inductive inferences are worthless. Hume was actually a closet "deductivist," where he meant to show that any method that does not rely on *a priori* principles is useless (e.g., Stove). (2) Others have alleged that Hume's negative argument only meant to show that we cannot use demonstrative reason to justify inductive inferences, but we can, apparently, justify them with probable reason (e.g., Beauchamp and Rosenberg, Arnold, Broughton, and Baier). (3) Still others argue that Hume's notion of justification (in regard to beliefs in general, including beliefs in causal inferences) should be understood in two stages in Book I of the *Treatise*. In the first, Hume does lay out a theory of justification. In the second (particularly in 1.4.7), he retracts it (e.g., Passmore, Immerwahr, Schmitt, and Loeb). (4) Finally, there are those who claim that no "justification" is needed for causal inferences. In fact, asking for it amounts to a misplaced demand for epistemic explanation; to some degree, this is what the negative argument shows us. What we must do instead is give a descriptive psychological explanation where this explanation consists of Hume's "positive" account of induction; see, for instance, *Treatise* 1.3.14, "of the idea of necessary connexion" (e.g., Strawson, Garrett, and Owen).

In the arguments that rule out demonstrative and probable reasoning, Hume assumes that the principle of uniformity is justified by, respectively, demonstrative reason and probable reason, and then he respectively shows why these assumptions are incorrect. In the concluding argument, he shows that this means that the principle of uniformity is not justified by reason, nor is the necessity that obtains of our causal inferences a function of reason. To do so, he draws on the premises established in his introduction and the conclusions established in the arguments that rule out demonstrative and probable reason.

> [We must now] discover the nature of that necessary connexion, which makes so essential a part of [the relation of cause and effect] [. . .]. Since it appears, that the transition from an impression present to the memory or senses to the idea of an object, we call cause and effect, is founded on past experience, and our resemblance of their constant conjunction, the next question is, whether experience produces the idea by means of the understanding or of the imagination; whether we are determin'd by reason to make the transition, or by a certain association of perceptions. If reason determin'd us, it wou'd proceed upon that principle, that instances, of which we have had no experience must resemble those, of which we have had experience, and that the course of nature continues always uniformly the same. In order therefore to clear up this matter, let us consider all the arguments, upon which such a proposition may suppos'd to be founded' and as these must be deriv'd either from knowledge or probability, let us cast our eye on each of these degrees of evidence, and see whether they afford any just conclusion of this nature. (Hume, 1.3.6.3, 1.3.6.4)

P1. When the mind makes what appears to be a necessary transition from a present impression, or a memory of an impression, to a given idea, we call that transition "cause and effect." The question is, on what is this seemingly necessary transition founded? Of what is it a function: understanding (i.e., reason) or the imagination?

P2. If reason does determine us to make these causal transitions, then this reasoning must proceed upon the principle that instances (e.g., particular associations of any two objects) that occurred in the past will continue to occur as such in the future (the principle of uniformity).

P3. If causal necessity is a function of reason, where that reason is based on the principle of uniformity, then the principle of uniformity must, in some fashion or other, be *justified*; it too must be "founded" on reason. In symbolic form, this reads $(N \supset P) \supset J$, where 'N' stands for causal necessity is a function of reason, 'P' stands for a principle of uniformity, and 'J' stands for "the principle of uniformity is justified by reason."

P4. There are only two kinds of reason that may justify a principle, including the principle of uniformity: (a) "knowledge" (demonstrative reasoning) or (b) "probable" reasoning.

P5. Assume that the principle of uniformity is justified by demonstrative reasoning.

P6. If the principle of uniformity is justified by demonstrative reasoning – in other words, it is an instance of demonstrative reasoning – then the principle of uniformity cannot be imagined otherwise.

P7. We can imagine that nature will not continue uniformly in the future, while simultaneously imagining that nature has always continued the same in the past, without contradicting ourselves.

  C1. The principle of uniformity is not proved; that is, justified by demonstrative reasoning (*modus tollens*, P6, P7).

P8. The principle of uniformity is justified by probable reasoning (assumption for *reductio*).

P9. Probable reasoning is actually causal reasoning, since both are cases where we are automatically led to think of an idea in virtue of experiencing an impression or remembering an impression.

P10. If the reasoning at hand is an instance of causal reasoning, then such reasoning is justified by the principle of uniformity.

  C2. Probable reasoning is justified by the principle of uniformity (*modus ponens*, P9, P10).

  C3. The principle of uniformity is justified by probable reasoning (i.e., causal reasoning) *and* justifies probable reasoning (i.e., causal reasoning) (conjunction, P7, C2).

  C4. The principle of uniformity is not justified by probable reason (*reductio*, P7–C3).

  C5. The principle of uniformity is not justified by either demonstrative or probable reasoning (conjunction C1, C4).

P11. If the principle of uniformity is not justified by either demonstrative or probable reasoning, then we must reject the claim that the principle of uniformity is justified by reason.

  C6. We must reject the claim that the principle of uniformity is justified by reason (*modus ponens*, C5, P11).

P12. If we must reject the claim that the principle of uniformity is justified by reason, then we must reject the claim that the necessity that seems to accompany causal relations is a function of reason.

  C7. We must reject the claim that the necessity that seems to accompany causal relations is a function of reason (*modus ponens*, P12, C6).

46

Argument by Analogy in Thales and Anaximenes

Giannis Stamatellos

Aristotle. *On the Heavens*, translated by W. K. C. Guthrie. Cambridge, MA: Harvard University Press, 1939.

Barnes, Jonathan. *The Presocratic Philosophers*. London: Routledge, 1979.

Diels, Hermann. *Die Fragmente der Vorsokratiker*, 6th edn., revised with additions and index by W. Kranz. Berlin: Weidmann, 1951–52. (DK)

Kirk, Geoffrey Stephen, John Earl Raven, and Malcolm Schofield. *The Presocratic Philosophers*. Cambridge, UK: Cambridge University Press, 1983.

Lloyd, Geoffrey Ernest Richard. *Polarity and Analogy: Two Types of Argumentation in Early Greek Thought*. Bristol: Bristol Classical Press, 1992.

Pachenko, Dmitri. "Thales and the Origin of Theoretical Reasoning." *Configurations* 3 (1993): 387–484.

Wright, M. R. *The Presocratics*. Bristol: Bristol Classical Press, 1985.

If x is P and Q, and y is P, we infer that y is also Q.

An argument by analogy relies on inductive inference. Arguing by analogy is arguing that since things are similar or alike in certain respects, they are similar or alike in others. An analogical argument is based on hypothetical similarities between distinct cases: in other words, since things are similar in certain observable or identified cases, they are also similar in some other unobservable or unidentified cases.

Just the Arguments: 100 of the Most Important Arguments in Western Philosophy, First Edition. Edited by Michael Bruce and Steven Barbone.
© 2011 Blackwell Publishing Ltd. Published 2011 by Blackwell Publishing Ltd.

An argument by analogy is not deductively valid. It is considered as a weak form of argumentation due to the arbitrary presupposition of similarities between things. However, analogy is not only used in literal cases but also in cases of metaphor and explanatory purposes. Moreover, an argument by analogy is considered as an indispensable accompaniment of scientific thought as far as induction forms the basic scientific method.

In early Greek philosophy, analogy is a pattern of thought that underlies the first attempts for an explanation of the cosmos. This is initially found in the Milesians thinkers Thales (*fl. c.* 585 BCE) and Anaximenes (*fl. c.* 546 BCE). Thales argued that "as a piece of wood floats on a pond, so the whole earth floats on water" (DK 11A14; cf., DK 11A12). According to Aristotle:

> Others say that the earth rests on water. For this is the most ancient account we have received, which they say was given by Thales the Milesian, that it stays in place through floating like a log or some other such thing (for none of these rests by nature on air, but on water) – as though the same argument did not apply to the water supporting the earth as to the earth itself. (Aristotle B13, 294a28)

Thales' inductive reasoning reflects an argument by analogy: if two things have certain properties in common on a small scale, then they have the same properties in common on a cosmic scale:

Small scale: a piece of wood floats on a pond.
Large scale: the Earth floats on Okeanos.

Likewise, Anaximenes claims an analogy between human soul and the cosmos:

> As our soul, which is air, maintain us, so breath and air surround the whole world. (DK, 13B2)

Anaximenes offers an argument by analogy:

Small scale: the human soul (human breath) maintains the single individual organism (microcosm).
Large scale: the soul of the cosmos (universal breath) surrounds and maintains the whole universe.

Analogy as a pattern of thought seems to underlie Anaximenes' inductive thinking used for rhetorical, metaphoric, and explanatory purposes. This is evident in some of his extant fragments and testimonies (*Die Fragmente der Vorsokratiker*):

The stars move around the earth, just as turban winds round our head. [A7]

The universe whirls like a mill-stone. [A12]

The stars are fixed in the crystalline in the manner of nails. [A14]

The sun is flat like a leaf. [A15]

In the above examples, analogy is used by Anaximenes to explain macrocosm through common observation. Thales' and Anaximenes' arguments by analogy are considered as one of the first incidences of inductive reasoning. The relationship between microcosm (small scale) and macrocosm (cosmic scale) reflects Thales' hylozoism and mathematical expertise (e.g., measurement of the pyramids and predictions of the eclipses) and Anaximenes' natural philosophy and cosmological discoveries. Early Greek philosophical argumentation by analogy, as a form of induction, marks the beginning of scientific explanation and thought.

47

Quine's Epistemology Naturalized

Robert Sinclair

Quine, W. V. "Epistemology Naturalized," in *Ontological Relativity and Other Essays*, 69–90. New York: Columbia University Press, 1969.

Gregory, Paul. *Quine's Naturalism: Language, Theory and the Knowing Subject*. New York: Continuum, 2008.

Roth, Paul. "The Epistemology of 'Epistemology Naturalized'." *Dialectica* 53 (1999): 87–109.

In his highly influential article "Epistemology Naturalized," W. V. Quine argued that the problems found in the history of modern empiricism should lead us to rethink the overall aims of contemporary epistemology. More specifically, he offered a historical reconstruction of post-Humean empiricism, highlighting where attempts to support or to justify our knowledge of the world through sensory experience fell into insurmountable problems and suggesting further the need to locate the grounds of knowledge within science itself. On his view, epistemology should then be "naturalized" in the sense that it becomes a scientific project where philosophers must use the resources of science to explain, to describe, and to justify our knowledge of the world.

His basic argument appeals to an analogy between studies in the foundations of mathematical knowledge and the empiricist attempt to provide a sensory foundation for scientific knowledge. The project in the philosophy

Just the Arguments: 100 of the Most Important Arguments in Western Philosophy, First Edition. Edited by Michael Bruce and Steven Barbone.
© 2011 Blackwell Publishing Ltd. Published 2011 by Blackwell Publishing Ltd.

of mathematics that is Quine's focus is known as "logicism," which held that mathematical truths could be defined in terms of a more basic logical language. Here, on what Quine calls the "conceptual" side, mathematical concepts could be rewritten and, in that sense, reduced to what was thought to be a more certain and obviously true logical vocabulary. This would also help deal with a further "doctrinal" concern over the justification of mathematical truths, since they could be restated as basic logical truths with a similar degree of logical certainty. Unfortunately, this project cannot be completed, since the proposed reduction of mathematical concepts requires set theory, which contains its own logical paradoxes and does not then have the same obviousness or certainty assumed to be had within logic. Moreover, Gödel's famous incompleteness theorems undermine the doctrinal aim, since they demonstrate that no logical rendering of all the truths of mathematics is possible.

With this as background, Quine proceeds to develop further his analogy between logicism and empiricism. Like logicism, the empiricist attempt to validate scientific truths within sensory experience contains a conceptual side focused on defining concepts in sensory terms and a doctrinal side that seeks to justify truths of nature through sensory experience. However, these two aims cannot be met. The conceptual side falters because of "holism," the view that terms and sentences have implications for experience only through their interconnections and never by themselves in isolation. What this suggests is that, in general, no concept or theoretical claim has its own consequences for experience, and thus no single concept or statement could then be assigned to or reduced to its own specific element of experience.

The doctrinal aim fails because of what Quine calls "Hume's problem," where even simple general claims based on our experience of things claim much more than any empirical evidence we could have to justify them. So, empiricism suffers from incompleteness in an analogous way to logicism in the philosophy of mathematics, but, importantly, Quine suggests that the epistemology of empirical knowledge is no worse off than mathematical knowledge (see Roth, 96). Studies in mathematics lowered its epistemic standards in fruitful ways, and given this analogy, empiricism can follow suit. This requires moving from the attempt to reconstruct science logically from experience, something which Quine accepts would be more epistemologically adequate, and instead seeking a validation for scientific knowledge from within the methods of science.

Quine's argument is then an invitation for us to reconsider what empiricist epistemology looks like once we adopt a holistic view of human knowledge and accept the way this undermines an empiricist reduction of knowledge to experience, while further viewing science as providing the best remaining resources for addressing justificatory issues in epistemology (see Roth, 96–100). Within such constraints, he stresses the importance of using the methods of science to justify scientific truths and to develop explanatory accounts of the causal mechanisms responsible for the creation of scientific theories.

The influence of this argument can be measured in terms of two contrasting responses, one positive, the other critical. With regard to the first, Quine's suggested reconstruction of epistemology has spawned numerous attempts to offer more empirically informed accounts of human knowledge. Such views appeal to a variety of different sciences such as evolutionary biology, psychology, and neuroscience, and in the field of philosophy of science further use has been made of history and sociology. More generally, Quine's philosophical naturalism, where philosophy is to be conceived as part of empirical science, has further influenced the development of work in the philosophy of mind, language, ethics, and elsewhere. The second more critical response has claimed that Quine's suggested naturalization of epistemology results in a curt dismissal of the central aims of epistemology. Here, much of the attention has focused on Quine's apparent rejection of the normative aims of justification leading to what many have viewed as a radical changing of the subject. The result is the so-called "replacement interpretation," where Quine is taken as advocating the replacement of normative epistemology, which seeks to assess critically and rationally the evidential basis of our beliefs, with a psychological description of the causal processes of belief acquisition (Gregory, 85–121).

Recent scholarship has suggested that this critical reading is mistaken and has further emphasized that, in general, Quine's proposal does not seek to eliminate such normative concerns but, rather, explains how epistemology can still remain normative in light of empiricism's failures and the ongoing progress of science.

> [T]here remains a helpful thought, regarding epistemology generally, in that duality of structure which was especially conspicuous in the foundations of mathematics. I refer to the bifurcation into a theory of concepts, or meaning, and a theory of doctrine, or truth; for this applies to the epistemology of natural knowledge no less than to the foundations of mathematics. The parallel is as follows. Just as mathematics is to be reduced to logic, or logic and set theory, so natural knowledge is to be based somehow on sense experience. This means explaining the notion of body in sensory terms; here is the conceptual side. And it means justifying our knowledge of truths of nature in sensory terms; here is the doctrinal side of the bifurcation. [. . .] Philosophers have rightly despaired of translating everything into observational and logico-mathematical terms. They have despaired of this even when they have not recognized, as the reason for this irreducibility, that the statements largely do not have their private bundles of empirical consequences. And some philosophers have seen in this irreducibility the bankruptcy of epistemology [. . .] But I think at this point it maybe more useful to say rather

that epistemology still goes on, through in a new setting and a clarified status. Epistemology, or something like it, simply falls into place as a chapter of psychology and hence of natural science. It studies a natural phenomenon, viz., a physical human subject. This human subject is accorded a certain experimentally controlled input – certain patterns of irradiation in assorted frequencies, for instance – and in the fullness of time the subject delivers as output a description of the three dimensional external world and its history. The relation between the meager input and the torrential output is a relation that we are prompted to study for somewhat the same reasons that always prompted epistemology; namely, in order to see how evidence related to theory, and in what ways one's theory of nature transcends any available evidence. (Quine 71, 82–3)

P1. There are important parallels between studies in the foundations of natural science and studies in the foundations of mathematics that can help illuminate the epistemology of empirical knowledge.

P2. The logicist project of constructing logical procedures for the codification of mathematical truths contained two elements: a conceptual one that defined mathematical notions in terms of logic, and a doctrinal component that derived mathematical truths using logical techniques.

   C1. The empiricist attempt to provide an evaluation or derivation of scientific truths on the basis of sensory experience contains the same general features: a conceptual side concerned with the definition of concepts in sensory terms, and a doctrinal side focusing on the justification of truths of nature in sensory terms (analogy, P1, P2).

P3. If the empiricist program is to be successful, it then needs to address:

   (A) The conceptual requirement of showing how theoretical concepts (e.g., body) can be defined in terms of sensory experience.

   (B) The doctrinal requirement of showing how scientific laws or generalizations can be derived from sense experience.

P4. (A) cannot be achieved because concepts and sentences have experiential consequences only as a collective body, and not in isolation from each other (holism). (B) cannot be achieved because even the simplest generalizations based on experience outrun the empirical evidence (Hume's problem).

   C2. No independent philosophical foundation for science is then available within empiricism (*modus tollens*, P3, P4).

P5. There are no better standards of justification available between formal derivation and the standards of empirical science itself (Quine's scalar hypothesis; see Roth 98).

P6. If empiricism cannot successfully implement its foundationalist project and there is no better justificatory standards than those found in science, then epistemology should appeal to science in justifying scientific results and practices.

P7. No independent philosophical foundation for science is then available within empiricism, and there are no better standards of justification available between formal derivation and the standards of empirical science itself (conjunction, C2, P5).

C3. Epistemology becomes science self-applied where we use the methods of science to justify scientific truths and develop an explanatory account of the causal mechanisms responsible for the development of scientific theories. In sum, epistemology should be naturalized (*modus ponens*, P6, P7).

48

Sellars and the Myth of the Given

Willem A. deVries

Sellars, Wilfrid. "Empiricism and the Philosophy of Mind," in *Minnesota Studies in the Philosophy of Science*, vol. I, edited by Herbert Feigl and Michael Scriven, 253–329. Minneapolis: University of Minnesota Press, 1956. (EPM) Reprinted with additional footnotes in *Science, Perception and Reality*. London: Routledge & Kegan Paul, 1963; reissued by Ridgeview Publishing Company in 1991. (SPR) Published separately as *Empiricism and the Philosophy of Mind: With an Introduction by Richard Rorty and a Study Guide by Robert Brandom*, edited by Robert Brandom. Cambridge, MA: Harvard University Press, 1997. Also reprinted in W. deVries and T. Triplett, *Knowledge, Mind, and the Given: A Reading of Sellars' "Empiricism and the Philosophy of Mind."* Cambridge, MA: Hackett, 2000. (KMG)

Alston, William P. "What's Wrong With Immediate Knowledge?" *Synthese* 55 (1983): 73–96. Reprinted in *Epistemic Justification: Essays in the Theory of Knowledge*. Ithaca, NY: Cornell University Press, 1989.
____. "Sellars and the 'Myth of the Given'," 1998. http://www.ditext.com/alston/alston2.html (accessed July 27, 2010).
Meyers, R. G. "Sellars' Rejection of Foundations." *Philosophical Studies* 39 (1981): 61–78.

Just the Arguments: 100 of the Most Important Arguments in Western Philosophy, First Edition. Edited by Michael Bruce and Steven Barbone.
© 2011 Blackwell Publishing Ltd. Published 2011 by Blackwell Publishing Ltd.

Knowledge has a structure: there are relations of dependency among a person's (and a community's) cognitive states. Skeptical challenges easily arise; for example, if every piece of knowledge is dependent on others, how could we acquire our first piece of knowledge (#38)? Many philosophers have held that knowledge has a hierarchical structure not unlike that of a well-built house. There must be some cognitive states that are in direct contact with reality, and that form a firm foundation that supports the rest of our knowledge. For obvious reasons, this has been called the "foundationalist picture" of knowledge's structure. Philosophers cash this metaphor out via two requirements on knowledge, as follows. (1) There must be cognitive states that are basic in the sense that they possess some positive epistemic status independently of their epistemic relations to any other cognitive states. Call this the Epistemic Independence Requirement [EIR]. Positive epistemic statuses include being an instance of knowledge, being justified or warranted, or (more weakly) having some presumption in its favor. (Many have claimed that basic cognitions must possess an *unassailable* epistemic warrant – certainty, incorrigibility, or even infallibility.) Epistemic relations include deductive and inductive implication. (2) Every nonbasic cognitive state with positive epistemic status possesses that status only because of the epistemic relations it bears, directly or indirectly, to basic cognitive states. Thus the basic states provide the ultimate support for the rest of our knowledge. Call this the Epistemic Efficacy Requirement [EER]. Call such basic – that is, independent and efficacious – cognitive states the "given." Many philosophers have believed that there has to be such a given if there is to be any knowledge at all.

The EIR and the EER together put constraints on what could play the role of basic knowledge. Traditionally, philosophers required that basic knowledge have an unassailable warrant. Although Sellars was a fallibilist and believed that any cognitive state could be challenged, his argument against the given, contrary to some interpretations, does not worry about this issue. If there are no foundations, we need not worry about the strength of foundational warrant.

A foundationalist structure has been attributed to logical and mathematical knowledge, which is formal and *a priori*, as well as to empirical knowledge. For millennia, Euclidean geometry, which starts with definitions and axioms and derives numerous theorems by long chains of reasoning, has provided a paradigmatic foundationalist structure. But no axioms – self-evident general truths – seem adequate to provide the basis for empirical knowledge. Rather, the common assumption is that particular truths can be known through direct experience and provide the basis for all empirical knowledge. Thus, experience supposedly provides us with epistemically independent and efficacious cognitive states that form the foundation of empirical knowledge. Empiricism claims that all substantive knowledge rests on experience.

Sellars' argument against the given denies not only that there must be a given but that there can be a given in the sense defined. It is thus an attack on the foundationalist picture of knowledge, especially its empiricist version. The argument claims that nothing can satisfy both EIR and EER. To satisfy EER, a basic cognition must be capable of participating in inferential relations with other cognitions; it must possess propositional form and be truth-evaluable. To meet EIR, such a propositionally structured cognition must possess its epistemic status independently of inferential connections to other cognitions. No cognitive states satisfy both requirements.

Many philosophers have believed in self-evident cognitive states that are epistemically independent. Mathematical axioms were traditionally called self-evident, but is any empirical proposition self-evident? According to Sellars, the standard candidates for basic empirical knowledge (knowledge of sense-data, knowledge of appearances, etc.) all presuppose other knowledge on the part of the knower and thus fail EIR. He argues that such states count as cognitive states only because of their epistemic relations to other cognitive states. Because he argues by cases, it is unclear whether some other candidates might pass EIR. For instance, some claim that externalism evades his critique because then the epistemic status of basic cognitive states is determined solely by their causal status and they pass EIR (see Meyers). Just assuming that there are (much less must be) Epistemically Independent cognitive states, however, begs the question against his argument. A final resolution of this dispute requires a positive theory of the sufficient conditions for possessing a positive epistemic status (see Alston). Sellars offers one, but this reaches beyond the critique of the given. At very least, Sellars' critique of the given shifts the burden of proof onto those who believe in epistemically independent cognitive states. They owe us a good theory of such states and why they have their epistemic status.

Some foundationalists believe that basic cognitive states are not propositionally structured but are cases of direct knowledge of an object – what Russell called "knowledge by acquaintance." Such states violate EER: How could such knowledge justify further knowledge? If John knows O, for some object O, no proposition seems to be warranted for John solely on that basis.

If Sellars' argument works, knowledge cannot be acquired incrementally from initial encounters with the world in experience that are already full-fledged cognitive states. The epistemic status of our perceptions and introspections belongs to them because they belong in a complex system of mutually supporting cognitive states that mediate our practical engagement with the world around us – though Sellars also rejects standard coherentism as well. The argument is not a conclusive, once-and-for-all refutation of the foundationalist picture of knowledge, but it is a significant challenge to that picture. Sellars' argument, in combination with arguments by Quine and Davidson, among others, have put foundationalism on the defensive since, roughly, the mid-point of the twentieth century.

Sellars' argument has influenced a wide range of late-twentieth-century philosophers, including Richard Rorty, Paul and Patricia Churchland, Laurence Bonjour, David Rosenthal, Jay Rosenberg, John McDowell, and Robert Brandom.

> If I reject the framework of traditional empiricism, it is not because I want to say that empirical knowledge has no foundation. For to put it this way is to suggest that it is really "empirical knowledge so-called," and to put it in a box with rumors and hoaxes. There is clearly some point to the picture of human knowledge as resting on a level of propositions – observation reports – which do not rest on other propositions in the same way as other propositions rest on them. On the other hand, I do wish to insist that the metaphor of "foundation" is misleading in that it keeps us from seeing that if there is a logical dimension in which other empirical propositions rest on observation reports, there is another logical dimension in which the latter rest on the former.
>
> Above all, the picture is misleading because of its static character. One seems forced to choose between the picture of an elephant which rests on a tortoise (What supports the tortoise?) and the picture of a great Hegelian serpent of knowledge with its tail in its mouth (Where does it begin?). Neither will do. For empirical knowledge, like its sophisticated extension, science, is rational, not because it has a foundation but because it is a self-correcting enterprise which can put any claim in jeopardy, though not all at once. (EPM VIII, §38, in SPR, 170; in KMG, 250)

The doctrine of the given requires that for any empirical knowledge P, some epistemically independent knowledge G is epistemically efficacious with respect to P.

P1. If X cannot serve as a reason for Y, then X cannot be epistemically efficacious with respect to Y.

P2. If X cannot serve as a premise in an argument for Y, then X cannot serve as a reason for Y.

P3. If X is nonpropositional, then X cannot serve as a premise in an argument.

P4. If X is nonpropositional, then X cannot serve as a reason for Y (hypothetical syllogism, P3, P2).

    C1. If X is nonpropositional, then X cannot be epistemically efficacious with respect to Y (hypothetical syllogism, P1, P4).

P5. If X cannot be epistemically efficacious with respect to Y, then the nonpropositional cannot serve as the given.

C2. The nonpropositional cannot serve as the given (*modus ponens*, C1, P5).

P6. No inferentially acquired, propositionally structured mental state is epistemically independent.

P7. The epistemic status of noninferentially acquired, propositionally structured cognitive states presupposes the possession by the knowing subject of other empirical knowledge, both of particulars and of general empirical truths.

P8. If noninferentially acquired empirical knowledge presupposes the possession by the knowing subject of other empirical knowledge, then noninferentially acquired, propositionally structured cognitive states are not epistemically independent.

C3. Noninferentially acquired, propositionally structured cognitive states are not epistemically independent (*modus ponens*, P7, P8).

P8. Any empirical, propositional cognition is acquired either inferentially or noninferentially.

C4. Propositionally structured cognitions, whether inferentially or noninferentially acquired, are never epistemically independent and cannot serve as the given (conjunction, P6, C3).

P9. Every cognition is either propositionally structured or not.

C5. Neither propositional or nonpropostitional cognitions can serve as the given (conjunction, C2, C4).

P10. If neither propositional nor nonpropostitional cognitions can serve as the given, then it is reasonable to believe that no item of empirical knowledge can serve the function of a given.

C6. It is reasonable to believe that no item of empirical knowledge can serve the function of a given (*modus ponens*, C5, P10).

49

Sellars' "Rylean Myth"

Willem A. deVries

Sellars, Wilfrid. "Empiricism and the Philosophy of Mind," in *Minnesota Studies in the Philosophy of Science*, vol. I, edited by Herbert Feigl and Michael Scriven, 253–329. Minneapolis: University of Minnesota Press, 1956. (EPM) Reprinted with additional footnotes in *Science, Perception and Reality*. London: Routledge & Kegan Paul, 1963; reissued by Ridgeview Publishing Company in 1991. (SPR) Published separately as *Empiricism and the Philosophy of Mind: With an Introduction by Richard Rorty and a Study Guide by Robert Brandom*, edited by Robert Brandom. Cambridge, MA: Harvard University Press, 1997. Also reprinted in W. deVries and T. Triplett, *Knowledge, Mind, and the Given: A Reading of Sellars' "Empiricism and the Philosophy of Mind."* Cambridge, MA: Hackett, 2000. (KMG)

____. "Intentionality and the Mental," a correspondence with Roderick Chisholm, in *Minnesota Studies in The Philosophy of Science*, vol. II, edited by Herbert Feigl, Michael Scriven, and Grover Maxwell, 507–39. Minneapolis: University of Minnesota Press, 1957. Reprinted in *Intentionality, Mind and Language*, edited by Ausonio Marras. Chicago: University of Illinois Press, 1972.

Marras, Ausonio. "On Sellars' Linguistic Theory of Conceptual Activity." *Canadian Journal of Philosophy* 2 (1973): 471–83.

____. "Reply to Sellars." *Canadian Journal of Philosophy* 2 (1973): 495–501.

____. "Sellars on Thought and Language." *Nous* 7 (1973): 152–63.

____. "Sellars' Behaviourism: A Reply to Fred Wilson." *Philosophical Studies* 30 (1976): 413–18.

____. "The Behaviourist Foundation of Sellars' Semantics." *Dialogue* (Canada) 16 (1977): 664–75.

Perner, Josef. *Understanding the Representational Mind.* Cambridge, MA: The MIT Press, 1991.

Just the Arguments: 100 of the Most Important Arguments in Western Philosophy, First Edition. Edited by Michael Bruce and Steven Barbone.
© 2011 Blackwell Publishing Ltd. Published 2011 by Blackwell Publishing Ltd.

Triplett, Timm, and Willem deVries. "Is Sellars's Rylean Hypothesis Plausible? A Dialogue," in *The Self-Correcting Enterprise: Essays on Wilfrid Sellars*, Poznan Studies in the Philosophy of the Sciences and the Humanities, vol. 9, edited by Michael P. Wolf, 85–114. New York: Rodopi, 2006.

Wellman, Henry M. *The Child's Theory of Mind*. Cambridge, MA: The MIT Press, 1990.

The Cartesian tradition teaches that people have direct, privileged knowledge of their own mental states and that such knowledge possesses the highest epistemic warrant. For example, Descartes' wax example argument in the Second Meditation concludes that he knows his own mental states "first and best." The concepts employed in such knowledge are usually assumed to be either innate or derived by abstraction from the occurrence of those mental states. This is crucial to theories that make our knowledge of our own subjective mental states *basic*, for the foundation of our knowledge must be independent of all other knowledge. Thus, according to such foundationalist theories, both our knowledge of particular mental states and our knowledge of the concepts employed in the knowledge of particular mental states are "givens." [See the argument that the given is a myth (#48).]

Early in "Empiricism and the Philosophy of Mind," Sellars attacked the idea that there could be a given in the sense that the Cartesian tradition demands, but that critique could not be very convincing without an alternative explanation of how we acquire concepts of the mental and why knowledge of our own mental states is immediate and privileged. So Sellars needs to establish that there is a coherent alternative to the traditional view that mentalistic concepts are given, either innately or abstracted directly from particular mental states. This is the point of the Rylean Myth. The Rylean Myth and the critique of the Myth of the Given reinforce each other, strengthening the conclusion that not even knowledge of subjective mental states is given.

Concepts of the mental, therefore, are not fundamentally different in kind or mode of acquisition and application from other empirical concepts. Early-twentieth-century psychology (#93) sought to legitimate the empirical investigation of mind by construing psychology as the science of behavior and eschewing the need to talk of inner, subjective states. But by the time of Sellars' essay, it was increasingly acknowledged that a narrowly behavioristic approach to mind, both in philosophy and in psychology, was inadequate. Sellars' Rylean Myth shows how intersubjective, empirical concepts of subjective states are possible, arguing that they are like theoretical concepts. If so, the mental is as open to intersubjective empirical investigation as any other realm within the empirical world. Furthermore, if our concepts of the mental are empirical concepts acquired via theory postulation, like the concepts of unobservable micro-objects postulated in the natural sciences, then there is little reason to think that they apply to objects of an entirely different kind from other natural objects. This removes a motivation for Cartesian dualism.

Sellars' approach to mentalistic concepts has been important for cognitive science, for it legitimates a naturalistic approach to the mind that nonetheless respects the internality of mental states. Indeed, it inspired the "theory theory" approach to folk psychology, a research program in cognitive science that develops the idea that in early childhood people acquire and learn to apply a theory-like conceptual structure that enables them to interpret the behavior of other people (see Perner and Wellman).

Sellars' argument takes the form of a thought experiment. He asks us to imagine a community that lacks concepts of inner psychological states, although it possesses a complex language for describing and explaining objects and events in the world. This community also possesses a behaviorist's ability to describe and to explain human behavior, as well as metalinguistic abilities to describe and to prescribe linguistic behavior. Such a community, Sellars then argues, can reasonably increase its explanatory resources by extending its language/conceptual system by postulating unobservable states internal to each person. Further, there is a motive to postulate two different kinds of internal states: one kind – thoughts – has properties modeled on the semantic properties of overt linguistic events, while the other – sense impressions – has properties modeled on the properties of perceptible objects. If Sellars' story is coherent, then the traditional view that our concepts and knowledge of the mental is simply given is not compulsory.

The principal objections to Sellars' Rylean Myth have been that the situation described in his thought experiment is either incoherent (Marras) or so empirically implausible as to be unworthy of serious consideration (Chisholm, Triplett). Could there really be people who have a rich physical language as well as a metalanguage yet lack all conception of internal psychological states, thoughts, and sense impressions?

> We [can] characterize the original Rylean language in which they described themselves and their fellows as not only a behavioristic language, but a behavioristic language which is restricted to the non-theoretical vocabulary of a behavioristic psychology. Suppose, now, that in the attempt to account for the fact that his fellow men behave intelligently not only when their conduct is threaded on a string of overt verbal episodes – that is to say, as we would put it when they "think out loud" – but also when no detectable verbal output is present, Jones develops a theory according to which overt utterances are

but the culmination of a process which begins with certain inner episodes. And let us suppose that his model for these episodes which initiate the events which culminate in overt verbal behavior is that of overt verbal behavior itself. In other words, using the language of the model, the theory is to the effect that overt verbal behavior is the culmination of a process which begins with "inner speech." (EPM §56, in SPR, 186; in KMG, 266–67)

P1. Concepts of mental states can be acquired only innately or by direct and privileged access to and abstraction from immediate experience of mental states, which are given by direct intuition (assumption for *reductio*).

P2. Consider a community of behaviorists with an intersubjectively available language that contains, besides object-level concepts, semantic (*ergo* metalinguistic) concepts as well. Such a community would possess no concepts of the psychological.

P3. Such a community would have available to it only the resources of narrow behaviorism to explain human behavior.

P4. The resources of narrow behaviorism are not sufficient to explain all human behavior.

P5. If such a community would have available to it only the resources of narrow behaviorism to explain human behavior, then such a community would, therefore, face substantial puzzles about numerous forms of human behavior.

C1. Such a community would, therefore, face substantial puzzles about numerous forms of human behavior (*modus ponens*, P4, P5).

P6. Such a community could enrich its explanatory resources by utilizing postulational scientific methodology.

P7. If such a community could enrich its explanatory resources by utilizing postulational scientific methodology, then using utterances as a model, this technique could give rise to concepts of inner, speech-like episodes that cause some of the puzzling forms of behavior, and, indeed, cause as well the overt linguistic episodes they are modeled on.

C2. Using utterances as a model, this technique could give rise to concepts of inner, speech-like episodes that cause some of the puzzling forms of behavior, and, indeed, cause as well the overt linguistic episodes they are modeled on (*modus ponens*, P6, P7).

P8. If other puzzling behaviors need to be explained, then the application of normal postulational scientific methodology, using perceptible objects as a model, could give rise to concepts of inner, qualitative states that are normally present when one perceives the perceptible object that is its model but can be present in one when the external object is absent.

P9. If (P6) such a community could enrich its explanatory resources by utilizing postulational scientific methodology, and using utterances as a model, this technique could give rise to concepts of inner, (C2) speech-like episodes that cause some of the puzzling forms of behavior, and, indeed, cause as well the overt linguistic episodes they are modeled on, and (P8) the application of normal postulational scientific methodology can explain other puzzling behaviors, then it is possible (and not in the sense of bare logical possibility, but in the sense that there is a coherent story with some empirical plausibility) that our concepts of the psychological are acquired in perfectly normal, intersubjectively available, empirical ways.

C3. It is possible (and not in the sense of bare logical possibility, but in the sense that there is a coherent story with some empirical plausibility) that our concepts of the psychological are acquired in perfectly normal, intersubjectively available, empirical ways (*modus ponens*, P9, conjunction, P6, C2, P8).

P10. It is not the case that concepts of mental states can be acquired only innately or by direct and privileged access to and abstraction from immediate experience of mental states which are given by direct intuition (*reductio*, P1–P9).

50
Aristotle and the Argument to End All Arguments

Toni Vogel Carey

Aristotle. *Metaphysics*, translated by W. D. Ross. Oxford: Clarendon Press, 1908.

Friedman, Milton. *Essays in Positive Economics*. Chicago: University of Chicago Press, 1953.

Mill, John Stuart. *A System of Logic: Ratiocinative and Inductive*, in *Collected Works of John Stuart Mill*, vols. VII and VIII, edited by J. Robson. Toronto: Toronto University Press, 1973.

Parsons, Charles. "Reason and Intuition," *Synthese* 125 (2000): 299–315.

This argument, which comes down from Aristotle, is one of the most fundamental in the history of thought. It is also one of the most abbreviated, however, which makes it easy to overlook. In the *Metaphysics*, Aristotle merely says:

> It is impossible that there should be demonstration of absolutely everything; [for then] there would be an infinite regress, so that there would still be no demonstration. (1006a, 8–10)

Here is an abridged version of Aristotle's implicit *reductio ad infinitum* argument:

Just the Arguments: 100 of the Most Important Arguments in Western Philosophy, First Edition. Edited by Michael Bruce and Steven Barbone.
© 2011 Blackwell Publishing Ltd. Published 2011 by Blackwell Publishing Ltd.

P1. For any *p*, if *p* is a proposition, then reasons can be given for/ against *p*.

P2. *p* is a proposition.

    C1. Reasons can be given for/against P (*modus ponens*, P1, P2).

P3. *q* and *r* are reasons for/against *p*.

P4. If *q* and *r* are propositions, then reasons can be given for/against *q* and *r*.

P5. *q* is a proposition.

    C2. Reasons can be given for/against *q* (*modus ponens*, P1, P5).

P6. *s* and *t* are reasons for/against *q*.

P7. If *s* and *t* are propositions, then reasons can be given for/against *s* and *t*.

P8. *s* is a proposition.

    C3. Reasons can be given for/against *s* (*modus ponens* P1, P8).

P9. *u* and *v* are reasons for/against *s*.

P10. If *u* and *v* are propositions, then reasons can be given for/against *u* and *v*.

P11. *u* is a proposition.

    C4. Reasons can be given for/against *u* (*modus ponens*, P1, 11).

And so on, *ad infinitum* (omitting *r*, *t*, and *v* for the sake of brevity).

If we demand reasons for/against every proposition, in other words, we will be stuck in an endless process of justification, unable to assert anything at all. As the philosopher of logic and mathematics Charles Parsons put it, "The buck has to stop somewhere."

This argument does not, of course, prevent us from giving reasons for many, indeed most, propositions. And even where we cannot give reasons for a proposition, it does not follow that we are therefore unjustified in believing it. Some propositions may be self-evident – known intuitively, as "evident without proof or reasoning," to quote *Webster's Ninth*. That is how Aristotle viewed the logical law of noncontradiction and how others have treated moral rules like promise keeping. The American Declaration of Independence famously begins: "We hold these truths to be self-evident."

Then, too, while the buck has to stop somewhere, it need not always stop in the same place. We can assume the truth of a proposition merely conditionally, for the sake of argument. We can even assume that *p* is true for one argument and false for another. As the economic theorist Milton Friedman notes in his *Essays in Positive Economics*, "there is no inconsistency in regarding the same firm as if it were a perfect competitor for one problem, and a monopolist for another, just as there is none in regarding the same chalk mark as a Euclidean line for one problem, a Euclidean surface for a second, and a Euclidean solid for a third" (36).

It is important, though, to know what proposition(s) one is taking as given. People are often unaware of their underlying premises or think them too obvious to mention. But marriages, friendships, and political alliances can come to a bad end simply because of unarticulated disagreements about where the buck stops.

We hold some truths to be more self-evident than others, not only for the sake of argument, but without qualification. Scientists operate on the assumption that whatever laws hold for the universe today will continue to hold tomorrow. And that the buck has to stop somewhere is even more foundational than this principle of induction. Philosophers have tradition-ally supposed there are some necessary truths; that is, propositions that could not, in any possible world, be false. If so, the Aristotelian argument we are considering is one of these.

On the other hand, in "Two Dogmas of Empiricism," the philosopher W. V. Quine put forward the idea that so-called necessary truths are merely those propositions we would be most reluctant to give up (#44). For many, the existence and benevolence of God is a belief to keep when all else fails. For Quine, though, no statement, not even a law of logic, is "immune to revision."

The argument we are considering is important because it shows that there are limitations to what reasoning can accomplish, which goes against our cherished belief that the exercise of reason can, in principle, settle all disputes. If the buck has to stop somewhere, then even in logic the ultimate appeal is not to reason, deductive or inductive, but to something closer to intuition. Aristotle had no trouble accepting this; nor, for that matter, did Einstein. But John Stuart Mill and others have made 'intuition' a term of ill repute – notwithstanding Mill's assertion in *A System of Logic* that "truths known by intuition are the original premises from which all others are inferred" (§4).

The trouble with intuition is that people are often loath to brook any challenge, however well taken, to their entrenched intuitive beliefs, making further discussion pointless, if not impossible; and this can lead to toxic forms of fanaticism. That one bases a belief on intuition does nothing to guarantee its truth. But fallible, and even dangerous, as intuitive beliefs can be, it does not follow that intuition should simply be discredited. As George Bealer notes in his entry on "Intuition" in the Supplement to the *Encyclopedia of Philosophy*, perception too is fallible (even dangerous at times), but no one thinks we should therefore discount it. On the contrary, it is a truism that "seeing is believing."

Valid logical inference is safe, while the appeal to intuition carries some risk. But what Aristotle's argument shows is that valid logical inference itself rests on propositions (axioms) whose truth we accept intuitively; that is perforce where the buck stops.

Part IV
Ethics

51

Justice Brings Happiness in Plato's *Republic*

Joshua I. Weinstein

Plato. *Republic*, translated by G. M. A. Grube and C. D. C. Reeve. Indianapolis: Hackett, 1992.

Cooper, John. "Plato's Theory of Human Motivation." *History of Philosophy Quarterly* 1 (1984): 3–21.

Korsgaard, Christine. "Self-Constitution in the Ethics of Plato and Kant." *Journal of Ethics* no. 3 (1999): 1–29.

Sachs, David. "A Fallacy in Plato's Republic. *Philosophical Review* 72 (1963): 141–58.

Santas, Gerasimos. *Understanding Plato's* Republic. Oxford: Wiley-Blackwell, 2010.

In its 300-plus pages, Plato's *Republic* addresses nearly every topic under the sun: tyranny and democracy, feminism and abortion, Homer and carpentry, musical scales and solid geometry, immortality and the afterlife, and why we hate ourselves for screwing up. But all these issues come up in the context of answering one big question: How should one live? What is the best kind of life to lead? In particular, why should one live a life of justice if the wicked seem to be better off?

The main claim in the dialogue is that justice is an excellence or virtue (*aretê*) that brings *eudaimonia*, some integration of happiness, success, and contentment; one lives well if and only if one is a just person. Justice, on

Just the Arguments: 100 of the Most Important Arguments in Western Philosophy, First Edition. Edited by Michael Bruce and Steven Barbone.
© 2011 Blackwell Publishing Ltd. Published 2011 by Blackwell Publishing Ltd.

Plato's account, is founded on how a person's soul or psyche holds together, since only a person whose priorities are all straight can be counted on to behave properly. Also, only such a person can really live life to its fullest.

The significance of this argument extends beyond the fact that the *Republic* has been one of the most influential texts in the history of philosophy. Arguments of this general kind become more important as one becomes less confident that God rewards the virtuous and punishes the wicked. This argument had many successors in the ancient world and has been taken up in various ways in contemporary thought. (For a fuller introduction to the *Republic* and its main argument, see Santas. For a contemporary use of the *Republic*'s strategy, see Korsgaard.)

The basic sketch of the argument is presented by Socrates at the end of Book 1, where he introduces the concept of *ergon*, the activity, work or function that typifies a thing:

> And could eyes perform their function (*ergon*) well if they lacked their peculiar virtue (*aretê*) and had the vice instead?
>
> How could they, for don't you mean if they had blindness instead of sight? [...]
>
> So ears, too, deprived of their own virtue perform their function badly?
> That's right. [...]
>
> Come, then, and let's consider this: Is there some function of a soul that you couldn't perform with anything else, for example, taking care of things, ruling, deliberating, and the like? Is there anything other than a soul to which you could rightly assign these, and say that they are its peculiar function?
>
> No, none of them.
>
> What of living? Isn't that a function of the soul?
> It certainly is.
>
> And don't we also say that there is a virtue of the soul?
> We do.
>
> Then, will a soul ever perform its function well, Thrasymachus, if it is deprived of its own peculiar virtue, or is that impossible?
> It's impossible.
>
> Doesn't it follow, then, that a bad soul rules and takes care of things badly and that good soul does all these things well?
> It does.
>
> Now we agreed that justice is a soul's virtue, and injustice its vice?
> We did.
>
> Then, it follows that a just soul and a just man will live well, and an unjust one badly.
>
> Apparently so, according to your argument.
>
> And surely anyone who lives well is blessed and happy (*eudaimôn*), and anyone who doesn't is the opposite.
> Of course.

Therefore, a just person is happy, and an unjust one wretched.
So be it.
It profits no one to be wretched but to be happy.
Of course.
And so, Thrasymachus, injustice is never more profitable than justice.

(Plato, 353b–354a)

P1. Every thing performs its activity or function (*ergon*) well if and only if it has its virtue or excellence (*aretê*).
P2. The activity of the soul is to live; that is, one lives by the soul.
    C1. One lives well if and only if one has the virtue of the soul (instantiation, P1).
P3. Justice is the virtue of the soul.
    C2. One lives well if and only if one is just (substitution, P3 into C1).
P4. One who lives well is happy; one who lives poorly is miserable.
    C3. The just person lives happily, the unjust lives miserably (substitution, P4 into C2).

This sketch leads into the main body of the dialogue, which elaborates, clarifies, and defends these premises and conclusions (among many other things!) Even the seemingly innocuous P4 comes in for examination (578a–592b). Though one might also wonder about P2 (does one really live only by the soul and not at all by the body?), the main difficulty in this argument is clearly P3: how is *justice* the specific virtue of the soul? Much of the *Republic* is devoted to explaining and defending this premise.

The defense of P3 is based on an analysis of the human psyche or soul. In particular, a human being is shown to be full of conflicting impulses and abilities so that only by ordering and integrating them can a person be "at one." Thus, for example, one can both feel a bodily thirst and simultaneously know (say, from a medical expert) that it would be bad to drink (439a–d). Conflicts such as this need to be resolved by the principle that each part of oneself does what it should and does not meddle in the business of the other parts. Deciding is the job of reason, not of thirst. This principle makes possible self-unification and psychic health, and when it is identified as justice, P3 begins to look somewhat better:

> Even if one has every kind of food and drink, lots of money, and every sort of power to rule, life is thought to be not worth living when the body's nature is ruined. So even if someone can do whatever he wishes [...] how can it be worth living when his soul – the very thing by which he lives – is ruined and in turmoil? (Plato, 445a)

The fuller version of the argument, as it appears in Book 4 (434d–445b), can be analyzed like this:

P1′. The activity of the soul is to live.

P2′. Living consists of potentially contradictory sub-activities.

   C1′. The soul performs potentially contradictory activities (substitution, P2′ into P1′).

P3′. Everything that performs potentially contradictory activities consists of parts.

   C2′. The soul is composed of parts (instantiation, P3′).

P4′. Everything that is composed of parts performs its activity well if and only if each of its parts performs, and only performs, its own activities.

   C3′. The soul performs its activity well if and only if each of its parts performs, and only performs, its own activity (instantiation, P4′).

P5′. Justice is doing what is one's own, and not doing what is not one's own.

   C4′. The soul performs its activity well if and only if it is just (substitution, P5′ into C3′).

   C5′. One lives well if and only if one is just (substitution, P1′ into C4′).

P6′. One who lives well is happy, one who lives poorly is miserable.

   C6′. The just person lives happily, the unjust lives miserably (substitution, P6′ into C5′).

This version of the argument is far more muscular and compelling than the original. The range of impulses it claims to integrate includes everything from the desire for sweet pastries and attractive partners, through the competitive urge to succeed and be respected (especially according to one's parents' expectations), and on to the desire to overcome perplexity, escape one's own ignorance, and contemplate eternity.

But this version also has problems which remain hotly contested to this day. P3′ and the inference to C2′ are defended in a complex and controversial argument based on the principle that no one thing can do or undergo both one thing and its opposite at the same time in the same sense and respect (436b–441c). This sub-argument is notable for probably being the first recorded use of the principle of noncontradiction. Plato also argues here that the number of activities – and hence parts of the soul – is exactly *three*: sustenance by the appetites; control and stability by the spirited part; and guidance through deliberation and reason. (Cooper is a good place to begin examining this tripartition of the soul.) C4′ has also drawn much fire, since it seems to depend on an equivocation on the meaning of a soul's being "just." Can one be just because all of one's psychic parts work properly and together, even as one goes out to rob, cheat, and steal? Or is Socrates right in asserting that this is impossible? (See Sacks.)

Do living well and treating others properly both depend on "justice in the soul"; that is, minimizing internal discord and being "in tune" with oneself? Freudian psychoanalysis and Eastern schools of yoga or meditation derive much of their appeal from similar arguments: "You can't live well without being an authentic, honest, person." "A thief never sleeps well at night." "You must find inner peace and be at one." Plato's version is not only older and more deeply rooted in Western culture, but the *Republic* also includes a detailed explication of how philosophy, politics, and pleasure all fit into the one whole thing which is "living one's life well through achieving psychic harmony" – that is, justice.

52
Aristotle's Function Argument

Sean McAleer[1]

Aristotle. *Aristotle: Nicomachean Ethics*, translated by Terence Irwin. Indianapolis: Hackett, 1999.

The *Nicomachean Ethics* of Aristotle (384–322 BCE) remains influential today, especially among advocates of virtue ethics (roughly, the view that moral philosophy should focus primarily the virtues rather than on duties or rights or good consequences). The Function Argument – so-called because it relies on the notion of a thing's function or characteristic activity – is the centerpiece of the first of the *Nicomachean Ethics*' ten books; Aristotle spends the remaining nine books elaborating on its conclusion by investigating its key terms (soul, virtue, etc.). The Function Argument concerns the nature of happiness (*eudaimonia*), which for Aristotle means not a momentary psychological state or mood but a life of flourishing or well-being. We all want to be happy, Aristotle thinks; happiness is the final good or end that we seek, the ultimate reason we choose other things and which we don't choose for the sake of anything else. But these formal features of happiness don't give us a clear target to aim at in leading our lives. The task of the Function Argument, an ambitious and influential attempt to

[1] Work on this chapter was supported by the University of Wisconsin – Eau Claire Faculty Sabbatical Leave Program, for which the author is most grateful.

Just the Arguments: 100 of the Most Important Arguments in Western Philosophy, First Edition. Edited by Michael Bruce and Steven Barbone.

arrive at moral truths by considering human nature, is to provide such a target; it boldly concludes that human beings can't be happy without being virtuous.

Some more conceptual background might be helpful. For Aristotle, the essence of a thing isn't what it's made of, or its DNA or chemical structure, but what activities it characteristically performs and ends it characteristically pursues: in other words, its function (*ergon*). This organ is a heart because its function is to pump blood, while that organ is a kidney because its function is to clean blood. Once you know a thing's function, you have a standard by which to evaluate it: something is good when it performs its function well – when it achieves the good it characteristically seeks. For example, a knife's function is to cut, so a good knife cuts well. A virtue or excellence (*aretê*) is the condition or state that enables a thing to perform its function well. Thus the virtue of a knife is sharpness, since being sharp is what enables a knife to cut well. Aristotle takes these insights about the functions of artifacts and organs and applies them to human beings. He argues that human beings have a distinctive function, "activity of the soul in accord with reasons" – what we'll simply call "rationality," remembering that it has both theoretical and practical (action-oriented) aspects. Since the good for human beings is happiness, and the human function is rationality, Aristotle concludes that happiness is rationality in accord with virtue – though he concedes that external factors beyond our control can affect whether we flourish.

Aristotle's claim that rationality is the human function is controversial. Some philosophers think that human beings are too complex to have a single, distinctive function; others doubt that the function is rationality. Readers will also want to be sensitive to the various senses 'good' can have: a teleological sense, in which a good is an end or goal pursued or desired; a beneficial sense, in which a thing is good for someone; an evaluative sense, in which a thing is good when it performs its function well; a moral sense, which goes beyond mere functional efficiency.

> But presumably the remark that the best good is happiness is apparently something generally agreed, and we still need a clearer statement of what the best good is. Perhaps, then, we shall find this if we first grasp the function of a human being. For just as the good, i.e., doing well, for a flautist, a sculptor, and every craftsman, and, in general, for whatever has a function and characteristic action, seems to depend on its function, the same seems to be true for a human being, if a human being has some function [...].
>
> Now we say that the function of a kind of thing – of a harpist, for instance – is the same in kind as the function of an excellent individual of the kind – of an excellent harpist, for instance. And the same is true without qualification in every case, if we add to the function the superior achievement in accord with the virtue; for the function of a harpist is to play the harp, and the

function of a good harpist is to play it well. Moreover, we take the human function to be a certain kind of life, and take this life to be activity and actions of the soul that involve reason; hence the function of the excellent man is to do this well and finely.

Now each function is completed well by being completed in accord with the virtue proper to that kind of thing. And so the human good proves to be activity of the soul in accord with virtue, and indeed with the best and most complete virtue, if there are more virtues than one. (I.7: 1097b23–1098a18)

P1. The good for members of a kind is to perform well the function distinctive of their kind.
P2. To perform well the function distinctive of one's kind is to perform it in accord with the relevant virtue(s).
  C1. The good for members of any kind is to perform their distinctive function in accord with the relevant virtue(s) (transitivity of identity, P1, P2).
P3. The function distinctive of humans is rationality.
  C2. The good for humans is rationality in accord with virtue (substitution, C1, P3).
P4. Happiness is the good for humans.
  C3. Happiness is rationality in accord with virtue (transitivity of identity, C2, P4).

53

Aristotle's Argument that Goods Are Irreducible

Jurgis (George) Brakas

Aristotle. *Nicomachean Ethics*, translated by W. D. Ross, revised by J. O. Urmson, and edited by Jonathan Barnes. Princeton, NJ: Princeton University Press, 1984.

Brakas, Jurgis. *Philosophiegeschicte und logische Analyse/Logical Analysis and History of Philosophy*, VI (2003): 23–74.

For most philosophers seeking to discover the nature of the good, the assumption underlying their quest is that the good is one thing – certainly when they are seeking the good for human beings, if not the good in general. This is a very natural assumption to make. If you say "health is a good (or a value)," "wealth is a good," and "my life is a good," it is reasonable to think that "a good" (or "a value") means the same thing when you make such claims. Aristotle, however, disagrees. While discussing the good for humanity in the *Nicomachean Ethics*, he suddenly shifts to a discussion of the good in general and argues that it cannot be one thing. In other words, for Aristotle, the senses of the good – or "value" – are irreducible (#60). His target here is not just his teacher, Plato, who did believe that the good is one thing (the Form of the good), but, more broadly, anyone who believes that the good is one thing (whatever that may be). Many would say that this is a very undesirable outcome, since it would mean that goods by nature

Just the Arguments: 100 of the Most Important Arguments in Western Philosophy, First Edition. Edited by Michael Bruce and Steven Barbone.
© 2011 Blackwell Publishing Ltd. Published 2011 by Blackwell Publishing Ltd.

are "fragmented," not capable of being placed in a hierarchy consistently derived from one fundamental good.

Aristotle's basic strategy is to argue that goods fall into every one of his categories of being – that is, into substance (or "the what"), quality, quantity, and the rest because "the good" signifies things in all of them. If they really do fall into all the categories, then they cannot be reduced to one thing, since they do not have anything in common. For example, although human being and ox can be reduced to animal (a substance) and blue and yellow to color (a quality), human being and blue cannot be reduced to one thing because they have no genus in common. There is just one problem here: why does Aristotle believe that goods exist in all the categories if "the good" signifies things in all of them? You can make any word signify whatever you please, but that does not mean that what it signifies exists – in the categories or anywhere else. However, a good case can be made that "the good" signifying things in all the categories that Aristotle has in mind here is the one signifying real, not apparent, goods – doing so by using his method of *endoxa* (interpreted in a certain way), a method which allows him to separate opinion from knowledge and the apparent from the real.

The interpretation offered here of the passage where Aristotle makes this argument is new. The passage has been remarkably resistant to satisfactory interpretation, defying the efforts of scholars for about a century (see Brakas).

> [S]ince "the good" is uttered signifying something in as many ways as "being" [is] {for it is uttered signifying things in [the category of] the "what" (for example, god – that is, mind) and in [the category of] quality (the virtues) and in [the category of] quantity (the moderate[-amount]) and in [the category of] the relative (the useful) and in [the category of] time ([the] opportune-time) and in [the category of] place ([an] abode) and other things such as these}, it is clear that it cannot be some common universal – that is, one thing; for [then] it would not be uttered signifying things in all the categories but in one only. (Aristotle A6: 1096a23–9; author's translation)

In fairness to Aristotle, I must add that he does not remain content with this negative conclusion. After having fielded five or six arguments to prove that the good cannot be one thing, he goes on in the same chapter to ask:

> But what, then, does ["the good"] signify?[1] It certainly is not like the things bearing the same name by chance. But then do absolutely all goods belong to one class at least by being [derived] from one thing or [by being] relative to one thing? Or [do they belong to one class] rather by analogy (for as sight

---

[1] Literally: "But how, then, is it uttered signifying something?"

is in the body, so reason is in the soul, and so on in other cases)? (Aristotle, 1096b26–9; author's translation)

He dismisses such questions "for now," since exact statements about them "would be more appropriate to another branch of philosophy" (Aristotle, 1096b30–1). His promise, unfortunately is not fulfilled – at least not in the extant works. Even so, I believe a plausible reconstruction of his answers to these questions can be given. However, no such reconstruction is in print yet.

P1. "The good" signifies things in all the categories of being.
P2. If "the good" signifies things in all the categories of being, then goods exist in all the categories of being.
  C1. Goods exist in all the categories of being (*modus ponens*, P2, P1).
P3. If goods exist in all the categories of being, then goods cannot be reduced to some universal common to all goods.
  C2. Goods cannot be reduced to some universal common to all goods (*modus ponens*, P3, C1).
P4. If goods cannot be reduced to some universal common to all goods, then the good is not one thing.
  C3. The good is not one thing (*modus ponens*, P4, C2).

54

Aristotle's Argument for Perfectionism

Eric J. Silverman

Aristotle. *Nicomachean Ethics*, translated by Martin Ostwald. Upper Saddle River, NJ: Prentice Hall, 1999.

Anscombe, G. E. M. "Modern Moral Philosophy." *Philosophy* 33, 24 (1958): 1–19.

Aquinas, Thomas. *Treatise on Happiness*, translated by John A. Oesterle. South Bend, IN: University of Notre Dame Press, 1983.

Broadie, Sarah. *Ethics with Aristotle*. Oxford: Oxford University Press, 1993.

Cahn, Steven M., and Christine Vitrano. *Happiness: Classic and Contemporary Readings in Philosophy*. Oxford: Oxford University Press, 2008.

One long-disputed issue in ethics concerns the nature of the supreme good for humanity. In other words, what is the best possible life that a person can lead? This supreme good is commonly referred to as "happiness" or "the happy life." Several of the ancient Greek philosophers held a view called "perfectionism," which claims that the ongoing exercise of moral and intellectual virtue constitutes the best possible life for humanity. Aristotle's *Nicomachean Ethics* offers the most influential of the ancient arguments for viewing the life of virtue rather than the life of pleasure, wealth, honor, or amusement as humanity's supreme good. Aristotle's perfectionistic views influenced the ethics of medieval theists such as Thomas Aquinas and Moses Maimonides. While his views were less influential

Just the Arguments: 100 of the Most Important Arguments in Western Philosophy, First Edition. Edited by Michael Bruce and Steven Barbone.
© 2011 Blackwell Publishing Ltd. Published 2011 by Blackwell Publishing Ltd.

during the modern era, some of them were reintroduced when G. E. M. Anscombe's "Modern Moral Philosophy" inaugurated the contemporary virtue ethics movement.

Aristotle's argument for perfectionism is grounded in a controversial account of human nature. Since he holds a teleological view of the universe, he claims that all things – including human beings – have an ultimate function or purpose for which they exist. Aristotelian terminology refers to this ultimate purpose as a "final cause." Therefore, he claims that the supreme good for humanity is to achieve this ultimate purpose. He establishes two criteria for recognizing the supreme good for humanity: it must be desired as an end in itself rather than as a means to some further good, and it must be sufficient in itself for making life good. Finally, he claims that the virtuous life fulfills humanity's ultimate purpose by actualizing the intellectual and moral potentials distinctive of our species. Accordingly, he argues that the virtuous life better fits the criteria for happiness than other lifestyles.

> Since there are evidently several ends, and since we choose some of these – e.g., wealth, flutes, and instruments generally – as a means to something else, it is obvious that not all ends are final. The highest good, on the other hand, must be something final. Thus, if there is only one final end, this will be the good we are seeking; if there are several, it will be the most final and perfect of them. We call that which is pursued as an end in itself more final than an end which is pursued for the sake of something else; and what is never chosen as a means to something else we call more final than that which is chosen both as an end in itself and as a means to something else. What is always chosen as an end in itself and never as a means to something else is called final in an unqualified sense. This description seems to apply to happiness above all else: for we always choose happiness as an end in itself and never for the sake of something else. Honor, pleasure, intelligence, and all virtue we choose partly for themselves – for we would choose each of them even if no further advantage would accrue from them – but we also choose them partly for the sake of happiness, because we assume that it is through them that we will be happy. On the other hand, no one chooses happiness for the sake of honor, pleasure, and the like, nor as a means to anything at all.
>
> We arrive at the same conclusion if we approach the question from the standpoint of self-sufficiency. For the final and perfect good seems to be self-sufficient. (Aristotle, 1097a26–1097b8)

P1. There is a supreme good for humanity, commonly referred to as happiness.

P2. If a good is desired as an end in itself and is sufficient for making life good, then that good constitutes happiness.

P3. The virtuous life fulfills a human being's function by actualizing that person's full potential.

P4. If some good fulfills a human being's function by actualizing that person's full potential, then that good is desired as an end in itself.

C1. The virtuous life is desired by human beings as an end in itself (*modus ponens*, P3, P4).

P5. If some good fulfills a human being's function, then it is sufficient for making that being's life good.

C2. The virtuous life is sufficient for making a human being's life good (*modus ponens*, P3, P5).

C3. The virtuous life is desired as an end in itself and is sufficient for making life good (conjunction, C1, C2).

C4. The virtuous life constitutes happiness, the supreme good for humanity (*modus ponens*, P2, C3).

55

Categorical Imperative as the Source for Morality

Joyce Lazier

Kant, Immanuel. *The Metaphysics of Morals*, translated by Mary Gregor. New York: Cambridge University Press, 1991.

Kant's deontological ethical theory relies on two assumptions used to deduce the categorical imperative. The first is that morality is for all, or what is wrong for one to do is wrong for everyone to do. The second is that morality is grounded on reason and not experience. Combining these two assumptions, Kant arrives at the categorical imperative. The following reconstruction of Kant's arguments for the categorical imperative brings to the forefront two major problems. First, the use of disjunction opens up Kant's argument to the fallacy of the excluded middle, and second, the reconstruction also makes more apparent Kant's reliance on teleology. Not many thinkers today believe that everything has a specific, defined end that belongs only to it. The arguments are taken from *The Metaphysics of Morals*, parts 216, 222, and 225.

> But it is different with the teachings of morality. They command for everyone, without taking account of his inclinations, merely because and insofar as he is free and has practical reason. He does not derive instruction in its laws from observing himself and his animal nature or from perceiving the ways of the world what happens and how men behave (although the German word *Sitten*, like the Latin *mores*, means only manners and customs). Instead,

Just the Arguments: 100 of the Most Important Arguments in Western Philosophy, First Edition. Edited by Michael Bruce and Steven Barbone.
© 2011 Blackwell Publishing Ltd. Published 2011 by Blackwell Publishing Ltd.

reason commands how men are to act even though no example of this could be found and it takes no account of the advantages we can thereby gain, which only experience could teach us. For although reason allows us to seek our advantage in every way possible to us and can even promise us, on the testimony of experience, that it will probably be more to our advantage on the whole to obey its commands than to transgress them especially if obedience is accompanied with prudence, still the authority of its precepts as commands is not based on these considerations. Instead it uses them (as counsels) only as a counterweight against inducements to the contrary, to offset in advance the error of biased scales in practical appraisal, and only then to ensure that the weight of a pure practical reason's a priori grounds will turn the scales in favor of the authority of its precepts. (216)

An imperative is a practical rule by which an action in itself contingent is made necessary. An imperative differs from a practical law in that a law indeed represents an action as necessary but takes no account of whether this action already inheres by an inner necessity in the acting subject (as in a holy being) or whether it is contingent (as in man); for where the former is the case there is no imperative. Hence an imperative is a rule the representation of which makes necessary an action that is subjectively contingent and thus represents the subject as one that must be constrained (necessitated) to conform with the rule. A categorical (unconditional) imperative is one that represents an action as objectively necessary and makes it necessary not indirectly through the representation of some end that can be attained by the action but through the mere representation of this action itself (its form), and hence directly. No other practical doctrine can furnish instances of such imperatives than that which prescribes obligation (the doctrine of morals). All other imperative are technical and are, one and all, conditional. The ground of the possibility of categorical imperative is this: that they refer to no other property of choice (by which some purpose can be ascribed to it) than simply to its freedom. (222)

The categorical imperative, which as such only affirms what obligation is, is: Act upon a maxim that can also hold as a universal law. You must therefore first consider your actions in terms of their subjective principles; but you can know whether this principle also holds objectively only in this way: That when your reason subjects it to the test of conceiving yourself as also giving universal law through it, it qualifies for such a giving of universal law. (225)

P1. A human is free and has practical reason.
P2. Either practical reason or experience uses perceptions of the ways of the world and actions of humans as sources of its laws.
P3. Practical reason does not use the ways of the world and actions of humans as sources of its laws.
  C1. Experience uses perceptions of the ways of the world and actions of humans as sources of its laws (disjunctive syllogism, P2, P3).

P4. Either practical reason or experience teaches us how to act given the advantages we can gain.

P5. Practical reason does not teach us how to act given the advantages we can gain.

    C2. Experience teaches us how to act given the advantages we can gain (disjunctive syllogism, P4, P5).

P6. Either practical reason or experience bases the authority of its precepts on how much advantages we can gain.

P7. Practical reason does not use perceived advantages as the basis of the authority of its commands.

    C3. Experience does use perceived advantages as the basis of the authority of its commands (disjunctive syllogism, P6, P10).

P8. Either experience or *a priori* grounds are the source of practical reason's authority.

P9. Experience is not the source of practical reason's authority.

    C4. *A priori* grounds are the source of practical reason's authority (disjunctive syllogism, P8, P9).

P10. If practical reason's source of authority is *a priori*, then it commands for everyone without taking into account one's inclinations.

P11. Practical reason's source of authority is *a priori* (C4).

    C5. Practical reason commands for everyone without taking into account one's inclinations (*modus ponens*, P10, P11).

P12. Either morality comes from experience or it comes from practical reason.

P13. The teachings of morality do not stem from experience.

    C6. The teachings of morality stem from practical reason (disjunctive syllogism, P12, P13).

P14. If practical reason is the source of morality's commands, then morality commands for everyone without taking into account one's inclinations.

P15. Practical reason is the source of morality's commands.

    C7. The teachings of morality command for everyone without taking into account one's inclinations (*modus ponens*, P14, P15).

P16. If a law represents an action as necessary, then it is not a practical law.

P17. Imperatives are laws that represent an action as necessary

    C8. Imperatives are not practical laws (*modus ponens*, P16, P17).

P18. If something is an imperative, then it necessitates an action.

P19. If something necessitates an action, then it must constrain the subject to conform to that rule.

    C9. If something is an imperative, then it is a rule that necessitates an action through constraint of the subject to conform to that rule (hypothetical syllogism, P18, P19).

P20. If an imperative is categorical, then it represents an action as objectively necessary.

P21. If an action is represented as objectively necessary, then it is not because of some end that can be attained.

    C10. If an imperative is categorical, then it is not because of some end that can be attained (hypothetical syllogism, P20, P21).

P22. If an imperative is categorical, then it makes an action necessary directly through representation of the action itself (its form).

P23. If an action is made necessary directly through representation of the action itself (its form), then it is grounded in freedom of choice (and not a subjective end).

    C11. If an imperative is categorical, then it is grounded in freedom of choice (and not a subjective end) (hypothetical syllogism, P22, P23).

P24. If an imperative is grounded in freedom of choice (and not some subjective end), then reason subjects the maxim of action as conceiving itself as a universal law.

P25. If the maxim of action can be conceived as a universal law, then it holds objectively.

    C12. If an imperative is grounded in freedom of choice, then it holds objectively (hypothetical syllogism, P24, P25).

P26. A categorical imperative is grounded in freedom of choice.

    C13. A categorical imperative holds objectively (*modus ponens*, C12, P26).

P27. If the categorical imperative holds objectively, then it is the source of morality.

    C14. A categorical imperative is the source of morality (*modus ponens*, P27, C13).

56

Kant on Why Autonomy Deserves Respect

Mark Piper

Guyer, Paul. "Kant on the Theory and Practice of Autonomy," in *Autonomy*, edited by Ellen Frankel Paul, Fred D. Miller, Jr., and Jeffrey Paul, 70–98. Cambridge, UK: Cambridge University Press, 2003.

Kant, Immanuel. *Groundwork of the Metaphysics of Morals*, translated and edited by Mary Gregor. Cambridge, UK: Cambridge University Press, 1998.

According to a widespread view, there is something important about autonomy in virtue of which it deserves special respect. More often than not, the claim that autonomy deserves respect comes into play in relation to particular autonomous choices or acts of will. An autonomous choice is not a thoughtless or offhand choice; rather, it is a choice that expresses a person's nature, freedom, preferences, or values – a person's "deep self" – in a powerful and significant way. As such, it is a choice that seems, according to many philosophers and nonphilosophers alike, to generate special demands of respect on others. This notion of the special respect owed to autonomy is pervasive throughout popular culture and philosophical discourse. It has application in debates concerning the ground of human dignity, the ground of human rights (including the defense of specific rights such as the right to free speech), the limits of intersubjective interference, medical ethics debates (including debates surrounding euthanasia and the physician–patient relationship), the justification of liberal education, the justification of liberal government, and the justification of the wrongness of paternalism. The classic source for the view that autonomy deserves special respect is Immanuel Kant, and the following is a reconstruction of the core aspects

---

Just the Arguments: 100 of the Most Important Arguments in Western Philosophy, First Edition. Edited by Michael Bruce and Steven Barbone.
© 2011 Blackwell Publishing Ltd. Published 2011 by Blackwell Publishing Ltd.

of Kant's argument for this claim. It should be noted that the reconstruction of this argument is, given Kant's dense and sometimes labyrinthine writing style, a difficult task, sometimes requiring reading between the lines or supplying premises that Kant does not provide explicitly. The key to the argument is Kant's insistence that the only acts of will that deserve respect are those acts of will that are truly free (according to Kant's understanding of "freedom"). It should quickly be added that Kant understood the concept of "respect" in a very robust way: according to Kant, to say that something deserves respect is to say that it is an object of true and proper esteem. Moreover, it is important to note that for Kant, what it means for a person to be free is for that person not to be dominated by his or her inclinations or desires but rather to will and to act in accordance with universal laws of reason. Lastly, it should be noted that a number of philosophers have agreed with Kant that autonomy deserves respect but have disagreed with Kant about what autonomy fundamentally is. More specifically, some philosophers have claimed that it is possible for autonomous acts of will to contain, or to be based on, inclinations.

> For an object as the effect of my proposed action I can indeed have inclination but never respect, just because it is merely an effect and not an activity of the will. In the same way I cannot have respect for inclination as such, whether it is mine or that of another; I can at most in the first case approve it and in the second sometimes even love it, that is, regard it as favorable to my advantage. Only what it connected with my will solely as ground and never as effect, what does not serve my inclination but outweighs it or at least excludes it altogether from calculations in making a choice – hence the mere law for itself – can be an object of respect and so a command. (Kant AK 4:400)

P1. If an act of will is free, then it deserves respect.

P2. If an act of will is not free, then it does not deserve respect.

P3. If an act of will is dependent on an object of desire, then it is not a free act of will.

P4. If an act of will is in no way influenced by any object of desire but is rather exercised in accordance with its own law, then it is a free act of will.

P5. An inclination is dependent on objects of desire.

    C1. Inclinations are not free acts of will (*modus ponens*, P3, P5)

    C2. Inclinations do not deserve respect (*modus ponens*, P2, C1).

P6. An autonomous act of will is in no way influenced by any object of desire but is rather exercised in accordance with its own law.

    C3. Autonomous acts of will are free acts of will (*modus ponens*, P4, P6).

    C4. Autonomous acts of will deserve respect (*modus ponens*, P1, C3).

57

Mill's Proof of Utilitarianism

A. T. Fyfe

Mill, John Stuart. "Of What Sort of Proof the Principle of Utility Is Susceptible," in *Utilitarianism*. London: Parker, Son, and Bourn, 1863.
____. "Excerpt from a Letter to Henry Jones," in *The Classical Utilitarians: Bentham and Mill*, edited by John Troyer. Indianapolis: Hackett, 2003.

Millgram, Elijah. "Mill's Proof of the Principle of Utility." *Ethics* 110 (2000): 282–310.
Sayre-McCord, Geoffrey. "Mill's 'Proof' of the Principle of Utility: A More than Half-Hearted Defense." *Social Philosophy & Policy* 18, 2 (2001): 330–60.

Utilitarianism, as summarized by one of its chief proponents, John Stuart Mill (1806–73), is the moral theory that "actions are right in proportion as they tend to promote happiness, wrong as they tend to produce the reverse of happiness." Therefore, viewing matters as Mill would, Robin Hood is not immoral for stealing from the rich to give to the poor, because in doing so he is able to produce more happiness in the world than would have otherwise existed. Likewise, if I possess excess wealth, it would be immoral of me to withhold that wealth from others for whom it would do more good. If, for example, I am considering new shoes when my present pair is fully functional, I should instead donate that excess wealth to famine relief. In both instances, Mill would have the agent in question perform whichever available action would best reduce unhappiness and promote happiness in the world.

Just the Arguments: 100 of the Most Important Arguments in Western Philosophy, First Edition. Edited by Michael Bruce and Steven Barbone.
© 2011 Blackwell Publishing Ltd. Published 2011 by Blackwell Publishing Ltd.

Utilitarianism is generally understood to be the combination of two separate moral theories. First, utilitarianism is a form of "consequentialism," since it holds that the rightness or wrongness of an action depends solely upon the goodness or badness of that action's consequences. Second, utilitarianism is a form of "welfarism," since it holds that the goodness or badness of an action's consequences depends solely upon the amount of happiness and unhappiness brought about by that action (i.e., the action's effect on people's welfare). Therefore, any argument for utilitarianism must aim to prove not one but two separate claims: a consequentialist "theory of the right" (i.e., what is right and wrong) and a welfarist "theory of the good" (i.e., what is good and bad).

Examining J. S. Mill's famous argument for utilitarianism, it is clear that Mill simply takes for granted a consequentialist theory of the right rather than providing an argument for it. As a result, even if Mill's argument for utilitarianism succeeds, it will only prove half of what utilitarianism consists in, a welfarist theory of value. Taking what Mill says at face value, his argument begins with the claim that the only way we come to know that something is visible or audible is through seeing or hearing it. Mill then concludes, by analogy, that the only way to prove that something is desirable (i.e., worth desiring; good) is by appealing to what we actually do desire. After using this analogy with audibility and visibility to establish the only method for proving that something is desirable, Mill argues that happiness is the only intrinsic good in existence since (1) people do desire it, and (2) it is the only thing that people desire for its own sake. With this result in hand, Mill then concludes his argument for utilitarianism – or at least utilitarianism's welfarist aspect – by inferring that since an increase in a person's happiness is good for that person, an increase in all persons' happiness is good for all persons.

This is a notoriously bad argument. If this straightforward reading accurately reflects the argument Mill means to give, then he has committed a number of elementary logical mistakes. In the first part of his argument, Mill states that because people desire happiness, it follows that happiness must be "desirable." However, "desirable" has two possible meanings, and Mill seems to be equivocating between them. Since "audible" just means "possible to hear" and "visible" just means "possible to see," in order for his analogy to work, Mill must mean "possible to desire" when he talks of something as being "desirable." However, to prove that what we desire is good, by "desirable" Mill must mean "worthy of desire" or "good." While it is possible that Mill is not confused and not equivocating between these two senses of "desirable," this would only mean that he is instead guilty of committing the "naturalistic fallacy"; that is, the fallacy of either inferring how things should be merely from how things actually are (in this case, what we should desire from what we do desire) or trying to define a moral concept with a nonmoral concept (in this case, Mill would be defining "worthy of desire" and "good" as just amounting to "desired").

Mill's apparent logical errors continue when, at the tail end of his argument, Mill seems to commit the "fallacy of composition." One commits this fallacy whenever one tries to infer something about a whole simply because it is true of the whole's parts. For example, I would be guilty of the fallacy of composition if I were to infer that tables were invisible to the naked eye just because tables are made of atoms, and atoms are invisible to the naked eye. Mill seems to be committing this fallacy when he infers that the general happiness is good for the group of all persons simply from the fact that he has proven that personal happiness is good for an individual person.

Is this straightforward reading of Mill's argument for utilitarianism correct? Did Mill really put forth an argument for half of utilitarianism that is itself riddled with the simplest of logical mistakes? This is unlikely. As a result, philosophers have developed a number of more charitable alternative interpretations in an attempt to uncover what Mill actually intended. One possible way in which philosophers have thought to alter our interpretation of Mill's argument for the better is by taking his analogy to be an attempt to show that desire functions as an "indicator" or "evidence" of goodness. For example, when someone thinks she hears something and there is no reason to think that she is mistaken, then it plausible for us to conclude that there actually is a sound present. On this reading of Mill's argument, desire similarly serves as an indicator of something worthy of desire actually being present. Such an interpretation would avoid equivocating between the two senses of "desirable" and would also prevent Mill from falling prey to the naturalistic fallacy. This more charitable interpretation also has the advantage of fitting in well with Mill's empiricist philosophical attitude.

Another way in which we might alter our interpretation of Mill's argument for the better is by reinterpreting his apparent commitment of the fallacy of composition to instead be an argument concerning how the value of happiness for an individual must depend on its intrinsic value. Specifically, Mill could be interpreted as arguing that if happiness is good for an individual to possess, then happiness itself must be good. But if happiness itself is good and if we are to judge the moral rightness of our actions by how much good they produce, then the rightness of my actions would depend not only on how much of my happiness they result in, but also on how my actions affect the happiness of others.

However, this does not exhaust the numerous alternative interpretations of Mill's argument. In fact, Mill's remarks about the impossibility of providing a proof of utilitarianism have led some philosophers to conclude that Mill never meant to be giving an argument for utilitarianism in the first place. Of course, no matter how successful Mill's argument for utilitarianism might be under some particular interpretation (if we interpret him to be giving one at all), Mill is still only arguing for utilitarianism's welfarist aspect. As we noted at the outset, Mill's argument fails to address consequentialism entirely. Mill simply takes for granted that it is "the doctrine of rational persons of all schools" that "the morality of actions depends on the consequences which they tend to produce." This has become increasingly regrettable, since much of the controversy surrounding utilitarianism has come to concern precisely its consequentialist aspect, something that Mill found so uncontroversial that he didn't even provide an argument for it.

> The only proof capable of being given that an object is visible, is that people actually see it. The only proof that a sound is audible, is that people hear it: and so of the other sources of our experience. In like manner, I apprehend, the sole evidence it is possible to produce that anything is desirable, is that people do actually desire it. If the end which the utilitarian doctrine proposes to itself were not, in theory and in practice, acknowledged to be an end, nothing could ever convince any person that it was so. No reason can be given why the general happiness is desirable, except that each person, so far as he believes it to be attainable, desires his own happiness. This, however, being a fact, we have not only all the proof which the case admits of, but all which it is possible to require, that happiness is a good: that each person's happiness is a good to that person, and the general happiness, therefore, a good to the aggregate of all persons. Happiness has made out its title as one of the ends of conduct, and consequently one of the criteria of morality. (Mill "Of What Sort of Proof," 61)

> As to the sentence [. . .] when I said the general happiness is a good to the aggregate of all persons I did not mean that every human being's happiness is a good to every other human being, [. . .] I merely meant in this particular sentence to argue that since A's happiness is a good, B's a good, C's a good, etc., the sum of all these goods must be a good. (Mill "Excerpt from a Letter," 270)

Generic Argument for Traditional Utilitarianism

P1. Consequentialist Theory of the Right. An action is right for someone to perform if and only if, of the available actions, it is the action that would maximize total net good over bad in existence – otherwise, the action is wrong.

P2. Welfarist Theory of the Good. The only intrinsic good is someone's happiness while the only intrinsic bad is someone's unhappiness.

  C1. Traditional Utilitarianism. An action is right for someone to perform if and only if, of the available actions, it is the action that would maximize total net happiness over unhappiness in existence – otherwise, the action is wrong (substitution, P1, P2).

Mill's Proof of Utilitarianism (Straightforward Interpretation)

P1. The only proof that an object is visible is that people actually see it.
P2. The only proof that a sound is audible is that people actually hear it.
   C1. The only proof that a thing is desirable is that people actually desire it (analogical inference, P1, P2).
P3. If the only proof that a thing is desirable is that people actually desire it and each person actually desires happiness for herself, then each person's happiness is desirable for herself.
P4. Each person actually desires happiness for herself.
   C2. The only proof that a thing is desirable is that people actually desire it and each person actually desires happiness for herself (conjunction, C1, P4).
   C3. Each person's happiness is desirable for herself (*modus ponens*, P3, C2).
   C4. The general happiness is desirable for the aggregate of all persons (fallacy of composition, C3).

Mill's Proof of Utilitarianism (One Alternative Interpretation)

P1. The only proof that a visible thing exists is that people actually see it and there is no reason to think they are mistaken.
P2. The only proof that an audible sound exists is that people actually hear it and there is no reason to think they are mistaken.
   C1. The only proof that a desirable thing exists is that people actually desire it and there is no reason to think they are mistaken (analogical inference, P1, P2).
P3. Each person actually desires happiness for himself and there is no reason to think he is mistaken.
   C2. Each person's happiness is desirable for himself (semantic consequence, C1, P3).
P4. If each person's happiness is desirable for himself, then happiness is a desirable thing itself.
P5. If happiness is a desirable thing itself, then the general happiness is desirable.
   C3. If each person's happiness is desirable for himself, then the general happiness is desirable (hypothetical syllogism, P4, P5).
   C4. The general happiness is desirable (*modus ponens*, C2, C3).

Mill's Proof of Utilitarianism (Another Alternative Interpretation)

P1. If everyone desires happiness for herself, then everyone thinks of happiness itself as good and everyone selfishly wants happiness for herself.
P2. Everyone desires happiness for herself.
  C1. Everyone thinks of happiness itself as good and everyone selfishly wants happiness for herself (*modus ponens*, P1, P2).
  C2. Everyone thinks of happiness itself as good (simplification, C1).
P3. If everyone thinks of happiness itself as good, then everyone should think of the happiness of herself and others as good.
  C3. Everyone should think of the happiness of herself and others as good (*modus ponens*, C2, P3).
P4. No one desires anything other than happiness for herself and/or happiness for others.
P5. If no one desires anything other than happiness for herself and/or happiness for others, then no one should think of anything other than the happiness of herself or others as good.
  C4. No one should think of anything other than the happiness of herself or others as good (*modus ponens*, P4, P5).
  C5. Everyone should think of the happiness of herself and others as good, and no one should think of anything other than the happiness of herself or others as good (conjunction, C3, C4).

58

The Experience Machine Objection to Hedonism

Dan Weijers

Nozick, Robert. *Anarchy, State, and Utopia*. New York: Basic Books, 1974.

De Brigard, Filipe. "If You Like It, Does It Matter if It's Real?" *Philosophical Psychology* 23, 1 (2010): 43–57.
Kymlicka, Will. *Contemporary Political Philosophy: An Introduction*. New York: Oxford University Press, 1990.
Sobel, David. "Varieties of Hedonism." *Journal of Social Philosophy* 33, 2 (2002): 240–56.

Robert Nozick's Experience Machine thought experiment describes a fantastic machine that can simulate any kind of experience for anyone who plugs herself into it. A life attached to an Experience Machine could be full of immensely pleasurable experiences; however (as Nozick correctly notes), the thought of actually living such a life is one that nearly everyone finds unappealing.

Although Nozick originally devised the Experience Machine thought experiment to make a point about how animals should be treated, it was quickly adopted by anyone who wanted to argue for the falsity of hedonism as a theory of the good. The Experience Machine thought experiment is equally effective against any kind of theory that posits the internal aspects of our experiences as the only valuable things in a life, but hedonism is

Just the Arguments: 100 of the Most Important Arguments in Western Philosophy,
First Edition. Edited by Michael Bruce and Steven Barbone.
© 2011 Blackwell Publishing Ltd. Published 2011 by Blackwell Publishing Ltd.

often singled out because it is the most widely discussed exemplar of this type of theory. The adoption of the Experience Machine thought experiment for the purpose of discrediting hedonism has been extremely successful. Indeed, virtually everyone who has written about hedonism since the mid-1970s cites the Experience Machine thought experiment as a (and often the) decisive objection against it. Hedonism comes in many guises, but all hedonistic theories share the foundational claims that pleasure is the only thing of intrinsic value in a life and that pain is the only thing of intrinsic disvalue. The reason why the Experience Machine Objection to Hedonism was (and still is) considered to be decisive is because the widespread judgment that a life plugged into an Experience Machine is not appealing is thought to give overwhelming reason to reject this central claim.

As with many other arguments in ethics, the Experience Machine Objection to Hedonism presents a thought experiment and relies on the readers' agreeing with the author's judgment about it. The Experience Machine Objection to Hedonism garners near-complete agreement on the judgment that a life plugged into an Experience Machine is not something that we would choose for ourselves. It should be noted that this widespread judgment arises despite Nozick's attempts to rule out some of the possible reasons that we might not want to plug in, such as allowing those who depend on us to plug in too. Even in modern reproductions of the Experience Machine Objection to Hedonism, which tend to place more emphasis than Nozick did on that fact that the experiences available in an Experience Machine would be far more pleasurable and less painful than those of a real life, hardly anyone admits to wanting to plug in to an Experience Machine.

Despite the nearly unanimous judgment that plugging into an Experience Machine for life would be a mistake, substantial disagreement remains on the question of why we think that our current life would be better for us than a life in an Experience Machine. Many philosophers have offered different suggestions as to why we do not, and should not, choose a life in an Experience Machine. Nozick's rationale is that plugging in would deprive us the chance really to do and be certain things (as opposed merely to having the internal experiences of doing and being them). Some (e.g., De Brigard) have suggested that the feelings we experience in response to the thought of the Experience Machine are based on an subconscious fear of change, as shown by reversing the thought experiment (imagine that you have actually been living an Experience Machine life all along). Until the disagreement about why nearly all of us judge a life plugged into an Experience Machine to be so ghastly is resolved, we cannot be confident that premise 3 of the argument (below) is correct or be sure that the Experience Machine Objection to Hedonism should really be considered as decisive as it generally is.

Suppose that there were an experience machine that would give you any experience you desired. Superduper neuropsychologists could stimulate your brain so that you would think and feel you were writing a great novel, or making a friend, or reading an interesting book. All the time, you would be floating in a tank, with electrodes attached to your brain. Should you plug into this machine for life, preprogramming your life's experiences? If you are worried about missing out on desirable experiences, we can suppose that business enterprises have researched thoroughly the lives of many others. You can pick and choose from their large library or smorgasbord of such experiences, selecting your life's experiences for, say, the next two years. After two years have passed, you will have ten minutes or ten hours out of the tank, to select the experiences of your next two years. Of course, while in the tank you won't know that you're there; you'll think it's all actually happening. Others can also plug in to have the experiences they want, so there's no need to stay unplugged to serve them. (Ignore problems such as who will service the machines if everyone plugs in.) Would you plug in? *What else can matter to us, other than how our lives feel from the inside?* Nor should you refrain because of the few moments of distress between the moment you've decided and the moment you're plugged. What's a few moments of distress compared to a lifetime of bliss (if that's what you choose), and why feel any distress at all if your decision is the best one? (Nozick, 42–3)

P1. Plugging into an Experience Machine would make the rest of your life dramatically more pleasurable and less painful than it would otherwise have been (stipulated in thought experiment).

P2. Given the choice to plug into an Experience Machine for the rest of your life, ignoring any responsibilities you might have to others, you would decline (appeal to readers' judgment).

P3. If, ignoring any responsibilities you might have to others, you would decline the chance to plug into an Experience Machine for the rest of your life, then pleasure and pain are not the only things of intrinsic value (or disvalue) in a life.

    C1. Pleasure and pain are not the only things of intrinsic value (or disvalue) in a life (*modus ponens*, P2, P3).

P4. If hedonism is true, then pleasure and pain are the only things of intrinsic value (or disvalue) in a life.

    C2. Hedonism is false (*modus tollens*, C1, P4).

59

The Error Theory Argument

Robert L. Muhlnickel

Mackie, John. "A Refutation of Morals." *Australasian Journal of Philosophy* 24 (1946): 77–90. Reprinted in *Twentieth Century Ethical Theory*, edited by Steven Cahn, Jeram Haber, and Joram Haber, 145–52. Upper Saddle River, NJ: Prentice-Hall, 1995.
____. *Ethics: Inventing Right and Wrong*. Harmondsworth: Penguin, 1977.

Metaethics is the philosophical inquiry into the nature and status of morality. A basic question about the nature and status of morality is whether expressions of moral approval and disapproval are objective. Moral objectivism, generally and simply stated, is the view that moral expressions (in speech, writing, or thought) are cognitive judgments, which are true or false because of their relations to moral facts. Moral skepticism is the view that there are no such moral facts. Many philosophers think that commonsense morality presumes moral objectivism, and many philosophers defend versions of moral objectivism. Defending moral skepticism requires showing that the belief that moral facts exist is in error, even though our ordinary language presumes they do exist. The aim of showing this belief as erroneous gives the argument its name. The error theory argument is a "destructive" argument; it aims to show that moral objectivism is false. J. L. Mackie defends the error theory argument and claims it shows that moral skepticism is more reasonable than moral objectivism.

The error theory argument first derives C1 by *modus ponens* that commonsense morality assumes and many moral philosophers defend moral objectivism. That C1 is the presumptive belief forestalls the objection that the error theory argument attacks a straw man. The error theory argument's

---

destructive aim is advanced by two component arguments: the argument from relativity and the argument from queerness.

The argument from relativity extends from P3 to C2. P3 states the unimpeachable fact of moral relativity: moral judgments observed in behavior, described in records of deliberation, and stated in authoritative moral codes of different societies and historical eras are different and often incompatible with one another. Moral skeptics and moral objectivists offer different explanations of the relativity of morals. Moral skeptics argue that moral relativity is best explained by the fact that there are no objective moral principles; rather, people assert moral codes based on their familiarity with the moral codes they learn in their societies (P4 (i)). Moral objectivists argue that factual differences in the circumstances of various societies result in different applications of objective moral principles. Such different applications yield distinct moral codes despite agreement on objective moral principles (P4 (ii)).

Mackie supports explanation (i) by appealing to a sentimentalist theory of the origins of moral expressions. Although Mackie does not call his argument an Inference to the Best Explanation, the reasoning here involves a comparative claim that the skeptical explanation accounts for the observed phenomena of moral expression better than the objectivist one. Inference to the Best Explanation arguments are comparisons of two or more explanations of observed phenomena and evaluations of each explanation on common standards. Commonly cited standards for comparing explanations are greater simplicity, greater explanatory power, and more coherence with other hypotheses and phenomena. Philosophers dispute what Inference to the Best Explanation argument implies, so the argument below includes P6 and C2 and P6* and C2* for comparison. P6 and C2 make a stronger claim, that explanation (i) shows that the belief in the existence of objective moral facts is unjustified, rather than merely not as well justified as disbelief in the existence of objective moral facts.

The objection to the argument from relativity on behalf of moral objectivism, though unsuccessful according to Mackie, leaves moral skepticism in need of further argument. The argument from queerness claims there are two necessary conditions of the existence of objective moral facts. The first condition is a claim about the ontology of moral facts. Putative moral facts would consist of a different kind of entity or relation than those known by scientific observation and hypothesizing, ordinary perception, and quasi-scientific methods. The second condition claims that mental ability humans would have to possess in order to have knowledge of moral facts would be something specifically moral. Such ability would be different in kind from other human mental abilities. Since neither necessary condition of the existence of objective moral facts is true, the antecedent of the conditional in P7 is false by *modus tollens*.

The error theory argument concludes in C4 by conjoining C3, that objective values no not exist, and C2, the belief that objective moral facts is not justified. The conjunction (C4) is put in the antecedent of a conditional (P9) to argue that the presumptive belief in the existence of object moral facts is erroneous. The presumptive belief is the target of the error theory argument, and the combined argument from relativity and argument from queerness presented here, form a valid argument that the presumptive belief is erroneous.

Mackie first presented the error theory argument in 1946 in "A Refutation of Morals." He expanded the argument in *Ethics: Inventing Right and Wrong* (30–42). The selections below are from the latter work. Mackie states that an error theory argument is required against moral objectivism:

> [T]he traditional moral concepts of the ordinary man as well as the main line of western philosophers are concepts of objective value. But it is precisely for this reason that linguistic and conceptual analysis are not enough. The claim to objectivity, however engrained in out language and thought, is not self-validating. But the denial of objective values will have to be put forward not as the result of an analytic approach, but as an 'error theory,' a theory that although most people in making moral judgments implicitly claim, among other things, to be pointing to something objectively prescriptive, these claims are all false. (*Ethics*, 35)

The argument from relativity follows:

> The argument from relativity has as its premiss the well-known variation in moral codes from one society to another and from one period to another, and also the differences in moral beliefs between different groups and classes within a complex community. Such variation is in itself merely a truth of descriptive morality, a fact of anthropology which entails neither first order nor second order ethical views. Yet it may indirectly support second order subjectivism: radical differences between first order moral apprehensions make it difficult to treat those judgments as apprehensions of objective truths. But it is not the mere occurrence of disagreements that tells against the objectivity of values. [...] Disagreement about moral codes seems to reflect people's adherence to and participation in different ways of life. The causal connection seems to be mainly that way round: it is that people approve of monogamy because they participate in a monogamous way of life rather than that they participate in a monogamous way of life because they approve of monogamy. (*Ethics*, 36)

Defenders of moral objectivism claim that moral relativity is explained by the application of objective moral principles to specific conditions rather than the nonexistence of objective moral principles. "It is easy to show,"

Mackie writes, "that such general principles, married with differing concrete circumstances, different existing social patterns, or different preferences, will beget different specific moral rules" (*Ethics*, 37). This argument fails, Mackie writes:

> [P]eople judge that some things are good or right, and others are bad or wrong, not because – or at any rate not only because – they exemplify some general principle for which widespread implicit acceptance could be claimed, but because something about those things arouses certain responses immediately in them, though they would arouse radically and irresolvably different responses in others. (*Ethics*, 37)

The argument from queerness:

> If there were objective values, then they would be entities or qualities or relations of a very strange sort, utterly different from anything else in the universe. Correspondingly, if we are aware of them, it would have to be by some special faculty of moral perception or intuition, utterly different from our ordinary ways of knowing anything else. [...] When we ask the awkward question, how we can be aware of this authoritative prescriptivity, of the truth of these distinctively ethical premises or of the cogency of this distinctively ethical pattern of reasoning, none of our ordinary accounts of sensory perception or introspection or the framing and confirming of explanatory hypotheses or inference or logical construction or conceptual analysis, or any combination of these, will provide a satisfactory answer; 'a special sort of intuition' is a lame answer, but it is the one to which the clear-headed objectivist is compelled to resort. (*Ethics*, 38)

P1. If ordinary language, commonsense morality, and philosophical theories indicate belief in objective moral facts, then there is a presumptive belief that objective moral facts exist.

P2. Ordinary language, commonsense morality, and philosophical theories indicate belief that objective moral facts exist.

　C1. There is a presumptive belief that objective moral facts exist (*modus ponens*, P1, P2).

P3. There is moral relativity among different societies and historical eras.

P4. Moral relativity is explained by either but not both of explanations (i) or (ii):

(i) People participate in different ways of life that lead them to believe that distinct moral rules are correct.

(ii) People apply objective moral principles to different circumstances.

P5. Explanation (i) is a better explanation of moral relativity than explanation (ii).

P6. If (i) explains moral relativity better than (ii), then the belief that objective moral facts exist is not justified.

> C2. The belief that objective moral facts exist is not justified (*modus ponens*, P5, P6).

P7. If there are objective moral values, then they are specifically moral entities or relations and we know of their existence by a specifically moral cognitive ability.

P8. There are no specifically moral entities or relations, and we have no specifically moral cognitive ability.

> C3. There are no objective moral values (*modus tollens*, P7, P8).
>
> C4. There are no objective moral values and the belief that objective moral facts exist is not justified (conjunction, C3, C2).

P9. If there are no objective values and the belief that objective moral facts exist is not justified, then the presumptive belief that objective moral facts exist is in error.

> C5. The presumptive belief that objective moral facts exist is in error (*modus ponens*, C4, P9).

P6*. If (i) explains moral disagreement better than (ii), then disbelief that objective moral facts exist is better justified than belief that moral facts exist.

> C2*. Disbelief that objective moral facts exist is better justified than belief that moral facts exist (*modus ponens*, C2, P5).

60

Moore's Open Question Argument

Bruno Verbeek

Moore, George E. *Principia Ethica*. Cambridge, UK: Cambridge University Press, 1903.

Frankena, W. K. "The Naturalistic Fallacy." *Mind* 48, 192 (1939): 464–77.

Miller, Alexander. *An Introduction to Contemporary Metaethics*. Cambridge, UK: Polity Press, 2003.

The Open Question Argument was first formulated by G. E. Moore in his *Principia Ethica* (1903). It marks the beginning of a branch of ethical theory now referred to as metaethics. One of the central problems in metaethics – or indeed the central problem for this sub-discipline – is an analysis of the central concepts and terms in ethics, such as 'ought' and 'good'. Moore argued that the property of goodness is an undefinable property. The reason, according to Moore, is that goodness is a simple, unanalyzable property. So-called "real definitions" of 'good', which attempt to define 'good' in terms of a kind with specific characteristics, will fail. Anyone who claims to give a definition of 'goodness' is attributing goodness to something rather than identifying what goodness is. Moral naturalists – that is, those philosophers who believe that moral properties exist and can be studied by the sciences – are particularly guilty of this fallacy: hence the name "naturalistic fallacy." As a result, the argument is typically invoked to reject moral naturalism. However, Moore was quick to point out that theists who

Just the Arguments: 100 of the Most Important Arguments in Western Philosophy, First Edition. Edited by Michael Bruce and Steven Barbone.
© 2011 Blackwell Publishing Ltd. Published 2011 by Blackwell Publishing Ltd.

claim that good is what God commands are prone to the same fallacy. (Note that a common misunderstanding is to think that the naturalistic fallacy is the invalid inference of an "ought" statement from factual ["is"] premises.)

The test that Moore proposed to determine whether an attempt at defining 'good' is correct and not an attribution in disguise is the so-called "Open Question Argument." The basic idea is that a correct definition of a term cannot be rephrased as a question without betraying conceptual incompetence. For example, the definition of a 'bachelor' is "unmarried man of the marriageable age." If I rephrase this definition as an open question ('Is a bachelor an unmarried man of the marriageable age?'), it shows that I don't know what a bachelor is (or 'man' or 'married', etc.). However, suppose somebody offers the following definition of 'good': "the property we refer to as 'good' is the property of being pleasurable," or "good is pleasurable" for short. If you rephrase this as an open question: "Is good pleasurable?" this does not indicate that I don't know what 'good' or what 'pleasurable' is. I am asking a meaningful question. This demonstrates, according to Moore, that the proposed definition is (at best) in fact an attribution of goodness to all pleasurable things.

> My point is that 'good' is a simple notion, just as 'yellow' is a simple notion; that, just as you cannot, by any manner of means, explain to any one who does not already know it, what yellow is, so you cannot explain what good is. Definitions of the kind that I was asking for, definitions which describe the real nature of the object or notion denoted by a word, and which do not merely tell us what the word is used to mean, are only possible when the object or notion in question is something complex. (Moore, 7)

> When a man confuses two natural objects with one another, defining the one by the other, if for instance, he confuses himself, who is one natural object, with 'pleased' or with 'pleasure' which are others, then there is no reason to call the fallacy naturalistic. But if he confuses 'good,' which is not in the same sense a natural object, with any natural object whatever, then there is a reason for calling that a naturalistic fallacy; its being made with regard to 'good' marks it as something quite specific, and this specific mistake deserves a name because it is so common. (Moore, 13)

The general form of the Open Question Argument is the following:

P1. Suppose that the predicate 'good' is synonymous with some other predicate N (e.g., 'pleasurable').
P2. 'X has the property N' will mean 'X is good'.
    C1. Anybody who would ask whether an X with property N is good, would *ipso facto* betray conceptual confusion. She is unaware what 'good' means (symmetry of identity, P2).

P3. However, for every N it is always an open question whether an X with property N is good. It is a meaningful question that does not demonstrate conceptual confusion.

P4. If for every N it is always an open question whether an X with property N is good, then 'N' cannot be synonymous with 'good'.

   C2. 'N' cannot be synonymous with 'good' (*modus ponens*, P3, P4).

P5. If N cannot be synonymous with 'good', then only 'good' can be synonymous with 'good'; therefore, good is a simple (primitive) concept and cannot be defined.

   C3. Only 'good' can be synonymous with 'good'; therefore, good is a simple (primitive) concept and cannot be defined (*modus ponens*, C2, P5).

The Open Question Argument is a very influential argument. It has motivated very diverse metaethical theories, such as noncognitivism, intuitionism, and anti-realist theories. It still figures prominently in virtually all textbooks on metaethics. However, the general opinion by now is that the argument does not work against naturalism. First, this is because it insufficiently distinguishes between conceptual or semantic naturalism (where "good" is defined in natural terms) and metaphysical naturalism (where "good" is analyzed as a natural kind, much as "water" is analyzed as H_2O).

The Open Question Argument works perhaps against the first kind of naturalism but not the second kind of naturalism, and this is the kind of naturalism that most moral naturalists defend. Second, it is by no means obvious that somebody who rephrases a definition as a question is conceptually confused. Some correct definitions are extremely complex; for example, 'knowledge is justified true belief'. Suppose this were correct; it still is not dead obvious to any competent speaker of English (Miller). Third, the argument in a deep sense begs the question against the naturalist (Frankena).

61

Wolff's Argument for the Rejection of State Authority

Ben Saunders

Wolff, Robert Paul. *In Defense of Anarchism*. New York: Harper & Row, 1970.

Graham, Gordon. *The Case against the Democratic State: An Essay in Cultural Criticism*. Thorverton: Imprint Academic, 2002.

Reiman, Jeffrey H. *In Defense of Political Philosophy: A Reply to Robert Paul Wolff's In Defense of Anarchism*. New York: Harper & Row, 1972.

Anarchism is traditionally associated with statelessness or resistance to coercive laws. Robert Paul Wolff defends what is sometimes known as "philosophical anarchism." This is not a view about political arrangements as such but, rather, an argument about the duties of the individual. Wolff, drawing on a Kantian idea of self-legislation, argues that each individual has a duty to be autonomous (#55). From this, it follows that no one ought to accept the authority of others, including that of the state.

This does not mean that one must disobey all laws – indeed, one may well conform to all laws – but one must never comply. (To conform is merely to do what the law says, for any reason, whereas to comply is to do so because that is what the law says.) That is, one must not unquestioningly obey the law because it is law but must always decide what to do for oneself. A just state's laws may well accord with what one ought to do anyway, for reasons of morality or prudence, while the threat of punishment will give one further reasons to do what the law requires. There is, however,

Just the Arguments: 100 of the Most Important Arguments in Western Philosophy, First Edition. Edited by Michael Bruce and Steven Barbone.
© 2011 Blackwell Publishing Ltd. Published 2011 by Blackwell Publishing Ltd.

no fundamental difference between being told not to steal by the state and being told that by a friend – neither actually gives you the reason in question.

The argument appears valid, but there are some problems with the premises; in particular, specifying exactly what Wolff means by autonomy. It is not easy to find a consistent interpretation that explains both why it is so important as to be the individual's primary obligation and incompatible with accepting authority. Even if something is in our interests, we do not ordinarily suppose it to be a duty for us.

> The defining mark of the state is authority, the right to rule. The primary obligation of man is autonomy, the refusal to be ruled. [...] Insofar as a man fulfils his obligation to make himself the author of his decisions, he will resist the state's claim to have authority over him. That is to say, he will deny that he has a duty to obey the laws of the state simply because they are the laws. (Wolff, 18)

P1. We have a higher-order interest in autonomy.
P2. If something promotes our higher-order interests, we have a duty to do it.
   C1. We have a duty to be autonomous (*modus ponens*, P1, P2).
P3. If we have a duty to be autonomous, then autonomy requires that we decide what to do for ourselves.
   C2. We should decide what to do for ourselves (*modus ponens*, C1, P3).
P4. If we accept the authority of others, then we are not autonomous.
   C3. We should not accept the authority of others (*modus tollens*, C1, P4).
P5. If we accept the authority of the law, then we accept the authority of others.
   C4. We should not accept the authority of the law (*modus tollens*, C3, P5).

62

Nozick's Taxation Is Forced Labor Argument

Jason Waller

Nozick, Robert. *Anarchy, State, and Utopia.* New York: Basic Books, 1974.

One of the most contentious issues in contemporary debates about distributive justice concerns the redistribution of wealth. Should the state tax richer citizens in order to provide various benefits (schools, medical care, job training, cash payments, housing subsidies, etc.) to poorer citizens? The traditional distinction between the political "right" and "left" turns largely (although, not exclusively) on this question. One of the most influential libertarian arguments concerning the redistribution of wealth is offered by Robert Nozick, who argues that all forms of redistribution are morally wrong. His general strategy is to show that taxation is a kind of forced labor (i.e., slavery). The argument has been influential because it seems to turn on an uncontroversial definition of forced labor and the seemingly undeniable claim that all forms of forced labor are immoral. Nozick concludes that when the state redistributes wealth from the rich to the poor, the poor are in fact unjustly enslaving the rich. This form of slavery is, of course, quite mild by comparison to past forms, but (at least according to Nozick) it is immoral just the same.

> Taxation of earnings from labor is on a par with forced labor. Some persons find this claim obviously true: taking the earnings of n hours of labor

Just the Arguments: 100 of the Most Important Arguments in Western Philosophy,
First Edition. Edited by Michael Bruce and Steven Barbone.
© 2011 Blackwell Publishing Ltd. Published 2011 by Blackwell Publishing Ltd.

is like taking *n* hours from the person; it is like forcing the person to work n hours for another's purpose. Others find the claim absurd. But even these, if they object to forced labor, would oppose forcing unemployed hippies to work for the benefit of the needy. And they would also object to forcing each person to work five extra hours each week for the benefit of the needy. (Nozick, 169)

P1. Forced labor (i.e., slavery) occurs anytime one (i) must perform some labor under threat of severe punishment (pain, prison, death, etc.) and yet (ii) the benefits of one's labor go to someone else.

P2. All forms of forced labor are immoral.

P3. The state requires all working citizens to pay certain taxes in order to benefit the needy or face severe punishment (i.e., prison time).

P4. A is a working citizen.

   C1. If citizen A does not pay taxes, then the citizen will receive severe punishment; that is, she will go to prison (material implication, P3).

P5. If citizen A does not work extra hours, then the citizen will not be able to pay her taxes.

   C2. If citizen A does not work extra hours at her job, then she will receive severe punishment; that is, she will go to prison (hypothetical syllogism, C1, P5).

P6. Citizen A receives no benefits for the extra hours spent earning the money to pay her taxes because this money goes to the needy.

   C3. During the time when citizen A is earning the money needed to pay her taxes, the citizen is (i) performing some labor under threat of severe punishment [by C2] and (ii) the benefits of her labor go to someone else, namely, the needy (conjunction, C2, P6).

   C4. During the time when citizen A is earning the money needed to pay her taxes, she is undergoing forced labor; that is, slavery (*modus ponens*, P1, C3).

   C5. Taxing citizen A to help the needy is immoral (instantiation, P2, C4).

P7. This same argument can be made for each taxpayer.

   C6. All instances of taxation are immoral (instantiation, C5, P7).

63

Charity is Obligatory

Joakim Sandberg

Singer, Peter. "Famine, Affluence, and Morality." *Philosophy and Public Affairs* 1 (1972): 229–43.
____. *Practical Ethics*, 2nd edn. Cambridge, UK: Cambridge University Press, 1993.
Sidgwick, Henry. *The Methods of Ethics*. Indianapolis: Hackett, 1981.
Unger, Peter. *Living High & Letting Die: Our Illusion of Innocence*. New York: Oxford University Press, 1996.

Most people think that it is good or charitable to give money to humanitarian aid agencies that provide food or shelter to people in need, and hence such agencies are referred to as charities. But couldn't it actually be a moral duty to give money to such agencies; that is, morally wrong not to do so? According to the present argument, most famously formulated by Peter Singer, relatively affluent people of developed countries are indeed under a moral duty to give a significant amount of their money to humanitarian aid agencies.

The argument turns on the seemingly uncontroversial principle (which can be found already in Sidgwick, 253) that it is wrong not to help others when helping is easy and cheap. Singer sometimes defends this principle by way of an example: Wouldn't it be wrong to refuse to save a child from drowning in a pond, say, simply because one is hesitant to get one's clothes dirty? The argument can be taken to exemplify philosophical reasoning in its most interesting form: going from seemingly uncontroversial premises to a largely controversial or unexpected conclusion. The conclusion is controversial because it basically requires us to – instead of spending our money on things for ourselves that we don't really need (nice clothes, coffee, beer,

Just the Arguments: 100 of the Most Important Arguments in Western Philosophy, First Edition. Edited by Michael Bruce and Steven Barbone.
© 2011 Blackwell Publishing Ltd. Published 2011 by Blackwell Publishing Ltd.

CDs) – give most of it away to people in remote parts of the world. And we are not even allowed to feel good about doing so – what we normally perceive as charitable (and thus beyond the call of duty) is really just morally obligatory. A number of slightly different formulations of the argument can be found in the literature, but we present it in its original form. All of the premises below have been scrutinized by critics in attempts to defuse the argument.

> I begin with the assumption that suffering and death from lack of food, shelter, and medical care are bad. I think most people will agree about this, although one may reach the same view by different routes. [. . .] My next point is this: if it is in our power to prevent something bad from happening, without thereby sacrificing anything of comparable moral importance, we ought, morally, to do it. By "without sacrificing anything of comparable moral importance" I mean without causing anything else comparably bad to happen, or doing something that is wrong in itself, or failing to promote some moral good, comparable in significance to the bad thing that we can prevent. This principle seems almost as uncontroversial as the last one [. . . but . . .] The uncontroversial appearance of the principle just stated is deceptive. If it were acted upon [. . .] our lives, our society, and our world would be fundamentally changed. [. . .] The traditional distinction between duty and charity cannot be drawn, or at least, not in the place we normally draw it. [. . .] When we buy new clothes not to keep ourselves warm but to look "well-dressed" we are not providing for any important need. We would not be sacrificing anything significant if we were to continue to wear our old clothes, and give the money to famine relief. By doing so, we would be preventing another person from starving. It follows from what I have said earlier that we ought to give money away, rather than spend it on clothes which we do not need to keep us warm. To do so is not charitable, or generous. Nor is it the kind of act which philosophers and theologians have called "supererogatory" – an act which it would be good to do, but not wrong not to do. On the contrary, we ought to give the money away, and it is wrong not to do so. (Singer "Famine," 231–5)

P1. Suffering and death from lack of food, shelter, and medical care are bad.
P2. If it is in one's power to prevent something bad from happening, without thereby sacrificing anything of comparable moral importance, one ought, morally, to do it.
　　C1. If it is in one's power to prevent suffering and death from lack of food, shelter, and medical care, without thereby sacrificing anything of comparable moral importance, one ought, morally, to do it (instantiation & *modus ponens*, P1, P2).
P3. By giving money to humanitarian aid agencies, one can prevent suffering and death from lack of food, shelter, and medical care.

C2. If one can give money to humanitarian aid agencies without thereby sacrificing anything of comparable moral importance (to suffering and death from lack of food, shelter, and medical care) one ought, morally, to do it (instantiation and *modus ponens*, C1, P3).

P4. We can give a substantial amount of our money away by simply giving up buying things that we do not really need; that is, without sacrificing anything of moral importance comparable to suffering and death from lack of food, shelter, and medical care.

C3. We ought, morally, to give a substantial amount of our money to humanitarian aid agencies (*modus ponens*, C2, P4).

64

The Repugnant Conclusion

Joakim Sandberg

Parfit, Derek. *Reasons and Persons*. Oxford: Clarendon Press, 1984.
Ryberg, Jesper, and Torbjörn Tännsjö (eds.). *The Repugnant Conclusion: Essays on Population Ethics*. Dordrecht: Kluwer, 2004.

When philosophers think about future generations and what sort of world we should try to create, they sometimes ponder issues in so-called population ethics. For example, "Would it be better if, in the future, a greater rather than fewer number of people lived?" and "Does the answer to this question depend further on who these people are and/or their quality of life?" The seminal work in this field is Derek Parfit's *Reasons and Persons*, and the present argument is its undisputed highlight. The argument addresses the issue of what the relative values are of the quantity of lives lived versus the quality of these lives and a seemingly straightforward position on this issue – the position that classical utilitarians take – is that quantity and quality should be given equal value.

Utilitarians typically compound these two factors into a measure of the overall utility, or "quantity of whatever makes life worth living," in a population. Parfit's argument against this view, however, takes the form of a *reductio ad absurdum*: If any loss in the quality of lives can be compensated for by a sufficient increase in the quantity of lives lived, then the best outcome could well be one in which an enormous amount of people lived lives that are barely worth living. This is what Parfit calls the "Repugnant Conclusion." Many ways of trying to get around the conclusion can be found in the literature. However, it may be noted that it has been surprisingly difficult to develop a theory that avoids this conclusion and at the same time doesn't imply equally counterintuitive conclusions. The field of population ethics thus continues to be challenging.

Just the Arguments: 100 of the Most Important Arguments in Western Philosophy, First Edition. Edited by Michael Bruce and Steven Barbone.
© 2011 Blackwell Publishing Ltd. Published 2011 by Blackwell Publishing Ltd.

In B there are twice as many people living as in A, and these people are all worse off than everyone in A. But the lives of those in B, compared with those in A, are more than half as much worth living. [. . .] Which would be the better outcome? [. . .] I can now state the [. . .] Impersonal Total Principle: If other things are equal, the best outcome is the one in which there would be the greatest quantity of whatever makes life worth living. [. . .] Z is some enormous population whose members have lives that are not much above the level where life ceases to be worth living. [. . .] In each of these lives there is very little happiness. But, if the numbers are large enough, this is the outcome with the greatest total sum of happiness. [. . .] The Impersonal Total Principle then implies The Repugnant Conclusion: For any possible population of at least ten billion people, all with a very high quality of life, there must be some much larger imaginable population whose existence, if other things are equal, would be better, even though its members have lives that are barely worth living. As my choice of name suggests, I find this conclusion very hard to accept. [. . .] If we are convinced that Z is worse than A, we have strong grounds for resisting principles which imply that Z is better. We have strong grounds for resisting the Impersonal Total Principle. (Parfit, 385–90)

P1. The "quantity of whatever makes life worth living" in a given population is a function of the quantity of its members and their quality of life.

P2. One can increase the quantity of whatever makes life worth living in a given population by simply adding people whose lives are worth living.

P3. If in one of two outcomes the quality of lives in a population is lower, the quantity of whatever makes life worth living can still be higher if sufficiently many people are added whose lives are worth living.

    C1. If A is a population of at least ten billion people with a very high quality of life, there must be some much larger imaginable population, Z, where the quantity of whatever makes life worth living would be greater even though its members have lives that are barely worth living (instantiation, P3).

P4. If, other things being equal, the best outcome would be the one in which there is the greatest quantity of whatever makes life worth living, one outcome is better than another if the quantity of whatever makes life worth living is greater.

    C2. If, other things being equal, the best outcome would be the one in which there is the greatest quantity of whatever makes life worth living, Z would be better than A (*modus ponens*, C1, P4).

P5. Z is worse than A.

    C3. It is not the case that, other things being equal, the best outcome would be the one in which there is the greatest quantity of whatever makes life worth living (*modus tollens*, C2, P5).

65

Taurek on Numbers Don't Count

Ben Saunders

Taurek, John. "Should the Numbers Count?" *Philosophy and Public Affairs* 6 (1977): 293–316.

Parfit, Derek. "Innumerate Ethics." *Philosophy and Public Affairs* 7 (1978): 285–301.

Sidgwick, Henry. *The Methods of Ethics.* Indianapolis: Hackett, 1981.

Wasserman, David, and Alan Strudler. "Can a Nonconsequentialist Count Lives?" *Philosophy and Public Affairs* 31 (2003): 71–94.

Consequentialists think that we have a moral duty to bring about the best outcomes possible. The idea of the overall best outcome, however, typically involves summing good and bad effects distributed over different individuals. It is therefore frequently objected that consequentialism is indifferent to the separateness of persons, ignoring the distribution of good and bad consequences and implying that a great loss to one person could be justified by smaller benefits to a great many others.

Nonconsequentialists have often argued that we should not engage in this interpersonal aggregation – that it makes no sense to speak of what's good or bad from "the point of view of the universe" (Sidgwick, 382). Sometimes, however, rejecting consequentialism leads to positions that conflict with common sense. In this much discussed article, Taurek rejects the idea that we have any obligation to save five people rather than one other, whom he calls "David." He argues that since there is no impersonal perspective from which we can judge either outcome better than the other, we are permitted to choose to bring about whichever outcome we prefer

Just the Arguments: 100 of the Most Important Arguments in Western Philosophy, First Edition. Edited by Michael Bruce and Steven Barbone.

– though if we want to show equal concern to all involved, he suggests that we toss a coin so everyone has a 50 percent chance of survival.

Not all aspects of Taurek's argument are entirely clear. For example, interpreters differ as to whether he denies any notion of impersonal "betterness" (even so-called Pareto improvements; i.e., those that are better for someone and worse for no one) or only denies the intelligibility of impersonal claims where there is a conflict of interests between two parties. Nonetheless, much ink has been spilled attempting to show that nonconsequentialists can resist his conclusion and justify saving a larger group of people without engaging in morally suspect aggregation.

> The claim that one ought to save the many instead of the few was made to rest on the claim that, other things being equal, it is a worse thing that these five persons should die than that this one should. It is this evaluative judgement that I cannot accept. I do not wish to say in this situation that it is a worse thing were these five persons to die and David to live than it is or would be were David to die and these five to continue living. I do not wish to say this unless I am prepared to qualify it by explaining to whom or for whom or relative to what purpose it is or would be a worse thing. (Taurek, 303–4)

P1. If we call one state of affairs (impersonally) better than another, then one ought (morally) to prefer it.

P2. It is not the case that David ought (morally) to prefer that he die so five others can be saved than the reverse (they die so he can be saved).

  C1. It is not the case that David's dying so five others can be saved is (impersonally) better than the reverse (they die so he can be saved) (*modus tollens*, P1, P2).

P3. If one state of affairs is not better than another, one is not required to bring it about.

  C2. David is not required to bring it about that he dies so five others can be saved (*modus ponens*, C1, P3).

P4. If it is permissible for David to choose to save himself, it is also permissible for a third party to save David.

  C3. It is permissible for a third party to save David (*modus ponens*, C2, P4).

P5. If it is permissible to save one rather than five, there cannot be any general obligation to save the greater number (in conflict cases).

  C4. There is no general obligation to save the greater number (in conflict cases) (*modus ponens*, C3, P5).

66

Parfit's Leveling Down Argument against Egalitarianism

Ben Saunders

Parfit, Derek. "Equality or Priority?" *Ratio* 10 (1997): 202–21. Originally published separately as "The 1991 Lindley Lecture." Lawrence: Department of Philosophy, University of Kansas, 1995. Reprinted in *The Ideal of Equality*, edited by M. Clayton and A. Williams. London: Palgrave Macmillan, 2002.

Frankfurt, Harry. "Equality as a Moral Ideal" *Ethics* 98 (1987): 21–42.
Jerome, Jerome K. "The New Utopia," in *Cultural Notes* no. 14. London: Libertarian Alliance, 1987.
Temkin, Larry. *Inequality*. Oxford: Oxford University Press, 1993.

Almost everyone these days affirms the moral equality of persons. Egalitarians hold that this has implications for distributive justice – that people's material conditions should be equalized, at least insofar as they are not themselves responsible for being better or worse off than others. Many philosophers have explored how best to interpret these egalitarian commitments; for instance, over what goods ought to be equalized and whether people ought to be made equal in outcomes or merely opportunities. Some, however, have rejected the idea that equality *per se* is of any moral significance. Harry Frankfurt, for instance, has argued that all that matters is that everyone has enough, citing the fact that we don't feel the need to redistribute from billionaires to millionaires. He claims that our concern is not really with inequality, but only with poverty.

Just the Arguments: 100 of the Most Important Arguments in Western Philosophy, First Edition. Edited by Michael Bruce and Steven Barbone.
© 2011 Blackwell Publishing Ltd. Published 2011 by Blackwell Publishing Ltd.

Frankfurt shows that we do indeed care about sufficiency, maybe more than about equality, but not that we do not care about equality as well. Derek Parfit, however, has advanced a famous argument to show that a commitment to equality has perverse consequences and ought to be rejected. He argues that anyone committed to equality must think that it is – at least in this one respect – better to bring everyone down to the same level (something he calls "leveling down") than to accept an inequality. This, however, seems perverse if no one is made better off as a result.

Suppose we think it unjust that some people are born with two healthy eyes and others with only one or none. In the absence of the technology required to perform eye transplants, there is nothing that we can do to make the blind better off. Thus, the only way to achieve equality between the blind and the sighted would be to blind those who can presently see (see Jerome's short story, "The New Utopia," which describes a dystopian future where such practices are carried out). Represented numerically, we could say that egalitarians think there is something better about a world where everyone has four units of good than a world where some have five and some have seven since, although everyone is better off in the latter world, it is unequal.

Note that Parfit is not saying that egalitarians are committed to this course of action all things considered, since most subscribe to values other than equality and think it is better for people to be able to see than not. What he is saying, however, is that *qua* egalitarians they are committed to accepting that this would be in one way good – there is some reason to do it – and he finds even this absurd. How could it be in any way good if it is, by hypothesis, worse for some people and better for none? (Temkin calls this premise, numbered P5 below, that the world cannot be better or worse without being better or worse for any individual, "the Slogan" and argues powerfully against it.)

While there are some who are completely untroubled by material inequalities between persons, no matter how large, Parfit's own positive view – which he calls the "Priority View" or prioritarianism, effectively a form of weighted utilitarianism – would be regarded by many as broadly egalitarian. Parfit thinks that it is morally more important to benefit someone the worse off he is. This view does not, however, require us to make comparisons between different people or posit that equality in itself has value, even if it will tend to have equalizing consequences in practice (because, where we can benefit one of two people, we ought to benefit the worse off until she becomes better off than the other).

> For true Egalitarians, equality has intrinsic value. [. . .] On the widest version of this view, any inequality is bad. It is bad, for example, that some people are sighted and others are blind. We would therefore have a reason,

if we could, to take single eyes from some of the sighted and give them to the blind [. . .]. Suppose that those who are better off suffer some misfortune, so that they become as badly off as everyone else. Since these events would remove the inequality, they must be in one way welcome [. . .] even though they would be worse for some people, and better for no one. This implication seems to many to be quite absurd. I call this the Levelling Down Objection. (Parfit *Idea*, 86, 97, 98)

P1. Egalitarianism implies that it is *pro tanto* (in one way) good to eliminate inequality.

P2. Inequality can be eliminated by bringing the worse-off up, and inequality can be eliminated by bringing the better-off down.

C1. Egalitarianism implies that it is *pro tanto* good to bring the worse-off up and that it is *pro tanto* good to bring the better-off down (conjunction, P1, P2).

C2. Egalitarianism implies that it is *pro tanto* good to bring the better-off down (simplification, C1).

P3. Simply bringing the better-off down does not make anyone better off.

P4. If no one is made better off, one state of affairs cannot be *pro tanto* better than another.

C3. Simply bringing the better-off down cannot be *pro tanto* better (*modus ponens*, P3, P4).

P5. If Egalitarianism is true, then it is *pro tanto* good to bring the better-off down.

C4. Egalitarianism is false (*modus tollens*, P5, C3).

67

Nozick's Wilt Chamberlain Argument

Fabian Wendt[1]

Nozick, Robert. *Anarchy, State, and Utopia*. New York: Basic Books, 1974.

Cohen, Gerald. "Robert Nozick and Wilt Chamberlain: How Patterns Preserve Liberty," in *Self-Ownership, Freedom, and Equality*. Cambridge, UK: Cambridge University Press, 1995.

Feser, Edward. *On Nozick*. Belmont, CA: Wadsworth, 2003.

Kymlicka, Will. *Contemporary Political Philosophy*. Oxford: Oxford University Press, 1990/2001.

Wolff, Jonathan. *Robert Nozick: Property, Justice, and the Minimal State*. Cambridge, UK: Polity Press, 1991.

Robert Nozick's Wilt Chamberlain Argument is notorious. It is very simple, and its premises sound fairly reasonable, but its conclusion is perplexing: Egalitarian (and other patterned) theories of justice are supposedly not acceptable. Many philosophers are convinced that there is something wrong with the argument, but it is not so easy to find a flaw in it. Nozick presents the argument in *Anarchy, State, and Utopia* after having introduced his own theory of justice, the entitlement theory. According to this theory, every

---

[1] I would like to thank Ali Behboud and Thomas Schramme for helpful comments on earlier versions of this text.

Just the Arguments: 100 of the Most Important Arguments in Western Philosophy, First Edition. Edited by Michael Bruce and Steven Barbone.
© 2011 Blackwell Publishing Ltd. Published 2011 by Blackwell Publishing Ltd.

distribution of property that arose from voluntary, free transfers of justly acquired property is just. The entitlement theory is, in Nozick's terminology, unpatterned; for a distribution of property to be just, it does not have to fit any particular pattern. The entitlement theory leads to a libertarian position in political philosophy, condemning redistributive welfare states as unjust. In contrast, egalitarians hold that a just state has to redistribute property in order to achieve an egalitarian distributional pattern in society. The egalitarian pattern can take many different forms. An egalitarian theory of justice may, for example, aim for equality of opportunity for welfare or, as in John Rawls' theory of justice, aim for equality of resources except when inequalities are to the benefit of the least advantaged.

The Wilt Chamberlain Argument is designed to show that all patterned theories of justice, including egalitarian theories as the most prominent subclass, are intuitively not acceptable. The basic outline of the argument is as follows. Intuitively, it is morally unproblematic freely to transfer property to other persons, for example, to pay Wilt Chamberlain for watching him play basketball. But free transfers of property will inevitably upset any distributional pattern. Liberty upsets patterns, as the title of the corresponding chapter in *Anarchy, State, and Utopia* says. If this is right, how could justice demand preserving a patterned distribution of property?

If patterned theories of justice are indeed not acceptable, then Nozick's unpatterned entitlement theory of justice would constitute the obvious alternative. But maybe this is too hasty. It seems to me that the Wilt Chamberlain Argument is most appealing when directed against egalitarian theories only, not against any form of patterned theories. In particular, premise P2 in the formalized version below is less convincing if D_1 in premise P1 is not specified as an egalitarian distributional pattern but as, for example, a distributional pattern prescribing that nobody should fall below a certain baseline of welfare. Nevertheless, a refutation of egalitarian theories of justice alone would still be a provocative result. Egalitarian critics of the argument will then probably have to reject either premise P3 or P4. If one wants a less limited version of the argument, one can simply substitute "egalitarian" by "patterned" in P1 and call it "patterned principle" instead of "equality principle."

> It is not clear how those holding alternative conceptions of distributive justice can reject the entitlement conception of justice in holdings. For suppose a distribution favored by one of these non-entitlement conceptions is realized. Let us suppose it is your favorite one and let us call this distribution D_1; perhaps everyone has an equal share, perhaps shares vary in accordance with some dimension you treasure. Now suppose that Wilt Chamberlain is greatly in demand by basketball teams, being a great gate attraction. (Also suppose contracts run for a year, with players being free agents.) He signs the following sort of contract with a team: In each home game, twenty-five cents from the

price of each ticket of admission goes to him. (We ignore the question of whether he is "gouging" the owners, letting them look for themselves.) The season starts, and people cheerfully attend his team's games; they buy their tickets, each time dropping a separate twenty-five cents of their admission price into a special box with Chamberlain's name on it. They are excited about seeing him play; it is worth the total admission price to them. Let us suppose that in one season one million persons attend his home games, and Wilt Chamberlain winds up with $250,000, a much larger sum than the average income and larger even than anyone else has. Is he entitled to this income? Is this new distribution D_2 unjust? If so, why? [...] If D_1 was a just distribution, and people voluntarily moved from it to D_2, transferring parts of their shares they were given under D_1 (what was it for if not to do something with?), isn't D_2 also just? (Nozick, 160–1)

P1. A society is just if and only if the distribution of property in the society has a certain egalitarian distributional structure D_1 (Equality Principle assumption).

P2. When people freely transfer their property to other persons, they change the distributional structure D_1 into a new distributional structure.

P3. It is not unjust for people freely to transfer their property to other persons (Liberty Principle).

P4. Whatever distributional structure results from a just distributional structure by not-unjust steps is itself just (Preservation Principle).

   C1. It is not unjust for people freely to transfer their property to other persons and whatever distributional structure results from a just distributional structure by not-unjust steps is itself just (conjunction, P3, P4).

P5. If P2 is true, then the following concretion of P2 is true as well: If people start from a just distributional structure like, presumably, D_1 and then freely transfer their property to Wilt Chamberlain, then the distributional structure in the society will have changed to a new distributional structure D_2.

   C2. If people start from a just distributional structure like, presumably, D_1 and then freely transfer their property to Wilt Chamberlain, then the distributional structure in the society will have changed to a new distributional structure D_2 (*modus ponens*, P2, P5).

P6. If C1 is true, then the following conditional is true as well: If people start from a just distributional structure like, presumably, D_1 and then freely transfer their property to Wilt Chamberlain, then the resulting distributional structure will be just.

   C3. If people start from a just distributional structure like, presumably, D_1 and then freely transfer their property to Wilt Chamberlain, then the resulting distributional structure will be just (*modus ponens*, C1, P6).

C4. If people start from a just distributional structure like, presumably, D_1 and then freely transfer their property to Wilt Chamberlain, then the distributional structure in the society will have changed to a new distributional structure D_2 and if people start from a just distributional structure like, presumably, D_1 and then freely transfer their property to Wilt Chamberlain, then the resulting distributional structure will be just (conjunction, C2, C3).

P7. If C4 is true, then D_2 is just.

C5. D_2 is just (*modus ponens*, C4, P7).

P8. If P1 is true, then D_2 is not just.

C6. D_2 is not just (*modus ponens*, P1, P8).

C7. D_2 is just and D_2 is not just (conjunction, C5, C6).

C8. P1 (the Equality Principle) is false (*reductio*, P1–C7).

68

Liberal Feminism

Julinna C. Oxley

Okin, Susan Moller. *Justice, Gender, and the Family*. New York: Basic Books, 1989.

Mill, John Stuart. *The Subjection of Women*, edited by Susan M. Okin, Indianapolis: Hackett, 1869/1988.
Wollstonecraft, Mary. *A Vindication of the Rights of Woman*. London: Joseph Johnson, 1792/London: Penguin, 2004.

First articulated in the late eighteenth century, liberal feminism is a political philosophy whose express aim is to free women from oppressive gender roles and achieve sexual equality (also called gender justice). Although women's social situation changes from one generation to the next – due in large part to the influence of liberal feminists – the message of liberal feminism remains the same: women, as rational human beings, are deserving of the same social and political rights as men, and gender justice is best achieved by modifying existing social institutions and political systems. The political agenda of liberal feminism addresses present-day inequalities: early liberal feminists sought to gain the right to vote and equal access to education, while contemporary liberal feminists aim to secure equal social, political, and economic opportunities, equal civil liberties, and sexual freedoms.

Perhaps the most controversial aspect of feminism is its claim that women are socially oppressed, especially since Western women in the twenty-first century do not appear to be oppressed. Yet contemporary liberal feminists contend that society is structured in ways that favor men.

Just the Arguments: 100 of the Most Important Arguments in Western Philosophy, First Edition. Edited by Michael Bruce and Steven Barbone.
© 2011 Blackwell Publishing Ltd. Published 2011 by Blackwell Publishing Ltd.

Many liberal feminists (such as Mill in the nineteenth century and Okin in the twentieth) argue that the primary source of woman's subordination is her social role in the family, not just her biological role in reproduction or the male tendency to sexual violence (other oft-cited explanations for why women are the "weaker" sex). Since liberal feminism is the oldest version of feminism, it is the target of much criticism, especially by other feminists who argue that liberal feminists overlook differences of race, socioeconomic status, and sexual orientation relevant to an accurate assessment of women's situation.

While liberal feminism is an active political movement with a variety of participants, all feminists agree that the aims of liberal feminism remain unfulfilled worldwide. For this reason, liberal feminism will continue to attract zealous adherents as well as vocal detractors.

Marriage continues the cycle of inequality set in motion by the anticipation of marriage and the related sex segregation of the workplace. Partly because of society's assumptions about gender, but also because women, on entering marriage, tend already to be disadvantaged members of the work force, married women are likely to start out with less leverage in the relationship than their husbands [. . .] In many marriages, partly because of discrimination at work and the wage gap between the sexes, wives (despite initial personal ambitions and even when they are full-time wage workers) come to perceive themselves as benefiting from giving priority to their husbands' careers. Hence they have little incentive to question the traditional division of labor in the household. This in turn limits their own commitment to wage work and their incentive and leverage to challenge the gender structure of the workplace. Experiencing frustration and lack of control at work, those who thus turn toward domesticity, while often resenting the lack of respect our society gives to full-time mothers, may see the benefits of domestic life as greater than the costs.

Thus, the inequalities between the sexes in the workplace and at home reinforce and exacerbate each other. It is not necessary to choose between two alternative, competing explanations of the inequalities between men and women in the workplace [. . .]. When the pivotal importance of gender-structured marriage and the expectation of it are acknowledged, these explanations can be seen, rather, as complementary reasons for women's inequality. *A cycle of power relations and decisions pervades both family and workplace, and the inequalities of each reinforce those that already exist in the other.* Only with the recognition of this truth will we be able to begin to confront the changes that need to occur if women are to have a real opportunity to be equal participants in either sphere [. . .].

The family is the linchpin of gender, reproducing it from one generation to the next [. . .] family life as typically practiced in our society is not just, either to women or to children. Moreover, it is not conducive to the rearing of citizens with a strong sense of justice. In spite of all the rhetoric about equality between the sexes, the traditional or quasi-traditional division of family labor still prevails [. . .]. Any just and fair solution to the urgent problem of women's and children's vulnerability must encourage and facilitate the equal sharing by men and women of paid and unpaid work, of productive and reproductive labor [. . .]. A just future would be one without gender. (Okin, 146–71)

P1. If a society is just and fair to women, then men and women will have equal social, political, and economic rights, liberties, and opportunities.
P2. But in many Western societies, men and women do not have equal social, political, and economic rights, liberties, and opportunities.
  C1. Many Western societies are not just and fair to women (*modus tollens*, P1, P2).
P3. If a society is to be just and fair to women, then it ought not promote or engage in practices that contribute to women's oppression.
P4. If a society does not promote or engage in practices that contribute to women's oppression, then its social, political, and legal institutions should be modified so as to eradicate features that contribute to women's oppression.
  C2. If a society is to be just and fair to women, then [Western] societies that seek gender justice should modify social, political, and legal institutions and eradicate features that contribute to women's disadvantage (hypothetical syllogism, P3, P4).

The Nature of Women's Disadvantage and Oppression

P1. If men and women do not spend the same amount of time performing domestic duties or doing unpaid labor in the home (including cooking, cleaning, raising children, etc.), then there will be an unequal distribution of labor in the family.
P2. In a traditional family, men and women do not spend the same amount of time performing unpaid labor in the home – women perform most of the domestic duties.
  C1. There is an unequal distribution of unpaid labor in the traditional family (*modus ponens*, P1, P2).
P3. If there is an unequal distribution of unpaid labor in the family, then this situation is unjust to women because the work is assigned in virtue of individual innate characteristics, and has long-term repercussions that make the woman vulnerable.
  C2. The traditional family is unjust to women because the work is assigned in virtue of individual innate characteristics, and has long-

term repercussions that make the woman vulnerable (*modus ponens*, P3, C1).

The Source of Women's Disadvantage and Oppression

P2. (repeated): In a traditional family, men and women do not spend the same amount of time performing domestic duties – women perform most of the domestic duties.

P5. Women perform the majority of domestic duties because men expect women to do most of the work in the home and are reluctant to contribute to household labor. These expectations inform the "gendered structure" of the family (causal reasoning for P2).

P6. If women spend more time working in the home than men, then they have less time to take advantage of opportunities to advance in the workplace than men do.

C3. Women have less time and thus fewer opportunities to advance in the workplace (*modus ponens*, P6, P2).

P7. If women have less time and thus fewer opportunities to advance in the workplace as men, they do not have equality of opportunity in social and political life.

C4. Women do not have equality of opportunity in social and political life (*modus ponens*, P7, C3).

P8. Women will have equality of opportunity in social and political life only if they do not perform the majority of the unpaid labor in the home (implied by P5–C4).

P9. For women not to perform a majority of the unpaid labor in the home, then men will have to be responsible for at least half of domestic duties (by definition).

C5. If domestic duties are defined by the "gendered structure" of the family, then men are not responsible for at least half of domestic duties (substitution, P5, P9).

C6. When men are not responsible for at least half of the domestic duties (the "gendered structure" of the traditional family), then women cannot achieve equality of opportunity in social and political life (*modus ponens*, P5, C5).

Achieving Gender Justice

P10. Gender roles, including norms and expectations regarding men's and women's roles in the family and in society, are learned in the family.

P11. If children are raised in traditional "gender-structured" families where women lack power and independence, then the children learn that inequalities between men and women are the norm and that they can be expected in social life (follows from P10).

P12. Many children are now raised in traditional "gender-structured" families where women are vulnerable because they lack power and independence.

C7. Many children will learn that inequalities between men and women are the norm, and that they can be expected in social life (*modus ponens*, P11, P12).

P13. If many children will learn that inequalities between men and women are the norm and that they can be expected in social life, then when they grow up and start their own families, many people will perpetuate the idea that inequalities between men and women are the norm and that this can be expected in social life (i.e., the cycle of inequality).

C8. When they grow up and start their own families, many people will perpetuate the idea that inequalities between men and women are the norm and that this can be expected in social life (i.e., the cycle of inequality) (*modus ponens*, P13, C7).

P14. A just and fair society seeks to eradicate inequality in its existing institutions, especially ones that perpetuate inequality.

P15. If the family is a social institution, then it should be an egalitarian structure.

P16. If the family is to be an egalitarian structure, then men and women will share equally the paid and unpaid work, productive and reproductive labor.

C9. If the family is a social institution, then men and women in the family will share equally the paid and unpaid work, productive and reproductive labor (hypothetical syllogism, P15, P16).

P17. The family is a social institution.

C10. A just society will encourage and facilitate the equal sharing by men and women of paid and unpaid work, of productive and reproductive labor (*modus ponens*, C9, P17).

P18. If a just society encourages and facilitates the equal sharing by men and women of paid and unpaid work, and of productive and reproductive labor, then it will do so by eliminating traditional gender roles and their corresponding expectations regarding work and family life.

C11. A just society will eliminate traditional gender roles and their corresponding expectations regarding work and family life; for example, by passing social policies that facilitate equally shared parenting, reorganizing work life to make parenting a priority, and educating children regarding the problems with gender stereotyping (*modus ponens*, P18, C10).

69

Moral Status of Animals from Marginal Cases

Julia Tanner

Bernstein, Mark. "Marginal Cases and Moral Relevance." *Journal of Social Philosophy* 33, 4 (2002): 523–39.

Narveson, Jan. "Animal Rights." *Canadian Journal of Philosophy* VII (1977): 161–78.

Porphyry. *On Abstinence from Animal Food*, translated by Thomas Taylor. London: Centaur Press, 1965.

Singer, Peter. *Animal Liberation*. London: Pimlico, 1995.

It matters a great deal whether animals have moral status. If animals have moral status, it may be wrong for us to use them as we currently do – hunting, farming, eating, and experimenting on them. The argument from marginal cases provides us with a reason to think that some animals have moral status that is equal to that of "marginal" humans.

Many of those who deny that animals have moral status argue that moral status depends on rational agency or the ability to use language or some other capacity/capacities that only humans have. There are many such capacities, so I shall use capacity X to stand in for them all.

But pinning moral status on X (rational agency or any capacity that is typical of normal adult humans) is problematic. Not all humans will have X (not all humans are normal adult humans). There are some humans, known as marginal humans, who do not possess, or do not fully possess, X. The reason that such humans are called "marginal cases" is that they

Just the Arguments: 100 of the Most Important Arguments in Western Philosophy, First Edition. Edited by Michael Bruce and Steven Barbone.

are atypical insofar as they do not possess the all-important capacity X. There are, broadly speaking, three types of marginal humans: pre-X – they have yet to acquire X, such as children; post-X – they have permanently lost X due to illness, accident, or old age; and non-X – they do not, never have had, and never will have X.

Those who argue that moral status depends on X are, therefore, faced with a dilemma. Either, they must admit that marginal humans lack moral status because they lack X, or they must concede that moral status depends on something other than X (I will call this "Z"). But some animals will also have Z. Thus, it must be conceded that those animals (with Z) have moral status too. This is the argument from marginal cases.

The argument from marginal cases has roots in ancient Greece. Porphyry was the first to make it (III. 19). But the term "argument from marginal cases" was coined more recently by Narveson (an opponent of the argument) (164). Peter Singer gives one of the earliest contemporary formulations (see below). Following Singer's version is a generic version of the argument.

> [H]uman beings are not equal [. . .] if we seek some characteristic that all of them possess [. . . it] must be a kind of lowest common denominator, pitched so low that no human being lacks it. The catch is that any such characteristic [. . .] possessed by all human beings will not be possessed only by human beings. (Singer, 237)

P1. If there is no morally relevant difference between marginal humans and some nonhuman animals, then if marginal humans have moral status, so do some nonhuman animals.
P2. There is no morally relevant difference between marginal humans and some nonhuman animals.
    C1. If marginal humans have moral status, then so do some nonhuman animals (*modus ponens*, P1, P2).
P3. Marginal humans have moral status.
    C2. Some nonhuman animals have moral status (*modus ponens*, C1, P3).

70

The Ethical Vegetarianism Argument

Robert L. Muhlnickel

Bentham, Jeremy. *The Classical Utilitarians*, edited by J. Troyer. Indianapolis: Hackett, 2003.

DeGrazia, David. *Taking Animals Seriously: Mental Life and Moral Status*. Cambridge, UK: Cambridge University Press, 1996.

Rachels, James. "The Basic Argument for Vegetarianism," in *The Legacy of Socrates*, edited by S. Rachels, 3–15. New York: Columbia University Press, 2007.

Singer, Peter. "All Animals Are Equal." *Philosophical Exchange* 1, 5 (1974): 103–16. Reprinted in *Unsanctifying Human Life*, edited by H. Kuhse. Oxford: Blackwell, 2002.

____. *Animal Liberation*. New York: Harper Perennial, 2009.

The ethics of relations between human and nonhuman animals is a minor topic in the history of Western moral philosophy. Philosophers have given it more attention since the 1970s, when Peter Singer's work prompted much thinking about the interests of nonhuman animals. Singer's signature claim is that the same interests of nonhuman animals and humans deserve the same degree of moral consideration. At the time, he pressed the analogy with contemporary liberation movements, saying that nonhuman animals were unfairly denied moral status just as women and people of color had been unfairly denied moral status. However, Singer's judgments of social status and claims of oppression contribute less to its philosophical merit

---

Just the Arguments: 100 of the Most Important Arguments in Western Philosophy, First Edition. Edited by Michael Bruce and Steven Barbone.
© 2011 Blackwell Publishing Ltd. Published 2011 by Blackwell Publishing Ltd.

than the impetus he gave to re-thinking the criteria of basic moral status. The argument presented here makes claims about moral status explicit.

This argument has had more influence among nonphilosophers than any philosophical argument of the past fifty years, with the possible exceptions of John Rawls' *A Theory of Justice* and Thomas Kuhn's *The Structure of Scientific Revolutions* (#90). Although the argument concludes that vegetarianism is morally required, the considerations adduced in its premises can be extended to moral judgments about using nonhuman animals in research, manufacturing, entertainment, and companionship.

The argument for ethical vegetarianism starts by asserting that the ability to suffer is the ground of basic moral consideration. A being deserves basic moral consideration if it deserves consideration for its own sake. In contrast, something deserves derivative moral consideration if it deserves consideration for the sake of something else. The Ethical Vegetarianism Argument aims to show that nonhuman animals deserve basic moral consideration.

A being deserves basic moral consideration just in case we are morally required to take its interests into account when deliberating about what to do. The ability to suffer is roughly co-extensive with sentience, the capacity to experience pain, pleasure, and frustration and satisfaction of desires. Anything that deserves basic moral consideration is said to have interests. If so, then any being that can suffer has an interest in avoiding suffering. Things that cannot suffer might merit derivative moral consideration even when they do not merit consideration for their own sakes.

Knowing that a being deserves moral consideration is necessary but not sufficient for moral judgment. In addition, we need to know how various beings' interests stand in relation to one another. The Equal Consideration of Interests Principle is an independent premise telling us that interests themselves are equal, regardless of the kind of being that has the interests. Thus, the Equal Consideration of Interests Principle asserts that the criterion of moral consideration, the ability to suffer, applies to both nonhuman and human animals. Thus, the same suffering ought to have the same weight in judging the rightness or wrongness of our actions, whether a human nonhuman animal experiences that suffering.

The argument derives C3 from P4 and P5, concluding that causing a being to suffer without adequate justification is morally wrong. P6 and P7 apply the Equal Consideration of Interests Principle, stated in P3, and C3 to eating meat, concluding that doing so is morally wrong. The premises introduce the factual claims that industrial production of meat involves confining, killing, and causing animals to experience pain and that by eating meat one participates in confining, killing, and causing pain.

Singer's earliest statement of the argument is his "All Animals Are Equal," published in 1974 in *Philosophical Exchange*. The journal is not widely available, but the article is frequently anthologized. The quotation below is from Singer's *Unsanctifying Human Life.*

> If a being suffers, there can be no moral justification for refusing to take that suffering into consideration. No matter what the nature of the being, the principle of equality requires that its suffering be counted equally with the like suffering – insofar as rough comparisons can be made – of any other being. If a being is not capable of suffering, or of experiencing enjoyment or happiness, there is nothing to be taken into account. This is why the limit of sentience (using the term as a convenient, if not strictly accurate, shorthand for the capacity to suffer or experience enjoyment or happiness) is the only defensible boundary of concern for the interests of others. To mark this boundary by some characteristic like intelligence or rationality would be to mark it in an arbitrary way. Why not choose some other characteristic, like skin color?
>
> The racist violates the principles of equality by giving greater weight to the interests of members of his own race, when there is a clash between their interests and the interests of those of another race. Similarly, the speciesist allows the interests of his own species to override the greater interests of members of other species. The pattern is the same in each case. Most humans are speciesists. I shall now briefly describe some of the practices that show this.
>
> For the great majority of human beings, especially in urban, industrialized societies, the most direct form of contact with members of other species is at mealtimes: we eat them. In doing so we treat them purely as means to our ends. We regard their life and well-being as subordinate to our taste for a particular kind of dish. I say "taste" deliberately – this is purely a matter of pleasing our palate. There can be no defense of eating flesh in terms of satisfying nutritional needs, since it has been established beyond doubt that we could satisfy our need for protein and other essential nutrients far more efficiently with a diet that replaced animal flesh by soy beans, or products derived from soy beans, and other high-protein vegetable products.
>
> It is not merely the act of killing that indicates what we are ready to do to other species in order to gratify our tastes. The suffering we inflict on the animals while they are alive is perhaps an even clearer indication of our speciesism than the fact that we are prepared to kill them. (84–5)

P1. If a being can suffer, then that being's interests merit moral consideration.

P2. If a being cannot suffer, then that being's interests do not merit moral consideration.

    C1. If a being's interests merit moral consideration, then that being can suffer (transposition, P2).

    C2. A being's interests merit moral consideration if and only if that being can suffer (material equivalence, P1, C1).

P3. The same interests merit the same moral consideration, regardless of what kind of being is the interest-bearer (equal consideration of interests principle).

P4. If one causes a being to suffer without adequate justification, then one violates that being's interests.

P5. If one violates a being's interests, then one does what is morally wrong.

C3. If one causes a being to suffer without adequate justification, then one does what is morally wrong (hypothetical syllogism, P4, P5).

P6. If P3, then if one kills, confines, or causes nonhuman animals to experience pain in order to use them as food, then one causes them to suffer without adequate justification.

P7. If one eats meat, then one participates in killing, confining, and causing nonhuman animals to experience pain in order to use them as food.

C4. If one eats meat, then one causes nonhuman animals to suffer without adequate justification (hypothetical syllogism, P6, P7).

C5. If one eats meat, the one does what is morally wrong (hypothetical syllogism, C3, C4).

71

Thomson and the Famous Violinist

Leslie Burkholder

Thomson, Judith Jarvis. "A Defense of Abortion." *Philosophy and Public Affairs* 1 (1971): 47–66.

"A Defense of Abortion." Available at http://en.wikipedia.org/wiki/A_ Defense_of_Abortion (accessed April 20, 2011)

There are many sources of opposition to abortion. Sometimes this opposition is based on thinking like the following: abortion results in the death of the fetus. But a fetus is a human being or person and all human beings, no matter what their age, have a moral right to continued life. So an abortion infringes on the right to continued life of a person, a human being. Of course the mother has rights too. She has a right to control what is done with and to her own body. Her having an abortion would be an exercise of this right. But the right to continued life is surely more important than anyone's right to control what is done to his body. So, even though the mother has this right, its exercise or use to have an abortion wrongfully violates another person's – the fetus' – right to continued life. This means that an abortion may not be done. It is ethically impermissible.

According to Judith Thomson, if this argument is deductively sound – if it is deductively valid with all true premises – then in the following imaginary case it would be morally impermissible to detach yourself from the famous violinist.

Just the Arguments: 100 of the Most Important Arguments in Western Philosophy, First Edition. Edited by Michael Bruce and Steven Barbone.
© 2011 Blackwell Publishing Ltd. Published 2011 by Blackwell Publishing Ltd.

You wake up in the morning and find yourself back to back in bed with an unconscious violinist. A famous unconscious violinist. He has been found to have a fatal kidney ailment, and the Society of Music Lovers has canvassed all the available medical records and found that you alone have the right blood type to help. They have therefore kidnapped you, and last night the violinist's circulatory system was plugged into yours, so that your kidneys can be used to extract poisons from his blood as well as your own. The director of the hospital now tells you, "Look, we're sorry the Society of Music Lovers did this to you – we would never have permitted it if we had known. But still, they did it, and the violinist is now plugged into you. To unplug you would be to kill him. But never mind, it's only for nine months. By then he will have recovered from his ailment, and can safely be unplugged from you." Is it morally incumbent on you to accede to this situation? No doubt it would be very nice of you if you did, a great kindness. But do you have to accede to it? What if it were not nine months, but nine years? Or longer still? What if the director of the hospital says, "Tough luck. I agree, but now you've got to stay in bed, with the violinist plugged into you, for the rest of your life. Because remember this. All persons have a right to life, and violinists are persons. Granted you have a right to decide what happens in and to your body, but a person's right to life outweighs your right to decide what happens in and to your body. So you cannot ever be unplugged from him." I imagine you would regard this as outrageous, which suggests that something really is wrong with that plausible-sounding argument I mentioned a moment ago. (Thomson, 48)

Thomson further says that you obviously have no moral obligation to stay attached to the violinist. The violinist is a human, and so she has a right to continued life, just as the fetus does. But that is not enough to prove that you may not have yourself detached. You can volunteer to stay attached and save the life of the violinist, but you are not ethically required to do this.

P1. All abortions are acts resulting in the death of some fetus.
P2. All acts resulting in the death of some fetus result in the death of some human being, person.
P3. Any act resulting in the death of some human being, person, is an infringement of the right to continued life of some person, human being.
   C1. If A is an abortion, then A results in the death of some fetus (universal instantiation, P1).
   C2. If A results in the death of some fetus, then A results in the death of some human being, a person (universal instantiation, P2).
   C3. If A results in the death of some human being, person, then A is an infringement of the right to continued life of some person, human being (universal instantiation, P3).

C4. If A is an abortion, then A results in the death of some human being, a person (hypothetical syllogism, C1, C2).

C5. If A is an abortion, then A is an infringement of the right to continued life of some person, human being (hypothetical syllogism, C3, C4).

C6. All abortions are infringement of the right to continued life of some person, human being (universal generalization, C5).

P4. All abortions are exercises of the mother's right to control of her own body.

P5. All exercises of the mother's right to control of her own body are exercises of some person's right to control of her own body.

C7. If A is an abortion, then A is an infringement of the right to continued life of some person, human being (universal instantiation, C6).

C8. If A is an abortion, then A is an exercise of the mother's right to control of her own body (universal instantiation, P4).

C9. If A is an exercise of the mother's right to control of her own body, then A is an exercise of some person's right to control of her own body (universal instantiation, P5).

C10. If A is an abortion, then A is an exercise of some person's right to control of her own body (hypothetical syllogism, C8, C9).

C11. Not A is an abortion or A is an infringement of the right to continued life of some person, human being (implication, C7).

C12. Not A is an abortion or A is an exercise of some person's right to control of her own body (material implication, C10).

C13. Both not A is an abortion or A is an infringement of the right to continued life of some person, and not A is an abortion or A is an exercise of some person's right to control of her own body (conjunction, C12, C11).

C14. Not A is an abortion or both A is an infringement of the right to continued life of some person, human being and A is an exercise of some person's right to control of her own body (distribution, C13).

C15. If A is an abortion, then both A is an infringement of the right to continued life of some person, human being, and A is an exercise of some person's right to control of her own body (material implication, C14)

P6. All acts that are an infringement of the right to continued life of some person, human being, and exercise of some person's right to control of her own body are wrongful infringements of the right to continued life of some person, human being, and may not be done.

C16. If A is an infringement of the right to continued life of some person, human being, and A is an exercise of some person's right to control of her own body, then A is wrongful infringement of the right to continued life of some person, human being, and may not be done (universal instantiation, P6).

C17. If A is an abortion, then A is wrongful infringement of the right to continued life of some person, human being, and may not be done (hypothetical syllogism, C15, C16).

C18. No abortion may not be done. All abortions are ethically impermissible (universal generalization, C17).

Thomson's argument against the argument above is deductively valid. So if its premises are both true, then its conclusion must be true. That would mean that the reasoning against abortion – the reasoning that says abortion is immoral and may not be done – would be unsound. But that reasoning is deductively valid. So if both the premises in Thomson's reasoning are true, at least one of the premises in the argument opposing abortion is false. It is pretty easy to see which one or ones that must be. It is premise P6. The fact that you may detach yourself in the imaginary case of the famous violinist shows that the rule stated in premise P6 is not true – someone else's right to life does not always outweigh the right to control what is done to your own body.

Not everyone accepts that the premises in Thomson's argument are both true. Some writers think you cannot detach yourself. In that case, premise P2 in Thomson's own argument would be false. Some others say that the conditional in premise P1 in her reasoning is false. The reasoning against abortion is sound, and yet you may detach yourself from the violinist. This is because there is some morally important difference between the case of a mother's aborting a fetus inside her and your detaching the violinist.

P1. If the reasoning opposing abortion is deductively sound, then you may not detach yourself from the famous violinist.

P2. You are allowed to detach yourself from the violinist. You are not ethically required to stay attached.

C. The reasoning opposing abortion is not deductively sound (*modus tollens*, P1, P2).

72

Marquis and the Immorality of Abortion

Leslie Burkholder

Marquis, Don. "Why Abortion Is Immoral." *The Journal of Philosophy* 86 (1989): 183–202.

Thomson, Judith Jarvis. "A Defense of Abortion." *Philosophy and Public Affairs* 1 (1971): 47–66.

According to Don Marquis, abortions are impermissible because of the following line of reasoning. Surely, sometimes killing a particular adult or child is wrong, seriously wrong. Probably, for example, killing you or me or your little brother right now would be wrong. What makes the killing so wrong, what explains its wrongness, is that it causes the loss of all the future experiences, activities, projects, and enjoyments that would be had by you or me or your little brother, and this loss is one of the greatest losses that can be suffered. But if that explanation is correct, then anything that causes the loss of all future experiences, activities, projects, and enjoyments is seriously wrong. Abortions of a healthy fetus cause just this loss. They cause the loss of all future experiences, activities, projects, and enjoyments the fetus would have were it not aborted. So abortions are not just ethically wrong but seriously wrong.

Marquis' argument is deductively valid. This means that if anything is wrong with the reasoning, one or more of its premises must be false. If they are all true, the conclusion would also have to be true. One premise that seems to be false is premise 3. It is a conditional. For it to be false, all that would need to happen is that the antecedent be true and the consequent be false. The antecedent in premise 3 is the consequent in premise 2. So it is

Just the Arguments: 100 of the Most Important Arguments in Western Philosophy, First Edition. Edited by Michael Bruce and Steven Barbone.
© 2011 Blackwell Publishing Ltd. Published 2011 by Blackwell Publishing Ltd.

easy to work out that it should be true. What about the consequent of premise 3? Look at the chapter in this volume examining Judy Thomson's famous violinist imaginary case (#71). Detaching yourself from the violinist would end all that individual's future experiences, activities, projects, and enjoyments. But would it be wrong for you to detach yourself? If not, then the consequent of premise 3 is false.

> What makes it wrong? Here's one central thing: killing us deprives us of the value of our future. It deprives us not only of what we value now and would have, given our current predilections, valued later, but also of what we would have come to value. (190)

P1. Killing this particular adult human being or child would be seriously wrong.
P2. What makes it so wrong is that it causes the loss of all this individual's future experiences, activities, projects, and enjoyments, and this loss is one of the greatest losses that can be suffered.
   C1. Killing this particular adult human being or child would be seriously wrong, and what makes it so wrong is that it causes the loss of all this individual's future experiences, activities, projects, and enjoyments, and this loss is one of the greatest losses that can be suffered (conjunction, P1, P2).
P3. If killing this particular adult human being or child would be seriously wrong and what makes it so wrong is that it causes the loss of all this individual's future experiences, activities, projects, and enjoyments and this loss is one of the greatest losses that can be suffered, then anything that causes to any individual the loss of all future experiences, activities, projects, and enjoyments is seriously wrong.
   C2. Anything that causes to any individual the loss of all future experiences, activities, projects, and enjoyments is seriously wrong (*modus ponens*, C1, P3).
P4. All aborting of any healthy fetus would cause the loss to that individual of all its future experiences, activities, projects, and enjoyments.
   C3. If A causes to individual F the loss of all future experiences, activities, projects, and enjoyments, then A is seriously wrong (particular instantiation, C2).
   C4. If A is an abortion of healthy fetus F, then A causes to individual F the loss of all future experiences, activities, projects, and enjoyments (particular instantiation, P4).
   C5. If A is an abortion of healthy fetus F, then A is seriously wrong (hypothetical syllogism, C3, C4).
   C6. All aborting of any healthy fetus is seriously wrong (universal generalization, C5).

73

Tooley on Abortion and Infanticide

Ben Saunders

Tooley, Michael. "Abortion and Infanticide." *Philosophy & Public Affairs* 2 (1972): 37–65.
____. *Abortion and Infanticide*. Oxford: Clarendon Press, 1983.

Thomson, Judith Jarvis. "A Defence of Abortion." *Philosophy & Public Affairs* 1 (1971): 47–66.

Abortion is understandably one of the more controversial ethical questions facing philosophers. Most refuse to take a stance on whether the fetus is a person. Thompson, for example, grants to her opponent that the fetus is indeed a person, but argues that abortion is nonetheless permissible, since one shouldn't be required to suffer great hardship for nine months in order to keep someone else alive.

Tooley argues that the fetus is not a person and nor in fact is a young infant. The argument depends on distinguishing between "human being" (which is a merely descriptive biological category) and "person" (which depends on self-awareness and implies a right to life). It is possible that not all persons are human – for instance, chimpanzees or dolphins may have the right to life – and that not all humans are persons; for instance, those in a persistent vegetative state. While the fetus or infant is undeniably human, Tooley argues that it does not acquire a right to life until it becomes self-aware. Before this point, it is permissible to kill the infant, even after

Just the Arguments: 100 of the Most Important Arguments in Western Philosophy,
First Edition. Edited by Michael Bruce and Steven Barbone.
© 2011 Blackwell Publishing Ltd. Published 2011 by Blackwell Publishing Ltd.

it is born. Tooley rejects the ideas that species membership or the mere fact of being born make any difference to an entity's rights, and he also argues that the mere potentiality of personhood is not sufficient to ground rights, since it would be permissible to kill a kitten that was going to become a person provided that one did so before it actually became a person.

The argument is important because it has implications not only for abortion but other areas such as our treatment of animals. The conclusion is obviously controversial, but that makes it all the more interesting if it can be established from the premises. It is unclear that it can, however, since it could be questioned whether the capacity to desire an object is, as Tooley suggests, a necessary condition for having a right to that object. If not, then he only succeeds in showing that fetuses and young infants do not satisfy certain sufficient conditions for a right to life (they are not persons and their mere potential for personhood is not itself sufficient to ground a right to life), but not that fetuses and young infants cannot have a right to life for other reasons.

> An organism possesses a serious right to life only if it possesses the concept of a self as a continuing subject of experiences and other mental states, and believes that it is itself such a continuing entity [...] [A] newborn baby does not possess the concept of a continuing self, any more than a newborn kitten possess such a concept. If so, infanticide during the time interval shortly after birth must be morally acceptable. (Tooley "Abortion," 62–3)

P1. If A has a morally serious right to X, then A must be able to want X.
P2. If A is able to want X, then A must be able to conceive of X.
  C1. If A has a morally serious right to X, then A must be able to conceive of X (hypothetical syllogism, P1, P2).
P3. Fetuses, young infants, and animals cannot conceive of their continuing as subjects of mental states.
  C2. Fetuses, young infants, and animals cannot want their continuing as subjects of mental states (*modus tollens*, P2, P3).
  C3. Fetuses, young infants, and animals do not have morally serious rights to continue as subjects of mental states (*modus tollens*, P1, C2).
P4. If something does not have a morally serious right to life, then it is not wrong to kill it painlessly.
  C4. It is not wrong to kill fetuses, young infants, and animals painlessly (*modus ponens*, C3, P4).

74

Rachels on Euthanasia

Leslie Burkholder

Rachels, James. "Active and Passive Euthanasia," *New England Journal of Medicine* 292 (1975): 78–80.

Beauchamp, Tom L. "A Reply to Rachels on Active and Passive Euthanasia," in *Medical Responsibility*, edited by Wade L. Robison and Michael S. Pritchard, 182–94. Clifton, NJ: The Humana Press, 1979.
Foot, Philippa. "Killing and Letting Die," in *Abortion: Moral and Legal Perspectives*, edited by James L. Garfield and Paul Hennessey, 177–85. Amherst, MA: University of Massachusetts Press, 1984.
Perrett, Roy W. "Killing, Letting Die, and the Bare Difference Argument," *Bioethics* 10 (1996): 131–9.

Active euthanasia happens when a medical professional or another kind of person deliberately does something that causes a person to die. Passive euthanasia, on the other hand, occurs when someone dies because medical professionals or others don't do something needed to keep the patient alive. This might include not starting a treatment that would prevent the person's death or not continuing with a procedure or treatment that is keeping a person or animal alive.

Just the Arguments: 100 of the Most Important Arguments in Western Philosophy, First Edition. Edited by Michael Bruce and Steven Barbone.
© 2011 Blackwell Publishing Ltd. Published 2011 by Blackwell Publishing Ltd.

Many medical professionals and others think that active euthanasia, even when it is done at the request of the person who dies, is morally wrong. They also think that passive euthanasia is morally right, at least when it is done following the wishes of the person who dies. This idea that the two are ethically different is reflected in the law in many countries. The law makes it a crime to commit active euthanasia but not a crime to perform passive euthanasia when the person who dies doesn't want to be kept alive. Is this idea about the ethical difference between active and passive euthanasia sound? According to Rachels' argument, it isn't.

One reason why so many people think that there is an important moral difference between active and passive euthanasia is that they think killing someone is morally worse than letting someone die. But is it? Is killing, in itself, worse than letting die? To investigate this issue, two cases may be considered that are exactly alike except that one involves killing whereas the other involves letting someone die. Then, it can be asked whether this difference makes any difference to the moral assessments. It is important that the cases be exactly alike, except for this one difference, since otherwise one cannot be confident that it is this difference and not some other that accounts for any variation in the assessments of the two cases. So, let us consider this pair of cases:

In the first, Smith stands to gain a large inheritance if anything should happen to his six-year-old cousin. One evening while the child is taking his bath, Smith sneaks into the bathroom and drowns the child, and then arranges things so that it will look like an accident.

In the second, Jones also stands to gain if anything should happen to his six-year-old cousin. Like Smith, Jones sneaks in planning to drown the child in his bath. However, just as he enters the bathroom Jones sees the child slip and hit his head, and fall face down in the water. Jones is delighted; he stands by, ready to push the child's head back under if it is necessary, but it is not necessary. With only a little thrashing about, the child drowns all by himself, "accidentally," as Jones watches and does nothing.

Now Smith killed the child, whereas Jones "merely" let the child die. That is the only difference between them. Did either man behave better, from a moral point of view? If the difference between killing and letting die were in itself a morally important matter, one should say that Jones's behavior was less reprehensible than Smith's. But does one really want to say that? I think not. In the first place, both men acted from the same motive, personal gain, and both had exactly the same end in view when they acted. It may be inferred from Smith's conduct that he is a bad man, although that judgment may be withdrawn or modified if certain further facts are learned about him – for example, that he is mentally deranged. But would not the very same thing be inferred about Jones from his conduct? And would not the same further considerations also be relevant to any, modification of this judgment? Moreover, suppose Jones pleaded, in his own defense, "After all, I didn't do anything except just stand there and watch the child drown. I didn't kill him;

I only let him die." Again, if letting die were in itself less bad than killing, this defense should have at least some weight. But it does not. Such a "defense" can only be regarded as a grotesque perversion of moral reasoning. Morally speaking, it is no defense at all. [...] I have argued that killing is not in itself any worse than letting die; if my contention is right, it follows that active euthanasia is not any worse than passive euthanasia. (Rachels, 78–80)

P1. Smith's killing the child is exactly like Jones's letting the child die except that Smith kills someone and Jones allows someone to die.

P2. What Smith did is morally as bad as what Jones did.

P3. If killing in itself is morally worse than letting die and Smith's killing the child is exactly like Jones' letting the child die except that Smith kills someone and Jones allows someone to die, then Smith's behavior should be more reprehensible than Jones'.

  C1. Not both killing in itself is morally worse than letting die and Smith's killing the child is exactly like Jones' letting the child die except that Smith kills someone and Jones allows someone to die (*modus tollens*, P2, P3).

  C2. Not killing in itself is morally worse than letting die or not Smith's killing the child is exactly like Jones's letting the child die except that Smith kills someone and Jones allows someone to die (De Morgan's, C1).

  C3. Not not Smith's killing the child is exactly like Jones' letting the child die except that Smith kills someone and Jones allows someone to die (double negation, P1).

  C4. Killing is not in itself morally worse than letting die (disjunctive syllogism, C2, C3).

P4. If there is an important moral difference between active and passive euthanasia, then killing someone is morally worse than letting someone die.

  C5. Active euthanasia is not any worse – ethically speaking – than passive euthanasia (*modus tollens*, P4, C4).

There is some ambiguity in the way some parts of the argument are stated. Formalizing the statements in a language for quantified first-order logic would bring out these ambiguities. For example, the final conclusion could mean that active euthanasia is never ethically worse than passive euthanasia, or it could mean that active euthanasia is not always ethically worse than passive euthanasia. It is pretty clear that Rachels has in the mind the second of these two. Again, the intermediate conclusion C1 might mean that killing is never ethically worse than otherwise identical instances of letting die. But Rachels does not intend this. All that he means is that killing is not always worse, morally speaking, than similar cases of letting die.

So long as these ambiguities are removed in a consistent way, this argument is deductively valid. So if there is anything wrong with the reasoning, it must be that one or more of the premises are false. If the ambiguities are not cleared up in the same way, then the argument will turn out to be invalid.

Part V
Philosophy of Mind

75

Leibniz' Argument for Innate Ideas

Byron Kaldis

Leibniz, G. W. *Discourse on Metaphysics and Other Essays*, edited and translated by Daniel Garber and Roger Ariew. Indianapolis: Hackett, 1991.

____. *New Essays on Human Understanding*, edited and translated by Peter Remnant and Jonathan Bennett. Cambridge, UK: Cambridge University Press, 1996.

____. *Philosophical Papers and Letters*, edited and translated by L.E. Loemker, 2nd edn. Kluwer: Dordrecht, 1969.

The importance of ideas, the cardinal building block in modern philosophy's theory of knowledge, can hardly be exaggerated. Equally important and vehement was the seventeenth-century debate over the status of certain principal ideas and special truths as either innate or not. Innatists and their opponents crisscross the dichotomy of rationalists/empiricists. A mental item can be innate in the sense of not acquired from extra-mental sources but also in the sense of discovered as stored in the mind since birth; obviously these two are not necessarily equivalent definitions. Nativists have standardly been distinguished between those who claim that the mind is actually aware of innate ideas and the more sophisticated ones, so-called dispositional innatists, such as Leibniz, who hold that the mind has the disposition or tendency to excavate certain ideas or principles it employs unconsciously or contains potentially.

Just the Arguments: 100 of the Most Important Arguments in Western Philosophy, First Edition. Edited by Michael Bruce and Steven Barbone.
© 2011 Blackwell Publishing Ltd. Published 2011 by Blackwell Publishing Ltd.

Leibniz, even more than Descartes before him, redrafts the issue of innateness by removing it from its ancient preoccupation with psychological origins only and redirects its emphasis mainly on the question of what the mind must be furnished with, seen that it, and not the senses, can access with remarkable epistemic success the modal status of necessary and universal truths.

Though not the only or the first champion of innate ideas in particular or of innate knowledge in general, Leibniz is the most intriguing and most vociferous defender of nativism (or innatism), both on the basis of his deep metaphysics as well as in terms of an argumentative strategy containing syllogisms designed specifically at rebutting Locke's well-known attack on nativism and the latter's attempt to reinstate the doctrine of the mind as a *tabula rasa*. The former, the metaphysical theses, are primarily found in Leibniz' *Discourse on Metaphysics* (1686) and other early metaphysical writings, while the latter, the syllogisms, are found in his celebrated *Nouveaux essais* [NE] in dialogue format (published posthumously in 1765 but composed around 1704–5), having Locke personally as their target and imaginary interlocutor. Leibniz' overall rationalist position aims at establishing that the validity of necessary truths in pure mathematics, metaphysics, logic, and even ethics, natural theology, and natural jurisprudence, cannot be proven in any other way but *a priori* or by means of reasoning only; that is, by what he calls the "natural light." In fact, the latter, innate natural reason that distinguishes humans from beasts is equivalent to the power of the understanding innate to us, or what comes to the same thing, of the "self." Hence, we have Leibniz' famed modification of the classic scholastic motto, "*nihil est in intellectu quod prius fuerit in sensu*," into "There is nothing in the understanding which has not come from the senses, except the understanding itself, *or the one who understands*" (*Philosophical Papers*, 549; emphasis added). This rich sense of "self" structured as containing fundamental notions, the so-called "intellectual ideas," of being, substance, unity, possibility, change, action, and so on, is deployed repeatedly by Leibniz in order to yield the innateness of these notions, being, after all, the ingredients of our self (hence "we are innate to ourselves" in this sense, too). So the possession of certain privileged intellectual ideas together with our epistemic access to the modal status of necessary truths, both unavailable by means of sense perception or induction, license belief in their innateness.

In his purely metaphysical mood where Leibniz goes as far as to maintain that, strictly, all ideas must be innate, his principal aim is to safeguard the immateriality of the mind and its cognitive autonomy or self-sufficiency. The mind, being a monad without any windows, cannot thereby receive any ideas from the outside by means of the senses. Influx of any sort is proscribed throughout Leibnizean metaphysics or physics, properly named "dynamics"; in a strict metaphysical sense, no created substance has any real influence upon any other. Although in the case of material things, mechanistic explanations in terms of transmission of influence (causation) may be acceptable since the things involved in such a causal contact are not real substantial unities; metaphysically speaking, this cannot be admissible, for genuine substances are real (i.e., self-enclosed) unities. At the same time, metaphysical theses such as the one just presented or that all substance whatsoever that is a genuine unity is essentially characterized by an inherent primary force or entelechy constantly operating – that is, it is perpetually acting or never without originating activity or "endeavor" (and therefore never comes into existence by generation nor goes out of extinction completely) – all such theses are constantly at the background or foreground in Leibniz' argumentative tactics in the *Nouveaux essais*. It must therefore be underlined that the earlier strictly metaphysical theses are never deactivated in the later *Nouveaux essais*, even when Leibniz is advancing arguments only in an epistemic or psychological vein.

Crucial to understanding Leibniz' nativism, avoiding making him sound unpalatable, is the particular manner in which he conceives of "thinking," "idea," and the unconscious in *dispositional* terms. For him, to learn something does not preclude it from being innate: Leibniz resists as invalid the entailment from "something is learned" to "it is not innate." Following Descartes but going one step further, Leibniz is prepared to bite the bullet and answer charges against the triviality or emptiness of any explanation that takes recourse to potentialities or dispositions. First, Leibniz never admits scholastic "bare faculties" – that is, mere potentiality or possibility – dismissing them as fictions. By contrast, active force or entelechy, inherent in substance, contains in itself a certain effort, "conatus," or "endeavor," striving toward actualization. In the particular case of the activity of the mind, this generic thesis is translated into the specific one whereby there is always a mental tendency to actualize the awareness of innate notions. In other words, the mind is never idle in the sense of having a mere "faculty" or potentiality that could remain unactualized. It never fails to activate its tendency; that is, the dedicated effort to unearth, or be aware of, innate notions and truths contained in it. Such a Leibnizian force ("endeavor") is predetermined never to fail to produce some actual activity, given the right conditions. By dint of attention or sense-probing, it acquires awareness of its otherwise unconscious innate mental contents. Second, and related to this, Leibniz never fails to emphasize well before the *Nouveaux essais* that by "idea" he does not understand an actualized occurrence or act of thought but a disposition to think in a certain way: "an idea consists not in some act, but in the faculty of thinking, and we are said to have an idea of a thing even if we do not think of it, if only, on a given occasion, we can think of it" (*Philosophical Papers*, 207). Given all this, third, for Leibniz, thinking does not amount to a constantly conscious series of occurrent mental acts with clarity and distinctness, since the soul's always being active *qua* substance can be said to still be active even during "confused" (i.e., less that fully clear) states, either as potentially striving toward such conscious attentive thinking episodes or as being most of the time at a steady-state attenuated potentiality only. But what safeguards such an attenuated state from being empty, thus threatening to undermine Leibniz' whole position, is that it contains one of his most innovative elements, what he famously called *"petites perceptions"*: innumerable minute imperceptible sensations, each one of which escapes our awareness yet contributes to the aggregate impression of which we are aware. The Leibnizean conception of the unconscious is used against Descartes' doctrine of constant or permanent thinking while at the same time avoiding on the other side Locke's doctrine that the mind can be, at periods, blank or inactive. That the *"petites perceptions"* turn out to be the capital pillar of Leibniz' defence of innateness in the *Nouveaux essais* becomes quickly apparent as he puts his invention to work in almost the whole range of his philosophy.

In the Preface to the *Nouveaux essais*, Leibniz advances three arguments corresponding to the following theses (suitably reconstructed in an organized form): (1) only innate principles ground our knowledge with demonstrative certainty of the modal status of specific truths as necessary and universally valid; (2) in self-reflection we become aware of possessing certain intellectual ideas (see above) being (a) immediately related to, and (b) always present to, the understanding, although we do not normally pay constant attention to these, since our everyday distractions and needs prevent our always being aware of them; and (3) as in a block of marble its veins predetermine the shape it may take, similarly our soul contains in an unconscious state innate items which it has the predetermined potentiality, tendency, or disposition to unearth, that is, become aware of – in support of this, the thesis of *petites perceptions* is employed. All these can be seen to be replies directed at the three prongs of Locke's attack on innatism: (1) together with (3) answer Locke's contention that necessary truths do not receive universal assent as they ought to if they were truly innate to all mankind; (2) together with (3) answer Locke's contention that our mind cannot possess something of which it is unaware; and (3) together with Leibniz' metaphysical theses about the nature of the mind (see above) answer Locke's contention that since the mind does not think all the time, it is possible for the mind to be empty. In the first chapter of Book I of the *Nouveaux essais*, Leibniz adds a new aspect to potentiality, this time regarding not just ideas but also our knowledge of truths and use of inferences: their enthymemic character.

The significance of Leibniz' argumentation cannot be overstated given the importance of the notion of the unconscious – something he did not invent but formulated in a novel and plausible manner, his influence on subsequent developments in German idealism, and, perhaps more importantly, its unnoticed relevance to recent discussions in the philosophy of mind and evolutionary psychology regarding nativism and concept-innatism, or current research in neurophysiology. It is worth pointing out that current neurobiological findings regarding motor cognition corroborate his view of the unconscious *petites perceptions* as neural activity falling below a minimum level or duration required to emerge into awareness. Similarly, in "subconcious pre-processing" during sense perception, it has been shown that we are not aware, for example, of the hairs of our inner ear that actually hear sounds but of the resultant aggregate acoustic sensation.

(1) [N]ecessary truths, such as we find in pure mathematics [. . .] must have principles whose proof does not depend on instances nor [. . .] on the testimony of the senses, even though without the senses it would never occur to us to think of them [. . .]. [S]o the proof of them can only come from inner principles described as innate. It would indeed be wrong to think that we can easily read these eternal laws of reason in the soul, as the Praetor's edict can be read on his notice-board, without effort or inquiry; but it is enough that they can be discovered within us by dint of attention [. . .] what shows the existence of inner sources of necessary truths is also what distinguishes man from beast. (2) [I]deas which do not originate in sensation come from reflection. But reflection is nothing but attention to what is within us, and the senses do not give us what we carry with us already [. . .] can it be denied that there is a great deal that is innate in our minds since we are innate to ourselves [. . .] and since we include Being, Unity, Substance [. . .] and hosts of other objects of our intellectual ideas? [. . .] (3) I have also used the analogy of the veined block of marble, as opposed to an entirely homogeneous block of marble, or to a blank tablet [. . .] if there were veins in the block which marked out the shape of Hercules rather than other shapes, then the block would be more determined to that shape and Hercules would be innate to it [. . .] even though labour would be required to expose the veins and to polish them to clarity, removing everything that prevents them from being seen. This is how ideas and truths are innate in us – as inclinations, dispositions, tendencies, or natural potentialities and not as action; although these potentialities are always accompanied by certain actions, often insensible ones, which correspond to them. (5) [. . . A]t every moment there is in us an infinity of perceptions unaccompanied by awareness or reflection; that is alterations in the soul itself, of which we are unaware because these impressions are either too minute and too numerous or else too unvarying [. . .]. But when they are combined with others they do nevertheless have their effect and make themselves felt. (6) [A] special affinity which the human mind has with [necessary truths . . .] is what makes us call them innate. So it is not a bare faculty [. . .] a mere possibility of understanding those truths; it is rather a disposition [. . .] a preformation which determines our souls and brings it about that they are derivable from it. (7) [A] "consideration of the nature of things" is nothing

but the knowledge of the nature of our mind and of those innate ideas, and there is no need to look for them outside oneself. (*New Essays*, 50–84)

Three Arguments

P1. The mind knows both truths of matter of fact and truths of reason.

P2. The mind knows truths of reason (simplification, P1).

P3. The truths of reason are necessary, universally valid (true in all possible words), and absolutely certain.

    C1. The mind knows necessary, universal, and absolutely certain truths (substitution, P2, P3).

P4. Necessity, universality, and certainty can either be established by means of induction from external sensory data, or they may originate from the mind itself.

P5. Induction is inadequate in yielding necessity, universal validity, and certainty.

    C2. Necessity, universal validity, and certainty of truths of reason can be original with the mind itself (disjunctive syllogism, C1, P4, P5).

P6. If necessity and certainty are original with the mind, then they are contained within it.

    C3. The mind contains these originally in itself (*modus ponens*, P6, C2).

P7. If the mind contains originally an item of knowledge, then the mind is not empty ever.

    C4. The mind is not empty ever (*modus ponens*, C3, P7).

P1. The mind has ideas by means of reflection.

P2. Ideas of reflection manifest the capacity of the mind to know itself.

P3. The mind can know itself inwardly either by relying on the senses for assistance or it is itself endowed with this capacity.

P4. The senses can deliver knowledge (ideas) regarding only the external world.

    C1. The mind's capacity for reflecting on itself is an endowed capacity (disjunctive syllogism, P3, P4).

P5. If the mind possesses an endowed capacity, then it contains it in itself without having it acquired.

    C2. The mind contains an endowed capacity without acquiring the reflecting capacity (*modus ponens*, C1, P5).

P6. If a mental item is contained in the mind without being acquired, then it is innate.

    C3. The mind's reflecting capacity is innate (*modus ponens*, C2, P6).

P7. If the mind has an innate item, then it cannot be empty at its inception.

P8. If the mind contains something innately (from its inception), then it contains it continuously.

C4. The mind is not empty ever (hypothetical syllogism, P7, P8).

P1. Either a mental faculty is a bare faculty or it is a predetermined, dedicated, capacity to search for specific objects [truths] in the mind.

P2. An epistemic faculty is a "bare faculty" if and only if it is merely an indeterminate disposition to receive truths (by definition).

C1. A mental faculty is either an indeterminate disposition to receive truths or a predetermined, dedicated, capacity to search for specific truths in the mind (substitution, P1, P2).

P3. The epistemic capacity of knowing necessary truths is a mental faculty.

C2. The epistemic capacity of knowing necessary truths is either a bare faculty or a predetermined dedicated capacity to search for specific such truths (substitution, C1, P3).

P4. If the epistemic capacity of knowing necessary truths is a bare faculty of receiving, then it is not the source of such truths.

P5. The mind is the source of the validity (proof) of necessary truths (as per above: first argument).

C3. The epistemic capacity of knowing necessary truths is not a bare faculty (*modus tollens*, P4, P5).

C4. The epistemic capacity of knowing necessary truths is a predetermined dedicated capacity to search for specific objects in the mind (disjunctive syllogism, P1, C3).

76

Descartes' Arguments for the Mind–Body Distinction

Dale Jacquette

Descartes, René. *Meditations on First Philosophy*, in *The Philosophical Works of Descartes*, translated by Elizabeth S. Haldane and G. R. T. Ross. Cambridge, UK: Cambridge University Press, 1931.

Almog, Joseph. *What Am I? Descartes and the Mind–Body Problem*. Oxford: Oxford University Press, 2001.

Beck, L. J. *The Metaphysics of Descartes: A Study of the Meditations*. Oxford: Oxford University Press, 1965.

Clarke, D. M. *Descartes's Theory of Mind*. Oxford: Oxford University Press, 2003.

Emmet, Dorothy. "Descartes on Body and Mind: After 300 Years." *Cambridge Journal* 4 (1950): 67–82.

Long, Douglas C. "Descartes' Argument for Mind–Body Dualism." *The Philosophical Forum* 1 (1969): 259–73.

Rozemond, Marleen. *Descartes's Dualism*. Cambridge, MA: Harvard University Press, 2002.

Ryle, Gilbert. *The Concept of Mind*. London: Hutchinson, 1949.

René Descartes' first argument in support of mind–body ontic nonidentity or substance dualism theory appears in Meditation 2 of his 1641 *Meditations on First Philosophy*. The argument is historically significant, if not obviously incorrect, and has earned its place as a focus of philosophical controversy for almost four centuries. If Descartes' reasoning is sound, then it answers the long-standing problem of understanding the relation between

Just the Arguments: 100 of the Most Important Arguments in Western Philosophy, First Edition. Edited by Michael Bruce and Steven Barbone.
© 2011 Blackwell Publishing Ltd. Published 2011 by Blackwell Publishing Ltd.

mind and body. Descartes believes that he has solved the mind–body problem in metaphysics that he revived from the time of the ancient Greeks, in keeping with certain religious beliefs about the soul's independence from material things, and especially from the physical human animal body it happens to inhabit.

Descartes applies the equivalent of Leibniz' Law – in particular, that half of the equivalence that is the conditional principle now often referred to as the "indiscernibility of identicals" – in a widely imitated general strategy for demonstrating the nonidentity of two distinct things by arguing for a difference in their properties. What is ahistorically called "Leibniz' indiscernibility of identicals principle" holds that for any A and B, if A = B, then A and B have all of their properties in common. Certainly Descartes would not have known the principle by either of these names but takes it for granted that distinctions between objects are drawn on the basis of a distinction among their properties. Descartes has the same intuitive grasp of the idea that identicals must have identical properties, and that any discrepancy among the properties of distinctly designated objects implies that the objects themselves are not identical. In order to prove that mind ≠ body in Meditation 2, Descartes claims to have found a difference in the properties of his mind and body, a property that his mind has but his body does not have, or conversely.

Descartes singles out the property that he argues distinguishes his body from his mind in two ways. He speaks of his mind as being "better knowable" or "more easily knowable" than his body and of his body as being such that its existence can be rationally doubted under the assumptions of a methodological skepticism while his mind is such that its existence cannot be rationally doubted, since entertaining doubt is a conscious state and in some cases an act of mind. The conclusion that Descartes can rationally doubt the existence of his body but not of his mind is supported, in turn, by Descartes' consideration that there might be an evil demon who systematically deceives him concerning the reality of any of his sense impressions that appear to reveal the existence and nature of an external world outside of, but correctly representing, the contents of his thoughts (the evil demon hypothesis). Descartes on pain of contradiction cannot consistently doubt the existence of his mind, since the actual entertainment of doubt would necessarily be an event actually occurring in and hence presupposing the existence of his mind (*Cogito, sum*, in Latin; or "When I think [including when I doubt], I exist") (#35, #36).

Descartes motivates his discussion of mind–body nonidentity in Meditation 2 by considering the sensible properties of a piece of wax that he invites the reader to imagine him describing as he holds and observes it in his hand. Descartes believes that the wax is better known to the intellect than by the senses because when the sensible properties of the wax all undergo change as the wax is gradually introduced to the heat of a flame, the senses alone do not tell us that it was the same wax that has undergone changes to its shape, size, color, smell, and other empirically perceivable properties. From this, Descartes draws the general conclusion that things known by the mind, including the mind itself, are better knowable than things, such as the body, known primarily or only with the aid of the senses. Descartes' proposition that his body but not his mind has the property of being such that its existence can be rationally doubted by his mind reinforces the argument's assumption that Descartes' mind is better knowable than his body, in the sense that he must infer the existence of his body from the evidence of the senses, while the existence of mind upon reflection is immediately known to itself and knows itself self-reflectively and introspectively, directly and without the intermediary of logical or inductive inference.

Descartes' first or Meditations 2's mind ≠ body argument has nevertheless been criticized as subject to a fatal dilemma. The kind of property Descartes maintains his mind has but his body does not have (better or easier knowability) or that his body has but his mind does not have (such that its existence is capable of being rationally doubted by his own mind) seems to involve a mistaken, excessively general, application of what with appropriate qualifications we shall continue to call "Leibniz' principle of the indiscernibility of identicals." Descartes' first or Meditation 2's argument for mind ≠ body depends on what is sometimes called a "converse intentional property," a property that belongs to an object by virtue of the intentional attitude that a thinking subject adopts or might adopt toward it. If I love Lisbon, then I have the intentional property of loving Lisbon, and Lisbon has the converse intentional property of being loved by me. If I doubt the existence of my body, then I have the intentional property of doubting the existence of my body, and my body has the converse intentional property of being such that its existence is doubted by me. Entities are distinguished when they can be shown not to share all of their properties. If it is a property of Lisbon that it is loved by me, and if I do not equally love London, then, if converse intentional properties are included among the shared properties of identical objects prescribed by Leibniz' Law, it should follow in this case that Lisbon ≠ London. If I equally loved London and Lisbon, then fortunately there would still remain many differences between them by which their nonidentity could be established as a consequence of Leibniz' Law. Lisbon and London have many things in common despite being different cities, so why shouldn't they have my equal love for each of them in common?

Descartes' first mind ≠ body (Meditation 2) argument makes a philosophically more unfortunate use of converse intentional properties in applying the indiscernibility of identicals principle. His argument is sometimes said to commit an "intensional fallacy." The objection is that by definition converse intentional properties do not belong intrinsically to objects but only as a consequence of the extrinsic circumstance of being thought of in a certain way by certain thinking subjects. Changes in object A's and object B's converse intentional properties as a result would seem to leave the object itself completely untouched as to the satisfaction or not of its intrinsic identity conditions. We know that $1 + 1 = 2$, for example, even though someone might doubt that $1 + 1$ is a prime number despite not doubting that 2 is a prime number. We know that Mark Twain = Samuel Clemens, regardless of whether or not someone happens to believe that Mark Twain wrote *Tom Sawyer* while doubting that Samuel Clemens wrote *Tom Sawyer*. Converse intentional properties invalidate Leibniz' Law as a universal identity principle, which means that extrinsic converse intentional properties should be barred from its applications. Unfortunately, Descartes' first (Meditation 2) mind ≠ body argument commits precisely the "intensional fallacy" of deducing the nonidentity of body and mind on the basis of their failure to share certain converse intentional properties; in particular, the property of being better or more easily knowable, or of the mind's but not the body's being such that its existence cannot be rationally doubted by the same mind.

The dilemma for Descartes' first or Meditation 2 mind ≠ body argument is that it either relies on a false, unrestricted, or excessively general version of Leibniz' principle of the indiscernibility of identicals that allows nonidentity determinations on the basis of converse intentional properties, in which case the argument is unsound; or, in case a correct formulation of Leibniz' Law is imposed, excluding converse intentional properties from permitted applications of the indiscernibility of identicals, the argument is deductively invalid, in the sense that the truth of its conclusion that mind ≠ body is not guaranteed by the truth of the argument's corrected assumptions containing the properly restricted form of Leibniz' Law that excludes converse intentional properties from its permissible applications, just as we must in the case where $1 + 1 = 2$ and Mark Twain = Samuel Clemens.

Descartes' argument, conspicuous weaknesses notwithstanding, represents a highly instructive effort to mark an essential difference between the properties of body and mind and to answer the mind–body problem in such a way as to hold out the prospect of contra-causal freedom of will and the soul's immortality. Descartes' fascinating project of replacing Aristotle's metaphysics in the Scholastic synthesis of Aristotle and Holy Scripture, refined during the medieval period especially by Thomas Aquinas, with a new metaphysics or "first philosophy" of his own, remains a heroic episode in the history of early modern philosophy, with a more general moral concerning the attractions and limitations of rationalist attempts to argue philosophically for significant metaphysical truths to whatever extent possible exclusively from phenomenology and the resources of ingenious pure reason.

> I know that I exist, and I inquire what I am, I whom know to exist [. . .]. But I already know for certain that I am, and that it may be that all these images, and, speaking generally, all things that relate to the nature of body are nothing but dreams [and chimeras]. [. . .] For if I judge that the wax is or exists from the fact that I see it, it certainly follows much more clearly that I am or that I exist myself from the fact that I see it. For it may be that what I see is not really wax, it may also be that I do not possess eyes with which to see anything; but it cannot be that when I see, or [. . .] when I think I see, that I myself who think am nought. (Descartes, 152–6)

P1. My body has the property of being such that its existence can rationally be doubted by me (evil demon hypothesis).

P2. My mind does not have the property of being such that its existence can rationally be doubted by me (*cogito sum*).

P3. For any objects A and B, if A = B, then A and B have all of their properties in common and there is no difference in their properties (Leibniz' Law [naïve form] or principle of the Indiscernibility of Identicals [naïve form]).

    C1. My body has a property that my mind does not have, namely, the property of being such that its existence can be rationally doubted by me (conjunction, P1, P2).

    C2. My body ≠ my mind (*modus tollens*, P3, C1).

(Premises (P1) and (P2) can be reformulated alternatively to the same effect in terms of the mind's having the (converse intentional) property of being "better knowable" or "more easily known" than the body or the body's existence, unlike the mind's, being known only inferentially from the evidence of sensation or external empirical perception rather than immediately in consciousness by reflection on the occurrence of consciousness.)

In Meditation 6, Descartes returns to the mind–body problem and offers another argument for the distinction, different in substance while identical in basic logical structure to the first argument of Meditation 2. Here, significantly, Descartes, deliberately or not, avoids the "intensional fallacy" of his Meditation 2 proof. In Meditation 6, Descartes no longer attempts to apply Leibniz' Law of the indiscernibility of identicals by singling out a converse intentional property possessed by the body but not the mind, or the reverse, but instead fixes on an evidently nonconverse intentional property. He invokes the property of the body's divisibility and the mind's indivisibility. He argues that the body, unlike the mind, can be separated into distinct parts that will still be bodies in the sense of continuing to be spatially extended though now scattered material things. The mind, Descartes claims, cannot be so divided, but in the relevant sense is indivisible, possessing an essential unity. It is implicit in Descartes' second argument, moreover, that the soul is immortal, on the grounds that only something capable of being broken down into component or parts can be destroyed. Descartes may believe that in this way he secures a new Cartesian rather than Aristotelian metaphysical foundation for religious belief in the soul's survival of death and the body's destruction.

"Nature," Descartes says, teaches him these things about extended bodies. It is noteworthy that Descartes believes after Meditation 3 that he has dispelled the systematic doubt by which he had previously motivated his project to tear down the old Aristotelian edifice of knowledge and rebuild natural philosophy or science in a more contemporary sense on the foundations of his demonstration that a perfectly good and therefore veracious God exists, who would not allow us to be deceived even by an evil demon when we clearly and distinctly perceive the properties of what we take to be the external world. The Meditation 6 proof of mind–body nonidentity based on the divisibility of body and indivisibility of mind into like parts could therefore not have been presented in Meditation 2, prior to Descartes' vouchsafing the certainty of clear and distinct perceptions with the insights into the natural properties of such things as the human body that the later argument requires.

Descartes' thesis of the mind's indivisibility is as interesting as it is controversial. The mind can of course be divided into such faculties as memory, imagination, calculation, emotion, and will, or into distinct thoughts. However, this is not the division of the mind into smaller component self-subsistent minds as its continuing scattered parts. If Descartes is right, then there is an essential difference in the way that the body is supposed to be capable of being divided into smaller component bodies, limbs, organs, cells, and so on, all of which are bodies in the sense of being potentially simultaneously existing spatiotemporally extended things belonging to the same metaphysical category – in this case, of material entities. Where psychological entities are concerned, Descartes is emphatic that the mind cannot be similarly divided. As to the problem of split personalities, or multiple personal disorder (MPD), Descartes, as we should expect, has nothing to say. He could presumably argue that in such circumstances there must be distinct independent minds occupying the same body, perhaps at different times, each of which, again, unlike the body, remains indivisible into independently existent minds as self-subsistent continuing minds, rather than being unified distinct components of one and the same mind.

In order to begin this examination, then, I here say, in the first place, that there is a great difference between mind and body, inasmuch as body is by nature always divisible, and the mind is entirely indivisible. For, as a matter of fact, when I consider the mind, that is to say, myself inasmuch as I am only a thinking thing, I cannot distinguish in myself any parts, but apprehend myself to be clearly one and entire; and although the whole mind seems to be united to the whole body, yet if a foot, or an arm, or some other part, is separated from my body, I am aware that nothing has been taken away from my mind. And the faculties of willing, feeling, conceiving, etc. cannot be properly speaking said to be its parts, for it is one and the same mind which employs itself in willing and in feeling and understanding. But it is quite otherwise with corporeal or extended objects, for there is not one of these imaginable by me which my mind cannot divide into parts, and which consequently I do not recognise as being divisible; this would be sufficient to teach me that the mind or soul of man is entirely different from the body, if I had not already learned it from other sources. (Descartes, 196)

P1. My body has the property of being such that it is divisible, capable of being divided into like self-subsistent parts that are also component physical bodies (bodily divisibility).

P2. My mind does not have the property of being such that it is divisible in the comparable sense as that above into self-subsistent parts that are also component minds (mental indivisibility).

   C1. My mind ≠ my body (Leibniz' Law, P1, P2).

P3. Only entities constituted by like parts are capable of being destroyed (concept of destructibility).

   C2. My mind, unlike my body, is indestructible; from which it further follows that the mind or soul, unlike the body, as religion teaches as an article of faith, is immortal (P2, C1, P3).

77

Princess Elisabeth and the Mind–Body Problem

Jen McWeeny

Atherton, Margaret (ed.). "Princess Elisabeth of Bohemia," in *Women Philosophers of the Early Modern Period*, 9–21. Indianapolis: Hackett, 1994.

Descartes, René. *The Philosophical Writings of Descartes*, 3 vols., translated by John Cottingham, Robert Stoothoff, and Dugald Murdoch. Cambridge: Cambridge University Press, 1984–91.

Descartes, René. *Oeuvres de Descartes*, 5 vols., edited by Charles Adams and Paul Tannery. Paris: Librairie Philosophique J. Vrin, 1971–74.

Descartes, René and Princess Elisabeth. "Correspondence," in *Descartes: His Moral Philosophy and Psychology*, translated by John J. Blom, 105–17. New York: New York University Press, 1978.

Gassendi, Pierre. "Fifth Set of Objections," in *The Philosophical Writings of Descartes*, vol. 2, translated by John Cottingham, Robert Stoothoff, and Dugald Murdoch, 179–240. Cambridge, UK: Cambridge University Press, 1984.

Kim, Jaegwon. *Mind in a Physical World: An Essay on the Mind–Body Problem and Mental Causation*. Cambridge, MA: The MIT Press, 1998.

McGinn, Colin. "Can We Solve the Mind–Body Problem?" *Mind* 98 (1989): 349–66.

Montero, Barbara. "Post-Physicalism." *The Journal of Consciousness Studies* 8, 2 (2001): 61–80.

Tollefson, Deborah. "Princess Elisabeth and the Problem of Mind–Body Interaction." *Hypatia: A Journal of Feminist Philosophy* 14, 3 (1999): 59–77.

Just the Arguments: 100 of the Most Important Arguments in Western Philosophy, First Edition. Edited by Michael Bruce and Steven Barbone.
© 2011 Blackwell Publishing Ltd. Published 2011 by Blackwell Publishing Ltd.

The mind–body problem exposes the inconsistencies that arise when mind and body are conceived as ontologically distinct entities. Human experience clearly shows that our minds interact with our bodies. When we will to walk, our legs usually move in the intended direction; when we become ill, the sharpness of our cognitive capacities is often compromised; when we are sad, we are frequently moved to tears; and so on. Philosophers who reject the identity of mind and body or mind and brain face the task of explaining these relations by illuminating the precise manner in which the mind moves the body and the body affects the mind. It is unsurprising, then, that the mind–body problem was first articulated as a response to René Descartes' dualistic philosophy. For Descartes, mind[1] is *res cogitans*, a nonextended, immaterial substance whose essential nature is to think, and body is its conceptual opposite – *res extensa*, a material substance with a particular shape that is extended and located in space. In its Cartesian form, the mind–body problem asks how an immaterial thing can move a material thing.

Princess Elisabeth of Bohemia (1618–80), also known as "The Princess Palatine," was the first philosopher to articulate the mind–body problem in the form of an argument and the first to elicit Descartes' serious attention to the matter, although the mind–body problem is rarely attributed to her. Princess Elisabeth lived most of her life in Holland, after her father had lost the throne of Bohemia and her family was exiled from their Palatinate lands and residence in Heidelberg during the Thirty Years' War. She was renowned for her knowledge of classical languages and her intellectual precision. As Descartes writes in his dedication to Princess Elisabeth at the beginning of *The Principles of Philosophy*, "You are the only person I have found so far who has completely understood all my previously published works" (Descartes *Philosophical Writings*, 2: 192). For the last years of her life, Princess Elisabeth served as abbess at a convent in Herford, Westphalia, and had wide jurisdiction over the surrounding territories.

A few scholars – most notably Pierre Gassendi – expressed their doubts about the possibility of mind–body interaction to Descartes shortly before Princess Elisabeth did (Gassendi, 1: 238). However, Gassendi's criticism was raised through a series of questions rather than an argument, and Descartes did not think that these questions were enough to produce a true "objection" to his philosophy (Descartes *Philosophical Writings*, 1: 266). Princess Elisabeth formulates the mind–body problem in her very first letter to Descartes, which is dated May 16, 1643. The general strategy that she employs is to use Descartes' understanding of motion as expressed in his *Optics* to show the impossibility of the mind's moving the body as long as

---

[1]   In his discussion of the mind–body relation, Descartes makes no conceptual distinction between "mind" (French *l'esprit*, Latin *mens*) and "soul" (French *l'âme*, Latin *anima*).

the mind is conceived of as nonextended and immaterial.[2] In response, Descartes admits that Princess Elisabeth's criticism is justified in light of his previous writings because he has said "nearly nothing" of the union between body and soul that enables the two to act and to suffer together (Descartes and Princess Elisabeth, 107). He thus sets about this task in his ensuing correspondence with her and even devotes his final work, *The Passions of the Soul*, to devising a solution to Princess Elisabeth's query. All three of his "solutions" – the question has been improperly posed, the union of the mind and body cannot be known by the intellect, and "the seat of the soul" is the brain's pineal gland – have been deemed largely unsatisfying by the majority of commentators, including Princess Elisabeth.

That Descartes himself was unable to produce a viable solution to the mind–body problem is indicative of its significance to his own thinking and to that of those philosophers who would follow him. Indeed, many of modern philosophy's innovations after Descartes, such as Spinoza's monism, Malebranche's occasionalism, Leibniz' monads, and Hume's skepticism, can be read as responses to this seemingly intractable problem generated by the Cartesian system. Moreover, the persistence of the mind–body problem has given rise to the area of contemporary analytic philosophy known as "philosophy of mind." Today, philosophers of mind most often frame the mind–body problem in terms of finding a physical explanation for mental phenomena, although some have preferred the term "nonmental" to "physical," because current physics makes it difficult to specify adequately what we mean by "physical" (see Kim and Montero). Still others have conceded that the problem cannot be solved (see McGinn). Whereas most contemporary philosophers of mind answer the mind–body problem by ascribing to some form of physicalism, they disagree as to what mental states actually are. In recent years, lively debates have developed as to whether mental states consist in behavioral dispositions, functional processes, neural states, or something else besides. Such disputes indicate that Princess Elisabeth's call for an explication of the manner in which the mind moves the body is far from answered. The mind–body problem therefore remains one of the most influential and long-standing arguments in the history of Western philosophy.

> I beseech you tell me how the soul of man (since it is but a thinking substance) can determine the spirits of the body to produce voluntary actions. For it seems every determination of movement happens from an impulsion of

---

[2]   Since Princess Elisabeth only refers to Descartes' *Meditations* in this early correspondence, there is some question as to whether she was indeed familiar with his physics when she wrote this letter. See Tollefson for an interpretation that indicates that Princess Elisabeth was referencing a passage in the *Optics*.

the thing moved, according to the manner in which it is pushed by that which moves it, or else, depends on the qualification and figure of the superficies of the latter. Contact is required for the first two conditions, and extension for the third. You entirely exclude extension from your notion of the soul, and contact seems to me incompatible with an immaterial thing. That is why I ask of you a definition of the soul more particular than in your Metaphysic – that is to say, for a definition of the substance separate from its action, thought. (Elisabeth, qtd. in Blom, 106)

P1. If movement of a thing occurs, it must have been caused by one of the following: (a) self-impulsion, (b) being pushed by something else, or (c) the quality and shape of its surface (e.g., a marble).

P2. Descartes defines the soul as nonextended and immaterial.

P3. If movement of a thing occurs and that movement is caused by self-impulsion or being pushed by something else, then contact is required.

P4. Nonextended and immaterial things (souls) cannot make contact with other things.

    C1. Nonextended and immaterial things cannot move themselves by self-impulsion and cannot move a thing by pushing it (*modus tollens*, P3, P4).

P5. If movement of a thing occurs by the quality and shape of its surface, then extension is required.

P6. Nonextended and immaterial things (souls) do not have extension.

    C2. Nonextended and immaterial things cannot move themselves by the quality and shape of their surface (*modus tollens*, P5, P6).

P7. If (C1) and (C2), then the soul (as it is defined by Descartes) cannot cause the body to move.

    C3. Nonextended and immaterial things cannot move themselves by self-impulsion and the quality and shape of their surface and cannot move a thing by pushing it (conjunction, C1, C2).

    C4. The soul (as it is defined by Descartes) cannot cause the body to move (*modus ponens*, P7, C3).

Implication: If the soul does cause the body to move, then Descartes' definition of the soul is incorrect.

78

Kripke's Argument for Mind–Body Property Dualism

Dale Jacquette

Kripke, Saul. *Naming and Necessity*. Cambridge, MA: Harvard University Press, 1980.

Ahmed, Arif. *Saul Kripke*. New York: Continuum, 2007.

Bayne, Steven R. "Kripke's Cartesian Argument." *Philosophia* 18 (1988): 265–9.

Feldman, Fred. "Kripke on the Identity Theory." *The Journal of Philosophy* 7 (1974): 665–76.

Fitch, G. W. *Saul Kripke*. London: Acumen, 2004.

Hughes, Christopher. *Kripke: Names, Necessity, and Identity*. Oxford: Oxford University Press, 2004.

Jacquette, Dale. *Philosophy of Mind: The Metaphysics of Consciousness*. New York: Continuum, 2010.

Preti, Consuelo. *On Kripke*. Cincinnati, OH: Wadsworth, 2002.

Saul A. Kripke offers a much-discussed argument against mind–body identity theory, supporting some type of property dualism, in his 1970 Princeton University lectures on *Naming and Necessity*. The argument purports to explain the relation between mind and body, solving the mind–body problem at a comparatively high level of abstraction within the context of a comprehensive philosophical treatment of the nature of transworld identity conditions and the theory of reference in logic, semantics, and philosophy of language. Kripke fashions an interesting argumentive methodology with important metaphysical conclusions based on independently defensible distinctions in modal logic and referential semantics. As such, Kripke's

Just the Arguments: 100 of the Most Important Arguments in Western Philosophy, First Edition. Edited by Michael Bruce and Steven Barbone.
© 2011 Blackwell Publishing Ltd. Published 2011 by Blackwell Publishing Ltd.

argument demonstrates unexpected connections between traditionally unrelated areas of inquiry in philosophy of language and the metaphysics of mind.

Kripke introduces the concepts and explores some of the applications of a distinction between rigid versus nonrigid designation. A rigid designator designates the same object in every logically possible world in which the object exists. According to Kripke, proper names such as 'Plato' and 'Barack Obama' are rigid designators in this sense. Nonrigid designators, in contrast, potentially designate different individuals in different logically possible worlds. Definite descriptions, whose content may apply to different objects in different worlds, in contrast with rigidly designative proper names, are generally nonrigid designators under Kripke's distinction. These standardly include such referring terms as 'The teacher of Aristotle' or 'The President of the United States in 2011', which could in principle refer to entirely different persons depending on with whom Aristotle happens to study or the logically contingent American election results as the election occurs in different logically possible worlds.

Kripke maintains that questions of transworld identity, of identifying precisely the same individual from one logically possible world to another, cannot be made with high-powered telescopes and cannot be justified on the basis of such superficial properties as external appearance, since these factors can differ radically across different logically possible worlds, obscuring the usual tests for identity and nonidentity that might be conducted in the actual world. Kripke proposes that transworld identity is a matter of stipulation, which is to say of decision rather than discovery. We do not look at alternative logically possible worlds and try to learn from our observations whether Aristotle exists in another logically possible world and what properties he might have there. We simply declare, laying it down as a kind of choice we have made, that there is a logically possible world in which Aristotle exists and has the following accidental properties different from those he possesses in the actual world. We must proceed by stipulation in order to make sense of transworld identities, according to Kripke, and we can only do so in thought and language by means of rigid designators.

The appeal to rigid designators further enables Kripke to mount an argument in support of mind–body dualism. The core of the argument is to say that, since we can consider without internal contradiction that the mind $\neq$ body, at least in the sense that corpses presumably exist without minds, and we can imagine the mind existing without being associated with a body, it is logically possible that mind $\neq$ body. If we rigidly designate an individual body and mind or type of brain and psychological entity or event, then, since in that case there is at least one logically possible world in which (rigidly designated) mind $\neq$ (rigidly designated) body, it must be true that (rigidly designated) mind $\neq$ (rigidly designated) body in every logically possible world. It follows, then, that mind and body are distinct entities universally in every logically possible world. It is logically necessary, and therefore *a fortiori* actually the case, that mind ≠ body. The least objectionable mind–body dualism to be accepted as a result of Kripke's argument is property dualism rather than substance or ontic (Cartesian) dualism, the latter of which has the additional burden of explaining causal interactions between the material body and the immaterial mind.

Kripke's argument delivers a powerful implication, supported by the general considerations that undergird his solution to the problem of understanding transworld identity and the considerable general utility of the distinction between rigid and nonrigid designation. Kripke's attitude toward the argument appears somewhat ambivalent, as in footnote 17 he seems to step away from the conclusiveness of his own inference when he adds these qualifications: "rejection of the [mind–body] identity thesis does not imply acceptance of Cartesian dualism [. . .] Descartes' notion seems to have been rendered dubious ever since [David] Hume's critique of the notion of a Cartesian self. I regard the mind–body problem as wide open and extremely confusing" (155).

> Descartes, and others following him, argued that a person or mind is distinct from his body, since the mind could exist without the body. He might equally well have argued the same conclusion from the premise that the body could have existed without the mind. Now the one response which I regard as plainly inadmissible is the response which cheerfully accepts the Cartesian premise while denying the Cartesian conclusion. Let 'Descartes' be a name, or rigid designator, of a certain person, and let 'B' be a rigid designator of his body. Then if Descartes were indeed identical to B, the supposed identity, being an identity between two rigid designators, would be necessary, and Descartes could not exist without B and B could not exist without Descartes. (Kripke, 144–5)

P1. Mind–body dualism is logically possible.

P2. If mind–body dualism is logically possible, then there is at least one logically possible world in which the mind is not identical to any material body, and mental events are not identical to any purely physical events.

P3. The concept of rigid designation implies that rigidly designated bodies and minds or mental and physical events, if nonidentical in any logically possible world, are necessarily distinct or nonidentical in every logically possible world in which they exist, and therefore *a fortiori* actually distinct or nonidentical in the actual world.

C1. Reductive mind–body physicalism or mind–body identity theory is therefore false, and some form of mind–body nonidentity, probably some type of property dualism, in particular, is true; (rigidly designated) mind ≠ (rigidly designated) body (*modus tollens*, P1, P2).

79

The Argument from Mental Causation for Physicalism

Amir Horowitz

Armstrong, David. *A Materialist Theory of the Mind.* London: Routledge & Kegan Paul, 1963.

Lewis, David. "An Argument for the Identity Theory." *Journal of Philosophy* 66 (1966): 17–25.

Kim, Jaegwon. *Mind in a Physical World.* Cambridge, MA: The MIT Press, 1998.

Rey, Georges. *Contemporary Philosophy of Mind.* Oxford: Blackwell, 1997.

Attempts to establish mind–body physicalism – the view that mental events are identical with physical events – often appeal to considerations pertaining to mental causation. The basic idea underlying the argument from mental causation in favor of physicalism (hereafter, "the argument from mental causation") is that physicalism is the only plausible explanation for the existence of mental causation. The expression "physical events" as it is employed here refers to events whose all properties are such that their instantiations are logically determined by instantiations of physical properties.

A similar idea served opponents of dualism ever since this thesis was officially launched by Descartes. These opponents of dualism argued that the interactions between nonphysical events and physical events cannot occur (due, e.g., to a conflict with the law of momentum, or the law of the conservation of mass and energy, or the alleged causal closure of the physical world). Since mental events are supposed by the dualist to be nonphysical, and since mental–physical interactions cannot be denied, dualism must be rejected. Put slightly differently, since physical events can only interact with physical events, the fact that mental events causally interact with physical events can only be accounted for by assuming that mental events are themselves physical events. The contemporary argument from mental causation employs this reasoning. In its simplest form, it asserts that mental events cause our actions and that brain events cause our actions; therefore, it is argued, mental events are in fact physical events. But such a version of the argument cannot do, for there are options in logical space in which nonphysical mental events as well as physical events cause actions (the same actions) without being identical. Thus, for the argument to go through, these options have to be ruled out. Various versions of the argument indeed rule such options out.

The argument has several versions. Some of them (e.g., Armstrong's) replace premise P2 with the premise that the concepts of mental events are concepts of specific causal roles, and they adjust premise P1 accordingly. Defenders of the argument also differ with respect to the way they rule out the options specified in (P3). Thus, option (3c) is sometimes ruled out by employing assumptions concerning the nature of the physical world (such as the causal closure principle), and sometimes by employing specific assumptions about our physiology. I believe that that sub-version of the version presented here that rules out option (3c) by employing specific assumptions about our physiology is superior to all alternatives. It employs neither controversial assumptions about the nature of mental concepts nor assumptions that are arguably biased concerning the nature of the physical world.

Let us say a few words about the argument's premises. P1 is a well-established scientific claim, one which no contemporary educated person would deny. P2 is a highly plausible claim, which everybody seems to know from personal experience: it is hard to deny (although there have been philosophers who do deny) that our actions are caused by our desires and our beliefs (regarding what would satisfy our desires). Now P1 and P2 together clearly entail C1. Assuming that P3 takes into account all options in which both mental events and physical events in the brain can be causes of our actions without being identical, the argument is formally valid. Of course, in order to persuade us, a convincing case should also be made in favor of its premises and in particular – since this is what is mainly at stake – in favor of ruling out those options mentioned in P3.

These options should be explained. In option (3a) – causal over-determination – actions are independently caused by both nonphysical mental events and by physical events; that is, they would have been caused by either. In option (3b) – "mental–physical causal cooperation" – non-physical mental events and physical events cooperate to cause actions by means of two separate causal chains – a nonphysical mental one and a physical one; that is, in the absence of either, the actions would not have been caused. In option (3c) – "mixed mental–physical causal chains" – nonphysical mental events and physical events are links in the same chains of events which bring about actions. We shall immediately illustrate this option.

So as said, all these options should be eliminated. Against option (3a) – that of causal over-determinism – it has been argued that nowhere in nature do we encounter such a phenomenon or that its occurrence is implausible from an evolutionary perspective. Option (3b) – that of mental–physical causal cooperation – is usually not taken seriously and is ignored. It is generally assumed that the question that lies at the heart of the argument from mental causation concerns the status of option (3c), that of mixed mental–physical causal chains. Armstrong describes this option thus, "Let us now consider the situation where a physical stimulus of some sort, say the sounds of a human voice, brings about certain mental events, say perceptions and thoughts, which then issue in further physical action. On the 'way up' there must be a last physical event in the brain before the mental events ensue. The mental events must then bring about a first physical event in the brain on the 'way down'" (62). In this case, mental causes intervene in the physiological chain of events.

The most promising way to rule this option out is along the following lines. First, it is argued that the idea that there is a mental intervention in the chain that leads to the action means that "a physical break" is involved in this chain. It means, that is, that the transition from the last brain event on the "way up" to the first brain event on the "way down" is not dictated by the laws of physics. Second, it is argued that the obtaining of such a physical break in the chain which leads to the action is empirically implausible.

> [I]t seems to be a striking fact about people and animals that all of their non-tendentiously described behavior could be explained in principle by reference to physical properties alone. All the motions of their bodies [. . .] could be perfectly well explained by reference to the electrical impulses along nerve fibers that precede them. These firings in turn could be explained by earlier neurological events, which in turn could be explained by earlier events. [. . .] We have absolutely no reason to believe that there is any break in the physical explanation of their motion. (Rey, 71)

According to this line of thought, since many physiological processes can be fully accounted for in physical terms and are completely dictated by physical laws, we seem to have good reasons to assume that no physical break obtains in the causal chains that lead to our actions. Both the way up (beginning with an external stimulus and ending with a mental event) and the way down (beginning with a mental event and ending with an action) are – it is hard to deny – purely physical. Is it plausible to assume that only in that short segment, which connects the last brain event on the way up and the first brain event on the way down, there is nonphysical intervention? Wouldn't it be plausible to infer from the complete control of physics over all other transitions that are involved in those processes that it controls this segment as well?

Opponents of the argument from mental causation might insist that, appearance to the contrary notwithstanding, the inference from the complete control of physics over all other transitions that are involved in physiological processes to its control over that segment is illegitimate since that segment is significantly different. It is significantly different precisely in that it involves a mental event, and the unique character of mental events – in virtue of their phenomenality and/or intentionality, and/or various epistemic characteristics, and so on – is granted even by physicalists (physicalists standardly maintain that mental phenomena are special physical phenomena). Once the uniqueness of mental events is admitted, there is no good reason to resist ascribing further uniqueness to the causal chains that include them, and assuming that these causal chains involve nonphysical links (namely, that those unique mental events that are included in those chains are unique also in being nonphysical). We shall leave it to the reader to estimate the strength of this objection to the argument from mental causation.

P1. Actions are caused by physical events in the brain.
P2. Actions are caused by mental events.
    C1. Either mental events are identical with physical events in the brain, or actions are caused both by mental events and physical events in the brain (conjunction, P1, P2).
P3. All of the options in which actions are caused both by mental events and by physical events in the brain while the mental events are not identical with brain events should be rejected:
    (a) causal over-determination;
    (b) "mental–physical causal cooperation";
    (c) "mixed mental–physical causal chains."
    C2. Mental events are identical with physical events in the brain (disjunctive syllogism, C1, P3).

80

Davidson's Argument for Anomalous Monism

Amir Horowitz

Davidson, Donald. "Mental Events," in *Essays on Actions and Events*, 207–24. Oxford: Clarendon Press, 1980.

How should one argue for a specific physicalist view of mentality such as token-physicalism – the view that mental events are physical events but what determines the mental type of a mental event (e.g., its being pain) is not its physical type?[1] The natural way for one to go, it seems, is first to establish physicalism and then show that, given the truth of this general view, the specific version in question is the most plausible one. But Davidson's argument for anomalous monism beautifully attempts to achieve both purposes in one stroke: his argument for physicalism assumes a rejection of strict mental–physical correlations, and thus the resulting physicalism is token-physicalism, or more specifically, Davidson's specific version of it, anomalous monism.

The general physicalist view that Davidson aims to establish (he refers to it as "the identity of the mental and the physical") is the view that mental events are identical with physical events.[2] A physical event, according to him, is an event that essentially has a physical description. Davidson avoids the jargon of properties, but it seems natural to take this characterization

---

[1] There is another use of "token-physicalism," in which it refers to the thesis that takes mental events to be identical with physical events but is neutral with respect to the question of mental types.

[2] To be more precise, Davidson confines his argument to those mental events that interact with physical events. Of course, if all mental events interact with physical events, this doesn't matter. In presenting Davidson's argument, I will ignore this point.

Just the Arguments: 100 of the Most Important Arguments in Western Philosophy, First Edition. Edited by Michael Bruce and Steven Barbone.
© 2011 Blackwell Publishing Ltd. Published 2011 by Blackwell Publishing Ltd.

to imply that a physical event is an event that has a physical property. An event that essentially has a physical description might also satisfy nonphysical descriptions, but Davidson certainly does not allow for such an event to have properties that are instantiated apart from physical space (this might explain his characterization of a physical event as an event that has only one physical description). He thus takes the thesis he argues to be a robust physicalist thesis that excludes not only Cartesian substance dualism but also property dualism.

One instructive way that Davidson presents the rationale of the argument concerns the reconciliation of the following three principles, all of which he takes to be true:

(a) (At least some) mental events interact causally with physical events.

(b) Causation is nomological: events related as cause and effect fall under strict deterministic laws.

(c) The mental is anomalous: there are no strict deterministic laws on the basis of which mental events can be predicted and explained. And in particular, there are no strict deterministic laws that connect events under their physical descriptions with events under their mental descriptions.

Principles (a) and (b) entail the obtaining of laws that connect mental events and physical events, but this seems to clash with (c), which seems to forbid mental–physical laws. How can this tension be resolved? Here is Davidson's brief presentation of his reasoning:

> Suppose *m*, a mental event, caused *p*, a physical event; then, under some description *m* and *p* instantiate a strict law. This law can only be physical [. . .]. But if *m* falls under a physical law, it has a physical description; which is to say it is a physical event. (224)

The basic idea is that there can be laws connecting mental events and physical events that do not mention the mental events as mental but rather as physical. We may call or refuse to call such laws "mental–physical laws"; the point is that the possibility of such laws ensures the consistency of principles a–c.

P1 and P2 (which express the above principles (a) and principle (b), respectively) straightforwardly entail C1, namely the claim that there must be strict deterministic laws that connect mental events with physical events. The crucial step of the argument comes next. P3 expresses principle (c) but also involves a generalization of it, namely the idea that all strict laws are physical laws – laws that employ physical descriptions of the events that they connect. So those laws that connect mental events with physical events also connect those events – the physical events as well as the mental events – under physical descriptions, and there are such laws (C2); *a fortiori*, these events have physical descriptions (C3) and so (if P5 is accepted) are physical. In short, it is the causal role of the mental that reveals its physical nature, for only the physical satisfies the nomological requirement for causality.

The argument's official conclusion is the physicalist thesis that mental events are physical events, but in fact the argument shows more. For the way to this conclusion goes through the assumption that the mental is anomalous – that it resists being predicted and explained by means of strict laws. Thus, according to this argument, the mental is both physical and anomalous, so the resulting view of the mental is anomalous physicalism, or as Davidson puts it, anomalous monism. Now, further, one aspect of the anomalous nature of the mental is that there can be no lawful connections between mental events with physical events. So anomalous monism excludes type-physicalism, which is committed to such lawful connections (it identifies mental types with physical types), and is a form of token-physicalism.

Since, as we saw, the conclusion of Davidson's argument follows from the premises and the argument is a formally valid one, the only direct way to attack it is to attack its premises. Indeed, attacks against the argument's premises have been launched, mainly against P2 and P3. The argument has also been attacked indirectly, by claiming that it has an arguably implausible implication, namely the "type-epiphenomenalist" view that the causal efficacy of mental events cannot be attributed to their mental properties. Whether or not this implication is to count as a *reductio ad absurdum* of the argument is a matter of dispute.

P1. Mental events bear causal relations to physical events.
P2. If there is a causal relation between events, then there is an implied existence of a strict deterministic law that connects those events.
   C1. There are strict laws that connect mental events with physical events (*modus ponens*, P1, P2).
P3. Strict laws only connect events under physical descriptions with events under physical descriptions.
   C2. There are strict laws that connect mental events under their (non-mental) physical descriptions with physical events (instantiation, P3, C1).
P4. If there are strict laws that connect mental events under their (nonmental) physical descriptions with physical events, then mental events have physical descriptions.
   C3. Mental events have physical descriptions (*modus ponens*, C2, P4).
P5. If a mental event has a physical description, then it is a physical event.
   C4. Mental events are physical events (*modus ponens*, C3, P5).

81

Putnam's Multiple Realization Argument against Type-Physicalism

Amir Horowitz

Putnam, Hilary. "The Nature of Mental States," in Hilary Putnam, *Mind, Language, Reality: Philosophical Papers*, vol. II, 429–40. Cambridge, UK: Cambridge University Press, 1975.
Fodor, Jerry. *Psychological Explanations*. New York: Random House, 1968.

Hilary Putnam's multiple realization argument aims to undermine the view nowadays known as "type-physicalism." According to type-physicalism, mental properties are physical properties; put differently, mental types are physical types, and what makes a mental state of a certain type belong to its type (e.g., its being a pain state) is its physical–chemical makeup. Putnam took this view, which he labeled "the brain state theory," to be the (then) standard physicalist view of mentality.

The argument is simple in structure. P1 exposes the real meaning of type-physicalism. This theory is committed to the claim that all pains share physical–chemical nature, one which only they have – this is what makes them states of pain; similarly all states of hunger share physical–chemical nature that only they have – this is what makes them states of hunger, and so on for other mental states. We may say that according to P1, type-physicalism is committed to the thesis of the single realization of mental properties. One might think that exposing this commitment of type-physicalism isn't exciting, but we should bear in mind that at the time Putnam's argument was first published there was no official statement of

Just the Arguments: 100 of the Most Important Arguments in Western Philosophy, First Edition. Edited by Michael Bruce and Steven Barbone.
© 2011 Blackwell Publishing Ltd. Published 2011 by Blackwell Publishing Ltd.

this theory, and Putnam elicited this commitment from what the champions of the prevalent physicalist view asserted (thus, in fact, exposing that they are type-physicalists).

According to P2, there are empirical reasons to doubt this hypothesis. P2 expresses the multiple realization thesis: it asserts that most likely mental properties such as being pain are multiply realizable, so that pain states do not share a unique physical nature. It is possible that my pain and the pain of another creature do not exclusively share any physical property whatsoever: mine is realized by the instantiation of one physical property; the other creature's by a different physical property. Now if type-physicalism is committed to the single realizability of mental properties but mental properties are (most probably) multiply realizable, then type-physicalism is (most probably) false. That is, C seems straightforwardly to follow from P1 and P2. The argument is valid. The validity of the argument is not affected by the fact that the multiple realization thesis is assumed to be only highly plausible – indeed, it is suggested as an empirical hypothesis, and not simply true, because the conclusion also claims for no more than high plausibility. Putnam strengthens his case against type-physicalism by comparing this theory to the thesis that mental properties are functional properties and showing the superiority – in terms of empirical likelihood – of the latter. Due to length, it will not be discussed here.

It is important to note that the multiple realization argument undermines only one (important as it is) physicalist thesis and does not undermine physicalist ontology. Its soundness is compatible with the idea that mental properties are realized physically, although they may be realized in different physical ways. Indeed, given the truth of physicalist ontology, the argument may be taken to establish that some nonreductive form of physicalism, such that endorses physicalist ontology but denies that mental types are – or are reducible to – physical types, is probably true. In fact, for many philosophers, this is the important import of the multiple realization argument.

Some philosophers have tried to downplay the argument's conclusion by saying that although Putnam's examples (such as that of octopus) suggest that not all pains exclusively share physical nature, it is still plausible that all human pains do. These philosophers thus endorsed a weak version of type-physicalism – species-specific-type-physicalism. According to species-specific-type-physicalism, all pains of members of the same species exclusively share physical natures, and the same holds for all the other mental states, of course. This view, however, has been challenged by the empirical finding that some areas of the brains of people who have suffered from some brain damage managed to "learn" to perform mental functions that were previously performed by other, physically different, areas of the brain. If so, it seems, the multiple realizability of mental properties penetrates also at the intra-species level.

In addition to undermining type-physicalism, Putnam's argument paved the way for the functionalist view of the mind. According to functionalism, mental properties are functional properties of organisms, the relevant functions being ones that connect perceptual inputs, behavioral outputs, and mental states. In fact, Putnam attempts to show not only that type-physicalism is not a very plausible theory but also that functionalism is more plausible and has to be preferred. Many philosophers were persuaded by Putnam's considerations, and as a result functionalism has acquired the status of the dominant theory of mind.

Putnam refers in the following passages to "brain states" and "mental states" rather than to properties, but the text clearly indicates that he takes the hypothesis he wishes to reject (namely the hypothesis that "every psychological state is a brain state") to be the one according to which what makes a psychological state belong to its mental type (e.g., its being a pain state) is the type of brain state that it is. So he is indeed discussing – and aims at undermining – type-physicalism.

> Consider what the brain-state theorist has to do to make good his claims. He has to specify a physical–chemical state such that any organism (not just a mammal) is in pain if and only if (a) it possesses brain of suitable physical–chemical structure; and (b) its brain is in that physical–chemical state [. . .]. At the same time, it must not be a possible (physically possible) state of any physically possible creature that cannot feel pain [. . .]. It is not altogether impossible that such a state will be found [. . .]. Thus it is at least possible that parallel evolution, all over the universe, might always lead to one and the same physical "correlate" of pain. But this is certainly an ambitious hypothesis.
>
> Finally, the hypothesis becomes still more ambitious when we realize that the brain state theorist is not just saying that *pain* is a brain state; he is, of course, maintained to concern that every psychological state is a brain state. Thus, if we can find even one psychological predicate which can clearly be applied to both a mammal and an octopus (say, "hungry"), but whose physical–chemical "correlate" is different in the two cases, the brain state theory has collapsed. It seems to me overwhelmingly probable that we can do this. (Putnam, 436)

P1. If type-physicalism is true, then every mental property can be realized in exactly one physical way.

P2. It is empirically highly plausible that mental properties are capable of multiple realizations.

  C1. It is (empirically) highly plausible that the view of type-physicalism is false (*modus tollens*, P1, P2).

82

The Supervenience Argument against Non-Reductive Physicalism

Andrew Russo

Kim, Jaegwon. "Mechanism, Purpose, and Explanatory Exclusion."
Philosophical Perspectives 3 (1989): 77–108.
___. *Mind in a Physical World*. Cambridge, MA: The MIT Press, 1998.
___. *Physicalism, or Something Near Enough*. Princeton, NJ: Princeton
University Press, 2005.

Davidson, Donald. "Mental Events" in his *Essays on Actions and Events*,
207–25. Oxford: Oxford University Press, 1980.
Putnam, Hilary. "The Nature of Mental States," in *Philosophy of Mind:
Classical and Contemporary Readings*, edited by David Chalmers, 73–9.
Oxford: Oxford University Press, 2002.
"Mental Causation." *The Stanford Encyclopedia of Philosophy*. (Summer
2008 edn.), edited by Edward N. Zalta, available at http://
plato.stanford.edu/entries/mental-causation/

How it is possible for the mind to be causally relevant to events in the
physical world has been recognized as a serious philosophical problem at
least since Descartes defended his unique form of substance dualism.
Nevertheless, it has become ironically clear that the problem of mental
causation is sticking around as a difficult problem in contemporary metaphysics of mind despite both Cartesian and non-Cartesian forms of substance dualism finding diminished proponents amongst most philosophical
circles. "Physicalism," the thesis that somehow or other everything is
dependent on the physical (and not the other way around), is motivated in
large part due to the inadequate explanations (or lack thereof) substance

dualists offer for how the mind could be causally relevant in the physical world. It is thought that if the mind just were something physical, then the problem of mental causation would simply be dissolved.

Various reasons against reductive versions of physicalism have led many to accept some form of "nonreductive physicalism," the view that despite everything somehow or other being dependent on the physical, it is not the case that mental properties are identical to physical properties (see Putnam and Davidson). The two most influential forms of nonreductive physicalism have been anomalous monism and functionalism. The importance of the supervenience argument lies in its conclusion that finding a place for the mind amidst the causal workings of the physical world is not possible simply by embracing one or the other version of nonreductive physicalism. In other words, the problem of mental causation remains a problem for the nonreductive physicalist.

If reductive physicalism no longer remains an option, then why not accept that the mind simply has no place amidst the causal workings of the physical world? One should admit this position is even more difficult to defend than reductive physicalism. Mental causation is crucial in our self-understanding as free, rational, morally responsible agents, and epistemically evaluable cognizers. So, if mental causation is not possible, then much of the picture of ourselves isn't possible either. The supervenience argument, then, poses a dilemma for the physicalist: embrace some form of reductionism *or* concede that the scientific conception of the world really does threaten the distinctiveness we take ourselves to have. This dilemma reveals an important point: it would be a mistake to think that the supervenience argument is an argument against mental causation *tout court*. Instead, the argument should be understood as calling into question how the mind could be causally relevant in the physical world supposing the truth of nonreductive physicalist.

P is a cause of P*, with M and M* supervening respectively on P and P*. There is a single underlying causal process in this picture, and this process connects two physical properties, P and P*. The correlations between M and M* and between M and P* are by no means accidental or coincidental; they are lawful and counterfactual-sustaining regularities arising out of M's and M*'s supervenience in the causally linked P and P*. These observed correlations give us an impression of causation; however, that is only an appearance, and there is no more causation here than between two successive shadows cast by a moving car, or two successive symptoms of a developing pathology. This is a simple and elegant picture, metaphysically speaking, but it will prompt howls of protest from those who think that it has given away something very special and precious, namely the causally efficacy of our minds. Thus is born the problem of mental causation. (Kim *Mind in a Physical World*, 21)

Kim presents his supervenience argument as a *reductio ad absurdum* of the assumption:

(CR) Mental properties are causally relevant properties.[1] More specifically, it is the assumption that some mental property M causes some physical property P*.[2] The following are the further assumptions he uses along the way to justify his premises:

(SS) The mental strongly supervenes on the physical; that is, for any object O and any time T, if O has a mental property M at T, then necessarily O has a physical property P at T and necessarily anything having P at T has M at T.

(NR) Mental properties are not reducible to physical properties in a sense of 'reduction' such that mental properties cannot be identified with physical properties.

(CE) Except for cases of genuine causal over-determination, no single property can have more than one sufficient cause at any given time (see Kim "Mechanism").

(CC) If a physical property has a cause at T, then its cause at T is a physical property.[3]

P1. M causes P* (CR = assumption for *reductio*).
P2. M has a supervenient base, call it P (SS).
   C1. P causes P* (P1, P2).[4]
   C2. M and P cause P* (conjunction, P1, C1).

---

[1] For the sake of clarity, I shall speak of properties causing other properties (alternatively, we can talk of states causing other states). But, according to Kim, it is more accurate to say that it is the *instantiation* of a property that causes the *instantiation* of another property. This is, of course, skirting over important issues in the metaphysics of causation.

[2] Nothing hangs on the fact that the assumption is a mental property *causing a physical property*. Kim's argument can be given (with minimal changes) if we were to begin with the assumption that a mental property causes another mental property.

[3] Take note that CC by itself does not rule out mental causation, since it allows the possibility of some physical property being causally overdetermined by another physical property and some mental property.

[4] One might question the move from P1 and P2 to C1. In other words, why think that just because P is the supervenient base of M and M causes P* that P deserves to be considered a cause of P*? Kim's answer is twofold. First, if you take causation to be grounded in nomological sufficiency, then P does deserve to be considered a cause of P*, since (a) any supervenient base is nomologically sufficient for what supervenes on it, (b) M is nomologically sufficient for P* by being a cause of P*, and (c) the relation of nomological sufficiency is transitive. Second, if you take causation to be grounded in counterfactuals then, again, P deserves to be considered a cause of P*, since (d) if the supervenient base had not occurred, then what supervenes on it would not have occurred, (e) if M had not occurred, then P* would not have occurred in virtue of M's causing P*, and (f) these particular counterfactuals are transitive. Either way you choose to ground causation results in P's deserving to be considered a cause of P* (see Kim *Mind in a Physical World*, 43).

P3. If M and P cause P*, then either (i) M and P are the same property or (ii) P* has more than one sufficient cause (plausibly true).

P4. M and P are not the same property (NR).

P5. P* does not have more than one sufficient cause, or P* is a genuine case of overdetermination (CE).

P6. P* is not a genuine case of overdetermination (stipulation).

    C3. P* does not have more than one sufficient cause (disjunctive syllogism, P5, P6).

    C4. M and P are not the same property and P* does not have more than one sufficient cause (conjunction P4, C3).

    C5. It is not the case that either (i) M and P are the same property or (ii) P* has more than one sufficient cause (DeMorgan's, C4).

    C6. It is not the case that both M and P cause P* (*modus tollens*, P3, C5).

    C7. M does not cause P* or P does not cause P* (DeMorgan's, C6).

P7. P does cause P* (CC and given that P* is caused).

    C8. M does not cause P* (disjunctive syllogism, C7, P7).

    C9. M does and does not cause P* (conjunction, P1, C8).

    C10. M does not cause P* (*reductio*, P1–C9).

Another way to understand Kim's supervenient argument is that the set of assumptions above is inconsistent; that is, (CR), (SS), (NR), (CE), and (CC) cannot all be true. In order to resolve the inconsistency, one must abandon one of the above assumptions. Many philosophers are committed to the truth of (CR) and at least some thesis on the dependence of the mind on the physical, for example, (SS). Presumably, no physicalist should find a problem with (CC), and (CE) has independent support (see note 4). Therefore, Kim urges that the best way of resolving the inconsistency is by rejecting (NR); that is, in some sense of 'reduction' we must accept the thesis that mental properties are reducible to physical properties.

83

Ryle's Argument against Cartesian Internalism

Agustin Arrieta and Fernando Migura

Ryle, Gilbert. *The Concept of Mind*. Chicago: University of Chicago Press, 2002.

Descartes, René. *Meditations on First Philosophy*, translated by John Cottingham. Cambridge, UK: Cambridge University Press, 1996.

Descartes put forward a conception of mind that has been sometimes described as "internalist." Actually, Descartes' conception of mind is dualist, and internalism is just an aspect of it. Internalism's main thesis claims that mental states are inner states. And, in Descartes' view, it goes on to claim that you alone have privileged access to your mental states: you are the only one who has authority about them.

Internalism has been criticized from different points of view. Logical behaviorism has been one of them. Not without controversy, Ludwig Wittgenstein and Gilbert Ryle can be considered as fathers of logical behaviorism. Ryle's criticism, in a nutshell, is that Cartesianism implies that there is an abyss between knowledge of my mind and knowledge of other minds. In other words, concerning knowledge of mind, the only authentic knowledge is self-knowledge. The problem is that, in Ryle's view, this conclusion is false; hence, Cartesian internalism is false.

Since the argument is valid, if someone wants to defend Cartesian internalism, he or she must reject some of the premises. It seems very difficult to regard as false the second and the third premises because they are just direct (or analytic) consequences of the definitions of the concepts we are using in such premises: privileged access, first-person introspection. In defense of Cartesian internalism, one can reject the fourth premise and

Just the Arguments: 100 of the Most Important Arguments in Western Philosophy, First Edition. Edited by Michael Bruce and Steven Barbone.
© 2011 Blackwell Publishing Ltd. Published 2011 by Blackwell Publishing Ltd.

assert that we do not have knowledge of the mental state of the others. As a Cartesian, one may defend the idea that (certain) knowledge is only possible concerning my own mental states (arguing in this way, one assumes a concept of knowledge linked to certainty). One accesses others' mental states just by analogy (or induction). But, actually, it seems difficult to accept as knowledge something which is justified upon induction from one unique case (induction from one's own case). In any case, Ryle defends the idea that that there is no such asymmetry between other minds and one's own mind.

It is important to distinguish between internalism and Cartesian internalism. The argument above does not apply to non-Cartesian internalism: the first premise is (can be) false if Cartesian internalism is substituted for internalism. For instance, let us suppose that mental states are (internal) brain states. If so, one does not have privileged access to these states. Presumably, a brain-expert would have access to such states. In that case, first-person privileges disappear.

> [Self-knowledge] is not attained by consciousness or introspection, as these supposed Privileged Accesses are normally described. [. . .] The sorts of things that I can find out about myself are the same as the sorts of things that I can find out about other people, and the methods of finding them out are much the same. A residual difference in degree between what I can know about myself and what I can know about you, but these differences are not all in favour of self-knowledge. In certain quite important respects it is easier for me to find out what I want to know about you than it is for me to find out the same sorts of things about myself. (Ryle, 155–6)

P1. If Cartesian internalism is true, then one has privileged access to one's mental states.

P2. That each one has privileged access to one's mental states means that first-person introspection is the only way to know what a person's mental states are. First-person introspection is the method to research the mind.

P3. If first-person introspection is the only way to know what a person's mental states are, then we cannot know the mental states of others (or in other words, there is a strong qualitative difference between knowledge of one's mind and knowledge of other minds).

P4. One has knowledge of the mental states of others (or in other words, there is, at most, a residual difference in degree between knowledge of other minds and self-knowledge).

P5. First-person introspection is not the only way to know what a person's mental states are (*modus tollens*, P3, P4).

P6. One does not privileged access to one's mental states (*modus tollens*, P2, P5).

C1. Cartesian internalism is false (*modus tollens*, P1, P6).

84

Jackson's Knowledge Argument

Amir Horowitz

Jackson, Frank "Epiphenomenal Qualia," *Philosophical Quarterly* 32 (1982): 127–36.

____. "What Mary Didn't Know," *Journal of Philosophy* 83 (1986): 291–5.

Horgan, Terence. "Jackson on Physical Information and Qualia," *Philosophical Quarterly* 34 (1084): 147–52.

Stoljar, D. and Y. Nagasawa (eds.). *There is Something about Mary: Essays on Phenomenal Consciousness and Frank Jackson's Knowledge Argument.* Cambridge, MA: The MIT Press, 2004.

Frank Jackson's Knowledge Argument (sometimes referred to simply as "the knowledge argument") aims at refuting physicalism and establishing mind–body dualism. Roughly, physicalism is the thesis that everything in the concrete world is physical and possesses only physical properties. Mind–body dualism denies physicalism: according to all its versions, mental states have nonphysical properties. The knowledge argument attempts to show that conscious experiences have nonphysical properties, thus vindicating dualism. (The argument deals with visual experiences but its reasoning can be applied to experiences of other kinds; e.g., audible experiences, bodily sensations such as pain, etc.).

Just the Arguments: 100 of the Most Important Arguments in Western Philosophy, First Edition. Edited by Michael Bruce and Steven Barbone.
© 2011 Blackwell Publishing Ltd. Published 2011 by Blackwell Publishing Ltd.

The knowledge argument belongs to a family of epistemological arguments. Epistemological arguments purport to derive ontological conclusions (conclusions about what there is) from epistemological premises (premises about knowledge). Other important arguments that belong to this family are the "zombie argument" (#85) and the explanatory gap argument that also seek to establish mind–body dualism. Moving from epistemological premises to ontological conclusion is no mean feat, and ingenuity is necessary in order to perform such a move without committing a fallacy. As we shall see, the knowledge argument is indeed ingenious. Nevertheless, some critics have argued that it rests on a fallacy.

The argument is based on a thought experiment: an (arguably) logically possible scenario is described in which a certain person knows everything there is to know about the physical properties of an experience yet lacks knowledge of another property of this experience. So experiences, it is inferred, have nonphysical properties.

Let us briefly review the steps of the argument. The assumption that upon her release, Mary acquires new information (P2) means that this information was not included in the information she had before her release. But since before her release she had all physical information (P1), it follows that she gains information that isn't physical. So C1 follows from P1 and P2. Now, the expression "physical information," as it is used in Jackson's argument, refers to information about physical properties (indeed, P1 means that Mary had information about all physical properties of the experience in question); and similarly, "nonphysical information" refers to nonphysical properties. So the claim (C1) that Mary acquired nonphysical information about the experience in question entails (in fact, means) that Mary acquired information about a nonphysical property of this experience. C2 thus seems to be warranted by the argument's premises. And if Mary acquires information about a nonphysical property of this experience, then *a fortiori* this experience has such a property, as C3 states. That, in turn, means that physicalism is false and dualism is true. As we see, the knowledge argument appears to be a formally valid argument.

According to one prominent objection, this argument is only valid if P2 is construed in a way in which it cannot be defended. This is the objection from the intentionality of knowledge and information (mainly due to Horgan). The intentionality of information consists in the fact that one can have the information that something has a property X without having the information that is has property Y even though (unbeknownst to one) X is identical with Y. For example, one can have the information that Superman can fly without having the information that Clark Kent can fly; this can happen when the property in question is presented via different modes of presentation (e.g., different concepts). Thus, it is possible that Mary's "new" information is new in a limited sense – it is about a property she knew all along from her scientific study of vision; it is just that before her release this property was presented in her knowledge by a physical concept, and after her release it is also presented in her knowledge by a mental (phenomenal) concept. How does this possibility affect the argument? According to this objection, P2 should be understood so as to concern "new" information in this limited sense only, and then P1 and P2 do not entail C1; for if the new information may be about the same property as the old information, then it may be about a physical property and thus not be nonphysical information.

It may be instructive to note that Mary's newly gained information may be said to be nonphysical in some sense, in the sense that it involves concepts that do not belong to physical theory – phenomenal concepts. But if "nonphysical information" in C1 is defined in this way, then, of course, C2 does not follow. Indeed, we can understand the intentionality objection as claiming that the knowledge argument illegitimately moves from an epistemological claim – a claim regarding the way in which information is given – to an ontological claim – a claim regarding what this information is about. Is it plausible to maintain that upon having for the first time the experience of seeing red (and shouting "Oh, this is what it is like to see red") Mary didn't learn about a new property? I will leave it to the reader to answer this question and thus to assess the strength of this objection.

> Mary is a brilliant scientist who is, for whatever reason, forced to investigate the world from a black and white room via a black and white television monitor. She specializes in the neurophysiology of vision and acquires, let us suppose, all the physical information there is to obtain about what goes on when we see ripe tomatoes, or the sky, and use terms like 'red', 'blue', and so on. She discovers, for example, just which wavelength combinations from the sky stimulate the retina, and exactly how this produces via the central nervous system the contraction of the vocal cords and expulsion of air from the lungs that results in the uttering of the sentence 'The sky is blue'. [. . .] What will happen when Mary is released from her black and white room or is given a color television monitor? Will she *learn* anything or not? It seems just obvious that she will earn something about the world and our visual experience of it. But then it is inescapable that her previous knowledge was incomplete. But she had *all* physical knowledge. Ergo there is more to have than that, and physicalism is false. (Jackson "Epiphenomenal Qualia," 130)

P1. Before her release from the black and white room, Mary had all physical information about the experience of seeing red.

C1. If Mary acquired new information outside the room, then that information would be nonphysical (by definition of P1).

P2. When released from the black and white room and having for the first time the visual experience of seeing red, Mary acquired new information about such experiences – she acquired information about the ("phenomenal") property of what it is like to see red.

C2. The information which Mary acquired about the experience of seeing red when released from the black and white room was nonphysical information (*modus ponens*, C1, P2).

P4. If Mary acquired nonphysical information, then that information is information about a nonphysical property of this experience.

C3. The information which Mary acquired about the experience of seeing red when released from the black and white room is information about a nonphysical property of this experience; that is, the experience of seeing red has a property that is not physical (*modus ponens*, C2, P4).

P5. If the experience of seeing red has a property that is not physical, then physicalism is false and dualism is true.

C4. Physicalism is false and dualism is true (*modus ponens*, P5, C3).

85

Nagel's "What Is It Like to Be a Bat" Argument against Physicalism

Amy Kind

Nagel, Thomas. "What Is It Like to Be a Bat?" *Philosophical Review* 83 (1974): 435–50.

___. *The View from Nowhere*. Oxford: Oxford University Press, 1986.

Physicalism – the claim that everything is physical – has been the dominant position in philosophy of mind since at least the middle of the twentieth century. Nonetheless, physicalism has long been accused of being unable to account satisfactorily for the qualitative or subjective aspect of experience, for example, the reddishness of one's visual experience of a ripe tomato or the painfulness of one's tactile experience of a sharp object. Many have charged that it is difficult to see how these aspects of experience could be accounted for in solely physical terms. Focusing specifically on the experience that a bat has when using its sonar, Thomas Nagel formulated this charge in a particularly powerful way. His argument is designed to show that subjective facts about experience, which are essential to it, cannot be captured in the objective language of physicalism. Although most philosophers assume that the argument, if successful, would show that physicalism is false, Nagel himself is careful to claim only that we currently lack the conceptual resources to see how physicalism could be true.

Just the Arguments: 100 of the Most Important Arguments in Western Philosophy, First Edition. Edited by Michael Bruce and Steven Barbone.

I assume we all believe that bats have experience. After all, they are mammals, and there is no more doubt that they have experience than that mice or pigeons have experience. [. . .]

[T]he essence of the belief that bats have experience is that there is something it is like to be a bat. Now we know that most bats (the microchiroptera, to be precise) perceive the external world primarily by sonar, or echolocation, detecting the reflections, from objects within range, of their own rapid, subtly modulated, high frequency shrieks. Their brains are designed to correlate the outgoing impulses with the subsequent echoes, and the information thus acquired enables bats to make precise discriminations of distance, size, shape, motion, and texture comparable to those we make by vision. But bat sonar, though clearly a form of perception, is not similar in its operation to any sense that we possess, and there is no reason to suppose that it is subjectively like anything we can experience or imagine. This appears to create difficulties for the notion of what it is like to be a bat. [. . .]

Whatever may be the status of facts about what it is like to be a human being, or a bat, or a Martian, these appear to be facts that embody a particular point of view. [. . .]

This bears directly on the mind–body problem. For if the facts of experience – facts about what it is like for the experiencing organism – are accessible only from one point of view, then it is a mystery how the true character of experiences could be revealed in the physical operation of that organism. The latter is a domain of objective facts par excellence – the kind that can be observed and understood from many points of view and by individuals with differing perceptual systems. (Nagel "What Is It," 438, 441, 442)

P1. Humans cannot experience anything like what it is like for a bat when it is using its sonar.

P2. Humans cannot imagine anything like what it is like for a bat when it is using its sonar.

P3. If P1 and P2, then what it is like to be a bat is fundamentally a subjective phenomenon, understood only from a single point a view (namely, the bat's).

P4. Humans cannot experience anything like what it is like for a bat when it is using its sonar and humans cannot imagine anything like what it is like for a bat when it is using its sonar (conjunction, P1, P2).

C1. What it is like to be a bat is fundamentally a subjective phenomenon, understood only from a single point of view (*modus ponens*, P3, P4).

P5. Physicalism takes the objective point of view.

P6. If physicalism takes the objective point of view, and what it is like to be a bat is a subjective phenomenon understood from only a single point of view, then physicalism cannot capture what it is like to be a bat.

P7. Physicalism takes the objective point of view and what it is like to be a bat is fundamentally a subjective phenomenon, understood only from a single point of view (conjunction, C1, P5).

C2. Physicalism cannot capture what it is like to be a bat (*modus ponens*, P6, P7).

P8. The fact that experience is subjective is an essential fact about experience.

C3. The subjectivity of what it is like to be a bat is an essential fact about it (semantic entailment, P8).

C4. Physicalism cannot capture what it is like to be a bat, and the subjectivity of what it is like to be a bat is an essential fact about it (conjunction, C2, C3).

P10. If physicalism cannot capture what it is like to be a bat, and that is an essential fact about it, then physicalism cannot capture all the essential facts about experiences.

C5. Physicalism cannot capture all the essential facts about experiences (*modus ponens*, C4, P10).

86

Chalmers' Zombie Argument

Amy Kind

Chalmers, David. *The Conscious Mind*. Oxford: Oxford University Press, 1996.
____. "Consciousness and Its Place in Nature," in *Philosophy of Mind: Classical and Contemporary Readings*, edited by David Chalmers, 247–72. Oxford: Oxford University Press, 2002.

Kirk, Robert. "Zombies versus Materialists." *Proceedings of the Aristotelian Society*, Supplement 66 (1974): 135–52.

In the late twentieth century, zombies began to play an important role in philosophical discussions about consciousness. But unlike the zombies of Hollywood, philosophical zombies are very much alive – or at least, they would be were they to exist. As philosophers use the term, a zombie is a creature that is microphysically identical to a human being – and thus produces behavior that is indistinguishable from that of a normal human being – but lacks any sort of consciousness in the phenomenal sense. Zombies behave as if they are in pain when you stick them with a pin, and they will report that they are in pain, but they don't experience any painful sensations.

Many philosophers have recently claimed that we can coherently imagine the existence of zombies. This claim is taken to imply the possibility of zombies, a claim that in turn is taken to imply the falsity of physicalism. The zombies, after all, are by definition exactly like us physically. But if

Just the Arguments: 100 of the Most Important Arguments in Western Philosophy, First Edition. Edited by Michael Bruce and Steven Barbone.
© 2011 Blackwell Publishing Ltd. Published 2011 by Blackwell Publishing Ltd.

two creatures alike physically can differ with respect to consciousness, then it seems to show that consciousness is something over and above the physical. The zombie argument is one of a class of arguments in philosophy of mind often referred to as "conceivability arguments." Such arguments start by claiming that some scenario is conceivable. The conceivability of the scenario is taken to imply that it is possible, and this is then supposed to show something about the actual nature of the mind. With respect to conceivability arguments in general, each of these moves is controversial, and the zombie argument is no exception. Some philosophers have questioned whether zombies are really conceivable. Others grant that zombies are conceivable but deny that it is appropriate to move from a claim about their conceivability to a claim about their possibility. Yet others grant that zombies are possible creatures but deny that this shows anything about physicalism.

> [I]t is conceivable that there be a system that is physically identical to a conscious being, but that lacks at least some of that being's conscious states. Such a system might be a *zombie*: a system that is physically identical to a conscious being but that lacks consciousness entirely. It might also be an *invert*, with some of the original being's experiences replaced by different experiences, or a *partial zombie*, with some experiences absent, or a combination thereof. These systems will look identical to a normal conscious being from the third-person perspective: in particular, their brain processes will be molecule-for-molecule identical with the original, and their behavior will be indistinguishable. But things will be different from the first-person point of view. What it is like to be an invert or a partial zombie will differ from what it is like to be the original being. And there is nothing it is like to be a zombie.
>
> There is little reason to believe that zombies exist in the actual world. But many hold that they are at least conceivable: we can coherently imagine zombies, and there is no contradiction in the idea that reveals itself even on reflection. As an extension of the idea, many hold that the same goes for a *zombie world*: a universe physically identical to ours, but in which there is no consciousness. Something similar applies to inverts and other duplicates.
>
> From the conceivability of zombies, proponents of the argument infer their *metaphysical possibility*. Zombies are probably not naturally possible: they probably cannot exist in our world, with its laws of nature. But the argument holds that zombies *could have* existed, perhaps in a very different sort of universe. For example, it is sometimes suggested that God could have created a zombie world, if he had so chosen. From here, it is inferred that consciousness must be nonphysical. If there is a metaphysically possible universe that is physically identical to ours but that lacks consciousness, then consciousness must be a further, nonphysical component of our universe. If God could have created a zombie world, then (as Kripke puts it) after creating the physical processes in our world, he had to do more work to ensure that it contained consciousness. (Chalmers "Nature," 249)

P1. I can conceive of zombies; that is, creatures that are microphysically identical to conscious beings but that lack consciousness entirely.

P2. If zombies are conceivable, then they are metaphysically possible.

C1. Zombies are metaphysically possible (*modus ponens*, P1, P2).

P3. If zombies are metaphysically possible, then consciousness is nonphysical.

C2. Consciousness is nonphysical (*modus ponens*, C1, P3).

Alternatively:

P1. I can conceive of a zombie world; that is, a world physically identical to ours but in which there is no consciousness.

P2. If a zombie world is conceivable, then it is metaphysically possible.

C1. A zombie world is metaphysically possible (*modus ponens*, P1, P2).

P3. If a zombie world is metaphysically possible, then facts about consciousness are facts over and above the physical facts.

C2. Facts about consciousness are facts over and above the physical facts (*modus ponens*, C1, P3).

P4. If physicalism is true, then there are no facts about consciousness over and above the physical facts.

C3. Physicalism is false (*modus tollens*, C2, P4).

87

The Argument from Revelation

Carlos Mario Muñoz-Suárez

Byrne, Alex and David Hilbert. "Color Primitivism," *Erkenntnis* 66 (2007): 73–105.

Campbell, John. "A Simple View of Colour," in *Reality, Representation and Projection*, edited by John Haldane and Crispin Wright, 257–68. Oxford: Oxford University Press, 1993. Reprinted in *Readings on Color*: vol. 1, *The Philosophy of Color*, edited by Alex Byrne and David R. Hilbert, 177–90. Cambridge, MA: The MIT Press, 1997.

____. "Transparency vs. Revelation in Color Perception," *Philosophical Topics* 105 (2005): 105–15.

Harman, Gilbert. "The Intrinsic Quality of Experience," in *Action Theory and Philosophy of Mind*, edited by James Tomberlin, 53–79. Philosophical Perspectives, vol. 4. Atascadero, CA: Ridgeview, 1990.

Johnston, Mark. "How to Speak of the Colors," *Philosophical Studies* 68 (1992): 221–63. Reprinted in *Readings on Color*, vol. 1: *The Philosophy of Color*, edited by Alex Byrne and David Hilbert, 137–72. Cambridge, MA: The MIT Press, 1997.

Loar, Brian. "Phenomenal States (Revised Version)," in *The Nature of Consciousness: Philosophical Debates*, edited by Ned Joel Block, Owen J. Flanagan, and Güven Güzeldere, 597–616. Cambridge, MA: The MIT Press, 1997.

Russell, Bertrand. *The Problems of Philosophy*. London: Oxford University Press, 1912.

Strawson, Gallen. "Red and 'Red'," *Synthèse* 78 (1989): 193–232.

Tye, Michael. *Consciousness, Color and Content*. Cambridge, MA: The MIT Press, 2000.

Just the Arguments: 100 of the Most Important Arguments in Western Philosophy, First Edition. Edited by Michael Bruce and Steven Barbone.
© 2011 Blackwell Publishing Ltd. Published 2011 by Blackwell Publishing Ltd.

The argument from revelation is one of the most controversial arguments in the contemporary philosophy of mind and metaphysics. The terminology is due to Mark Johnston, in the context of the so-called "philosophy of color." The argument tries to make explicit a basic conviction concerning our epistemic position with respect to what is known by having sensations, and it represents an effort to asking what knowledge our visual sensations of color provide us. Despite its apparent clarity, it is far from being an obviously sound argument with noncontroversial implications.

According to Johnston, Strawson describes the idea behind the argument as follows: "[C]olor words are words for properties which are of such a kind that their whole and essential nature as properties can be and is fully revealed in sensory-quality experience given only the qualitative character that that experience has" (224). An earlier version of the argument was sketched by Russell (47). The Argument from Revelation (henceforth AR) is not an argument concluding that revelation is true but takes this as a premise. According to Johnston, revelation is often understood as a "core belief" of our conception of colors: "[W]ere such beliefs to turn out not to be true we would then have trouble saying what they were false of, i.e., we would be deprived of a subject matter rather than having our views changed about a given subject matter" (137).

The AR is, in principle, an epistemological argument: it shows that the essential nature of that what sensations are about of is revealed to subjects merely by having such sensations. Hence, revelation concerns the relation between sensations and knowledge.

> [T]he nature of canary yellow is supposed to be fully revealed by visual experience so that once one has seen canary yellow there is no more to know about the way canary yellow is. Further investigation and experience simply tells us what further things have the property and how that property might be contingently related to other properties. (Johnston, 139–40)

Thus, for example, subjects having visual sensations of colors are epistemically related to the essential features of those colors and, generalizing this, to have sensations suffices to know what they are about in themselves without acquiring any theoretical knowledge. The argument might be synthesized as follows:

P1. If a subject, S, has the sensation, V, and V is a sensation as of X, then (by revelation) S will know the essential features of X.
P2. S has such a sensation.
 C1. S will know the essential features of X (*modus ponens*, P1, P2).

This argument can also be applied to sensations other than merely visual – for example, to sensations of itches and pains – for revelation is not thought to be a property of what sensations are about but a feature of the epistemic role of sensations.

The AR has been defended against "Type-type Physicalism" (henceforth TP): the metaphysical thesis that mental entities of some type (say, sensations) are necessarily identical to physical entities of some type (say, neurobiological). TP is a version of ontological monism; that is, the thesis that reality is objectively constituted only by physical entities (say, events, states of affairs, processes, properties, and so on). Accordingly, some philosophers claim that if TP is true, then by knowing the latter (e.g., neurobiological states) we will know *a priori* the former (e.g., visual sensations). If we accept such inference, we will obtain *a priori* physicalism (AP), the epistemological thesis that by knowing physical entities of some type (say, neurobiological), we will know *a priori* mental entities of some type (say, visual sensations). In this sense, we can derive the AR against Type-type *a priori* physicalism (henceforth ARP).

ARP *simpliciter* does not conclude that TP fails but that AP does. Thus, if someone defends a sort of TP dependent on the inference TP → AP, then this sort of physicalism will be denied by ARP. The AR is independent from ARP, for someone might accept TP to refute AP (Loar) or, for example, by accepting the thesis that the essential features of colors are *a posteriori* known as physical (Tye). The ARP might be synthesized as follows:

P1. If sensations of certain type, V, are (necessarily metaphysically) identical to physical entities of certain type, N, then knowing N *a priori* entails knowing V; that is, TP → AP.
P2. By merely knowing N, subjects will not know the essential features of V [Revelation].
C1. TP is false (*modus tollens*, P1, P2).

The AR is often viewed as framing Realist Primitivism (RP) (Byrne and Hilbert §2.2); that is, the thesis that properties – or example, colors – are *sui generis* external properties. RP agrees that "objects often do have the colors we take them to, and colors of objects often figure in causal explanations, in particular, that they figure in causal explanations of why things look to have the colors they do" (Campbell 178).

The main problem with revelation lies on the meaning of "essential features." This expression has, at least, two senses: (i) essential features of what sensations are about of and (ii) essential features of sensations as mental states. Sense (ii) should not be confused with sense (i) (Harman). In other words, essential features of contents of sensations cannot be confused with essential features of sensations as mental states. If one adopts the former, then AR favors a sort of infallibility of sensations in relation to properties appearing to be external ones (e.g., colors). Further on, if one accepts the latter, then sensations are self-revelatory. "Essential features" can also be understood as *phenomenal* or *perspectival* features that cannot be reduced to *physical* entities. So, if one accepts, for example, TP, then one will accept that essential features, either of sensations or of contents of sensations, are physical themselves. In principle, in talking about revelation we are talking about features in a phenomenal sense or features essentially phenomenal.

There is a version of the AR with the following conclusion: "S will know the complete set of truths about X" – call this version "ART." ART implies that the complete set of *linguistic* knowledge about, for example, colors is revealed to subjects merely by having sensations. Some philosophers have criticized ART (Campbell ibid.). The main difference between the AR and ART is that the former is an argument from revelation of essential features as qualitative ones, and the latter is an argument from revelation of true propositions about essential features.

88

Searle and the Chinese Room Argument

Leslie Burkholder

Searle, John. "Minds and Brains without Programs," in *Mindwaves*, edited by C. Blakemore and S. Greenfield, 209–33. Oxford: Blackwell, 1988.
____. "Minds, Brains, and Programs." *Behavioral and Brain Sciences* 3 (1980): 417–57.

Copeland, Jack. *Artificial Intelligence*. Oxford: Blackwell, 1993.

Is it possible to make a computer intelligent or give one a thinking mind just by having it run the right computer program? Strong AI believes that by designing the right programs with the right inputs and outputs, minds can be created in computers. John Searle's famous Chinese Room argument is intended to prove that this answer is wrong. Here are Searle's own words:

> Suppose that I'm locked in a room and given a large batch of Chinese writing. I know no Chinese, either written or spoken. Now suppose further that after this first batch of Chinese writing I am given a second batch of Chinese script together with a set of rules for correlating the second batch with the first batch. The rules are in English, and I understand these rules. They enable me to correlate one set of formal symbols with another set of formal symbols, and all that "formal" means here is that I can identify the symbols entirely by their shapes. Unknown to me, the people who are giving me all of these symbols call the call the [first] batch "questions." Furthermore,

Just the Arguments: 100 of the Most Important Arguments in Western Philosophy, First Edition. Edited by Michael Bruce and Steven Barbone.
© 2011 Blackwell Publishing Ltd. Published 2011 by Blackwell Publishing Ltd.

they call the symbols I give them back in response to the [first] batch "answers to the questions," and the set of rules in English that they gave me, they call "the program." Suppose also that after a while I get so good at following the instructions for manipulating the Chinese symbols and the programmers get so good at writing the programs that from the external points of view – that is, from the point of view of somebody outside the room in which I am locked – my answers to the questions are absolutely indistinguishable from those of native Chinese speakers. As regards the [claims of strong AI], it seems to me quite obvious in the example that I do not understand a word of Chinese. I have inputs and outputs that are indistinguishable from those of the native Chinese speaker, and I can have any formal program you like, but I still understand nothing. (Searle, 417–18)

Searle continues by saying that if he doesn't understand Chinese solely on the basis of running the right rules, then neither does a computer solely on the basis of running the right program. And what goes for Chinese goes for other forms of cognition as well. Just manipulating symbols according to a program is not enough by itself to guarantee cognition, perception, understanding, thinking, and so forth. So strong AI is decisively proved wrong.

P1. All things or people who have a rule book or computer program that allows them to respond to questions and comments in Chinese in a way that can't be distinguished from responses by someone who does understand Chinese satisfy the Turing test for having that ability.

P2. Searle has a rule book that allows him to respond to questions and comments in Chinese in a way that can't be distinguished from responses by someone who does understand Chinese.

C1. If Searle has a rule book that allows him to respond to questions and comments in Chinese in a way that can't be distinguished from responses by someone who does understand Chinese, then Searle satisfies the Turing test for understanding Chinese (instantiation, P1).

C2. Searle satisfies the Turing test for understanding Chinese (*modus ponens*, P2, C1).

P3. All things or people that satisfy the Turing test for understanding Chinese are following the right rules or program for understanding Chinese.

C3. If Searle satisfies the Turing test for understanding Chinese, then Searle is following the right rules or program for understanding Chinese (instantiation, P3).

C4. Searle is following the right rules or program for understanding Chinese (*modus ponens*, C2, C3).

P4. Searle doesn't understand Chinese. Nothing about the situation changes this.

C5. Searle is following the right rules or program for understanding Chinese and not Searle does understands Chinese (conjunction, C4, P4).

C6. Not either not Searle is following the right rules or program for understanding Chinese or Searle understands Chinese (De Morgan's, C5).

C7. It is not the case that if Searle is following the right rules or computer program for understanding Chinese then Searle understands Chinese (material implication, C6).

P5. If Searle doesn't understand Chinese solely on the basis of running the right rules, then neither does a computer solely on the basis of running the right program.

C8. A computer doesn't understand Chinese solely on the basis of running the right program (*modus tollens*, C7, P4).

P6. If no computer can understand Chinese solely on the basis of executing the right symbol-manipulating program or following the right symbol-manipulating rules, then no computer has any cognitive abilities just in virtue of executing the right program or following the right rules.

C9. Just manipulating symbols according to a program is not enough by itself to guarantee cognition, perception, understanding, thinking, and so forth; that is, the creation of minds (*modus ponens*, C8, P6).

P7. If strong AI is true, then if there are the right programs with the right inputs and outputs, then there is creation of minds.

C10. Strong AI is false. Strong AI is refuted (*modus tollens*, C9, P7).

Part VI
Science and Language

89

Sir Karl Popper's Demarcation Argument

Liz Stillwaggon Swan

Popper, Karl, R. "Philosophy of Science: A Personal Report," in *British Philosophy in Mid-Century*, edited by C. A. Mace, 104–30. London: George Allen & Unwin, 1957.
____. *Conjectures and Refutations: The Growth of Scientific Knowledge.* New York: Routledge & Kegan Paul, 1963.

Karl Popper (1902–94) is considered one of the most influential philosophers of science of the twentieth century. He is perhaps best known for his criterion of demarcation between science and pseudo-science. Troubled by the presumed scientific status of some theories popular in his time – most notably, Marx's theory of history, Freudian psychoanalysis, and Alfred Adler's individual psychology – Popper was determined to identify some criterion by which to distinguish scientific theories from pseudo-scientific theories. This criterion, known as falsifiability, was for Popper the mark of a scientific theory. According to Popper, a theory is scientific only if it makes predictions that can be tested and potentially shown to be false. If a theory is not falsifiable in this way and can only be confirmed with cumulative supporting evidence, then it is pseudo-scientific. For example, Einstein's theory of general relativity predicts that light rays from distant stars will be deflected by the sun's gravitational field. During a solar eclipse in 1919, astrophysicists confirmed that starlight was in fact deflected by the sun, and

Just the Arguments: 100 of the Most Important Arguments in Western Philosophy, First Edition. Edited by Michael Bruce and Steven Barbone.
© 2011 Blackwell Publishing Ltd. Published 2011 by Blackwell Publishing Ltd.

by almost precisely the amount predicted by Einstein. Einstein's theory of general relativity is a scientific theory, according to Popper's criterion, because it made a falsifiable prediction (that in fact was not falsified).

> The problem which troubled me at the time was neither, "When is a theory true?" nor, "When is a theory acceptable?" My problem was different. I *wished to distinguish between science and pseudo-science*; knowing very well that science often errs, and that pseudo-science may happen to stumble on the truth. (*Conjectures*, 44)

> As for Adler, I was much impressed by a personal experience. Once, in 1919, I reported to him a case which to me did not seem particularly Adlerian, but which he found no difficulty in analyzing in terms of his theory of inferiority feelings, although he had not even seen the child. Slightly shocked, I asked him how he could be so sure. "Because of my thousandfold experience," he replied; whereupon I could not help saying: "And with this new case, I suppose, your experience has become thousand-and-one-fold." (*Conjectures*, 368)

> The history of science, like the history of all human ideas, is a history of irresponsible dreams, of obstinacy, and of error. But science is one of the very few human activities – perhaps the only one – in which errors are systematically criticized and fairly often, in time, corrected. This is why we can say that, in science, we often learn from our mistakes, and why we can speak clearly and sensibly about making progress there. (*Conjectures*, 293)

P1. If a theory is scientific, then it makes claims or predictions that could be shown to be false.
P2. A theory that warrants only confirmation (and ignores falsifying evidence) cannot be shown to be false.
　C1. A theory that can only be confirmed and not falsified is not scientific but pseudo-scientific (*modus tollens*, P1, P2).

90

Kuhn's Incommensurability Arguments

Liz Stillwaggon Swan and Michael Bruce

Kuhn, Thomas S. *The Structure of Scientific Revolutions*. Chicago: The University of Chicago Press, 1963.
____. "Objectivity, Value Judgment and Theory Choice," in *The Essential Tension*, 320–39. Chicago: The University of Chicago Press, 1977.
____. *The Road since Structure*. Chicago: The University of Chicago Press, 2000.

Thomas Kuhn (1922–96) was trained as a historian of science, but is best known for his contributions to the philosophy and sociology of science. His *Structure of Scientific Revolutions* was one of the most important and most controversial books of twentieth-century philosophy of science, mainly because it so compellingly questioned the objectivity of science, which had previously been taken for granted especially in the foregoing philosophical tradition of logical positivism. Among Kuhn's many contributions to the philosophy of science, three of the most important are: (1) an analysis of scientific revolutions wherein a paradigm shift occurs that enables scientists to see the world in a new light; (2) the notion that science is not cumulative, as generally assumed, since newer paradigms are incommensurable with the old, and the methods employed in making observations and uncovering "truth" are relative to the reigning scientific paradigm; and (3) the insight that science is best understood as a socially and historically contextualized

Just the Arguments: 100 of the Most Important Arguments in Western Philosophy, First Edition. Edited by Michael Bruce and Steven Barbone.
© 2011 Blackwell Publishing Ltd. Published 2011 by Blackwell Publishing Ltd.

endeavor, which was in sharp contrast to the earlier positivist philosophy of science that saw science as divorced from the human narrative.

Rationality and Paradigm Shifts

[T]he choice [between paradigms] is not and cannot be determined merely by evaluative procedures characteristic of normal science, for these depend in part upon a particular paradigm, and that paradigm is at issue. (*Structure*, 88)

The competition between paradigms is not the sort of battle that can be resolved by proofs. (*Structure*, 148)

There must also be a basis, though it need be neither rational nor ultimately correct, for faith in the particular candidate chosen. Something must make at least a few scientists feel that the new proposal is on the right track, and sometimes it is only personal and inarticulate aesthetic considerations that can do that. (*Structure*, 158)

P1. If an emerging paradigm becomes the dominant one not by scientific proof but by majority acceptance or intuitive appeal, then the transition from one paradigm to another is not rationally decided.
P2. An emerging paradigm becomes dominant by majority acceptance or intuitive appeal.
  C1. The transition from one paradigm to another is not rationally decided (*modus ponens*, P1, P2).

Incommensurable Paradigms and Holism

The physical referents of these Einsteinian concepts are by no means identical with those of the Newtonian concepts that bear the same name. (Newtonian mass is conserved; Einsteinian is convertible with energy. Only at low relative velocities may the two be measured in the same way, and even then they must not be conceived to be the same). (*Structure*, 102)

Though subtler than the changes from geocentrism to heliocentrism, from phlogiston to oxygen, or from corpuscles to waves [as an account of the nature of light], the resulting conceptual transformation is no less decisively destructive of the preciously established paradigm. (*Structure*, 94)

Lavoisier [...] saw oxygen where Priestley had seen dephlogisticated air and others had seen nothing at all. (*Structure*, 118)

P1. Scientific terms refer to things and have meaning through a network of meaning.

P2. If paradigms were commensurable, then terms would still refer to the same things in new paradigms; for example, "mass" in Newton's theories would be equivalent to "mass" in Einstein's theories.

P4. Terms do not refer to the same things in new paradigms; for example, "mass" is not equivalent in Newton's and Einstein's theories (and neither is a special case of the other), and some things (e.g., phlogiston) are eliminated outright.

C1. Paradigms are incommensurable (*modus tollens*, P2, P4).

P5. If paradigms are incommensurable, then science does not more closely approximate the truth over time.

C2. Science does not more closely approximate the truth over time (*modus ponens*, P5, C1).

91

Putnam's No Miracles Argument

Liz Stillwaggon Swan

Putnam, Hilary. *Mathematics, Matter and Method: Philosophical Papers*, vol. 1. London: Cambridge University Press, 1975.

Boyd, Richard N. "The Current Status of the Issue of Scientific Realism," in *Erkenntnis* 19, 1–3 (May 1983): 45–90.
Worrall, J. "Structural Realism: The Best of Both Worlds?" *Dialectica* 43 (1989): 99–124.

Hilary Putnam (1926–) is a philosopher of language, mind, and science, who proposed the No Miracles argument in support of a realist understanding of the success of science. Realism holds that our best scientific practices and theories give us genuine knowledge about the world, and, in some cases, that the entities quantified over in scientific theories, such as electrons, subparticle strings, anti-matter, and mathematical laws, really do exist – or else our science would not be successful in teaching us about the world. The crux of the No Miracles argument is that the best explanation for the predictive and manipulative success of our scientific theories is that they are (at least approximately) true. (The opposing view – that of the anti-realist – is that the entities quantified over in our scientific and mathematical theories need not exist for the theories to be useful; or, in other words, that our theories are useful but not necessarily empirically accurate.)

The positive argument for realism is that it is the only philosophy that does not make the success of science a miracle. (Putnam, 73)

It would be a miracle, a coincidence on a near cosmic scale, if a theory made as many correct empirical predictions as, say, the general theory of relativity or the photon theory of light without what that theory says about the fundamental structure of the universe being correct or "essentially" or "basically" correct. But we shouldn't accept miracles, not at any rate if there is a non-miraculous alternative. If what these theories say is going on "behind" the phenomena is indeed true or "approximately true" then it is no wonder that they get the phenomena right. So it is plausible to conclude that presently accepted theories are indeed "essentially" correct. (Worrall, 101)

P1. If a scientific theory yields accurate observational predictions, then it must be (at least approximately) true.

P2. Many of our scientific theories yield accurate observational predictions.

    C1. Many of our scientific theories must be (at least approximately) true; otherwise, the success of science would be miraculous (*modus ponens*, P1, P2).

92

Galileo's Falling Bodies

Liz Stillwaggon Swan

Galileo. *Discorsi e Dimostrazioni Matematiche, Intorno à Due Nuove Scienze* 213, Leida, Appresso gli Elsevirii. Leiden: Louis Elsevier, 1638, or *Mathematical Discourses and Demonstrations, Relating to Two New Sciences*, translated by Henry Crew and Alfonso de Salvio. New York: Dover, 1914.

____. *Dialogue concerning the Two Chief World Systems*, translated from the *Dialogo* by S. Drake, 2nd rev. edn. Berkeley, CA: University of California Press, 1967.

Brown, James R. The *Laboratory of the Mind: Thought Experiments in the Natural Sciences*. New York: Routledge, 1991.

Galileo's (1564–1642) famous thought experiment concerning falling bodies appeared in his final work, *Discorsi,* which he wrote during his time under house arrest. It is generally considered to be one of the most compelling thought experiments from the natural sciences and exemplifies a rarity in the history of science in that it doubles as a *reductio ad absurdum* argument. Relying on nothing but logical reasoning, Galileo demonstrated that Aristotle's long-standing theory that heavy objects fall more quickly than light objects leads to a contradiction, so he supplanted it with his own theory that all objects fall at the same rate of speed regardless of their respective weights. Now demonstrable in the laboratory with vacuum tubes,

Just the Arguments: 100 of the Most Important Arguments in Western Philosophy, First Edition. Edited by Michael Bruce and Steven Barbone.
© 2011 Blackwell Publishing Ltd. Published 2011 by Blackwell Publishing Ltd.

Galileo's thought experimental insight is remarkable in that he used only logic to arrive at the correct solution hundreds of years before empirical proof was possible. Interesting to note is that in his time, Galileo was criticized for being overly confident in his *a priori* conclusion; yet, had he in fact carried out the experiments described in his Falling Bodies thought experiment, he would have confirmed Aristotle's, and not his own, insight, due to the natural effects of air resistance.

SALVIATI: If we take two bodies whose natural speeds are different, it is clear that on uniting the two, the more rapid one will be partly retarded by the slower, and the slower will be somewhat hastened by the swifter. Do you not agree with me in this opinion?

SIMPLICIO: You are unquestionably right.

SALVIATI: But if this is true, and if a large stone moves with a speed of, say, eight, while a smaller stone moves with a speed of four, then when they are united, the system will move with a speed of less than eight. Yet the two stones tied together make a stone larger than that which before moved with a speed of eight: hence the heavier body now moves with less speed than the lighter, an effect which is contrary to your supposition. Thus you see how, from the assumption that the heavier body moves faster than the lighter one, I can infer that the heavier body moves more slowly. [...]

And so, Simplicio, we must conclude therefore that large and small bodies move with the same speed, provided only that they are of the same specific gravity.

(Galileo *Dialogue*, 108)

P1. If the light ball falls more slowly than the heavy ball, then it acts as a drag on the combined system, causing it to fall more slowly than the heavy ball alone.

P2. But the combined system is itself a new, even heavier object that falls more quickly than the heavy ball alone.

C1. The light ball does not fall more slowly (*modus tollens*, P1, P2).

P3. If the light ball does not fall more slowly, then all objects fall at the same rate of speed regardless of their respective weights.

C2. Galileo concludes that the only logical solution is for all objects to fall at the same rate of speed regardless of their respective weights (*modus ponens*, P3, C1).

93

Eliminative Materialism

Charlotte Blease

Churchland, Paul M. "Eliminative Materialism and the Propositional Attitudes." *Journal of Philosophy* 78, 2 (1981): 67–90.
____. "Evaluating Our Self-Conception." *Mind and Language* 8, 2 (1993): 211–22.
Feyerabend, Paul. "Materialism and the Mind–Body Problem." *Journal of Metaphysics* 17 (1963): 49–66.

In the philosophy of mind, "eliminative materialism" is perhaps the most radical thesis that has ever been proposed by philosophers. It is the provocative claim that our "folk psychology" – that is, our commonsense understanding of our own and other people's behavior – is not only a theory but it is a false theory and will one day be eliminated in favor of a future, neuroscientific theory of the mind. The most recent and most vociferous eliminative materialist is Paul Churchland. Churchland argues that we need to overhaul our self-conception and eliminate such mental concepts as "beliefs," "desires," "wishes," and so on. The thesis therefore has grave consequences for ethics and the social sciences (psychology, sociology, history, economics, and anthropology) and their applications (psychiatry, law, politics, etc.), since these fields employ such commonsense mental terms in their explanations. Eliminative materialism has been challenged on the grounds that it is self-refuting: the eliminative materialist, it is argued, cannot believe that "beliefs" are not true. Churchland argues that it merely

Just the Arguments: 100 of the Most Important Arguments in Western Philosophy,
First Edition. Edited by Michael Bruce and Steven Barbone.
© 2011 Blackwell Publishing Ltd. Published 2011 by Blackwell Publishing Ltd.

shows how deeply entrenched such terms as "belief" are in our self-understanding. Other objections to eliminative materialism include rejecting the claim that folk psychology is a theory or rejecting the view that it is false theory. In any case, successfully challenging or grappling with eliminative materialism can fundamentally change the way we think about ourselves.

> Eliminative materialism is the thesis that our commonsense conception of psychological phenomena constitutes a radically false theory, a theory so defective that both the principles and the ontology of that theory will eventually be displaced, rather than smoothly reduced to a completed neuroscience. Our mutual understanding and even our introspection may then be reconstituted within the conceptual framework of completed neuroscience, a theory we may expect to be more powerful by far than the commonsense psychology which it displaces, and more substantially integrated within physical science generally. (Churchland "Eliminative Materialism," 67)

P1. Folk psychology is a theory.
P2. If folk psychology is a theory, then folk psychology is fallible; that is, eliminable.
  C1. Folk psychology is fallible; that is, eliminable (*modus ponens*, P1, P2).
P3. There are good grounds for believing that folk psychology is false.
P4. If (C1) and (P3), then folk psychology should be rejected as a false theory.
P5. (C1) and (P3) (conjunction).
  C2. Folk psychology should be rejected as a false theory (and thereby eliminated) (*modus ponens*, P4, P5).

94

Wittgenstein's Private Language Argument

George Wrisley

Wittgenstein, Ludwig. *Philosophical Investigations*, translated by G. E. M. Anscombe, P. M. S. Hacker, and Joachim Schulte, edited by P. M. S. Hacker and Joachim Schulte, rev. 4th edn. in German and English. Oxford: Wiley-Blackwell, 2009.

Candlish, Stewart, and George Wrisley. "Private Language." *The Stanford Encyclopedia of Philosophy* (Fall 2008 edn.), edited by Edward N. Zalta, available at http://plato.stanford.edu/archives/fall2008/entries/private-language/

Mulhall, Stephen. *Wittgenstein's Private Language: Grammar, Nonsense, and Imagination in Philosophical Investigations*. Oxford: Clarendon Press, 2007.

Stern, David G. *Wittgenstein's Philosophical Investigations: An Introduction*. Cambridge, UK: Cambridge University Press, 2004.

In section 243 of his *Philosophical Investigations*, Ludwig Wittgenstein (1889–1951) introduces the idea of a private language, a language that is supposed to refer to one's own immediate, private sensations in such a way that no one else could understand the language. Such a language would not be private in the weak sense of a secret code, since a secret code could be shared. The idea that concerns Wittgenstein is whether a *necessarily* private language, one that could never be shared, is possible or even conceivable.

Just the Arguments: 100 of the Most Important Arguments in Western Philosophy, First Edition. Edited by Michael Bruce and Steven Barbone.
© 2011 Blackwell Publishing Ltd. Published 2011 by Blackwell Publishing Ltd.

Often, section 258 is seen as a key remark in what is often called "the private language argument." However, the variety and complexity of issues discussed in the remarks from sections 243–315 suggest that there is not one single argument that could be labeled "the private language argument." Those remarks approach related issues from different directions rather than form a sustained critique of a single issue. Nevertheless, the argument contained in sections 256–258 is central to the overall consideration of the possibility of a private language, and it can be reconstructed.

The general strategy of sections 256–258 is to show: (1) how different a private language of sensations would have to be from our ordinary public language since it would require disconnecting our sensations from their natural expressions – for example, the expression of pain through crying, joy through smiling, and so on; and (2) that the conditions needed to establish a private language are not possible, or that the very notion of a "private language," one consisting of mere association of sign and private object, cannot be given meaning.

The philosophical implications of the arguments in the private language sections of *Philosophical Investigations*, particularly of those in sections 256–258, are many and varied, but two important ones concern:

Epistemology: Wittgenstein criticizes the idea that there is a sharp epistemological divide between knowledge of one's own "inner" states and knowledge of other's "inner" states. Descartes held that even if all he believed about the world external to his mind might be false, he could nevertheless not fail to know that he had certain sensations and thoughts and that he was consciousness. This implies that while I can know that I am in pain, I cannot know for certain of another person that she is in pain. Much of what Wittgenstein says on privacy seeks to undermine such a position. He questions whether it's not the other way around, namely, that we do very well know when others are in pain and it is questionable in what sense I can be said to know that I am in pain. His reasons for questioning knowledge claims about one's own pain are not easily summarized. However, they stem, in part, from observations about the differences in context and use between such claims as "I know my car is running; I just turned the key" and "I know my tooth hurts; I feel it."

Metaphysics and the Philosophy of Language: Wittgenstein has a general criticism of what might seem like a commonsensical view of the relationship between language and world; that is, he challenges the view that the world divides naturally into objects to which we then simply attach labels (names). One consequence of his consideration of ostensive definitions (defining/explaining a word by pointing to what it refers) is that referring to the world is only possible when a language is in place to fix the reference. Thus the foundation of a language cannot simply be a matter of looking around to see what there is and then attaching names to self-identifying objects.

In considering our sensation language, Wittgenstein similarly criticizes the idea that sensations are "self-identifying," providing their own criteria of identity, so that all that is required to talk about them meaningfully is to associate a name with a sensation. Because of how intimate we are with our sensations, we may believe that all it takes for the word *pain* to be meaningful is for us to associate the sign 'pain' with the sensation. The sensation is unique and self-identifying, so that the meaning of 'pain' is determined by the sensation. However, if Wittgenstein is right about naming and the way names and words refer, then objects and sensations do not pick themselves out as the objects and sensation that they are. Their identity is determinate only in relation to a language that can be used determinately to refer to them as conceived by the language. Sensation words are not meaningful because they refer to self-identifying, private sensations; rather, it is the public observable behavior that is the foundation for the use and meaning of sensation language.

> 256. Now, what about the language which describes my inner experiences and which only I myself can understand? How do I use words to signify my sensations? – As we ordinarily do? Then are my words for sensations tied up with my natural expressions of sensation? In that case my language is not a "private" one. Someone else might understand it as well as I. – But suppose I didn't have any natural expression of sensation, but only had sensations? And now I simply associate names with sensations, and use these names in descriptions. –

> 257. [. . .] When one says "He gave a name to his sensation" one forgets that much must be prepared in the language for mere naming to make sense. And if we speak of someone's giving a name to a pain, the grammar of the word "pain" is what has been prepared here; it indicates the post where the new word is stationed.

> 258. Let's imagine the following case. I want to keep a diary about the recurrence of a certain sensation. To this end I associate it with the sign "S" and write this sign in a calendar for every day on which I have the sensation. — I first want to observe that a definition of the sign cannot be formulated. – But all the same, I can give one to myself as a kind of ostensive definition! – How? Can I point to the sensation? – Not in the ordinary sense. But I speak, or write the sign down, and at the same time I concentrate my attention on the sensation – and so, as it were, point to it inwardly. – But what is this ceremony for? For that is all it seems to be! A definition serves to lay down the meaning of a sign, doesn't it? – Well, that is done precisely by concentrat-

ing my attention; for in this way I commit to memory the connection between the sign and the sensation. – But "I commit it to memory" can only mean: this process brings it about that I remember the connection correctly in the future. But in the present case, I have no criterion of correctness. One would like to say: whatever is going to seem correct to me is correct. And that only means that here we can't talk about 'correct'. (Wittgenstein)

P1. If a sensation is to be necessarily private, then it must not have a natural expression; for example, as pain is expressed through groans, screams, crying, and so on.

P2. Suppose that one were to want to begin a private language and did so by making a sign, "S," in a diary every time a particular sensation occurred.

P3. If "S" is to be given a meaning and if there is to be a criterion of correctness for the correct application of "S" in the future, then a definition of "S" must be formulatable, *or* If "S" is to be given a meaning and if there is to be a criterion of correctness for the correct application of "S" in the future, then "S" must be given an ostensive definition (i.e., a definition through pointing to the thing named while saying/writing its name).

P4. No definition for "S" can be formulated, for to do so would require the use of a public language, which would invalidate the language's privacy.

P5. Would it not be possible, nevertheless, ostensively to define "S" by concentrating one's attention on the sensation while writing the sign in the diary? No! Because:

5a. As mentioned in section 257, and defended in sections 27–37 of *Philosophical Investigations*, if an ostensive definition is to function, then a conceptual–linguistic context to determine the "object" of the pointing, or in this case, the concentration of one's attention, must exist.

5ai. Ostensive definitions cannot be used to ground meaning but, rather, act as a final step in making the already established meaning of a sign explicit.

5aii. Without a conceptual–linguistic context with which to determine the "object" of concentration, there is no determinate "pointing" to the sensation. Is it the sensation that is concentrated on, its duration, its intensity, the body minus the sensation, and so on?

C1. No ostensive definition is possible in the context of the private diarist (*modus tollens*, P5, 5a–5aii).

5b. In the context of the private diarist, there is no existing conceptual–linguistic context.

C2. The concentration of one's attention on a sensation while writing a sign does not establish a meaning, private or otherwise, for the sign (*modus tollens* 5a, 5b).

There is controversy among Wittgenstein scholars regarding whether the above line of reasoning (together with other things Wittgenstein writes) is meant to show that the idea of establishing a private language by private ostension is false or nonsense. In order to reflect that controversy, two different versions of this conclusion are given below.

C3. No meaning has been given to "S" and there is no criterion for the correct application of "S" in the future (destructive dilemma, P3, P4, P5).

P6. If (C3), then nothing meaningful will result.

C4. Nothing meaningful will result from the mere association of a sign with a sensation (*modus ponens*, C3, P6).

C5. Since we do speak meaningfully about sensations, sensation talk does not get its meaningfulness from the mere association of sign with sensations (instantiation, C4).

P7. Languages, even private ones, must be meaningful.

C6-Version 1 It is false that a private language consisting of mere association of sign and private object is possible (substitution, C5, P7).

C6-Version 2 Since we have failed to give any meaning to the notion of a necessarily private language, one consisting of mere association of sign and private object, it is not false that a private language consisting of mere association of sign and private object is possible; rather, it is not clear exactly what possibility is being ruled out. A necessarily private language is in effect nonsense (substitution, C5, P7).

95

Fodor's Argument for Linguistic Nativism

Majid Amini

Fodor, Jerry. *The Language of Thought*. Hassocks, Sussex, UK: Harvester Press, 1976.

Chomsky, Noam. *Knowledge of Language: Its Nature, Origin, and Use*. New York: Praeger, 1986.

Gopnik, Myran (ed.). *The Inheritance and Innateness of Grammars*. Oxford: Oxford University Press, 1997.

Bertrand Russell, one of the most influential philosophers of the twentieth century, is reputed to have remarked, "How comes it that human beings, whose contacts with the world are brief and personal and limited, are nevertheless able to know as much as they do know?"(qtd. in Chomsky xxv). This is what Noam Chomsky has canonized as "Plato's Problem," "How we can know so much given that we have such limited evidence" (Chomsky xxv). In a similar Russellian spirit, Myran Gopnik offers the following observation about language: "One of the puzzles about language is the fact that children do not speak when they are born, but by the time they are two they are using language and by four they are fluent speakers. How do they accomplish this amazing feat?" (Gopnik 3).

Historically speaking, the acquisition of language by human beings has been explained in terms of two contrasting and competing analogies. On the one hand, John Locke, in his classic work *An Essay concerning Human*

Just the Arguments: 100 of the Most Important Arguments in Western Philosophy, First Edition. Edited by Michael Bruce and Steven Barbone.
© 2011 Blackwell Publishing Ltd. Published 2011 by Blackwell Publishing Ltd.

Understanding (1689), contends that the mind of a child is like a *tabula rasa* or "blank slate," which passively receives the impressions of experience to form linguistic competence and performance. Basically, at birth, the mind is bereft of any understanding, and, subsequently, senses and experience inscribe linguistic marks on the empty tablet. Yet, on the other hand, Gottfried Leibniz, in his *New Essays concerning Human Understanding* (1703), explicitly inveighs against the Lockean blank slate analogy of language acquisition and argues that the mind of an infant is like a "veined block of marble" with its ingrained structure, whereby experience can only carve at certain pre-specified forms and patterns (see #75). On the Leibnizian account, the conceptual wherewithal of the mind is innate and pre-configured and the senses and experience only provide the occasion for the knowledge of language to arise.

Jerry Fodor has been one of the most prominent contemporary philosophers at the forefront of defending the innateness of language through a number of influential arguments that are rather less empirical in nature and more abstract in orientation. He attempts to argue for the existence of innate knowledge not only of the syntactic categories and structure of language but also of internal words in the following way:

> Learning a language (including, of course, a first language) involves learning what the predicates of the language mean. Learning what the predicates of a language mean involves learning a determination of the extension of these predicates. Learning a determination of the extension of the predicates involving learning that they fall under certain rules (i.e. truth rules). But one cannot learn that P falls under R unless one has a language in which P and R can be represented. So one cannot learn a language unless one has a language. (Fodor, 63–4)

The first premise lends itself to two readings, since there is an ambiguity in the premise.

A sentence is considered ambiguous when it can be read in at least two different ways. In the case of Fodor's argument, his first premise could be rendered either strongly or weakly, and accordingly the two different readings can be presented as follows:

(1) Strong Reading: There is a rule R such that one learns language L only if one learns R.
(2) Weak Reading: One learns language L only if there is a rule R such that one learns R.

The different readings of the first premise could be represented schematically by using the symbol for existential quantifier in modern logic – that is, $\exists R$ – in the following manner:

(1) ∃R (one learns L only if one learns R).
(2) One learns L only if ∃R (one learns R).

But, what is important to observe is that Fodor needs the strong version for sustaining his argument for nativism. What is required for the weak version is just to construe knowledge of language only as an ability to use language, that is, an ability to conform to some rules, which is not sufficient to support a nativist conception of language. Therefore, a weak reading of the first premise renders the argument invalid, unless one can show that an ability conception of language is untenable.

The second premise is also susceptible to various interpretations. For one thing, in characterizing a behavioral pattern, one has to distinguish between (i) being guided by a rule and (ii) fitting a rule. For instance, although a plant exhibits a regular behavior, it does not represent a rule. That is, a tree's behavior fits a rule but is not guided by the rule. Therefore, in the case of language, it may be claimed that although a child's speech pattern fits a certain rule, it does not follow that it is guided by it. The latter needs further justification.

However, what might be more damaging to the argument is an ambiguity in the premise. Again, there are two possible ways of reading the premise:

(A) Strong Reading: Coming to know a rule requires a prior ability to represent it.
(B) Weak Reading: If one has come to know a rule, one has to be able to represent it.

The problem is that although the weak version appears plausible, it does not entail the strong one. In other words, one may hold the weak version without subscribing to the other one, and the premise required for the nativist argument has to be in the strong sense. Again, if Fodor intends to insist on the strong reading of the premise, he needs to offer some further argument to rule out the weak reading of his second premise.

This premise is also in need of clarification, specifically about the notion of language invoked. For, if the notion of language is broadly interpreted, then the claim verges on banality in the sense that it would be general enough such as no one would object to it. But, in that case, it will not have sufficient strength to sustain innateness of language. However, Fodor's invocation of language is more substantial, and he has a highly detailed and complex understanding of it. Consequently, in support of his third premise, Fodor resorts to a number of other arguments, including the controversial idea of impossibility of learning, to defend his claim about linguistic nativism.

P1. If one is learning a language, then one is required to learn a rule.

P2. If one is learning a rule, then one is required to represent a rule.

P3. If one is learning a language, then one is required to represent a rule (hypothetical syllogism, P1, P2).

P4. If one is required to represent a rule, then one is required to already know a language.

    C1. If one is learning a language, then one is required to already know a language (hypothetical syllogism, P3, P4).

96

Fodor and the Impossibility of Learning

Majid Amini

Fodor, Jerry. "On the Impossibility of Acquiring 'More Powerful' Structures," in *Language and Learning: The Debate between Jean Piaget and Noam Chomsky*, edited by Massimo Piattelli-Palmarini, 142–62. London: Routledge & Kegan Paul, 1980.

Piatteli-Palmarini, Massimo. "Ever since Language and Learning: Afterthoughts on Piaget–Chomsky Debate," in *Cognition on Cognition*, edited by Jacques Mehler and Susana Franck, 376–78. Cambridge, MA: The MIT Press, 1995.

Since the middle of the twentieth century, there has been a steady stream of empirical research purporting to support the idea that much of our cognitive abilities rely on the existence of innate theories of some specific domain of knowledge (#75, #95). For example, it seems that children possess an innate basis of information about other minds whose disruption can ensue in states such as autism. Innate beliefs have also been invoked in the explanation of other domains of cognitive competence, such as our knowledge of basic properties of physical objects and of kinds of stuff: children's ability at exploiting limited information about numbers, set, and basic algebraic operations; adults' conception of numbers; music perception; naïve conceptions of the physical world; certain facial expressions of emotions; deductive inferences and our reasoning concerning actions and

Just the Arguments: 100 of the Most Important Arguments in Western Philosophy, First Edition. Edited by Michael Bruce and Steven Barbone.
© 2011 Blackwell Publishing Ltd. Published 2011 by Blackwell Publishing Ltd.

their practical consequences. Thus, without denying or diminishing the role of experience as input and environmental trigger, the picture presented by these empirical investigations is that much of our cognitive competencies is the result of native capacities rather than learning and acquisition.

Jerry Fodor, as one of the leading contemporary proponents of cognitive nativism, has been arguing that the cause of nativism is further strengthened when one realizes that, strictly speaking, learning is impossible. The argument revolves around the impossibility of changes in the representational system of an organism. Fodor argues that a stronger representational system cannot arise from a weaker one by means of general learning. In fact, the argument is applicable to any theory of learning couched in terms of conceptual enrichment. Fodor contends that nothing new could be acquired during cognitive development. Basically, the insight is that theories purporting to explain such new acquisition can offer explanation on pain of presupposing the availability of the very concepts involved in the new acquisition. However, the Achilles heel of Fodor's reasoning seems to be the argument's major assumption that knowledge and learning involve representations – a doctrine known as the representational theory of mind. One can talk about the process of learning involving changes in the representational system, as the first premise does, only if one has already assumed that learning cannot take place without representation. But, if one believes that knowledge and learning can happen without representations, then the first premise of the argument becomes untenable and thereby the argument collapses. Yet, the doctrine of representationalism is a presumption that is widely shared by a significant number of cognitive science practitioners and philosophers.

> Suppose we have a hypothetical organism for which, at the first stage, the form of logic instantiated is propositional logic. Suppose that at stage 2 the form of logic instantiated is first-order quantification logic. [. . .] clearly a case of a weaker system at stage 1 followed by a stronger system at stage 2. And, of course, every theorem of a propositional logic is a theorem of first-order quantificational logic, but not vice versa. Now we are going to get from stage 1 to stage 2 by a process of learning, that is, by a process of hypothesis formation and confirmation. Patently, it can't be done. Why? Because to learn quantificational logic we are going to have to learn the truth conditions on such expressions as "$(X)Fx$." And, to learn those truth conditions, we are going to have to formulate, with the conceptual apparatus available at stage 1, some such hypothesis as "$(X)Fx$" is true if and only if [. . .]. But of course, such a hypothesis can't be formulated with the conceptual apparatus available at stage 1; that is precisely the respect in which propositional logic is weaker than quantificational logic. Since there isn't any way of giving truth conditions on formulas such as all "$(X)Fx$" in propositional logic, all you can do is say: they include Fa and Fb and Fc, and so on. (Fodor, 148)

P1. If learning is possible, then it involves changes in the representational system of an organism.

P2. If there are changes in the representational system of an organism, then the representational system already has the required conceptual apparatus for the change.

P3. The representational system does not already have the required conceptual apparatus for the change.

    C1. There are not changes in the representational system of an organism (*modus tollens*, P3, P2).

    C2. Learning is impossible (*modus tollens*, C1, P1).

97

Quine on the Indeterminacy of Translation

Robert Sinclair

Quine, W. V. *Word and Object*. Cambridge, MA: The MIT Press, 1960.

Hylton, Peter. *Quine*. New York: Routledge, 2007.
Kemp, Gary. *Quine: A Guide for the Perplexed*. New York: Continuum, 2006.

In Chapter 2 of his magnum opus *Word and Object*, W. V. Quine famously attacked the scientific credentials of the concept "meaning" with his controversial argument for the indeterminacy of translation. The argument is set up in what Quine takes to be scientifically and empirically adequate terms, where the evidence for the assignment of meaning is viewed as objective and public, which is then captured in terms of dispositions to respond overtly to socially observable stimulations. He further emphasizes that the criteria available for isolating meanings, which are used to distinguish one meaning clearly from another, should also to be evaluated in terms of this public conception of empirical evidence. With this as background, Quine's critical argument against the empirical viability of "meaning" proceeds with his introduction of the thought experiment he calls "radical translation." In this idealized scenario, a field linguist seeks to translate an unknown language without the help of dictionaries or bilingual guides of any sort. It is within such a hypothetical situation, Quine suggests, that one can better

Just the Arguments: 100 of the Most Important Arguments in Western Philosophy,
First Edition. Edited by Michael Bruce and Steven Barbone.
© 2011 Blackwell Publishing Ltd. Published 2011 by Blackwell Publishing Ltd.

focus on the raw empirical data available for the assignment of meanings to the language in question. He concludes that the available data can only take the linguist so far, and that the completion of the translation requires the linguist to use his own subjective preferences or intuitions concerning how to understand the language. As a result, the unscientific nature of the enterprise is fully exposed, since the assignment of meaning largely involves matters of practical convenience and preference rather than scientific matters of fact. Translation is then indeterminate for Quine; a consideration of the evidence and methods available leaves translation unfinished, requiring the further introduction of the linguist's own preferences for its completion. He more dramatically makes this point by claiming that two rival translation manuals could be constructed that do justice to all the evidence yet offer inconsistent translations, and there is no further "fact of the matter" to decide between them. Many have missed or misunderstood the ontological upshot of this conclusion. By showing that "meaning" is unfit for philosophical and scientific purposes, Quine thinks he has given us reason to reject the idea that meanings are entities that somehow underlie the practice of translation and communication. This is because translation aims at establishing synonymy or sameness of meaning relationships between languages, which for Quine would provide us with criteria for the separate identification of meanings. Given the indeterminacy found within radical translation, there remains no adequate empirical clarification of this synonymy relation, so we lack identity criteria for meanings and then have no reason to suppose that "meanings" exist. Since some philosophers have claimed that meanings should be construed as propositions, Quine sometimes presents indeterminacy of translation as undermining this claim that meanings are propositions.

Given his interest in addressing semantical issues from a critical, scientific perspective and his specific view of the relevant evidence, Quine introduces several technical terms within his argument. The "stimulus meaning" of a sentence is the ordered set of sensory stimulations that would cause the acceptance or rejection of a sentence by a speaker. Importantly, stimulus meaning serves as the objective evidence from which the linguist proceeds to develop a translation manual. An "observation sentence" is an utterance that all speakers of the language would assent to when stimulated by the same situations or circumstances. Further, two sentences are said to be "stimulus-synonymous" when they are assented to under the same circumstances. A sentence is "stimulus-analytic" for a speaker if she would assent to that sentence in any situation whatsoever. Lastly, "analytical hypotheses" consist of the linguist's guesses concerning the meaning of elements of the native language and their correlation to English words and phrases. Quine's introduction of these terms indicates the type of empirical clarity he wished to inject into the philosophical (i.e., scientific) study of semantics or meaning.

For him, clarity is only achieved if our hypotheses, even the more abstract ones of philosophy, are described in terms of overt behavior and dispositions to such behavior. He takes the use of these terms as providing greater scientific and empirical clarity on these issues than mentalist approaches to mind and meaning, which he ultimately rejects as unexplanatory. Moreover, these terms help further to clarify the steps taken to complete the translation and to highlight in more explicit terms the exact ways in which the procedure falls short.

Of the many critical responses to this argument, perhaps the most obvious would stress that Quine ignores relevant empirical facts that may help to rule out competing translations, perhaps even determining just one. So, for example, one might argue that relevant features of human brains, such as the innate genetic endowment central for language acquisition, help to determine translation. However, if one accepts that the data to be explained with regards to meaning is public and empirical in the way emphasized by Quine, then it remains unclear how an appeal to such neurological features of the brain will help with the detection of meaning or with language translation. Quine himself thought that the indeterminacy thesis was plausible. Few have agreed. While some have taken the indeterminacy thesis as central to Quine's overall philosophy, at least one noted commentator questions this view. Even if translation was shown to be determinate along lines suggested by Quine, the notion of meaning that would emerge would be inadequate for the philosophical purposes usually assigned to propositions and meanings such as understanding a language. On this reading, Quine's reflections on indeterminacy would, at most, show the concepts of "meaning" and "proposition" as not empirically well grounded, but this by itself would have little impact on a view of propositions as nonempirical, abstract entities. For Quine's criticism of this use of proposition, one has to look elsewhere in his philosophy, specifically at his genetic view of language learning and how this account reveals no need for an appeal to this philosophical conception of meaning (Hylton, 225–30). Quine's recent rather agnostic description of indeterminacy as a conjecture would appear to offer some support for this interpretation.

> Known languages are known through unique systems of analytical hypotheses established in tradition or painfully arrived at by unique skilled linguists. To devise a contrasting system would require an entire duplicate enterprise of translation, unaided even by usual hints from interpreters. Yet one has only to reflect on the nature of possible data and methods to appreciate the indeterminacy. Sentences translatable outright, translatable by independent evidence of stimulatory occasions, are sparse and must woefully under-determine the analytical hypotheses on which the translation of all further sentences depends. To project such hypotheses beyond the independently translatable sentences at all is in effect to impute our sense of linguistic analogy unverifi-

ably to the native mind. Nor would the dictates even of our own sense of analogy tend to any intrinsic uniqueness; using what first comes to mind engenders an air of determinacy though freedom reign. There can be no doubt that rival systems of analytical hypotheses can fit the totality of speech behavior to perfection, and can fit the totality of dispositions to speech behavior as well, and still specify mutually incompatible translations of countless sentences insusceptible of independent control. (Quine, 72)

P1. Language is a social art. Acquiring it depends on intersubjective observable cues concerning what to say and when to say it; that is, it is here that we find empirical evidence relevant for the determination of meaning.

P2. If language is social in this specific sense, then understanding how "meaning" is acquired can only be clarified by an appeal to dispositions to respond overtly to socially observable stimulations; that is, verbal dispositions to overt behavior.

    C1. The type of empirical evidence relevant for clarifying the determination of meaning consists of verbal dispositions to overt behavior (*modus ponens*, P1, P2).

P3. To isolate better this data and the possible empirical limits of a scientific account of meaning, we can consider an account of translation called "radical translation" (RT), an idealized situation where we confront an unknown language and have no help from bilinguals or dictionaries. We then examine how far the evidence (i.e., verbal dispositions) preserves sameness of meaning across languages.

P4. Using the stimulus meanings of native utterances, the field linguist translates native utterances by observing interactions with the local environment. This method yields translations of observation sentences and logical connections between utterances. Even more generally, the linguist can judge whether two sentences are stimulus-synonymous – that is, when they share stimulus meanings – or stimulus-analytic; that is, when assented to following any stimulus.

    C2. At this point, translation can be more or less objectively determined, with most of the language in question still remaining untranslated. Further steps need to be taken to complete the translation (P4, detailed description of the steps in RT).

P5. If translation is to proceed beyond this stage, then the linguist must break down sentences further into words and assign independent significance to them, thereby developing a system of analytical hypotheses; that is, provide a translation manual.

    C3. The linguist completes a manual of translation using these analytical hypotheses (*modus ponens*, C2, P5).

P6. These hypotheses go beyond the available evidence (i.e., stimulus meaning) and are not then directly answerable to this evidence.

P7. If analytical hypotheses are not directly answerable to the data, then it is possible to construct rival systems of analytical hypotheses that are equally good translations of the language in question.

    C4. The result is translational indeterminacy: rival systems of analytical hypotheses are possible, each of which provides a translation manual that is equally successful in facilitating effective communication. There remains no further "fact of the matter" to distinguish one as the single best translation manual of the language. Synonymy or sameness of meaning across languages has not been empirically clarified (*modus ponens*, P6, P7).

P8. If we have translational indeterminacy and unclear standards of synonymy, then there is no good scientific or philosophical reason to posit the existence of meanings or propositions underlying the practice of translation and communication.

    C5. There are then no propositions or sentence meanings (*modus ponens*, C4, P8).

98

Davidson's Argument for the Principle of Charity

Maria Caamaño

Davidson, Donald. "Radical Interpretation," in *Inquiries into Truth and Interpretation*, 125–39. Oxford: Oxford University Press, 1984.

____. "On the Very Idea of a Conceptual Scheme," in *Inquiries into Truth and Interpretation*, 183–98. Oxford: Oxford University Press, 1984.

Hahn, Ludwig E. (ed.). *The Philosophy of Donald Davidson, The Library of Living Philosophers*, vol. XXVII. Chicago and La Salle: Open Court, 1999.

McGinn, Colin. "Charity, Interpretation and Belief." *Journal of Philosophy* 74 (1977): 521–35.

Ramberg, Bjorn. *Donald Davidson's Philosophy of Language*. Oxford: Blackwell, 1989.

Stich, Stephen. *The Fragmentation of Reason*. Cambridge, MA: The MIT Press, 1990.

Wilson, N. L. "Substance without Substrata." *Review of Metaphysics* 12 (1959): 521–39.

Davidson develops his argument for the Principle of Charity as a way to avoid appealing to intentional entities in his semantic theory while, at the same time, ruling out also the Quinean problem regarding the indeterminacy of translation (#97). The six premises formulated below correspond to six Davidsonian theses. The first establishes what evidence is available for interpreting. The second states that such evidence is insufficient, whereas

P3 points out a first requirement for interpreting, namely, the attribution of beliefs. The fourth and fifth premises point to a twofold problem arisen from the latter requirement, that is, the interdependence between belief and meaning and the inaccessibility of beliefs. In P6, a second condition is laid down in order to solve that problem: the application of the Principle of Charity. The conclusion makes reference to the consequence that follows from the fulfillment of the second condition: the translatability between the interpreter's language and the language of the person being interpreted. The dependence between the fulfillment of the first and the second requirements, being stated within Davidson's philosophical framework, is what determines the dependence of interpretation on translation. The argument follows a syllogistic strategy hinging on three main assumptions: one concerning the need of belief attribution for interpretation to be possible, one related to the inaccessibility of other agents' beliefs, and another regarding the interdependence between beliefs and meanings. It must be pointed out that Davidson drastically changed the original formulation of the Principle of Charity by N. L. Wilson: "We select as *designatum* [of a name] that individual which will make the largest possible number of [the speaker's] statements true" (532). Davidson introduces the Principle of Charity not only as a semantic rule to determine the referents of the nouns in the speaker's language but also as a necessary condition for recognizing a linguistic agent as such, that is, for recognizing any intentional behavior. Three main kinds of objections have being raised to Davidson's use of such principle: (1) the *a priori* character of the Principle of Charity, which lacks any empirical justification (Ramberg); (2) the high probability that the necessary agreement to interpret be much less than Davidson thinks (Stich); and (3) the existence of different patterns of rational behavior that can evolve along history, and even a certain degree of irrationality also obeying certain patterns that are amenable to evolution (McGinn).

> If we cannot find a way to interpret the utterances and other behaviour of a creature as revealing a set of beliefs largely consistent and true by our own standards, we have no reason to count that creature as rational, as having beliefs, or as saying anything. (Davidson "Radical Interpretation," 137)

The first part has to do with coherence. Thoughts with a propositional content have logical properties; they entail and are entailed by other thoughts. Our actual reasonings or fixed attitudes don't always reflect these logical relations. But since it is the logical relations of a thought that partly identify it as the thought it is, thoughts can't be totally incoherent [. . .]. The principle of charity expresses this by saying: unless there is some coherence in a mind, there are no thoughts [. . .]. The second part of the argument has to do with the empirical content of perceptions, and of the observation sentences that express them. We learn how to apply our earliest observation sentences from others in the conspicuous (to us) presence of mutually sensed objects, events, and features of the world. It is this that anchors language and belief to the world, and guarantees that what we mean in using these sentences is usually true. [. . .] The principle of charity recognizes the way in which we must learn perceptual sentences. (Davidson, qtd. in Hahn, 343)

P1. If something is evidence available for interpreting, then that is the agent's behavior in publicly observable circumstances.

P2. The only evidence available for interpreting is insufficient.

P3. If there is interpretation, then there is attribution of beliefs to the agents being interpreted.

P4. Belief and meaning are interdependent.

P5. Beliefs are not agent's behavior in publicly observable circumstances.

    C1. Beliefs are not evidence available for interpreting (*modus tollens*, P1, P5).

P6. If there is attribution of beliefs, then there is a maximization of the agreement between the interpreter's beliefs and the beliefs of the agents being interpreted.

    C2. If there is interpretation, then there is a maximization of the agreement between the interpreter's beliefs and the beliefs of the agents being interpreted (hypothetical syllogism, P3, P6).

P7. There is a maximization of the agreement between the interpreter's beliefs and the beliefs of the agents being interpreted (assumption).

    C3. There is maximization of agreement between the meaning of the interpreter's language and the meaning of language used by the agents being interpreted (substitution, P4, P7).

    C4. If there is maximization of the agreement between the beliefs, then there is maximization of agreement between meanings, that is, translation (substitution P7, C3).

    C5. (Principle of Charity): If there is interpretation, then there is translation. (hypothetical syllogism, C2, C4).

99
Frege's Argument for Platonism

Ivan Kasa

Frege, Gottlob. *Grundlagen der Arithmetik. Eine logisch mathematische Untersuchung über den Begriff der Zahl.* Breslau: W. Koebner, 1884.
____. *Begriffsschrift. Eine der arithmetischen Nachgebildete Formelsprache des reinen Denkens.* Halle: Louis Nebert, 1879.
____.*The Foundations of Arithmetic,* translated by J. L. Austin. Evanston, IL: Northwestern University Press, 1994.

Hale, Bob, and Crispin Wright. *The Reason's Proper Study.* Oxford: Oxford University Press, 2000.
Wright, Crispin. "Field and Fregean Platonism," in *Physicalism in Mathematics,* edited by A. Irvine, 73–94. Dordrecht: Kluwer, 1990.

Commonly, many mathematical statements are considered to be true. We learn to distinguish early on, for example, true arithmetical statements, such as "2 + 3 = 5," from false ones, such as "2 + 3 = 4." On a higher level of mathematical sophistication, but to a similar effect, professional mathematicians strongly appear to be in the business of articulating mathematical conjectures and proving their truth.

On the other hand, on any account of informal reasoning it holds that, in order for it to be the case that something is so-and-so, the thing so characterized has to exist. In formal theories of logical consequence, this is captured by rules of existential generalization. Expressible in quantified

Just the Arguments: 100 of the Most Important Arguments in Western Philosophy,
First Edition. Edited by Michael Bruce and Steven Barbone.
© 2011 Blackwell Publishing Ltd. Published 2011 by Blackwell Publishing Ltd.

predicate logic, existential generalization says that every formula of the form $\exists x P(x)$ (for P a predicate) is the logical consequence of any formula of the form Pa, where a is a constant term.

Interestingly, these elementary and uncontroversial contentions constitute premises for an argument that has a very controversial effect. To ask whether abstract objects, such as numbers, sets, or properties, exist means stepping into a traditional battleground of Western philosophy that is still vigorously contested. At the same time, the claim that there is something that is a number can be inferred from any trivial truth of arithmetic.

The following refinement of this short but important argument makes explicit some of the central assumptions commonly associated with the concepts involved. These are assumptions about how language is structured and how it relates to the world that can be invoked to justify the rules of inference mentioned above and are reflected in standard formal accounts of meaning. The development of such accounts began with Frege's analysis of elementary predication in function-argument form, whereby singular terms constitute a syntactically determinable category of expressions the members of which have the function to refer to entities in the world (see Frege's *Begriffsschrift*).

It is natural to suppose that reference is not successful if the entity purportedly referred to does not exist. Abstract singular terms are singular terms that purport to refer to abstract entities, that is, roughly entities that lack spatio-temporal location. On the traditional Fregean conception, objects are by definition precisely those entities we can refer to, that aspect of the world responsive to the syntactically characterizable category of singular terms. (Note that this makes the class of objects somewhat broad, including, for example, people's whereabouts.) In particular, Frege has argued that numerals are singular terms and numbers therefore are abstract objects (see Frege's *Grundlagen*).

> In arithmetic we are not concerned with objects which we come to know as something alien from without through the medium of the senses, but with objects given directly to our reason and, as its nearest kin, utterly transparent to it. (Frege *Foundations*, §105)

> Frege's belief that numbers are objects [. . .] is the product of a deceptively simple train of thought. Objects are what singular terms, in their most basic use, are apt to stand for. And they succeed in doing so when, so used, they feature in true statements. Certain sorts of expression, for instance the standard decimal numerals, and expressions formed by applying the numerical operator 'the number of . . . ', to a predicate, are used as singular terms in the pure and applied arithmetical statements of identity and predication in which they feature. Many such statements are true. So such terms do have reference, and their reference is to objects. (Wright, 154)

P1. If a sentence is true, all of its syntactic constituents have successfully discharged their semantic function.

P2. The semantic function of (abstract) singular terms is to refer to (abstract) objects.

   C1. If a sentence is true, all of its singular terms (if there are any) successfully refer to objects (substitution, P1, P2).

P3. If a singular term successfully refers, there is an object that it refers to.

   C2. If a sentence partly constituted by singular terms is true, there are objects that its singular terms refer to (hypothetical syllogism, C1, P3).

P4. There are true sentences partly constituted by abstract singular terms.

   C3. There are abstract objects (*modus ponens*, C2, P4).

100

Mathematical Platonism

Nicolas Pain

Benacerraf, Paul. "Mathematical Truth," *Journal of Philosophy* 70 (1973): 661–80.

Balaguer, Mark. *Platonism and Antiplatonism in Mathematics*. Oxford: Oxford University Press, 1998.

Gödel, Kurt. "What is Cantor's Continuum Hypothesis?" in *Kurt Gödel: Collected Works. Publications 1938–1974*, edited by Solomon Ferferman, John W. Dawson Jr., Stephen C. Kleene, Gregory H. Moore, Robert M. Soloway, and Jean van Heijenoort, vol. 2, 254–70. Oxford: Oxford University Press, 1995. Originally published in *Philosophy of Mathematics: Selected Readings*, edited by Paul Benacerraf and Hilary Putnam. Englewood Cliffs, NJ: Prentice-Hall/Oxford: Blackwell, 1964.

Parsons, Charles. "Mathematical Intuition," *Proceedings of the Aristotelian Society* 80 (1979–80): 145–68.

Mathematical Platonism's (MP) purpose is to justify mathematical knowledge and to explain why certain mathematical propositions are true and meaningful. It is the metaphysical and the epistemological claim: (1) that abstract objects exist, that is, objects that are neither spatio-temporal nor causal; (2) that true and meaningful mathematical propositions of high-order theory stand for or refer to abstract objects; (3) that we know when these propositions are true and meaningful because we have an access to abstract objects. Reference to abstract objects seems to appear in second- or

Just the Arguments: 100 of the Most Important Arguments in Western Philosophy, First Edition. Edited by Michael Bruce and Steven Barbone.

higher-order logical and mathematical theories, that is, in theories that do not quantify over individuals (e.g., "If there is an x such that $x \geq y$, then $x + z \geq y + z$"), but over properties of logical and mathematical items (e.g., in "Any natural number that has only two distinct natural number divisors, 1 and itself, is a prime," we quantify over the property 'to be a natural number'), or properties of properties. Because of mathematical evidence (the fact that we know for sure that certain mathematical propositions of second or higher order, e.g., "3 is a prime," are true), MP argues that we can infer from *the intuition of* these propositions being true, first, that we have *an intuition that* there are abstract objects that give them meaning, and, second, that we have, similarly to the perception of empirical objects, a specific cognitive faculty to perceive abstract objects, without which no intuition would be, cognitively speaking, likely to be possible (see Gödel and Parsons).

Whereas the metaphysical argument (see Benacerraf) against MP addresses statement (1), the skeptical argument against MP addresses statements (2) and (3). The key point of the epistemological argument against MP is the causal theory of knowledge (Benacerraf), whose purpose is to deny, first, the validity of the inference that goes from the *intuition of* to the *intuition that*, and, second, the existence of a specific cognitive faculty to perceive abstract objects. A human being X knows **P** (a proposition) if and only if X is, in an appropriate way, causally related to the fact that *p*. And from that premise, we infer, first, that human beings cannot obtain the knowledge of abstract objects, and, second, that human beings cannot obtain knowledge of mathematical propositions of second- or higher-order theory grounded on abstract objects. Therefore, MP is not true. And since we know for sure that certain propositions of second or higher order are true, even if we suppose that we do not know abstract objects, MP fails to explain mathematical evidence. Therefore, MP is not the best way to explain mathematical knowledge.

> [If X knows that *p*, it] must be possible to establish an appropriate sort of connection between the truth conditions of *p* (. . .) and the grounds on which *p* is said to be known, at least for propositions that one must come to know – that are not innate. In the absence of this no connection has been established between having those grounds and believing a proposition which is true. [. . .] This second condition on an account of mathematical truth will not be satisfied, because we have no account of how we know that the truth conditions for mathematical propositions obtain. (Benacerraf, 667)

P1. If Mathematical Platonism is true, then, if for any human being there is knowledge of mathematical propositions of second- or higher-order theory, then this knowledge is grounded on abstract objects.

P2. If S knows **P** (a proposition), then S's grounds for **P** are relevantly connected to the fact that *p*.

P3. For any X, if X is a spatio-temporal being, and for any **Q** (a proposition that describes a fact *q* about an abstract object), then X is not relevantly connected to the fact that *q* and, therefore, X does not know **Q**.

P4. Human beings are spatio-temporal beings.

    C1. Human beings are not relevantly connected to abstract objects and do not have any knowledge of abstract objects (*modus ponens*, P3, P4).

    C2. Human beings do not know any proposition grounded on abstract objects (*modus tollens*, P2, C1).

P5. If human beings have knowledge of mathematical propositions of second- or higher-order theory grounded on abstract objects, then human beings possess knowledge of abstract objects.

    C3. Human beings do not have any knowledge of mathematical propositions of second- or higher-order theory grounded on abstract objects (*modus tollens*, P5, C2).

    C4. Mathematical Platonism is not true (*modus tollens*, P1, C3).

Appendix A: Learning the Logical Lingo

A **statement** or **proposition** is a sentence that can either be true or false.

A **conditional statement** is a sentence that can be either true or false and has two parts: the antecedent and the consequent. A conditional statement generally has the form of an "If . . . , then . . . " statement.

An **argument** is a set of statements with at least one premise and one conclusion. The premises provide reasons or evidence for the truth of the conclusion.

A **deductive argument** has premises that guarantee the truth of the conclusion. An **inductive argument** is an argument where the premises provide reasons that the conclusion is probably true.

An argument is a **deductively valid argument** if and only if it is impossible for the conclusion to be false if the premises are true. An argument is called "**sound**" when it is deductively valid and the premises are in fact true. An **unsound** argument is either invalid, or valid with at least one false premise.

A **strong argument** is an inductive argument where the premises sufficiently support that the conclusion is probably true. The strength of an inductive argument is a matter of degree, and describing an argument as such does not imply that the premises are true.

Inductive arguments that are not strong, having unlikely conclusions given the premises, are therefore called "**weak**" arguments.

A **cogent argument** is a strong argument in which all the premises are in fact true. An uncogent argument is either weak or strong, with at least one false premise.

Just the Arguments: 100 of the Most Important Arguments in Western Philosophy, First Edition. Edited by Michael Bruce and Steven Barbone.
© 2011 Blackwell Publishing Ltd. Published 2011 by Blackwell Publishing Ltd.

Appendix B: Rules of Inference and Replacement

Modus ponens	$p \supset q$
	p
	$\therefore q$
Modus tollens	$p \supset q$
	$\sim q$
	$\therefore \sim p$
Hypothetical syllogism	$p \supset q$
	$q \supset r$
	$\therefore p \supset r$
Disjunctive syllogism	$p \vee q$
	$\sim p$
	$\therefore q$
Constructive dilemma	$(p \supset q) \cdot (r \supset s)$
	$p \vee r$
	$\therefore q \vee s$
Destructive dilemma	$(p \supset q) \cdot (r \supset s)$
	$\sim q \vee \sim s$
	$\therefore \sim p \vee \sim r$
Absorption	$p \supset q$
	$\therefore p \supset (p \cdot q)$
Simplification	$p \cdot q$
	$\therefore p$
Conjunction	p
	q
	$\therefore p \cdot q$
Addition	p
	$\therefore p \vee q$

Just the Arguments: 100 of the Most Important Arguments in Western Philosophy, First Edition. Edited by Michael Bruce and Steven Barbone.
© 2011 Blackwell Publishing Ltd. Published 2011 by Blackwell Publishing Ltd.

Any of the following logically equivalent expressions can replace each other:

De Morgan's Theorem	$\sim(p \cdot q) \equiv (\sim p \text{ v} \sim q)$
	$\sim(p \text{ v } q) \equiv (\sim p \cdot \sim q)$
Commutation	$(p \text{ v } q) \equiv (q \text{ v } p)$
	$(p \cdot q) \equiv (q \cdot p)$
Association	$[p \text{ v } (q \text{ v } r)] \equiv [(p \text{ v } q) \text{ v } r]$
	$[p \cdot (q \cdot r)] \equiv [(p \cdot q) \cdot r]$
Distribution	$[p \cdot (q \text{ v } r)] \equiv [(p \cdot q) \text{ v } (p \cdot r)]$
	$[p \text{ v } (q \cdot r)] \equiv [(p \text{ v } q) \cdot (p \text{ v } r)]$
Double negation	$p \equiv \sim \sim p$
Transposition	$(p \supset q) \equiv (\sim q \supset \sim p)$
Material implication	$(p \supset q) \equiv (\sim p \text{ v } q)$
Material equivalence	$(p \equiv q) \equiv [(p \supset q) \cdot (q \supset p)]$
	$(p \equiv q) \equiv [(p \cdot q) \text{ v } (\sim p \cdot \sim q)]$
Exportation	$[(p \cdot q) \supset r] \equiv [p \supset (q \supset r)]$
Tautology	$p \equiv (p \text{ v } p)$
	$p \equiv (p \cdot p)$

Symmetry of identity: If $a = b$, then $b = a$ (e.g., #21).
Transitivity of identity: If $a = b$ and $b = c$, then $a = c$.
Substitution: If $a = b$, then a can replace b (e.g., #9).

"Instantiation" reasons from the general to the particular: from "All men are mortal" to "Mike is mortal," where "Mike" is an instance of "men."

Reductio ad absurdum is an indirect strategy of proving a proposition to be true by assuming its contradiction (opposite) and then showing that this leads to a conclusion that is false, contradictory, or absurd, and thereby justifying the original proposition. Note that, for any proposition, either that proposition is true, or its negation is true.

Notes on Contributors

Scott F. Aikin, PhD, is a senior lecturer in philosophy at Vanderbilt University, Nashville, Tennessee. He is the author of *Epistemology and the Regress Problem* (forthcoming) and is the co-author (with Robert Talisse) of *Pragmatism: A Guide for the Perplexed* (2008).

Majid Amini, PhD, is a professor of philosophy at Virginia State University and has previously taught at the Universities of London and Manchester in the United Kingdom and the University of the West Indies in Barbados. He has published a number of papers and book chapters in the fields of epistemology, philosophical logic, philosophy of psychology, philosophy of religion, philosophy of education, history of modern and analytic philosophy, and postcolonial thought. His doctoral dissertation, which covers logico-linguistic nativism, was completed at the University of London, UK.

Agustin Arrieta, PhD, is a lecturer in logic and philosophy of science at the University of the Basque Country (Donostia-San Sebastián, Spain), and he also has a degree in computing sciences. His working interests are in history and philosophy of logic and in philosophy of language and mind. He is interested in Hume's philosophy, especially in his ethics.

David Baggett, PhD, has a degree from Wayne State University, Michigan. He is currently a professor of philosophy at Liberty University, Lynchburg, Virginia. His interests include moral philosophy, philosophical theology, philosophy and popular culture, and philosophy of religion.

Steven Barbone, PhD, is an associate professor at San Diego State University, where he occasionally has the good fortune to work with talented, able MA students, some of whom go on to produce original volumes such as this one. His major research area lies within the seventeenth century, primarily with Benedict Spinoza and more recently with Gabrielle Suchon.

Adrian Bardon, PhD, is an associate professor of philosophy at Wake Forest University, Winston-Salem, North Carolina. His academic interests include

Just the Arguments: 100 of the Most Important Arguments in Western Philosophy,
First Edition. Edited by Michael Bruce and Steven Barbone.
© 2011 Blackwell Publishing Ltd. Published 2011 by Blackwell Publishing Ltd.

the philosophy of time, the history of science, and philosophical naturalism.

Charlotte Blease, PhD, was born in Belfast, and her dissertation, *Paul Churchland's Arguments for Eliminative Materialism*, was done at Queen's University, Belfast, Northern Ireland. She is an assistant lecturer at Queen's University, and her main interests are in philosophy of psychology and philosophy of psychiatry.

Nicolas Bommarito, BA, is a PhD student at Brown University, Providence, Rhode Island. He did his undergraduate degree in philosophy at University of Michigan, Ann Arbor, and he also has a language degree from Tibet University in Lhasa. He is interested in ethics, epistemology, and moral psychology.

Montserrat Bordes, PhD, taught analytic philosophy in the Faculty of Letters and bioethics in the Faculty of Science at the University Pompeu Fabra in Barcelona. She authored several articles on ontology, philosophy of emotions and applied ethics, as well as of a book on political philosophy. She was a member of the Spanish Society for Analytic Philosophy (SEFA) and of the Committee for Ethics of Scientific Research of the Institute for Scientific Research of Barcelona (IMIM).

Jurgis (George) Brakas, PhD, earned his degree in philosophy at Columbia University, New York, in 1984 after earning an AB in philosophy at Princeton University in 1968. His main interests include Aristotle, ancient Greek philosophy, Rand, ethics and metaethics, and logic and philosophy of logic.

Michael Bruce, MA, earned his degree in philosophy at San Diego State University. He is the co-editor of this volume and has also edited with Robert M. Stewart *College Sex – Philosophy for Everyone: Philosophers with Benefits* (Wiley-Blackwell, 2010). Bruce has taught philosophy and mathematics courses at the University of Washington's Robinson Center for Young Scholars and has published essays in books, journals, and online.

Leslie Burkholder, PhD, earned the doctorate at the University of British Columbia, Canada, and now works there as a senior lecturer in philosophy. Her interests include applications of formal logic, computing, and philosophy.

Maria Caamaño, PhD, earned the degree at the University of Santiago de Compostela and is an associate professor at the University of Valladolid, Spain. Her research is mainly in the philosophy of science, including its interface with philosophy of language on topics such as the theory of change and referential change. She is also interested in issues related to naturalized epistemology.

Nicola Ciprotti, PhD, completed the degree at the University of Florence, Italy. He currently holds a senior fellowship at the University of Salzburg, Austria. He has published papers in metaphysics and philosophical logic.

John M. DePoe, candidate for the PhD, is at the University of Iowa, where he is finishing a dissertation in the fields of metaphysics and epistemology.

Willem A. deVries, PhD, earned a BA at Haverford College and both an MA and PhD at the University of Pittsburgh. He has taught at Amherst College, Harvard, Tufts, and the University of Vienna, Austria; since 1988, he has been teaching at the University of New Hampshire, where he holds the rank of professor. He is interested in philosophy of mind, metaphysics and epistemology, and the history of philosophy, especially German idealism. He has published a great deal on Wilfrid Sellars.

Luis Estrada-González, PhD student, studies contemporary philosophy at the Universidad Autónoma del Estado de Morelos (UAEM), Mexico, and for the academic year 2010–11 was on a research stay at the Bernoulli Research Institute of the University of Groningen, Netherlands. He has taught logic and philosophy of science in UAEM and the Universidad Iberoamericana, Puebla campus. His work is at the intersection of logic, philosophy of logic, and category theory. He is especially interested in the philosophical bases of general theories of logic and in the philosophical significance of category theory.

Matthew Frise, MA, is a philosophy PhD student at the University of Rochester, New York, where he specializes in epistemology and the philosophy of religion. He earned his MA in philosophy at the University of California, Santa Cruz; his thesis centered on offering a probabilistic interpretation of one of Moore's anti-skeptical strategies.

A. T. Fyfe, MA, teaches philosophy at Pierce College in Washington State. He has earned an MA at both the University of Miami and the University of Washington. He is currently pursuing a PhD.

Brett Gaul, PhD, is an assistant professor of philosophy at Southwest Minnesota State University in Marshall, Minnesota. He earned the PhD at the University of Iowa. His research interests include Augustine, ethics, and philosophy and popular culture. His work has appeared in *Augustinian Studies* and *The Proceedings of the American Catholic Philosophical Association*.

Jeffrey Gordon, PhD, holds the rank of professor of philosophy and is an NEH Distinguished Teaching Professor in the Humanities at Texas State University. His many essays and articles focus on issues pertinent to the meaning of life.

Tom Grimwood, PhD, was awarded his degree by Lancaster University, UK, where he currently teaches ethics in the Department of Philosophy, Politics, and Religion. His research concerns the philosophical relationship of interpretation, ethics, and ambiguity; he has published on this relationship in journals such as *The British Journal for the History of Philosophy*, *Angelaki*, and *The Journal of Cultural Studies*.

Gerald Harrison, PhD, earned the degree at the University of Durham, UK, in 2006. He is a lecturer in philosophy at Massey University, New Zealand, and an honorary research fellow at the University of Aberdeen, UK. His research interests lie in the metaphysics of free will, moral responsibility, and procreation ethics.

Deborah Heikes, PhD, earned a doctorate in philosophy at the University of Illinois and is currently an associate professor at the University of Alabama in Huntsville. Her primary research interest is the nature of rationality and feminist epistemology.

Julia Hermann, PhD candidate at the Department of Political and Social Sciences of the European University Institute in Florence, Italy, is writing her dissertation on moral justification and moral competence. Her main research interests are in moral and political philosophy, the issue of free will, and the philosophy of the later Wittgenstein.

Stephen Hetherington, PhD, is a professor of philosophy at the University of New South Wales, Australia, where he specializes mainly in epistemology. His degrees include a BPhil from Oxford and an MA and PhD from the University Pittsburgh. He has written six books, mostly on epistemology. Two of these are monographs: *Epistemology's Paradox* (1992) and *Good Knowledge, Bad Knowledge* (2001). Four of his books are introductory: *Knowledge Puzzles* (1996), *Reality? Knowledge? Philosophy!* (2003), *Self-Knowledge* (2007), and *Yes, But How Do You Know?* (2009). He has edited two epistemology collections – *Epistemology Futures* (2006) and *Aspects of Knowing* (2006) – and published over fifty papers, also mostly on epistemology.

Amir Horowitz, PhD, is an associate professor of philosophy at the Open University of Israel. His main research interest lies in the philosophy of mind and the philosophy of language. He is also interested in ethics, the philosophy of law, and the philosophy of sport.

Dale Jacquette, PhD, is Lehrstuhl ordentlicher Professur für Philosophie, Schwerpunkt theoretische Philosophie (Senior Professorial Chair in Theoretical Philosophy), at the University of Bern, Switzerland. He is the author of numerous articles on logic, metaphysics, and philosophy of mind, and has recently published *Symbolic Logic, Philosophy of Mind: The*

Metaphysics of Consciousness, Ontology, Wittgenstein's Thought in Transition, David Hume's Critique of Infinity, and *Logic and How It Gets That Way.* He has edited the Blackwell *Companion to Philosophical Logic* and the volume on *Philosophy of Logic* in the North Holland Handbook of the Philosophy of Science series.

Ludger Jansen, PhD, has a doctorate in philosophy as well as university degrees in philosophy and theology. He teaches philosophy at the University of Rostock and is managing director of the Centre of Logic, Philosophy, and History of Science (ZLWWG) at that university. Currently, his research focuses on ancient philosophy and metaphysics, especially on biomedical and social ontology.

Byron Kaldis, PhD, is Associate Professor of Philosophy at the Hellenic Open University, Greece, having previously taught at universities in the UK and the USA. His academic interests include metaphysics, the philosophy of the social sciences, the relationship of ethics and politics, and philosophical issues related to modern technology. He is the General Editor of the SAGE Encyclopedia of Philosophy and the Social Sciences and editor of a forthcoming Synthese Library volume on *Mind and Society: Cognitive Science Meets the Philosophy of the Social Sciences.*

Ivan Kasa, MA, who has a degree in philosophy and a diploma in mathematics, is a Marie Curie Early Stage Researcher in Philosophy at the University of Stockholm, Sweden. His current research investigates neo-Fregean and fictionalist theories within the philosophy of mathematics.

Amy Kind, PhD, is an associate professor of philosophy at Claremont McKenna College, California, where she teaches philosophy of mind, metaphysics, and logic. She earned her PhD at the University of California, Los Angeles. Her research interests include phenomenal consciousness, the imagination, and introspection, and her work has appeared in journals such as *Philosophy and Phenomenological Research, Philosophical Studies,* and *The Philosophical Quarterly.*

Joyce Lazier, PhD, earned her degree in 2003 at the University of Nebraska. Her dissertation concentrated on Kant's duties of right in the *Metaphysics of Morals.* She has articles and book chapters on Kantian ethics in all stages of publication. Currently, she is teaching at Indiana University, Purdue University Fort Wayne (IPFW), as a limited term lecturer.

Harry Lesser, PhD, retired as a senior lecturer in philosophy at Manchester University, UK, in 2008 and is now an Honorary Research Fellow. His teaching and publications have been mainly in the areas of ethics (especially medical ethics), philosophy of law, ancient philosophy, and philosophy and psychiatry; he has also taught philosophy of religion. An edited book,

Justice for Older People, is forthcoming, and he is currently working on a paper on international law.

Steven Luper, PhD, received his doctorate from Harvard University. He is professor and chair of the Philosophy Department at Trinity University, San Antonio, Texas.

Fauve Lybaert, PhD candidate, studies philosophy at the University of Leuven, Belgium. She is working on a dissertation on personal identity and the formal self. Within this framework, she examines contributions to the question of personal identity and self-consciousness from both the phenomenological tradition and analytic philosophy.

Sean McAleer, PhD, is an associate professor of philosophy at the University of Wisconsin, Eau Claire. His primary interests are ethical theory and the history of ethics. His work appeared in *The American Philosophical Quarterly*, *The Pacific Philosophical Quarterly*, *Utilitas*, and other journals.

Jen McWeeny, PhD, earned an MA in philosophy at the University of Hawai'i at Manoa in 2000 and the doctorate in philosophy at the University of Oregon in 2005. She is as associate professor of philosophy at John Carroll University, Cleveland, Ohio. Her research interests are in the areas of epistemology, emotion theory, phenomenology, feminist comparative philosophy, and early modern philosophy. She has published articles on Simone de Beauvoir, comparative methodology, epistemology, and emotion theory. Current projects include co-editing *Liberating Traditions: Essays in Feminist Comparative Philosophy* and writing articles on feminist phenomenology and embodied cognition.

Fernando Migura, PhD, is a lecturer in logic and philosophy of science at the University of the Basque Country (at Donostia-San Sebastián, Spain). He works on formal and informal logic, philosophy of logic, logical semantics and philosophy of language, and in the related areas of philosophy of mind. He is also interested in epistemology and ethics.

M. Joshua Mozersky, PhD, earned his doctorate in philosophy at the University of Toronto. He is an associate professor of philosophy at Queen's University, Kingston, where he holds the Canada Research Chair in Metaphysics and the Philosophy of Science. His research interests include the philosophy of language, metaphysics, and the philosophy of science.

Robert L. Muhlnickel, PhD, earned his doctorate at the University of Rochester, New York, and taught at the University of Wisconsin-Eau Claire and Colgate Rochester Crozer Divinity School. He is an assistant professor of philosophy at Monroe Community College in Rochester, New York. His specialty is in ethics, and he is interested in all areas of philosophy.

Carlos M. Muñoz-Suárez holds a PhD in both philosophy and psychology. His areas of specialization are philosophy of mind, philosophy of psychology, and neurosciences and neurosemantics, and his research topics are perception, sensations, sensory consciousness, and lexical retrieval. He is a researcher with Sensus Research Group, assistant professor at Universidad Icesi (Colombia), and professor at Universidad del Valle (Colombia).

Mark Nelson, PhD, earned a BA in philosophy at Wheaton College, Illinois, and an MA and PhD in philosophy at the University of Notre Dame, Indiana. He currently holds the Kenneth Monroe Endowed Chair in Philosophy at Westmont College in Santa Barbara, California. His research interests are primarily in ethics, epistemology, and philosophy of religion. Recent publications include "We Have No Positive Epistemic Duties" (*Mind*, 2010), "A Problem for Conservatism" (*Analysis*, 2009), "More Bad News for the Logical Autonomy of Ethics" (*Canadian Journal of Philosophy*, 2007), and "Moral Realism and Program Explanation" (*Australasian Journal of Philosophy*, 2006).

Julinna C. Oxley, PhD, is an assistant professor of philosophy and the director of the Women's and Gender Studies Program at Coastal Carolina University. Her interests include topics in ethics and political philosophy, feminism, the family, emotions, moral psychology, and applied ethics. Her book, *Understanding Others: Empathy and Ethical Thought*, is forthcoming. She is also co-director of the Jackson Family Center for Ethics and Values' Summer Ethics Academy, a program that teaches ethics to sixth graders, and she has a one-year-old daughter.

Nicolas Pain, MA, has earned MA degrees in both philosophy at Lyon 3 Jean Moulin University and in French modern literature at Paris-IV-Sorbonne. He is an independent researcher, working in the history and philosophy of logic and mathematics, philosophy of biology, and cognitive anthropology.

Timothy J. Pawl, PhD, obtained a BA at Valparaiso University, Indiana, in 2003 and both an MA and doctorate at St. Louis University in 2007 and 2008, respectively. He is an assistant professor of philosophy at the University of St. Thomas, Minnesota. His main research interests include metaphysics, philosophy of religion, and the thought of Thomas Aquinas. Some of his recent work has appeared in *Faith and Philosophy* and *The Australasian Journal of Philosophy*.

Tommaso Piazza, PhD, earned both his BA and doctorate at the University of Florence, Italy. He subsequently spent two years in Salzburg, Austria as a research fellow. He is currently a researcher (C-2007, co-financed by FSE and POPH) at the Institute of Philosophy of the University of Oporto, Portugal. His main interests are epistemology and metaphysics. He is now working on a research project (*Secret and Memory in the Information Era*), which deals with the epistemological status of *prima facie* unjustifiable empirical claims (for instance about miracles or conspiracies).

Mark Piper, PhD, is an assistant professor of philosophy at James Madison University, Virginia. His primary area of research is normative ethics, with special concentration in autonomy studies, theories of well-being, and virtue theory (see his web site at https://sites.google.com/site/philosophymarkpiper/).

Stefanie Rocknak, PhD, earned her advanced degree at Boston University, where she studied with Jaakko Hintikka. She is currently an associate professor of philosophy and the director of the Cognitive Science Program at Hartwick College, Oneonta, New York. Her interests include Hume, the philosophy of art, analytic philosophy, and the philosophy of mind. She is also a professional sculptor.

Agnieszka Rostalska, a PhD student at the Jagiellonian University, Faculty of International and Political Studies, Department of Middle and Far East Studies, Kraków, Poland, obtained her MA in philosophy after having studied for three years at Gdansk University in Poland and for two years at the University of Calgary in Canada. In her MA thesis, she worked on analytic philosophy of mind (Richard Swinburne's arguments for dualism in particular). Currently, she's focusing on Indian philosophy, especially the interplay of the notions of self, causality, and freedom in Samkhya-Yoga and Nyaya-Vaisesika.

Andrew Russo, PhD student of philosophy at the University of Oklahoma, is interested the philosophy of mind and the philosophy of language. In particular, he enjoys working on issues in the metaphysics of mind, theories of mental content, and the nature of mental representations. He also has a growing interest in topics concerned with philosophical methodology.

Joakim Sandberg, PhD, is a Research Fellow in Practical Philosophy at the University of Gothenburg, Sweden, and Honorary Research Fellow in Global Ethics at the University of Birmingham, UK. His main academic interests are moral philosophy, political philosophy, and economics – especially the intersections among these subjects. He also serves as president of the Philosophy Society at the University of Gothenburg and as a member of the Gothenburg Animal Research Ethics Committee.

Ben Saunders, PhD, wrote his contributions while a departmental lecturer at the University of Oxford, UK, where he completed his doctorate in 2008. Beginning September 2010, he became a lecturer in philosophy at the University of Stirling, Scotland. His interests cover most areas of political and normative moral philosophy, particularly democracy, distributive justice, and the thought of J. S. Mill. He has published in journals including *The Journal of Applied Philosophy, Utilitas, The Journal of Medical Ethics*, and *Ethical Theory and Moral Practice*.

Eric J. Silverman, PhD, is an assistant professor of philosophy and religious studies at Christopher Newport University, Virginia. His doctorate in philosophy is from St. Louis University. His research interests include medieval philosophy, ethics, and philosophy of religion. His first monograph, *The Prudence of Love: How Possessing the Virtue of Love Benefits the Lover* (2010), defends a Thomistic–Aristotelian account of the virtue of love and argues that love typically increases the lover's overall well-being.

Robert Sinclair, PhD, is an assistant professor in the Department of Philosophy at Brooklyn College, City University of New York. His research examines the interconnections among analytic philosophy, pragmatism, and naturalism in twentieth-century American philosophy. His most recent work discusses aspects of Quine's and Dewey's naturalistic philosophies.

Giannis Stamatellos, PhD, earned his degree at the University of Wales, Lampeter (2005). He is the author of *Plotinus and the Presocratics* (2007) and currently a post doc at the Centre for Neoplatonic Virtue Ethics, University of Copenhagen, Denmark. His research interests include ancient Greek philosophy and computer ethics.

Grant Sterling, PhD, earned a BA in philosophy at Eastern Illinois University and a doctorate in philosophy at the University of Iowa. He is currently an assistant professor of philosophy at Eastern Illinois. His main interests are in medieval philosophy and ethics, especially issues regarding free will and moral responsibility.

Liz Stillwaggon Swan, PhD, earned her degree in philosophy from the University of South Carolina in 2008. She holds a history and philosophy of science postdoctoral fellowship at the Center for the Humanities at Oregon State University. Her philosophical research draws on neurobiology and biosemiotics in an effort to understand the origins and evolutionary development of human cognition.

Julia Tanner, PhD, recently completed her doctorate in philosophy at the University of Durham, UK. Her dissertation focused on animals' moral status, and she has written a number of articles defending the moral status of animals.

James E. Taylor, PhD, earned his advanced degree at the University of Arizona. He is a professor of philosophy at Westmont College in Santa Barbara, California. His primary research interests are in epistemology and philosophy of religion. He teaches courses in these areas and also in philosophy of language and modern and contemporary philosophy.

Sara L. Uckelman, PhD, worked in logic at the Institute for Logic, Language, and Computation, University of Amsterdam, The Netherlands, where she now works as a post-doctoral researcher in the Dialogical Foundations of Semantics project. She is interested in dynamic and dialogical aspects of medieval and modern logic.

Rafal Urbaniak, PhD, specialized in logic and philosophy of mathematics at the University of Calgary. After having spent some time at Bristol University, UK, as a British Academy Visiting Fellow, he's now an assistant professor at Gdansk University, Poland, and postdoctoral researcher at Centre for Logic and Philosophy of Science, Ghent University, Belgium. Apart from philosophy of mathematics, he is interested in logical aspects of philosophical arguments, especially in philosophy of religion.

David **Vander Laan**, PhD, is Associate Professor of Philosophy at Westmont College, Santa Barbara, California. He received his PhD from the University of Notre Dame, where he wrote a dissertation entitled *Impossible Worlds*. His primary research interests are in metaphysics, particularly in ontology, philosophical theology, and the borderlands of metaphysics and logic.

Bruno Verbeek, PhD, teaches ethics and political philosophy at Leiden University, The Netherlands. He is interested in the relations between metaethics, political theory, action theory, and moral psychology with decision and game theory. He is the author of *Moral Philosophy and Instrumental Rationality* (2002) and *Reasons and Intentions* (2008).

Toni Vogel Carey, PhD, who earned the philosophy degree at Columbia University in 1976, writes as an independent scholar about philosophy and the history of ideas. Her work appears in scholarly journals as well as in *Philosophy Now*, where she serves as an editorial advisor. Her writings range from metaethics (her dissertation is entitled *Deontic Perfection* and deals with the is–ought relation) to philosophy of science (Galilean idealization, natural selection) to the Scottish Enlightenment (Adam Smith, Thomas Reid) to traditional philosophical problems (skepticism, the ontological argument). She now is working on two books, one on independent scholarship and its practitioners (Darwin, Lyell, Galileo, William and John Herschel – the list is long), and the other is on the philosophical relation between real and ideal (see her web site at http://mysite.verizon.net/toni. carey).

Jason Waller, PhD, is an assistant professor of philosophy at Eastern Illinois University. His research interests are in political philosophy and early modern philosophy. He has recently published articles in the *British Journal for the History of Philosophy*, *Iyyun: The Jerusalem Philosophical Quarterly*, and *The Internet Encyclopedia of Philosophy* among others. He is currently co-authoring a book for Routledge on Spinoza's political philosophy.

Dan Weijers, BA, is a lecturing assistant and PhD candidate in the Philosophy Department at Victoria University of Wellington and a co-founding editor of the *International Journal of Wellbeing*. His main area of interest is inter-disciplinary research on well-being, especially happiness, hedonism, and pleasure.

Joshua I. Weinstein, PhD, studied physics, philosophy, and Talmud in the United States and in Israel, and he earned his PhD from the Hebrew University of Jerusalem. He is an associate fellow of the Institute for Philosophy, Political Theory, and Religion at the Shalem Center in Jerusalem. His research interests include Greek psychology, ethics, and politics; foundations of mathematics, evolution, and neuroscience; Nietzsche and phenomenology; and comparative theology.

Fabian Wendt, PhD, is currently an assistant professor (*Wissenschaftlicher Mitarbeiter*) at the University of Hamburg, Germany. In 2008, he earned his PhD from the Ludwig Maximilian University of Munich. His doctoral dissertation was on libertarian political philosophy; his interests include political philosophy, normative ethics, and metaethics.

George Wrisley, PhD, earned his degree in philosophy at the University of Iowa. He currently teaches at North Georgia College and State University. His research interests are in metaphysics, the philosophy of language, and ethics. He has published on Wittgenstein in *The Australasian Journal of Philosophy* and (with Stewart Candlish) in *The Stanford Encyclopedia of Philosophy*.

Index

Entries in **bold** refer to the rules found in Appendix B.

Just the Arguments: 100 of the Most Important Arguments in Western Philosophy,
First Edition. Edited by Michael Bruce and Steven Barbone.
© 2011 Blackwell Publishing Ltd. Published 2011 by Blackwell Publishing Ltd.

This index was prepared by Neil Manley.